D0899220

This study explores the relationship between the poetic language of Donne, Herbert, Milton, and other British poets, and the choral music and part-songs of composers including Tallis, Byrd, Gibbons, Weelkes, and Tomkins. The seventeenth century was the time in English literary history when music was most consciously linked to words, and when the mingling of Renaissance and "new" philosophy opened new discovery routes for the arts. McColley offers close readings of poems and the musical settings of analogous texts, and discusses the philosophy, performance, and disputed political and ecclesiastical implications of polyphony. She also enters into current discourse about the nature of language, relating poets' use of language and composers' use of music to larger questions concerning the arts, politics, and theology.

POETRY AND MUSIC IN
SEVENTEENTH-CENTURY ENGLAND

POETRY AND MUSIC IN SEVENTEENTH-CENTURY ENGLAND

DIANE KELSEY McCOLLEY

Rutgers University

CAMBRIDGE
UNIVERSITY PRESS

PUBLISHED BY THE PRESS SYNDICATE OF THE UNIVERSITY OF CAMBRIDGE
The Pitt Building, Trumpington Street, Cambridge CB2 1RP, United Kingdom

CAMBRIDGE UNIVERSITY PRESS
The Edinburgh Building, Cambridge CB2 2RU, United Kingdom
40 West 20th Street, New York, NY 10011–4211, USA
10 Stamford Road, Oakleigh, Melbourne 3166, Australia

First published 1997

Printed in the United Kingdom at the University Press, Cambridge

Typeset in Baskerville no. 2 11/12.5   [SE]

A catalogue record for this book is available from the British Library

Library of Congress cataloguing in publication data

McColley, Diane Kelsey, 1934–
Poetry and music in seventeenth-century England / Diane Kelsey
McColley.
p.   cm.
Discography
Includes bibliographical references and index.
ISBN 0 521 59363 8 (hardback)
1. Music and literature – History – 17th century.   2. Vocal music
– England – 17th century – History and criticism.   3. English poetry
– Early modern, 1500–1700 – History and criticism.   4. Music –
England – 17th century – Philosophy and aesthetics.   I. Title
ML3849.M35   1997
782.4′3′094209032–dc21   97–7581 CIP MN

ISBN 0 521 59363 8 hardback

Contents

Musical examples

Acknowledgments

My hope in writing this book has been to demonstrate ways of discovering relations between words and music and to increase readers' enjoyment of these relations in part-music and poetry. I would like to thank those I have sung with chorally, those I have sung with metaphorically as part of a community of scholars, and those who have provided practical support.

The National Endowment for the Humanities supplied a grant, supplemented by the Research Council of Rutgers University, which also provided two sabbatical semester leaves with research stipends. The Newberry Library in Chicago and the William Andrews Clark Memorial Library in Los Angeles provided one-month fellowships, the Newberry for use of its collection of Italian liturgical and secular part-music and the Clark for study of late seventeenth-century English musical life. I am grateful for the hospitality of Lucy Cavendish College in the University of Cambridge, its President, Dame Anne Warburton, and its Fellows, especially Mindele Treip, Marie Lawrence, and Jillinda Tiley, during a term I spent there as Visiting Fellow, and to the American Philosophical Society for a grant enabling me to undertake this fellowship. While in Cambridge I received gracious advice from Professor John Stevens, Dr. Jeremy Maule, and the late Dr. Peter le Huray, whose premature death the world of music mourns. My experience of seventeenth-century liturgical music was richly increased in Cambridge at the daily services offered by the choirs of St. John's College, directed by Dr. George Guest, and of King's College, directed by Stephen Cleobury, and by other choirs, particularly Trinity's, under Richard Marlow, and St. Catharine's, under Peter le Huray, which have admitted women while preserving Renaissance intonation. I am immensely grateful to these choirs and the many others whose live and recorded performances have brought to my ears the beauty of the music described in this book. I would also like to thank Polly and John Mander for arranging a visit to the Mander Organ Works in London and its manager, Ralph Beddoes, for an explanatory tour.

Numerous literary colleagues have supported this work by their scholarly friendship and expertise, among them Cedric and Nicola Brown, Gardner Campbell, Mario A. DiCesare, Donald M. Friedman, Albert C. Labriola, Barbara Lewalski, Michael Lieb, Mary Ann Radzinowicz, Joseph Summers, and Kathleen Swaim. Three anonymous readers for Cambridge University Press, literary and musicological, made valuable suggestions and prevented many inaccuracies. My thanks go as well to Josie Dixon, Senior Commissioning Editor, for her support and advice, and to Alan Finch for attentive and consultative copy-editing.

I am grateful to Stainer and Bell and Oxford University Press for permission to quote musical examples and the following editors and publishers for permission to use revised excerpts from previous work: "The Poem as Hierophon: Musical Configurations in George Herbert's 'The Church,'" in *A Fine Tuning: Studies of the Religious Poetry of Herbert and Milton*, edited by Mary A. Maleski (Binghampton: Medieval and Renaissance Texts and Studies, 1989); "'The Copious Matter of My Song,'" in *Literary Milton: Text, Pretext, Context*, edited by Diana Treviño Benet and Michael Lieb (Pittsburgh: Duquesne University Press, 1994); and "'How All Thy Lights Combine': Herbert and King's," in *George Herbert: Sacred and Profane*, edited by Helen Wilcox and Richard Todd (Amsterdam: VU University Press, 1995).

My first-hand experience of choral singing began in the Oratorio Society of the University of Illinois at Urbana-Champaign, led by Harold Decker and Louis Halsey, and in the choir of Emmanuel Memorial Episcopal Church, Champaign, which gave the pleasure not only of choral music but also of choral friendship and of singing with my family. Some of its directors, especially Larry Brandenberg, Patrick O'Shea, Debra Cairns, and Kiren Nielson, have been particularly helpful. Sue Dürr first drew my attention to the relation of words and music in Renaissance songs forty years ago, and Olivann Hobbie has aided and encouraged this interest. Nicholas Temperley and Herbert Kellman of the University of Illinois School of Music also gave advice, as did Robert McColley, whose knowledge and collection of recorded music provided my first guided tour of the aural cosmos.

Editions and abbreviations

Quotations not cited in the notes are from these editions. Music collections are cited here by series and parenthetically in the text by volume number; titles and editors of separate volumes are listed in the bibliography under series title.

LITERARY WORKS

Cowley, Abraham. *The Complete Works in Verse and Prose*, ed. Alexander B. Grosart. 2 vols. New York: AMS Press, 1967. Vol. II includes *Davideis: A Sacred Poem*.

Donne, John. *The Complete Poetry*, ed. John T. Shawcross. Garden City, NY: Doubleday, 1967.

The Sermons of John Donne, ed. George Potter and Evelyn M. Simpson. 10 vols. Berkeley: University of California Press, 1953–62.

Dryden, John. *The Works of John Dryden*, gen. ed. H. T. Swedenberg, Jr.; vol. III, ed. Earl Miner. Berkeley: University of California Press, 1969.

Herbert, George. *The English Poems of George Herbert*, ed. C. A. Patrides. London. Dent, 1974.

Herrick, Robert. *The Poems of Robert Herrick*, ed. L. C. Martin. London: Oxford University Press, 1965.

[*Lawes*] Hooker, Richard. *Of the Lawes of Ecclesiastical Polity*, ed. Georges Edelen. *The Folger Library Edition of the Works of Richard Hooker*, gen. ed. W. Speed Hill. Vols. I and II. Cambridge, MA: The Belknap Press, 1977.

Marvell, Andrew. *The Complete Poems*, ed. Elizabeth Story Donno. Harmondsworth: Penguin Books, 1978.

Milton, John. *Samson Agonistes and Shorter Poems*, ed. A. E. Barker. Arlington Heights: AHM Publishing Corporation, 1950.

[*CM*] *The Works of John Milton*, gen. ed. Frank Allen Patterson.

18 vols. + index. New York: Columbia University Press, 1931–40.

[*PL*] *Paradise Lost*, ed. Merritt Y. Hughes. New York: The Odyssey Press, 1962.

[*SM*] *The Student's Milton*, ed. Frank Allen Patterson. New York: Appleton-Century-Crofts, 1933.

[*YP*] *The Complete Prose Works of John Milton*, gen. ed. Don M. Wolfe. 8 vols. New Haven: Yale University Press, 1953–82.

Shakespeare, William. *The Complete Works*, ed. G. B. Harrison. New York: Harcourt, Brace, 1952.

Traherne, Thomas. *Centuries, Poems, and Thanksgivings*, ed. H. M. Margoliouth. 2 vols. Oxford: At the Clarendon Press, 1958.

Vaughan, Henry. *The Complete Poems*, ed. Alan Rudrum. New Haven: Yale University Press, 1981.

MUSIC, SCRIPTURE, AND LITURGY

[AV] The Holy Bible, containing the Old and New Testaments, in the Authorized or King James Version [1611]. Philadelphia: A. J. Homan, n.d.

[*BCP*] *Book of Common Prayer, 1559*, ed. John E. Booty. Washington: The Folger Shakespeare Library, 1976. [This scholarly edition does not include the Coverdale Psalter, which is quoted from various editions.]

[*BE*] *The Byrd Edition*, gen. ed. Philip Brett. London: Stainer and Bell, 1963–.

[*BF*] *The Collected Works of William Byrd*, ed. Edmund H. Fellowes. London: Stainer and Bell, 1937– .

[*EECM*] *Early English Church Music*, gen. ed. Frank Ll. Harrison. London: Stainer and Bell, 1962– .

[*EL*] *English Lute-Songs*, ed. Edmund H. Fellowes, rev. Thurston Dart. London: Stainer and Bell, *c.* 1959– .

[*EM*] *The English Madrigal School*, ed. Edmund H. Fellowes. London: Stainer and Bell, 1913–24; revised as *The English Madrigalists* by Thurston Dart, 1956– .

Fellowes, E. H. *English Madrigal Verse, 1588–1632*. Third edition, revised and enlarged. Oxford: Clarendon Press, 1967.

[*Grove*] *The New Grove Dictionary of Music and Musicians*, ed. Stanley Sadie. 20 vols. Washington, DC: Grove's Dictionaries of Music, 1980.

[*MB*] *Musica Britannica.* London: Stainer and Bell, 1951– .
Purcell, Henry. *The Works of Henry Purcell.* 32 vols. London:
    Novello, 1878–1965. vol. VIII: *An Ode on St. Cecilia's Day
    (1692),* ed. J. A. Fuller Maitland, 1897.
[*TCM*] *Tudor Church Music,* ed. P. C. Buck, E. H. Fellowes, A.
    Ramsbotham, R. R. Terry, S. Townsend Warner. London and
    New York: Published for the Carnegie United Kingdom Trust
    by the Oxford University Press, H. Milford, 1922–29.

Note on musical editions

Assiduous scholarship has made modern editions of seventeenth-century choral music possible and is behind the splendid performances, live and recorded, through which twentieth-century audiences may experience it. For the examples and descriptions of musical works included here, apart from photographs, I have used twentieth-century scholarly editions. Readers should be aware that these editions may vary from the original notation. Editing early music requires complex and sometimes controversial editorial choices concerning pitches, time values, accidentals, and variant manuscripts. On the basis of scholarship, church music is frequently raised to a minor third higher than secular music, and smaller note values are supplied because of changes in the notation of time values since the seventeenth-century. Editors have also added bar lines, which should not necessarily be read as indicating regular metrical stress, and in some cases transpositions and other helps to modern performers and interpreters. Some editorial additions are aids to intelligibility; others, such as dynamics indications, are matters of opinion; and some editorial decisions have to be made on the basis of performance experience. In the examples used here, reduction of note values varies; dynamic indications, breath marks, and other modern additions have been removed; and piano accompaniments for rehearsal only are omitted.

David Wulstan discusses editorial issues in chapters 7 and 8 of *Tudor Music,* and includes critiques of some of the editions used here; Roger Bowers raises disagreements in "To chorus from quartet." Further information may be found under "Editing," "Pitch," and "Tempo" in *The New Grove Dictionary of Music* and, on the technicalities of editing, in John Caldwell's *Editing Early Music.* Recent essays on performance history, providing new scholarship and questioning older views, may be found in *English Choral Practice, 1400–1650,* edited by John Morehen.

Note on orthography

Quotations retain original spellings, with modern forms for letters and abbreviations no longer in use. I have added accent marks on a few syllables and lined out and punctuated texts available only as underlay. In the musical examples, some rehearsal accompaniments are omitted from modern editions.

Titles are italicized regardless of the length of the work, but titles that are first words of poems or musical works are in quotation marks.

Introduction

This book is about the musical experience of seventeenth-century poets and ways it gets into their poems. It is addressed primarily to readers of poetry, but I hope that musicians, and especially choir members, interested in relations between words and music will also be interested in what a literary interpreter has to say about them.

Even though their era is regarded as the golden age of English Church music, little has been written about connections between poetry and the work of composers such as Byrd, Gibbons, Weelkes, and Amner, who provided the music of college chapels and cathedral churches and were included in books of madrigals, songs, and psalms that poets are likely to have used. Because others have dealt with solo song and the music of court and theatre, my own contribution concerns mainly the part-music seventeenth-century poets are likely to have known intimately as participants in private musical gatherings and in the liturgy.

Primary consideration is given to Donne, Herbert, and Milton, with some attention to Marvell, Dryden, and others. These poets, though Donne perhaps only briefly, were associated with Cambridge University, and I have therefore made Cambridge the principal location of historical and cultural contexts. However, most major composers were members of the Chapel Royal, and their music was performed throughout the realm. Herbert and Milton were accomplished musicians, and Donne wrote poems that were set and sung. All three expressed interest in liturgical music, composed "hymns," versified psalms or scriptural songs, and wrote poems for the seasons of the liturgical year that the music of those seasons often illuminates.

Chapter 1 discusses the theory and practice of relating texts and music by word-painting, structure, and expressiveness to show how close listening to the music of this period can enrich close reading of its poetry. Chapter 2 discusses relations among poetry, choral music, and the visual arts as epitomized in King's College Chapel; continuities and changes in the treatment of words in English polyphony; and the church music controversy of the Reformation. The next three chapters are devoted to Donne, Herbert, and Milton in turn. The last chapter looks at musical encomia in which the praise of music reaches a formal zenith but begins to become detached from earlier interest in its relation to words and treats it as a separate art.

Scholars have devoted much study to ways in which words affect Renaissance and early baroque music, but less to ways in which music affects words. Many poems are charged with music that we cannot hear unless we know the music their authors heard and sang. Musical genres bring a wealth of connotation to poems that adopt or allude to them just as literary genres do; and musical culture affects language not only by providing rhythm, imagery, and metaphor but by entering into diction, form, nuances of prosody, and configurations of words. I have given close analysis to poems and musical analogues and provided historical contexts addressed to the general reader concerning philosophy, politics, and performance practice. The comparisons of particular compositions and poems are not meant to demonstrate explicit "influence" or authorial intention, but to let readers share poets' experience and to consider ways that music may affect language as represented by these examples. My attention to English polyphony is not meant to subordinate solo song, theatre music, classical and Renaissance rhetoric and poetics, and other contexts, but to show how church music and other part-music contribute to the verbal close-weaving of seventeenth-century verse.

Of the three poets discussed in depth, Herbert and Milton are the most intrinsically musical, but musical culture has an important part in Donne's poetry as well. The *Songs and Sonets* often respond to popular lute songs and madrigals and the divine poems to church music; and these musical awarenesses bear on Donne's renovations of language and the complex tonalities of his poems. Herbert and Milton incorporated qualities of music into their poems that helped to give the English language extraordinary fullness, refinement, and resilience by weaving together resonant words and forms as polyphony weaves sounds. While it may be argued that any good poetry does so, poems of this period, and theirs especially, have a density and a plenitude of connections that go beyond verbal coherence and suggest a musical kind of writing. Like polyphony, their poems have complex structural as well as conceptual significance and are composed in vertical harmonies, as well as linear verses, with finely tuned overtones as well as fundamentals. Verbal resonance may not have the simultaneity of musical chords; but, much as the singer of a motet or a madrigal has to keep to a particular line but can with increasing familiarity increasingly hear its relations to all the others, so a reader of poetic lines harmonically in tune with each other, though reading linearly, can increasingly hear those resonances as verbal concords: an experience able to cure overly linear thinking and expand awareness of multiple connections in the nature of things.

"Just concent" is the harmony produced by the pure intonation in which Renaissance and early baroque music was sung and played and which links it to the numerical proportions observable in nature. Seventeenth-century poetry absorbs this art and endues language with a kind of precise diction that tunes words to each other as pure intonation tunes both the fundamentals and the overtones (which include dissonances) of musical chords. This precision does not decrease, but increases, the polysemousness of words, much as pure intonation increases the audibility of parts. The more words "concent" together – the more exactly tuned they are to each other's sounds and meanings – the more connections they reveal. Virtually all memorable poetry has links to music; but the music of the sixteenth and seventeenth centuries, when music was most consciously being wedded to words by musical humanism and church music reform, appears to have given these poets a heightened consciousness of the resources of musical experience not only for form and prosody but also for the harmonic concinnities of words.

This project raises at least three theoretical questions. First, can one argue from contemporary settings of analogous texts that Herbert's hymns or Milton's angelic anthems are permeable to the music of Tallis, Tomkins, or Monteverdi? The proof will be in the listening, and my hope is that readers will find their readings of poems enriched and germinated, critical puzzles untangled, and the significance of poetic forms expanded by the examples offered here. Second, can argument by analogy demonstrate actual connections? While there is always some slippage when comparing different arts, I think that musical analogy is a natural part of the production of language by poets immersed in a musical and religious culture. It is more reasonable to compare language and musical proportion in the work of artists who believe that a creator designed the cosmos and the perceiving mind with natural correspondences than in the work of those who believe that the universe is a flux of phenomena upon which we impose structures devised by minds that are also fluxes of phenomena. Most poets are analogists, as metaphor requires, but Renaissance poets were philosophical ones, believing that art participated in a divine creative process and discerning analogies between the design of the cosmos and the design of the mind. "Analogy" means according to, or with, *logos*, which means both "word" and "ratio," reason and proportion. Whether there is any "real" connection is a theological question. Third, what are the implications of the relation between words and music for the views that all human language is "fallen," "meaning" is inaccessible, or significance has little relation to what an author does in the act of composition?

The numerical proportions of music, supposed eternal, cannot be intrinsically fallen, though music, like language, can be deceptively used. Words cannot be put to mathematical proof and declared universal, as musical proportions can, but the doctrine of the Fall did not require seventeenth-century poets to believe that all language since Adam's remains fallen, since the doctrine of regeneration also applied. Some theorists thought that "the language of Adam" was univocal and all polysemousness a mark of fallenness. But that assumption implies a static creation by an authoritarian God. For poets, multiple meanings, though corruptible, are no more intrinsically fallen than partials within musical notes; they are elements of creativity, part of the generative and regenerative potency for discovery and connection endowed by a creative Logos.

The conception of cosmic concinnity produced a fecund mating of matter and spirit in the arts partly because it was undergoing ferment and change. The new philosophy had been disrupting static ideas of nature for half a century when the earliest poems included here were written, and the sense of process produced by telescopic and microscopic observation may be seen in experiments in language, music, and political revolution. Musical poetic language not only sounds musical but operates, as music does, as cosmic discovery. Musicians explore the world of mathematical proportions made audible in consonant (and dissonant) sound, and poets explore the world of language and find that it provides not just linear but harmonic constructions that, like the harmonies of music, result in more than parallel lines of signification. Works of art having complex concinnities of sound and significance produce new places in the universe – lodgings, Herbert calls them – that are not just manipulations of parts but new areas of consciousness. The oceanic change where Renaissance and "new" philosophy still mingled, and reason was not yet confined to rationality, opened new discovery routes for exploring the significance of creation.

Like any literary study, this one offers one voice among many. Other writers have addressed the historical and artistic relations between poetry and music from different but related points of view. James Winn in *Unsuspected Eloquence* considers relations between words and music from ancient to modern times. S. K. Heninger, Jr. in *Touches of Sweet Harmony* elucidates the effects of cosmology on poetics. Music scholars who discuss the setting of texts include David Wulstan in *Tudor Music*, Joseph Kerman in *The Elizabethan Madrigal* and *The Masses and Motets of William Byrd*, and Peter Phillips in *English Sacred Music, 1549–1649*. Among literary scholars, John Stevens studies relations between poetry and music in medieval and early Tudor courts; Bruce Pattison gathers information about the secular and social musical environment of Elizabethan poetry; and Gretchen Finney's *Musical Backgrounds for English Literature, 1580–1650* discusses music theory with special reference to Milton. Wilfred Mellers evocatively describes the relations of music to text and society in *Harmonious Meeting*, and John Hollander's *The Untuning of the Sky* brings formidable scholarship to words about music. Winifred Maynard's *Elizabethan Lyric Poetry and its Music* studies lyric verse of Tudor and Stuart song-books, miscellanies, ballads, masques, and plays, and Robert Toft's study of song performance, *Tune Thy Musicke To Thy Heart*, compares verbal and musical rhetorical figures. Elise Bickford Jorgens and Louise Schleiner show how composers interpret the verses they set, and Schleiner makes extended comparisons of Milton's verse with Italian monody. Other work on musical settings and contexts includes John Caldwell, Edward Olleson, and Susan Wollenberg,

The Well-Enchanting Skill: Music, Poetry, and Drama in the Culture of the Renaissance; Rivkah Zim, *English Metrical Psalms: Poetry as Praise and Prayer, 1535–1601*; Mary Chan, *Music in the Theatre of Ben Jonson*; Willa Evans, *Ben Jonson and Elizabethan Music* and *Henry Lawes: Musician and Friend of Poets*; and the work of Thomas O. Calhoun and Thomas King on settings of poems by Abraham Cowley in *The Collected Works*, II:1.

During the twentieth century, music scholars have greatly increased the availability of Renaissance and early baroque choral music by assembling and editing part-books and, especially in the past twenty years, reforming performance practice. Polyphonic music grows more beautiful the better one knows it, and the best ways to know it are to sing it, to hear live performances, and to follow scores while listening to recorded ones, paying attention to each part and particularly to the inner ones. A beginner might try Dowland's setting of the hundreth psalm (from Ravenscroft's *Whole Book of Psalmes*, 1621, in Diana Poulton's modern edition) in which the familiar Sternhold and Hopkins tune ("Old Hundredth") appears in the tenor voice. Readers who do not read musical notation can still hear performances and find increased pleasure in the music of poetry. Performances, to which I am much indebted, of most of the musical works mentioned in this study are cited in the discography. Also appended are a list of selected poetry, music, and iconography for the liturgical year, a chronology of historical, biographical, architectural, musical, and poetic events, and a glossary of musical and liturgical terms.

CHAPTER 1

Nature's voice: concent of words and music

In Henry Purcell's setting of Nicholas Brady's *Ode on St. Cecilia's Day*, the chorus apostrophizes Music:

> Soul of the World! inspir'd by thee,
> The jarring Seeds of Matter did agree,
> Thou didst the scatter'd Atoms bind,
> Which, by the Laws of true proportion join'd,
> Made up of various Parts one Perfect Harmony.

Brady's words sum up a musical conception of the cosmos, and Purcell's music offers auricular proof: jarring chords by tremulous strings on "jarring Seeds" beg for resolution, voices agree homophonically on "agree" and scatter in separate lines on "scatter'd," various voice parts sing "various Parts," modulation displays harmonic proportions on "true proportion," and a lingering cadence on "one Perfect Harmony" ends with one perfect tonic chord. "Inspir'd" – from *in* and *spirare*, to breathe in or into, as God is said to animate Adam – receives an animated series of rising phrases between which the singers may quickly breathe in: Purcell fills the musical metaphor with both the spiritual and the physical meaning of the word to show the power of music as the "anima" that orders and moves the physical world.

Seventeenth-century minds and ears perceived music as the formative soul of the cosmos made audible. In the shifting world of sense and intellection, music witnesses to something real: number, hence rhythm and harmonic proportion, hence music, are everlasting. Since these actualities are infinitely recombinable, the unchangeable gives room for, in fact makes possible, unlimited creativity. Harmony allows "various Parts." Remarkably, when music combines with words, these differing substances can be felicitously matched to animate and confirm each other. Because of the variety of ways in which musical treatment of words strikes the mind and senses as congruent, the "concent" between words and music reveals correspondences between cosmic design and the design of the mind. If both the universe and the human soul are "inspir'd" with the musical proportions of universal numbers, the fundamentals of creation, music can heal the soul by retuning it to those intervals and rhythms that make audible the design of the world and the attributes of the designer. "The heavens are telling the glory of God" sings the Psalmist; and as the celestial bodies in their orderly yet varied motions display glory visibly, the orderly plenitude of music displays it audibly. While astronomers with their optic glasses searched the body of the cosmos, composers of music investigated its soul.

Music is said to encompass three levels: the music of the spheres, or abstract eternal numbers; the music of the soul; and practical or audible music.[1] The music of the spheres is that set of proportions in the arrangements of the heavenly bodies which, Pythagoras taught, corresponds with the concords of music, so that, as Adam and Eve describe them in *Paradise Lost*, they "move / In mystic Dance not without Song" (5.177–78).[2] The Ptolemaic cosmic map corresponds with the Pythagorean musical scale, in which only fourths, fifths, and octaves are considered consonant; but Kepler understood the universe as sun-centered and believed that the cosmos corresponded with the "just intonation" of polyphony: that is, in a heliocentric universe, his measurements of the relations of the planets corresponded with the mathematical proportions in which thirds and sixths are most consonant.[3] The new cosmology, by throwing all in doubt, both created new anxieties and opened new possibilities for the mind, the body politic, and the arts, and these corresponded with an intonation whose mathematics requires that voices must constantly adjust to each other to produce "perfect harmony."

The music of soul is the set of proportions in which, Plato believed, a human being is composed. When discomposed they can be reharmonized by music. Just as "*God's Poem*" is made of elements corresponding with choral voices, the microcosm Man "is all o'er *Harmony*," Abraham Cowley writes in *Davideis* (1.451–76): "*Storehouse* of all *Proportions! single Quire!*" whom in the beginning "*God's Breath* did tunefully inspire." The charms of music can therefore heal both body and soul, as David's music healed Saul's, "Not by their *Force*, but *Party* that's within."

Practical music is the music we can hear. Everything in nature has the capacity to make it. Wood, metal, skin, flesh, bones – all things that can be made to vibrate – set the air in motion in various timbres; wind, water, and ingenuity can extract this intrinsic music. For Henry Vaughan in *The Morning-Watch*, all nature and all creatures sing to God as a "quick" manifestation of the inaudible cosmos:

> In what rings,
> And *hymning circulations* the quick world
> Awakes, and sings;
> The rising winds,
> And falling springs,
> Birds, beasts, all things
> Adore him in their kinds.
> Thus all is hurled
> In sacred *hymns*, and *order*, the great *chime*
> And *symphony* of nature.

Thomas Traherne, contemplating the hymn "of every creature" (Rev. 5.13) in *Thanksgivings for the Glory of God's Works*, exults that what Milton in *At a Solemn Musick* calls "the fair musick that all creatures made" at the first creation shall be renewed:

> That we shall hear all Creatures
> In Heaven and Earth
> So praising thee,
> Plainly sheweth, that we shall
> Understand their Natures,
> See their Beings,
> Know their Excellencies,
> Take Pleasure in them.

For many poets and composers, human beings are artist-priests of nature's voice because they can shape music into articulate language. The human body is a delicately constructed musical instrument, having pipes, strings, bellows, resonating chambers, and a mouthpiece that can shape music into words and so join the beauty of number with the beauty of thought, which move the heart and mind in concordant ways. Joining words to music is a fundamental human vocation. William Byrd prefaces his *Psalmes, Sonets, and Songs* (1588) with "Reasons . . . to perswade euery one to learne to sing," one being that "The better the voice is, the meeter it is to honour and serue God there-with; and the voyce of man is chiefly to be imployed to that ende." James Clifford asserts that since choral singing will be our "employment in Heaven, it will be a wretchless and unexcusable neglect not to mind it here on earth."[4] John Donne describes himself in a *Hymne to God my God, in my sicknesse* as an instrument preparing to join God's "Musique." George Herbert claims in *Providence* that "Beasts fain would sing; birds dittie to their notes"; since only "Man" can do both, he is "Secretarie" of creation's praise. Milton's Adam and Eve join their "vocal Worship to the Choir / Of Creatures wanting voice" and invoke "all ye Creatures" to join their orisons (9.197–99; 5.164).

Brady addresses Music: "Thou tun'dst this World below, the Spheres above, / Who in the Heavenly Round to their own Music move": when both worlds are tuned by music they are tuned to each other. Purcell illustrates with apt pitches for "below" and "above" and gives "World" and "Spheres" similar yet inverse melodies. A new variation of the figure appears on "Round" while the triple rhythm imitates the swing and recurrence of their round dance. These two lines, utterly natural and charming, are sung first by a soprano or cantus voice and then by the four-part chorus; when in performance these lines are repeated, the first (about the two worlds) occurs twice each time, and the second (about the spheres) four times, so that eight repetitions of the second line, with variations (like Donne's "trepidation of the spheares" or Milton's "vicissitude"[5]), represent the eight spheres moving in parts "to their own Music." "Move" runs up and down, but more up than down, in swingingly extended figures on lilting dotted notes, so that the "Heavenly Round" seems to dance in expanding circles.

While the spheres were being retuned – not untuned – by the new philosophy, seventeenth-century writers and composers intensified this sense of relation among creator, cosmos, soul, music, and language. Sir Thomas Browne denies the audibility of cosmic music but affirms its intelligibility:

[T]here is a musicke where-ever there is a harmony, order or proportion; and thus farre we may maintain the musick of the spheares; for those well ordered motions, and regular paces, though they give no sound unto the eare, yet to the understanding they strike a note most full of harmony. Whatever is harmonically composed delights in harmony; which makes me much distrust the symmetry of those heads which declaime against all Church musicke . . . [E]ven that vulgar and Taverne Musicke, which makes one man merry, another mad, strikes in mee a deepe fit of devotion, and a profound contemplation of the first Composer; there is something in it of Divinity more than the eare discovers. It is an Hieroglyphicall and shadowed lesson of the whole world, and [the] Creatures of God, such a melody to the eare, as the whole world well understood, would afford the understanding. In briefe it is a sensible fit of that Harmony, which intellectually sounds in the eares of God.[6]

The cosmographer Robert Fludd used Ptolemaic cosmic maps with a human figure superimposed to show correspondences between the human body and the macrocosm and between the faculties of the soul and the angelic choirs arranged in nine supracosmic spheres. ("It is too little to call man a little world," Donne remarks; "except God, man is diminutive of nothing."[7]) Another figure shows the hand of God tuning a monochord on which the planets are disposed as the notes of the musical scale.[8] Vetruvius in *De Architectura* depicts a similarly spreadeagled human body against a circle within a square, showing humankind as both earthly (the square) and spiritual (the circle).[9] Music corresponds to this symbolic geometry when words having to do with earth are set in duple or quadruple rhythm and those having to do with heaven in threes: triple or "perfect" time being represented in Renaissance notation by a circle. For Herbert in *Mans medley*, humanity's vocation is to unite the two worlds:

> To this life things of sense
> Make their pretence:
> In th' other Angels have a right by birth:
> Man ties them both alone,
> And makes them one,
> With th' one hand touching heav'n, with th' other earth.

This tie is one that the union of words and music is especially equipped to effect.

Readers of poets' verbal music need to be aware of several qualities of Renaissance and early baroque practical music.[10] First, "concent" is singing (or playing) in harmony and exactly in tune. When choirs concent together, they sing in a pure intonation that also concents with the cosmos. Choral singing, and as far as possible instrumental music as well, was performed in natural tuning: that is, in the simplest possible mathematical proportions. Pitches are composed of a fundamental sound and its partials or over-tones; in pure intonation the partials are in tune with each other. Modern ears are used to equal temperament, the tuning of the keyboard, a compromise that allows instruments with fixed tuning to modulate freely over a wide range of keys and pitches by spreading evenly the mathematical inequalities of natural tuning in different octaves.[11] Human voices (and other unstopped instruments) do not need this adjustment because they can continually readjust to the consonances of natural tuning. (Organs were tuned to a mean-tone scale that provided natural thirds in the church modes.)

"Just" or "natural" intonation requires beginning each note exactly on pitch, pronouncing vowels uniformly, and singing without vibrato, an embellishment of monody, because fluctuating pitches disturb the consonances and reduce the clarity of polyphonic lines. In just concent, voices in close harmony, like Milton's embracing angels, remain distinct while they intermix. Since numbers are eternal (Pythagoras, Plato, and Kepler would say), singers in natural intonation are literally in tune "with angels and archangels, and with all the company of heaven"[12] while the hearer's eardrums, nerves, and bones vibrate in "concent" with the physical matter of the cosmos. What Milton in *At a Solemn Musick* calls "keeping in tune with Heav'n" is a literal as well as a spiritual act. This musical relation of the eternal and material worlds, which for Milton differ only in degree, depends on the "pure concent" which "we on Earth with undiscording voice" may learn through the "mixt power" of "Voice, and Vers" to "rightly answer."

Second, the pulse or measure allows for flexible rhythms and modes for flexible tonalities. Modern singers, guided by bar-lines, often count metrical beats. Sixteenth- and early seventeenth-century singers saw no bar-lines and no time signatures within a piece to signal rhythmic changes. Instead, the leader beat or the singer felt a steady silent pulse, and the music on the page appeared in phrases shaped by the words, flowing supply between duple or triple measures. Similarly, modal music sounds less tonally centered than music controlled by a diatonic keynote, and many compositions modulated freely within their modes to suit the words.

Third, in polyphonic and much homophonic music, all voice parts have melodic interest. The performance is also egalitarian.

The tuning of each voice depends on listening and responding to each other voice; Giovanni de' Bardi, leader of the Florentine Camerata, taught that

one should not imitate those who, when they sing in parts, as though the whole company had come only to hear their creaking, think only of making their own voices heard, not knowing or perhaps not remembering that good part-singing is simply joining one's voice with the voices of others and forming one body with these . . . with all the suavity and sweetness in his power.[13]

At the same time, in many musical genres each voice or voice part frequently emerges from the texture. This practice is most often associated with early baroque music, like Monteverdi's *concertante* style, but had been part of English choral music at least since Dunstable and is the outstanding feature of a particularly English pair of genres, the verse anthem and verse service.[14] Like its measure and tonalities, the voicing of seventeenth-century part-music is responsive to words. Solo voices or sections may alternate with full choir, vocal textures may be sparse or full, instruments may double vocal lines or have parts of their own. This diversity of equal parts all carefully balanced in response to each other, and each having its moments of prominence, intimates "the fair musick that all creatures made" before "disproportion'd sin" broke it and that Milton and others think art can teach us to make again.

During the Middle Ages the work of liturgical music was to show forth God's glory by making the beauty of cosmic numbers audible. When the Reformation refocused on God's word and provided the liturgical community with a vernacular liturgy, reformers objected to choral music in church because words set to the overlapping lines of polyphony lack intelligibility. The medieval reliance on number and proportion to display the Logos gave way to words. But apart from some extreme simplification in the early years of the Reformation, English composers developed ways to call attention to words without abandoning the beauty, the expressive resources, and the numerical proportions of polyphony. Such settings may still be unintelligible to the passive listener. They rely on audiences acquainting themselves with the scriptural and liturgical texts and listening with the kind of responsive engagement that painting and poetry of the period also require.

Whether people can understand the words of a choral piece depends on performance and on familiarity. Despite the reverberation time of cathedrals and large chapels, even polyphonic musical lines, when sung in just intonation, keep the voice parts distinct enough to let familiar texts be recognized. The singers themselves were the main beneficiaries of the verbal content of Latin services,[15] but the hearer who knew the shape of the liturgy could follow its outlines, and once the sung portions had become familiar through chant (alternated with polyphonic sections in Tudor times), and even more after they had been translated into the vernacular, moderately polyphonic settings were still moderately intelligible, especially when composers used such techniques as exposing the words homophonically before repeating them in more elaborate polyphony.

In the early seventeenth century, university students, therefore many of the poets discussed here, were required to attend daily morning and evening prayer in the colleges and services at the University Church on Sundays. When they attended choral services, many of the texts would be engraved in memory. The most familiar sung texts would be the canticles and some of the prayers of the daily office; then the Psalms, the whole book being said or antiphonally chanted through during each month and frequently read and sung privately, and the ordinary of the communion service; and then the proper, or sections of a service sung only once a year, such as occasional collects and "Christ Rising Again" and "Christ is risen again" for Easter Day, the only anthems authorized within the liturgy and incorporated into the Book of Common Prayer. Even during the earlier Reformation's fervor for clarity, John Sheppard's five-part setting of the Lord's Prayer, Peter Phillips observes, "is a model of clearly-written pervasive imitation, with hardly a bar of homophony in it."[16] Yet once the "Our Father" has been intoned in close succession by the first two voices of the counterpoint – each of the five parts entering with the leap of a fifth to illustrate the lifting up of the prayer – the congregation would be able to follow the words through the overlapping voices which appropriately convey the experience of their own multiplicity.

Numerous aids to intelligibility are available in polyphonic music: the incipits, to start with; passages for solo voice or voice section; and structural and expressive conventions that alert the listener to key words or dramatic moments. The beginning of a new sentence or clause may be marked by homophony or reduced voicing, the end by full choir, an elongated or melismatic cadence, that distinctive penultimate dissonance called "the English cadence," or all of these. These devices were used expressively even before the Reformation: a shift to fewer voices at "Qui tollis peccata mundi" or "Et incarnatus est" alerts the listener to moments of meditative intensity, while full and perhaps homophonic choral singing expresses "pleni sunt caeli et terra gloria tua" with a plenitude that the listener expects and recognizes. In Taverner's *Missa Gloria Tibi Trinitas* (*EECM* xx) solo voices, and hence words, frequently emerge from the polyphony in extraordinary sonic flights. "Et incarnatus est" is preceded by silence and expressed with slow, thoughtful declamation by multiple voices; "Crucifixus etiam pro nobis" is also preceded by a silence, then the bass entrance gives weighty sobriety, followed by a plaintive treble, and the other parts enter like mourners gathering around the cross.

After the publication of the Book of Common Prayer in 1549, English Church music had to be re-noted, and composers were exhorted to set words simply so that they could be understood. Beginning with Marbecke, they started to compose plainchant and homophonic syllabic settings, but such limitations have never succeeded for long in repressing musical variety. Instead, musicians found more ways of increasing intelligibility without sacrificing musical diversity. Declaiming a line of text monophonically or homophonically and then repeating it polyphonically achieves intelligibility while retaining varied sources of expressiveness; widely spaced imitative entrances let the gist emerge before more voices join; widely spaced intervals for these entrances, for example the basses entering first, then the means, give contrast that helps keep the lines clear; marking verbal emphases with harmonic modulations, and clauses with cadences, matches musical and verbal structure.

When composers are at their best, the delights of symbolic structure and formal unity, melodic and harmonic beauty, word-painting, and expressiveness occur simultaneously. "Lift up your hearts" set on a mimetically rising figure might also express and elicit jubilation harmonically and melismatically and contribute to structural unity by points of imitation. When sung in pure intonation by diverse but unified voices, and when, Herbert says in "A true Hymne," "the soul unto the lines accords," such a passage constitutes six kinds of "concent": of vocal parts with each other, of structural proportion with cosmic design, of intonation with the mathematics of that design, of music with words, of heart with art, and of the singers joined in what Hooker calls "a league of inviolable amitie" (*Lawes* II:154). Similarly, when poets are at their best, form, structure, verbal melody, imagery, prosodic word-painting, expressiveness, and an empathetic interchange with the reader or hearer conjoin.

The examples of relations between music and words that follow come from the two hundred years of English music, both secular and sacred, from Taverner to Purcell. Although the Reformation effected great changes, and although English choirs had a predilection for contemporary and local composers, the continuity of English choral traditions allows works of both centuries to chime with seventeenth-century poems.[17]

ONE DOUBLE STRING: MIMETIC CONCINNITY

Word-painting,[18] by which composers imitate the action or imagery of texts, is the best known connection of words and music, but the least respected because "madrigalisms" may interfere with structural and expressive unity. However, skillful composers use word-painting, structural unity, and expressiveness in mutually enhancing ways. Word play and music play and their interplay, displaying the interconnectedness of the design of the world and the workings of the mind, produce unexpected insights and awareness of real connections. Such text illumination provides delight because the mind revels in its expansion into a creation of which it is a freely creative part.

Since composers did not divide their stylistic resources into secular and sacred kinds, musical mimesis includes both secular witticisms and holy wit. Unlike strophic songs, madrigals are through-composed, with attention to words throughout, and some strophic ballets like Weelkes' "Hark, all ye lovely saints above" use only stanzas whose words are parallel in mood and fit the same music. The anthems and service music of the English Church were also through-composed, giving words musical figures specifically suited to them.

John Stevens points out that the earliest word-painting in English music precedes the Renaissance and is naturalistic, giving a poignant example from William Cornysh's setting of "Woefully arrayed," in which the speaker is Christ nailed to the cross and a "rare melodic leap" imitates the tactile piercing of the nailing.[19] Clearly, such detail is expressive of emotion as well as sensation. Hugh Benham gathers other early examples of "love of 'natural detail'" such as "the odd *stand*still, with semibreves in both parts, on the first syllable of 'Stabas' in Browne's six-part *Stabat virgo mater Christi* and "Fawkyner's depiction of the serpent in the undulating phrase at bars 91–94 of *Gaude rosa sine spina*."[20]

Renaissance and Reformation respect for language much increased the mimetic musical treatment of words. While each figure is a fresh variation, each composer being at pains to provide new twists, word-painting also became conventionalized as to kinds, so that for people who sing (including many poets discussed here) certain words take on musical expectations that flow into poetry. I shall give examples of kinetic, sensuous, and conceptual word-painting, though these will often overlap.

Thomas Morley gives a simple principle:

[Y]ou must have a care that when your matter signifieth "ascending," "high," "heaven," and such like you make your music ascend; for as it will be thought a great absurdity to talk of heaven and point downwards to the earth, so it will be counted a great incongruity if a musician upon the words "he ascended into heaven" should cause his music descend, or by the contrary upon the descension should cause his music to ascend.[21]

Accordingly, in Thomas Tomkins' "Arise, O Lord, into thy resting-place" (*EECM* XXXVII) the notes rise, linger on "rest," and lower as if settling into "place." Leighton's "Drop, drop slow tears" (*EECM* XI) descends the scale: music that drops in pitch does not *sound* like tears, but imitates the way they move. Lachrimae like Dowland's "Flow my Tears" and John Bennett's "Weep O mine eyes and cease not" combine long and short descending notes that imitate tears as they gather and fall, and Bennett sets "To swell so high" on ascending notes that peak on "high" and adds voice parts on "swell." A poem like Phineas Fletcher's "Drop, drop, drop" reads better if such music lingers in its pauses. Robert Herrick mimes a dropping tear with gentle humor in his epigram *Upon His Spaniel Tracy*:

Now thou art dead, no eye shall ever see,
For shape and service, *Spaniell* like to thee.
This shall my love doe, give thy sad death one
Tear, that deserves of me a million.

Some mimetic settings have the added pleasure of "eye music," since the notes visually ascend or descend the staves. In John Amner's Song of Moses,[22] on the words "the horse and him that rode vpon him, hath he ouerthrowne in the sea" the notes roll up and down the staff like big waves, with the lowest point at the end of "ouerthrowne," representing in sight and sound the Red Sea overwhelming Pharaoh's army. In Michael East's "When Israel came out of Egypt" (example 1) the verse "The mountains skipped like rams" makes tonal leaps on the very page, and these leaps are also mimed for the ear by the wide interval on "skipped," while "the little hills" skip "like young sheep" in upward runs and dotted rhythm; and these figures form peaks and ridges on the staves.

Hieroglyphic poems use analogous devices. In *Divination by a Daffadill*, Herrick contrives mimesis for the eye but not the ear:

When a Daffadill I see,
Hanging down his head t'wards me;
Guesse I may, what I must be:
First, I shall decline my head;
Secondly, I shall be dead;
Lastly, safely buryed.

The visual decline occurs in lines of exactly the same number of syllables.

In addition to eye music, singers sometimes experience other kinetic figures that listeners might miss. If you have ever been part of an amateur music group sight-reading Handel's "All we like sheep have gone astray" you know exactly what he means. Composers traditionally set the words "Let me not be confounded" as a fugue, so that the singers, fitting their similar lines into different parts of the texture, have an actual experience (one hopes) of not being confounded.

Kinetic mimesis includes moving-notes on words like "move" and separate voice parts on words like "part." Thomas Campion's song "When to her lute Corinna sings" begins syllabically but quickens melismatically on "revives." John Wilbye's "Adieu, sweet Amaryllis" mimes "to part" with separated voice parts and weights "O heavy tiding" with chromatic suspensions. "Yet once again ere

Example 1. Michael East, Psalm 114, "When Israel came out of Egypt," part 1, quintus part

that I part with you" is, of course, repeated several times, followed by a rest in all voices – a full break, like a parting of hands – and a change of mode for the final, repeated, reluctant adieux.

Henry Peacham notices in Vecchi's "S'io potessi raccor'i mei sospiri" "the breaking of the word sospiri with crotchet and crotchet-rest into sighs."[23] Campion's "Corinna" adapts the device to a one-syllable English word by inserting a rest after each repetition of "sighs." The word-painting is literally as well as metaphorically imitative, since the singer can inhale during the rest. George Herbert creates a verse analogue in the first stanza of *Sighs and Grones*:

> O do not use me
> After my sinnes! look not on my desert,
> But on thy glorie! then thou wilt reform
> And not refuse me: for thou onely art
> The mightie God, but I a sillie worm;
> O do not bruise me!

If Herbert had justified the lines in the usual way, they would be end-stopped, metrically smoother, lacking visual and kinetic interest, and far less expressive; a lesser poet might write

> According to my sins, O do not use me!
> Look not on my desert, but on thy glorie!
> Then thou wilt reform and not refuse me:
> For thou art mighty God, and I am only
> A poor and sillie worm; O do not bruise me!

Instead, by beginning the first line in the middle of the page Herbert throws all the stops into the middles of the lines to make caesuras that act like madrigalian "sighs." This pattern is emphasized by the internal rhyme of "refuse me" which would have formed a closing rhyme with "bruise me" if Herbert had not broken his lines in two. As it is, the first line does not find its resolving rhyme until the last, providing another gap, and also giving a sense of enclosure rather than fatal closure. By suggesting within itself a restructuring that leaves traces of a less interesting possibility, the stanza not only mimes the "Sighs" of the title but discloses a revision by which the miming is achieved; thus the stanza also mimes hieroglyphically the gist of the prayer, which is "reform."

Other instances of word-painting respond sensuously to sensory images: aural, tactile, olfactory, and visual. Settings of words having to do with the senses often alert the faculty addressed by ornamental, structural, or harmonic emphasis, a point worth remembering when reading poems. Taverner's "Audivi vocem de Caelo" (*EECM* xxx: "I heard a voice from heaven") gives nearly a third of the motet's music to "Audivi" and sets "Ecce," "Behold," on two long chords. Byrd ends a highly melismatic Christmas anthem sung "By angels" on over seventy notes in each part for "Lend us your listening eares" with extended repetitions and melisma on "listen."[24]

The mimesis of sound is of course native to music, and examples are legion. Psalms 96, 98, and 149, all beginning "O sing unto the Lord a new song," challenge each composer to set these words in new ways and thus obey them. Psalms 81, "Sing we merrily unto God our strength," and 150, "O praise God in his sanctuary," list musical instruments whose timbres choral composers imitate in the voice parts. In "This sweet and merry month of May," a tribute to Queen Elizabeth, William Byrd introduces "Eliza" by voicing that imitates a trumpet flourish, and on "O beauteous Queen" offers a broad homophonic fanfare. Milton imitates this kind of imitation by the tongue-exercise of "Trumpets' sound throughout the host" (*Paradise Lost* 1.754) and mimes the broadness of the "Trumpet's regal sound" when "four speedy Cherubim / Put to thir mouths the sounding Alchemy" (2.515–17).

The sounds of nature often enter music through pastoral poetry and romance as set by Italian madrigalists and their English followers. For Guarini's "A un giro sol de'begl'occhi lucenti," in which the beloved's lucent glance brightens the surroundings, calms the waves and winds, and irradiates the sky, Monteverdi in his *Quatro libro dei madrigali* (1603) paints the waves with rolling runs, the wafting winds with lighter ones, and the sky with twinkling points of imitation. Marenzio's setting of Tasso's "Vezzosi augelli" (*Primo libro dei madrigali*, 1585) includes avian melodies, leafy lightness, and rolling floods. In Adriano Banchieri's *Contrapunto Bestiale alla Mente* the cuckoo, the screech-owl, the cat, the dog, and the drunkard make comic polyphony of their diverse cries. Josquin des Près' *El Grillo* (The Cricket) scrapes and chirps, and Claude Le Jeune's "Petite importune mouch" and "Une puce" both audibly pester the speaker or his mistress in ways that foretell Donne's *The Flea*: the first speaker envies the fly's licence in touching his beloved everywhere, and the second has a flea in his ear that itches and bites in a way only the mistress can relieve. William Byrd imitates both song and flight in "The Nightengale so pleasant" (reminding one of Milton's poetic emblem) and Thomas Weelkes in "The nightengale, the organ of delight" puts "all the pretty quiristers of flight" together in an exuberant chorus silenced finally by the cuckoo. Vautor's "Sweet Suffolk Owle" sings "Te whit, te whoo," Gibbons' "Silver Swanne" glides, Wilbye's "Sweet hony sucking Bees" dart and buzz, and *The Cats* of William Lawes caterwaul.

Musical imitations of touch often occur in settings of love poems. In Dowland's "Come again" a panting ascent climaxes on "die" followed by a descending subsidence. In "A little pretty bonny lass" John Farmer's syncopation on the words "I took her by the hand" suggests an impulsive gesture. Weelkes' "Four arms, two necks, one wreathing" weaves sensuous homophonic harmonies, with an occasional brief emergence of separate voices to indicate the two-ness within the one-ness: in the words of Donne's *Exstasie*, a "dialogue of one." In Wilbye's "Lady your words do spite me" the words "kiss" and "kisses" get extra length, or pressure.

Musical treatment of visual experience frequently includes "eye music" in two senses. Italian madrigalists liked to set "occhi," eyes, on pairs of whole notes, miming the lovers' long gaze, so that a pair of eyes seems to gaze at the singer from the page. (Since in Renaissance notation notes are commonly lozenge or diamond-shaped, the Petrarchism of eyes like diamonds is literalized.) When one voice part is singing these long notes, the other voices may be creating intensity and vivacity by means of runs, suspensions, and dissonances, recreating the complexity of emotions in the long-held look. In Marenzio's "Occhi lucenti e belli" the cantus sings whole notes clear through – apart from some long rests like sighs – while the other voice parts represent the various expressions in those eyes and the vagaries of passion, hope, and pain in the heart of the lover. Words like "lucenti," "vaghi," and "allegri" get lightsome runs, while a suspension on "crudele" provides a suspenseful dissonance and leading tone. Intensity builds in ascending harmonic progressions while the whole notes continue with maddening persistence, until one feels acutely the lover's plea that since by them he will live or die, those dear eyes should be serene and clear, a hope which the harmonies of the final line fulfill.

Olfactory word-painting is rarer, but notable instances in settings of the Easter respond "Dum transisset Sabbatum" represent the aromatic spices brought by the three Marys to Christ's tomb. Taverner (followed by Tallis, Shephard, and Robert Johnson) sumptuously ornaments "aromata," dwelling on the syllables as if to savor the scent and cadencing with a richly harmonized melisma and a modulation to a higher key as the spicy fragrances rise. Sweet smells also melodically rise in settings of verses from the Song of Songs such as "Let him kiss me with the kisses of his mouth" (AV Song of Solomon 1.2–4):

> Osculetur me osculo oris sui;
> Quia meliora sunt ubera tua vino.
> Fragrantia unguentis optimis,
> Oleum effusum nomen dilexerunt te.
>
> Trahe me, post te curremus
> In odorem unguentorum tuorum . . .

In Palestrina's setting, the harmony sharpens on "vino" and rises lushly on "Fragrantia"; on "post te curremus" the voices follow each other in runs, and these prepare for the captivation of a more nearly homophonic harmonic richness for "In odorem unguentorum tuorum." Thomas Tomkins' "My beloved spake" (*EECM* x i v) harmonically expresses "give a sweet smell" with a rich rising modulation.

Kinetic, sensuous, and pictorial treatments of words one need only notice or feel. Conceptual musical metaphor depends on construing. Giles Farnaby's "Construe my meaning" has odd tonalities and chromaticisms that make the music as puzzling as the text. In "A little pretty bonny lass" John Farmer ornaments the verb "devise," which in its substantive form meant emblematic ornament.

Numerical and relational concepts are often expressed by voicing: multiplicity polyphonically, unity homophonically, both by "full" sections where other passages are assigned to fewer voices. Thomas Greaves' "Come away sweet love and play thee" is homophonic until the words "running in and out," where the voice lines break apart and run in and out of each other. At "Leave off this sad lamenting," Greaves reverts to homophony and interpolates a modal harmony that would now be called "minor" on "lamenting," which is immediately "left off" for a return to cheerful tonalities on "And take thy hearts contenting." Wilbye's masterful "Oft have I vowed," after abundant polyphonic repetition on "millions of tears" (the repeated *t*'s splashing audibly), a heaving prolongation on "sighs," and heavily declining notes as the lover's heart pines, suddenly bares the bass line on "barren hopes." In a sacred madrigal by Michael East,[25] voice parts represent body parts. Two middle voices, quintus and tenor, sing "To thee O Jesus I direct mine eyes." The higher cantus sings "to thee my handes" – uplifted, we suppose – and the solo moves down to the tenor for "To thee my humble knees." Quintus and cantus together sing "To thee my harte shall offer sacrifice" and all members make one body for "to Thee, my all, my selfe and all I giue."

Much word-painting crosses the line, if there is one, between mimetic and rhetorical metaphor. Thomas Tomkins' two settings of "Turn thou us, O good Lord," from the prayer book "Commination against Sinners," treat the conception of turning in several ways. The first (*EECM* xiv),[26] a verse anthem in five parts, begins with a simple alto solo in C minor (in the modern edition), which goes up the scale, then turns and comes down on "and so shall we be turned," with syncopation giving momentum. Then the full choir repeats the words, moved up to F minor which at the cadence confirms "so shall we be turned" by pivoting (with the middle voice decorating the word while providing the preparatory $E_\natural$) into an affirmative F major chord, so that the singers are literally con-verted (turned together). Meanwhile, however, the organ part executes more complicated melodic and harmonic turns over and under the simple voice parts, as if the spirit, or the Spirit, were at work above and beneath the plain words. The voicing of the second version (*EECM* xxvii) is more complicated: it is a canon, so that the voice parts circle in a round, each voice taking the melody in turn; melodically, each voice in its turn turns down, and then up, in rhythmically mirroring figures, and while some voices are turning down, others are turning up; the line modulates and re-turns harmonically while the lower parts complete "so shall we be turned." Of course, any of these strategies could occur in a piece that was not about turning, but the fact that they turn up together gives an intellectual delight to match the kinetic sensation, and so joins body and soul by letting us perceive physically and mentally the spiritual act requested.

The treatment of abstractions such as mercy and justice also engages the listener's rational faculties. Descending notes represent God's mercy dropping down from heaven, often chromat-

ically, as Monteverdi sets "misericordia" in Psalm 112 (AV 113): a
kind of figure which might have made Milton remove the phrase
"harsh chromatick jars" from a draft of *At a Solemn Musick*.[27] Since
justice demonstrates uprightness and makes straight the ways of
the Lord, "just" and "justitia" are often "justified," in the printer's
sense of the word, in homophony – chords vertically aligned and
thus visually justified on the page, as at the beginning of Byrd's
"Justorum animae." In Orlando Gibbons' "O Lord, I lift my heart
to thee" (example 2) voices that had been weaving polyphonically
end on "just" in an open fifth. Not only are the notes "justified" on
the page, but the voices are so exposed that if the singers are not
precisely in "just concent" they immediately become aware of it.
Tuning is a metaphor for justice in Plato's definition of the just
man: one in whom the parts of the heart are in harmonious proportion.

A madrigal in Francis Pilkington's *Madrigals and Pastorals I à
3,4,5*, 1613 (example 3) combines several of these kinds of
mimetic figures.

> Have I found her? O rich finding!
> Goddess-like for to behold,
> Her fair tresses seemly binding
> In a chain of pearl and gold:
> Chain me, chain me, O most fair,
> Chain me to thee with that hair.

The conventional text is unprepossessing, but the setting is witty.
It begins with a timid but excited "Have I found her?" in the upper
voice only, in a tentative minor, followed by a promising but incomplete major chord on "O" in the lower voices and a satisfyingly full
four-voiced tonic chord on "rich," which changes to, or finds, the
dominant on "finding." The voices then repeat "Have I found her"
on quick notes, each part entering before the preceding one has
finished, with a sense of growing eagerness. "Goddess-like for to
behold" continues the part-singing, but with two voices at a time
singing the words together until all four join on "behold" (bar 16),
like lovers' eyes joining: "[O]ur eye-beames twisted," as Donne
puts it in *The Exstasie*, "and did thred / Our eyes, upon one double
string." In addition, the two middle parts exchange places, the
tenor singing above the alto, as if to mime the exchange of looks:
as Prospero observes of Ferdinand and Miranda, "They have
changed eyes."

Example 2. Orlando Gibbons, "O Lord, I lift my heart to thee," bars 12–21

Example 3a. Francis Pilkington, "Have I found her?", bars 10–16

Next, Pilkington musically strokes the lady's hair on "seemly tresses" with smooth descending whole notes, given a pleasing roughness by syncopation in the lower voices. On "In a chain of pearl and gold" (bars 32–48) he devises a conceptual metaphor. Henry Peacham describes a comparable figure from a madrigal by "mine own master, Horatio Vecchi of Modena" where on the words "I die enchained" Vecchi "driveth a crotchet through many minims, causing it to resemble a chain with links."[28] Pilkington forges the chain by clearly separated but interlinking figures. Not only is the figure conceptually chain-like, but the repetitions of "chain" as each voice enters provide the chinking *sound* of a chain. Then on "Chain me, chain me, O most fair" a strong homophony in dancing triple rhythm represents the binding of the lover with the tresses of his beloved. Here the metaphor of the chain, not the hair it complements, gets the word-painting.

Example 3b. Francis Pilkington, "Have I found her?", bars 32–41

How do such complex musical devices get into poetry? Since they are composed in response to words, music is imitating language; but in seventeenth-century poetry, especially, words also imitate music in so many ways that the influence is surely reciprocal. For those who have sung madrigals and anthems, captivating harmonies linger around comparable verbal figures and often appear to have given poets specific techniques for miming images and concepts in sound and syntax. Although mimetic prosody is dependent only on the properties of language, English poetry became extraordinarily rich in mimetic forms at the same time that the madrigal became naturalized in England and the connection between words and music was strongest in both secular and sacred music. The experience of musical mimesis surely enriched poets' stock of prosodic possibilities, structural proportions, and harmonic resonances and gave language a fullness, flexibility, and precision incorporating the conceptual and expressive qualities of music.

HOLY MATHEMATICS: STRUCTURAL CONCINNITY

While an informal series of musical images can be graceful in a short form like the madrigal, larger works need structural unity, a long-term mustering of energies and a deployment of form driven by the unfolding power of the music itself. In Renaissance music, contrapuntal imitation provides unity and elegance, a kind of "simplicity" within complexity; works not so organized may be built of musical blocks fitted together by repetition, variation, parallel motives and rhythms, harmonic development, tension, and resolution. At the same time, many composers managed to word-paint individual phrases within the integrity of larger structures[29] and even to unify structure by means of musical figures responsive to verbal ones. William Byrd is best known for excellences of structure and expression yet uses word-illumination, not as disparate decorations but as integral architectural forms.

In Byrd's Second Service, the emphasis listeners expect on words about perception applies to God's regard (in both senses) in the Magnificat: "For thou hast regarded the lowliness of thy handmaiden." An emphatic harmonic change on "regarded" makes singers and listeners aware of God's gaze, directed toward the handmaiden who speaks and toward the listener who hears. Byrd then repeats the harmony, with a slight variation, on "handmaiden," so that the regard and its object, the perceiver and the perceived, nearly become one, and the response of the handmaiden, the spokeswoman for right responders, is literally put in tune with God's regard. Her response and the cosmic structures that make music possible fuse. This treatment of words helps unify both the idea and the musical form and energize the line's movement toward its cadence. By this tuning of God's regard and the response of its recipient, the listener's perceptions are also being set, as Milton said poetry sets our affections, "in right tune."

Poets and composers match structure to meaning in comparable ways. Analysing the harmonic, melodic, and motivic structure of Byrd's "Ne irascaris Domine" (*BE* 11), Joseph Kerman comments, "Over . . . remarkably firm structural underpinnings Byrd spread a musical surface that is just as remarkable for its gentle iridescent quality"; the music emerges from "supple cells" into luminous cadences.[30] "Supple cells" is a felicitous phrase for formally structured yet subtle stanzas, such as Andrew Marvell's, as well. Meditating upon the "sober frame" of Appleton House and the magnitude of its inhabitants, Marvell remarks,

> Humility alone designs
> These short but admirable lines,
> By which, ungirt and unconstrained,
> Things greater are in less contained.
> Let others vainly strive t'immure
> The circle in the quadrature!
> These holy mathematics can
> In every figure equal man.

The form of Marvell's stanzas (or rooms) imitates the conception. Each has eight short lines of eight syllables, conceptually forming a square or quadrature (visually, too, if the manuscript lines were justified). The eight lines also suggest an octave or diapason, mirroring the eight spheres of the visible world. Each line has four stresses, and each stanza has four couplets. Four is the microcosmic number, eight the macrocosmic one. Humility recognizes that the heavenly circle cannot be walled into the earthly dwellings of and for the human body, for which, he says in the previous stanza, people should build "fit cases," as other animals do; the just man – in this case the Lord General Fairfax – constructs both his temperament and his house in fit proportions. Yet the dwellers therein are "ungirt" and the mathematics holy "in every figure." "Figure" means number, proportion, shape, architectural design, trope, scheme, and allegory. Just as in the architecture of the material house that contains the infinity of the human soul "Things greater are in less contained," so Marvell's stanzas contain unconstrained polysemousness, issuing out of the language itself, within "cases fit."

If the beauty of the created world displays an image of its creator, and composers and poets participate in creativity as his images, then number and proportion, the mathematical basis of creation, reside in each artist's bag of splendors. Musical intonation and verbal consonance supply one set of analogous effects. Musical and poetic structure supply another. Some composers of the Eton Choirbook retained a complex iconic numerology, but increasingly, composers sought structural clarity that imaged the proportions of the created world while simultaneously offering symbolic significance. The triad, for instance, is a mathematical fact of a musical scale in which thirds are consonant, and, as was often observed, three voices can produce all the consonances of the diatonic scale. If a composer gives words concerning the Trinity a three-part structure or three voices or triple measure, these threes are not arbitrary numerical icons but acknowledgments of the correspondence of mind and matter that Kepler said was not a necessity of creation but "a splendour of its form."[31] If the composer combines all three, this triune triplicity corresponds with the nine choirs of angels and the nine celestial spheres (including the *primum mobile*). Such "holy mathematics," as Marvell called fitness of form and substance with regard to architecture, may be seen in the structural similarities in three works of art: the windows of King's College Chapel, Taverner's *Missa Gloria Tibi Trinitas*, and Herbert's *Trinitie Sunday*.

The architecture of the chapel provides a visual analogy for music like Taverner's, contemporary with its completion: soaring yet rooted, symbolically proportioned but unified, and elaborate in elegant detail that refrains from obscuring its structural clarity. The program of the windows represents "the olde lawe and the new lawe."[32] The twelve bays contain twelve windows on each side, each having ten vertical lights, perhaps suggesting the ten commandments of "the olde lawe" and the twelve apostles of the new. At the same time, twelve is divisible by both three and four, a combination of symbolic numbers corresponding numerically with the intersection of heaven and earth in the geometry of the perpendicular style. The double twelve is also an astronomical number, as in Spenser's *Epithalamion*, whose twenty-four stanzas match the hours of the cosmic clock, and an epic one, Homer's epics having twenty-four books, Vergil's and Milton's twelve, Spenser's proposed one twelve or twenty-four.

The east window, however, alters the plan. Liturgically, the altar of a Christian church is always in the east, so that (symbolically if not actually) the congregation faces towards the earthly and, typologically, the heavenly Jerusalem and the rising sun and Son: God and nature joined. Instead of ten typological lights, this window has two rows of nine lights each, divided into three groups of three. A third set of lights at the top of the window is also divided by the tracery into three threes, and these further divide into fourteen lights in the center section and nine on each side; these nine correspond with the three lights in the sections below them, so that the triples triple.

Taverner's *Missa Gloria Tibi Trinitas* is a richly polyphonic piece in balanced sections in each of which (with the exception of one free-composed section of the Agnus Dei) the "mean" or lower treble voices state the cantus firmus three times. The words "et ascendit" in the Credo are set not only on rising notes in each of the nine voice parts but also on nine rising points of imitation. While each voice word-paints the action, the points of imitation provide unity, and the ascent of those points from bass to treble also corresponds with the sense of the words. The structural unity achieved by the imitation is given symbolic significance by the compass of nine notes, a triple trinity.[33] One might compare Dante's soul passing through the spheres and the music of the nine spheres answering to the music of the nine choirs of angels in Milton's *On the Morning of Christ's Nativity*.[34] The hearer is aware of the expressive quality of the music, achieved partly by the melodic ascent, the first two parts rising in sonorous and symbolic thirds, and partly by the less obvious quick ascent of the points of imitation from the lowest to the highest voice part. Although the words may be lost and the ascent so swift that only the singers may discern its complexities, any listener familiar with the Credo would receive a strong impression that an ascension is going on.

The cantus firmus of this mass setting, composed for Trinity Sunday during Taverner's tenure at Christ Church, Oxford, is an antiphon for that day from the Sarum Antiphoner: "Gloria tibi Trinitas aequalis una Deitas et ante omnia saecula et nunc et in perpetuum." Like the Gloria Patri, the antiphon joins the "nunc" of the present time with the eternity that subsumes time, another instance of the "perpendicular." The mass setting, like the architecture of the chapel, combines an ordered serenity with variety of detail; and its expressive beauty is enriched by its form. Solo voices thread the polyphonic weaving so that one is aware of individuality and community, specificity and continuity, temporality and eternity, at once. The phrases swell and subside like winged flight. In the last movement, on the last "Dona nobis pacem," Taverner changes to compound triple time with, Peter Phillips says, "magical effect"[35]: a structural analogue of the pattern of the east window of the chapel.

This kind of symbolic structuring, which does not interfere with the flow or expressiveness of the music but deepens its connections to the cosmos and divine numbers, is also a feature of Herbert's poem for the same occasion, *Trinitie Sunday.*

> Lord, who hast form'd me out of mud,
> And has redeem'd me through thy bloud,
> And sanctifi'd me to do good;
>
> Purge all my sinnes done heretofore:
> For I confesse my heavie score,
> And I will strive to sinne no more.
>
> Enrich my heart, mouth, hands in me,
> With faith, with hope, with charitie;
> That I may runne, rise, rest with thee.

The poem is structured in three stanzas of three lines, like a ninefold Kyrie, each triplet underscored and unified by end-stopped rhymes and the three visually unified as well, by their projecting first words that sum up the prayer: "Lord, Purge, Enrich." The three lines of the first stanza acknowledge the three operations of the Trinity – addressed in its unity as "Lord" with a singular "thee" – as creator, redeemer, and sanctifier. The three lines of the second stanza contain the speaker's plea for purification, his confession, and his resolution to "strive to sinne no more," each of these addressed to the whole of the Trinity and each of its persons: asking the Creator for re-creation, confessing to the Redeemer, and promising to strive in the Spirit. But the third stanza, like Taverner's Agnus Dei, triples, and becomes ninefold itself. The plea "Enrich my heart, mouth, hands" – the agents of the "thought, word, and deed" of the prayerbook's general confession – parallels the qualities the faith, hope, and charity sought, "That I may runne, rise, rest with thee." This tripling is particularly appropriate to the plea, "Enrich," answered by the increase and acceleration of the tripled series of words. "Runne, rise, rest," with its triple alliteration, speeds to the climactic "rest" or stay of the conclusion.

Whether, at Trinity College or elsewhere, Herbert heard or took part in a private reading of Taverner's mass is unknowable, but it seems likely that similar musical structures affected his poems. The "Trinity Sunday" in the Williams manuscript, not included in *The Temple*, does not have this structure, and it may be that he responds in the later poem to the kind of musical form he experienced at those "musick meetings" Walton speaks of following Evensong at Salisbury Cathedral, the home church of the Sarum Antiphoner. He observes the architectural symbolism of Cambridge chapels in several poems, and he possessed a sense of form like Taverner's "holy mathematics," as did many composers whose English service music he certainly heard. Through the correspondences of architectural, musical, and poetic form, the poem, in all its simplicity, participates in the richness of its liturgical contexts.

HEART AND ART: EXPRESSIVE CONCINNITY

Music can either express emotional states, create them, or revise them. Brady's and Purcell's *Ode on St. Cecilia's Day*, alluding to Orpheus, demonstrates this power:

> 'Tis Nature's Voice, thro' all the Wood
>   Of Creatures understood,
>   The Universal Tongue, to none
>   Of all her num'rous Race unknown.
>   From her it learn'd the mighty Art
>   To court the Ear and strike the Heart,
>   At once the Passions to express or move:
> We hear, and straight We grieve or hate, Rejoice or love:
>   In unseen Chains it does the Fancy bind.
>   At once it charms the Sense and captivates the Mind.

Purcell's melismatic setting for solo voice – in the original performance his own – demonstrates each affect and ends with a captivating example of what Milton in *L'Allegro* called "linckèd sweetnes long drawn out." A later section ("Wondrous Machine") contrasts the organ with other instruments, each illustrated with vocal melodies accompanied and recapitulated by the appropriate instruments: lute and viol "court the cruel fair, or praise Victorious Kings," flute and guitar labor to "inspire / Wanton Heat and loose Desire," and the fife attempts to stir up warlike passions, all in vain, while the organ, which contains them all, is "to more noble Uses bent" and its sounds "compose and charm."

The claim that music can cause or allay particular emotional states is based on both classical and scriptural ideas of the tuning of the soul. In *The Republic* Plato defines the well-tempered person by analogy to musical temperament. The three parts of the soul – reason, appetite, and a mediating spirit that can encourage or rebuke them – are like the intervals of a musical scale:

The just man does not allow the several elements in his soul to usurp one another's functions; he is indeed one who sets his house in order, by self-mastery and discipline coming to be at peace with himself, and bringing into tune those three parts, like the terms in the proportion of a musical scale, the highest and lowest notes and the mean between them, with all the intermediate intervals.[36]

The Bible applies music to a distempered soul in the story of David's healing of Saul: "David took an harp, and played with his hand: so Saul was refreshed and was well, and the evil spirit departed from him" (1. Sam. 16.23). The power of music to heal the soul was asserted in defenses against puritan opponents of church music and in seventeenth-century poetry, which was at the same time defending itself. Robert Herrick's epigrams *To Musique, to becalme his Fever* and *To Musick, to becalme a sweet-sick-youth* invoke music to allay the body's pain as well, and his charming epigram *To Musick* addresses music's power to create emotional states.

Just as Sidney recognizes that poetry can be well used or abused, Brady and Purcell recognize that certain kinds can stir up undesirable moods. (Morley in his *Plain and Easy Introduction* uses "mood" interchangeably with "mode.") The association of certain tonalities with moral slackness goes back at least as far as Plato's recommendation to avoid "slack" modes associated with "drunkenness, effeminacy, and inactivity" when training warriors.[37] In Marvell's *Dialogue, between the Resolved Soul and Created Pleasure*, music is the most seductive temptation "Created Pleasure" can produce. Visual artists recognized that music can incite to violence, wantonness, or idleness by including musical instruments in *Vanitas* paintings, and Hieronymus Bosch in *The Earthly Paradise* (like Milton) puts them in Hell.

On the other hand, artists represented the harmony of heaven by endowing good angels with various musical instruments, not only biblical ones – some depicted medieval and Renaissance instruments meticulously enough to provide models for modern reconstructions – and for innumerable poets music can both "lift our thoughts to Heaven" (*PL* 4.688) and fit our hearts for life on

earth. Richard Hooker, defending the music of the English
Church against reformers' zeal for plainness, says of harmony
that "such is the force thereof and so pleasinge effectes it hath
even in that verie parte of man which is most divine, that some
have bene thereby induced to thinke that the soule it selfe by
nature is, or hath in it harmonie." Harmony delights because of
"an admirable facilitie which musique hath to expresse and
represent to the minde more inwardlie than any other sensible
meane . . . all the passions whereunto the minde is subject," and
can either confirm or change them, since "In harmonie the verie
image and character even of vertue and vice is perceived" and by
it the mind is led to love either; "For which cause there is
nothinge more contagious and pestilent then some kindes of harmonie; then some nothinge more stronge and potent unto
good." And as Milton says that poetry has power to "set the affections in right tune" (*SM* 525), Hooker says of music even apart
from words:

[T]he verie harmonie of soundes beinge framed in due sorte and carryed
from the eare to the spirituall faculties of our soules is by a native puis-
sance and efficacie greatlie available to bringe to a perfect temper whatsoever is there troubled, apt as well to quicken the spirites as to allay that
which is too eger, soveraigne against melancolie and despaire, forcible to
drawe forth teares of devotion if the minde be such as can yeld them, able
both to move and to moderate all affections. (*Lawes* II:152)

The musical expression of emotion is often thought imported
into England from Italy in the sixteenth century. But although the
expressiveness of English music and poetry was enlarged by continental "musical humanism," earlier native developments and the
Reformation's attention to words are fundamental. John Stevens
finds no emotional connection between words and music in the
Middle Ages; rather, there may be a correspondence, because the
author and the composer are contemplating the same thing. From
the late fourteenth century, a few composers, such as Dunstable
and Ockeghem, imitated the "natural accent" of human speech by
passionate declamation. By the end of the fifteenth century word-
painting did not just imitate sounds but made music "symbolically
representative of texts." Of Cornysh's "Woefully arayed," when
Christ on the cross speaks, "So pained, so strained," Stevens writes,
"long notes with pauses are introduced in every voice: the per-
former sees an elongated shape on the page . . . the listener hears

a note stretched out"[38] – like the "stretchèd sinews" of Christ on the cross in Herbert's *Easter* .

Originally it was settings of texts associated with Mary that received expressive treatment, such as Dunstable's *Quam pulchra es*, other texts from the Song of Songs, and the Salve Reginas and Stabat Maters of the Eton Choirbook; her love and suffering moved composers to use the emotive resources of love songs. The second stanza of Cornysh's *Stabat Mater* contains a musical figure of extreme anguish, expressing the words "Cuius animam gementem, / Contristantem et dolentem, / Pertransivit gladius": Through her trembling soul, agonized and grieving, passed a sword. According to Peter Phillips, Cornysh's effects "would have made him perfectly suited to the madrigal a hundred years later."[39] When Renaissance musical humanism arrived on the scene, then, earlier English composers had prepared a way for it, and the native flavor reemerged in the English madrigal and verse anthem.

Wilfred Mellers describes the entrance of "humanistic pathos" into the timelessness of polyphony in the Agnus Dei of Byrd's Mass for Five Voices:

The form of this Agnus, as of the whole Mass . . . is an incarnation of Oneness, not an expression of human feeling: indeed a single theme dominates not only this movement, but the complete Mass . . . Entirely without metrical stress or harmonic implication, it is simply a stepwise undulation below and above the fifth: a suspiration as inevitable as the pulse or heart-beat, god-like because it seems equated with the mysterious source from which it flows. With the words "qui tollis peccata mundi," however, we turn from the contemplation of Godhead to our sinful selves.

Here Byrd introduces increasingly conflicting chromatic notes as each voice enters, a change which "effects a gradual increase in tension; the words 'miserere nobis' are set to a simple declining scale; but, entering in canon, the parts do not droop simultaneously. One is held while another falls, so that passing dissonances of minor ninth and minor second pierce our nerves." Whereas "the modal, non-harmonic nature of the individual lines, the fluidity of the rhythms, release us, as does the plainsong, from the burden of personality . . . the dissonant texture . . . imbues the music with a sense of suffering; and this dissonance – the concept of the suspension itself – is inseparable from an awareness of periodic Time."[40] Like Herbert's Man "With th'one hand touching heav'n, with th'other earth," Byrd's Mass joins the contrasts and the ties between divinity and humanity.

While musical expressiveness in the seventeenth century is often associated with monody, in which dramatic characters render words feelingly as musical humanists believed the music of Greek drama to do, part-music can also express and create profound emotion. Monteverdi's *Orfeo* alternates madrigals and declamation within a symmetrical structure, and it seems likely that the lost context of the *Lamento d'Arianna* – which he also rewrote in parts and set to a new text as a sacred madrigal – did the same. For some kinds of feeling, part-singing is more apt than monody. The experience of the intertwined lovers in Weelkes' musical embrace, "Four arms, two necks, one wreathing," could hardly be so movingly conveyed by one voice. The intensity of feeling vocal harmonic tensions allow may be heard in sacred madrigals by Weelkes and Tomkins on David's lament for Absalom (2. Sam. 18.93), mourning the death of Prince Henry in 1612 by the association of King James (who wrote metrical psalms) with David.

Musical ways of expressing words include modal changes, consonance and dissonance, rhythms and tempi, melisma and other kinds of ornamentation, and voicing, of which examples follow. But, as Henry Raynor says, music and words do not merely adorn or express each other, and neither is subservient; vocal music achieved a "complete union of words and music sharing the same expressive life."[41]

MODALITY

Much early seventeenth-century music was still modal, rather than tonal. Zarlino offers the simple principle, reminiscent of Morley's for word-painting, that "the harmony . . . should be so adapted . . . to the words, that in joyous matters the harmony will not be mournful, and vice versa, that in mournful ones the harmony will not be joyful."[42] To modern ears, the easiest distinction is between minor and major keys. But Zarlino's application of modes is less simple and composers' uses are highly adaptable. Although there were rules about beginning and ending compositions in related modes, modal music is not so tonally centered as the music that became dominant later in the century and raises expectations of resolution in a controlling key. Poems, too, such as Donne's *Songs and Sonets*, may have unexpected progressions and not wind up in the mood where they began.

Morley describes the eight modes, moods, tones, or tunes, as they were variously called, in the "Annotations" to part 3 of his obscure and complicated *Plaine and Easie Introduction*. Much more simply, according to William Duckworth and Edward Brown, the modes are "based on a pattern of five whole-steps and two half-steps; the changing placement of the half-steps gives each mode its own unique sound." Some slight idea of them may be gained by playing scales on the white keys of a piano, starting with each note from D to C, producing something like the ancient Dorian, Phrygian, Lydian, Mixolydian, Aeolian, Locrian, and Ionian modes,[43] but the church modes were the first four of these and their plagal versions. Plato, whose attitude toward music is at best austere, defined the use of modes according to the emotion to be aroused and found most of them unworthy.[44] "Song," Socrates says, "consists of three elements: words, musical mode, and rhythm . . . And the musical mode and the rhythm should fit the words . . . Which are the modes that express sorrow?"

[GLAUCON:] Modes like the Mixed Lydian and Hyperlydian.

[SOCRATES:] Then we may discard those; men, and even women of good standing, will have no use for them . . . Which are the modes expressing softness and the ones usual at drinking-parties?

[GLAUCON:] There are the Ionian and certain Lydian modes which are called "slack."

[SOCRATES:] You will not use them in the training of your warriors?

[GLAUCON:] Certainly not. You seem to have the Dorian and the Phrygian left.

[SOCRATES:] . . . two modes you must leave: the two which will best express the accents of courage in the face of stern necessity and misfortune, and of temperance in prosperity won by peaceful pursuits.

[GLAUCON:] The modes you want . . . are just the two I mentioned.

Hence Milton's demons march "to the Dorian mood / Of Flutes and soft Recorders," choosing the mode of "deliberate valor" (1.550–51, 1.554) through the instruments of Marsyas (as Socrates calls them) rather than Apollo. The playing of the martial mode on instruments that can "inspire / Wanton heat and loose desire" may be part of Milton's infernal humor.[45]

Reformation psalm-singing assigned expressive connotations to the church modes and psalters provided tables showing which tunes and meters fit which psalms. The Thomas Tallis wrote fine four-part harmonies for "Meane, Contra tenor, Tenor, Base" for the eight tunes (and his well-known Ordinal) for Archbishop Parker's *Whole Psalter translated into English metre* (*c.* 1567), which prescribes that "The Tenor of these partes be for the people when they will syng alone, the other parts, put for greater queers or to suche as will syng or play them priuately." The Psalter provides the psalms with symbols for appropriate modes; none of them is associated with lasciviousness, but the variety of other human emotions includes some that readers with a lugubrious idea of religious expressiveness might not expect.

1. The first is meeke: devout to saie,
2. The second sad in maiesty,
3. The third doth rage; and roughly brayth,
4. The fourth doth fawne; and flattrye playth.
5. The fyfth deligth: and laugheth the more,
6. The sixt bewayleth; it wepeth full sore,
7. The seuenth tredeth stoute in forward race,
8. The eyghthe goeth milde; in modest pace.

Consonance, Dissonance, and Chromaticism

Like any symbol, musical proportions have multiple interpretations. Simultaneous notes less than a minor third or more than a major sixth apart, "forbidden" intervals such as the tritone, and especially the "false relation" of a note with its sharpened or flattened namesake, such as C and C$_\sharp$, may be used to represent distress, discord, or the "barbarous dissonance" of Comus' monsters in Milton's *Mask* or "that wild Rout that tore the *Thracian* Bard" in *Paradise Lost* (7.30). But dissonance, and even the censorious-sounding "false relation," may represent intense awe and devotion as well. In Tallis' "Loquebantur variis linguis" (*TCM* VI) the repetitions of "magnalia Dei" culminate in the marvelous clash of G with F and A in the upper parts, followed by F$_\sharp$ in the Superius while the bass F is still sounding, and Tomkins' "O sing unto the Lord a new song" employs chromatic dissonance in its remarkable alleluias.

The use of false relations just before the close of a piece or section was so popular among English composers as to be called "the English cadence." A good example comes at the end of Tallis' "Spem in alium." When perfectly in tune, the effect is not unpleas-

ant, but thrilling. The use of dissonance gave English music distinction during the Middle Ages and a source of expressiveness
rooted in that native tradition during the Renaissance. Some of
the strength of English poetry, too, derives from a preference for
close and sometimes clashing sounds over tyrannical mellifluous-
ness.

Chromaticism, or the use of "accidentals" (marked with sharps
or flats) not found in the mode or key in which a piece is composed, is often used to express grief. Byrd exhibits the convention
musically (*BE* xiv):

> Come, woeful Orpheus with thy charming Lyre,
> And tune my voice unto thy skilful wire,
> Some strange Chromatic Notes do you devise,
> That best with mournful accents sympathize,
> Of sourest Sharps and uncouth Flats make choice,
> And I'll thereto compassionate my voice.

This highly chromatic piece not only demonstrates "sourest
Sharps and uncouth Flats" and, in contrast, "tune," but also, by
taking the voices through numerous mode changes on repetitions
of "And I'll thereto compassionate my voice" gives an Orphic
singing-lesson.

Like dissonance, chromaticism is by no means always negative.
Monteverdi uses falling chromatic notes on "misericordia" and
rising ones on "O dulcis Virgo Maria." His chromaticism can also
be profoundly sensuous, even sensual, as in *L'incoronazione di
Poppea*. Chromatic runs and accidentals are frequent in English
madrigals and anthems. Amner's "Come let's rejoice" uses accidentals festively and Weelkes' "Hark all ye lovely saints above" uses
chromatic descent on "Then cease, fair ladies: why weep ye?" to
represent tears but begins it on "fair ladies" to express compassion.

Rhythms, Tempi, Syncopation, and Melisma

Because there is usually no regularly stressed metrical beat,
rhythms are free to respond to verbal phrases and accented syllables. Some are symbolic; rhythmic groups of three, a dance-
rhythm, might be used for words about heaven (represented by
dance itself in, for example, Fra Angelico's *Last Judgment* and
Paradise Lost) and groups of four for words about the more pedestrian earth with its four corners, elements, humours, and winds

Example 4. William Byrd, Te Deum from the Great Service, bars 4–10

and its bilaterally symmetrical gaits. The Te Deum of Byrd's Great Service, on "All the earth doth worship thee, the Father ever-lasting," moves into triple rhythm on "Father" (example 4, bars 4–10). Sometimes movement between rhythmic groups is made by means of a hemiola, a figure in which groups of two and three equal note values take the same amount of time.

Syncopation expresses excitement or, by providing suspensions, allows dissonance. Quick tempi may express joy and slow ones grief, but not necessarily. Other rhythmic expressions include quickly moving notes on words about moving and awakening, slow ones for naming, lamentations, or lovers' gazes, quick notes for numerousness and slow ones for magnitude. In Victoria's "O magnum mysterium" both whole notes and the large interval of an octave express "magnum" and evoke a feeling of mysterious depth. Byrd's "Ave verum corpus" begins on slow chords that ascend in descending pairs, conveying gravity and intensity, with harmonic progressions so close that the ear, retaining the previous chord, hears the next as a dissonance that is, nevertheless, mysteriously harmonious, while on "corpus" the rhythm quickens: a eucharistic metaphor for incarnation and sacrifice.

Melisma, having many notes to a syllable, expresses jubilation and is one of the earliest forms of expressiveness. As James Winn explains, "The early Christian liturgy was evidently patterned on Jewish synagogue practice . . . Though quite different in detail from ancient Greek practice, Jewish liturgical song reflects a similarly oral origin, and therefore a similar closeness of text and tone." But the cantillation of psalms must have "sounded strange to Western ears," and

the elaborate, ecstatic melismata sung to the words *alleluia* and *amen* must have sounded stranger, since we know of no ancient pagan music in which a single syllable of text was extended by many notes of melody . . . The fact that both Hebrew words have remained untranslated throughout the Christian tradition indicates the primacy of music in this form, but the longer such melodies became, the stronger was the temptation to set new words to them.

These "songs of gladness without words," as Augustine called them, grew. "In the eighth and ninth centuries, new, longer melismata were added; unlike the Gregorian chants to which they were appended, these melodies had a musical form, not a verbal one: they were constructed in shapely melodic phrases, each of which was repeated, often antiphonally."[46] Eventually, words were added. These developments brought music forward in beauty, form, and complexity, but also began the separation of words and music which the Reformation and to some extent the Counter-Reformation labored to reunite. But in the music of the English Reformation *Amen* and *Hallelujah* (the preferred Reformation spelling, since it retains the Hebrew name of God, Jah) remain freely melismatic, and other words expressing joy, jubilation, and other quickenings of emotion or motion may receive moderate melisma.

Voicing

Ordinarily in choral churches and chapels of the Church of England the choir (architecturally speaking) is divided into two sets of stalls facing each other across the chancel aisle leading to the altar or communion table, and the singers are disposed in two choirs (vocally speaking) with all the voice parts represented on each side. English Reformation church music is usually scored for four voice parts, subdivided in works for five or more parts. The two sides are called the cantoris, the side on which the Cantor sits (the north or Gospel side, where the Gospel was read) and the decani, the side on which the Dean sits (the south or Epistle side). Typically the highest parts are for boys' voices, designated "means" because they originally came between trebles and altos; in Reformation music the high treble parts of pre-Reformation music were rarely used, perhaps because the virtuosity they required went against the spirit of greater simplicity. The three men's parts are for altos or countertenors (that is, high men's voices), tenors, and basses. These parts are identified in historically informed editions as MATB. In the case of secular music, which might be sung by both men and women, the upper voice is usually called the cantus,[47] and part-books for works of five and six parts add quintus and sextus. In much music of this period each voice part has a comfortable range, often an octave or a little over, inducing vocal serenity. Clarity of tone and enunciation and attention to pitch and pulse are the basic requirements; part-singing is a companionable activity rather than an exhibition.

Polyphony also allows for multiple personae. For example, many anthems represent angels and men singing together or responsively, with the boy singers cast as angels – whom Milton's Satan, no judge of music, calls "the minstrelsy of heaven" (*PL* 6.168). Orlando Gibbons' verse anthem "Lord, grant grace" (example 5) may serve as an example of apt voicing. It alludes to Revelation, like Milton's *At a Solemn Musick*, but relies on the music to do for paraphrased words what Milton's words do for themselves.

> Lord, grant grace we humbly beseech thee
> That we with thine angels and saints may sing to thee continually:
> Holy, holy, holy, Lord God of hosts.
> Glory, honour and power be unto thee
> O God the Creator, O Lord Jesu the Redeemer, O Holy Spirit the Comforter.
> And let everything that hath breath praise and magnify the same Lord.

The text is a miniature liturgy, opening with a brief collect, freely rendering the mixed choruses in Revelation, and ending with the last line of the last psalm. The musical rhythms correspond with both the verbal phrases, accented as they would be spoken, and the verbal concepts.

Example 5a. Orlando Gibbons, "Lord, grant grace," bars 31–35

Beginning with a vocal duet and reticent viols, Gibbons sets the words "Lord, grant grace we humbly beseech thee" in duple rhythm, with dissonances expressing both lowliness and the tension of the plea. "That we with thine angels and saints may sing to thee continually" is in triple rhythm. The Sanctus that the singers hope to join angels and saints in singing syncopates to conjoin the two kinds of time. Then, in full choir – the prayer mimetically answered – this integration of heaven and earth is achieved by hemiolas. On "Glory, honour and power," expressed strongly in threes, the choirs divide, but not, as would be usual, into cantoris and decani choirs. Instead, the phrase is sung antiphonally by two voices from one side and one voice from the other: two high voices and one low voice, then the remaining two low voices and one high one, troping humans and angels singing together ("we with thine angels and saints") in an integrated way.

Gibbons names the three persons of the Trinity musically. Eight voice parts, entering three at a time, sing in triple time, with actively moving parts, on "God the Creator." "Jesu" has four pulses in most voices, marking the Incarnation. "Comforter" (Latin *cum*, with, and *fortis*, strong) reaches a strong and satisfying resolution. By means of moderate polyphony, the three names of God are perfectly distinct, yet overlapped: a musical expression of three-in-one.

For the final verse, the choir in five parts sings first in homophonic chords, representing the unanimity of "everything that hath breath," and then repeats in polyphony, representing the diversity of "all creatures." The rhythms alter freely yet flow together serenely. These effects are achieved in an anthem that makes no virtuosic demands on the musicians. Each voice is comfortably at home in its range, and each makes its contribution to the music of "everything that hath breath" on an equal footing.

Naming

Early and continuous use of expressiveness occurs on sacred names, epithets, and pronouns: to take a familiar example, Vivaldi's dance of joy on "Domine Fili Unigenite Jesu Christe" in the *Gloria*. The use of evocative rhythms for attentive naming goes back to the Old Hall Manuscript, Dunstable, the Eton Choirbook, and the Fayrfax Manuscript. Although Marian antiphons were the richest early source of expressive naming, early Tudor composers used such expressiveness for the names of Jesus well before Marian antiphons were declared illegal in the English Church. Sheryngham ends both the verses and the refrains of his dialogue carol for Passiontide, "Ah, gentle Jesu," on chords that imitate a humble pity in which the speaker is literally reharmonized. Fayrfax reduces the five-part texture of "Aeternae laudis lilium," beginning with exquisite duets, for an account of the lineages of Jesus, through Mary, from Jesse's line and of John the Baptist; each name receives a distinct rhythmic signature. Taverner sets "Jesu" in his motet "Mater Christi sanctissima" and in his mass settings on two long chords which by a downward shift in the middle voices moves in the pattern of a now conventional *Amen*, but without its sense of closure (example 6 bars 24 and 31). The effect mimetically expresses the thought (Phil. 2.10) that "at the name of Jesus every knee should bow." After the liturgy was Englished his anthems could be translated without losing this expressive

Example 5b. Orlando Gibbons, "Lord, grant grace," bars 43–54

match of words and music. Byrd carries on the tradition in "Ave verum Corpus" on the climactic "O dulcis, O pie, O Jesu fili Mariae" with prolonged notes rising to a climax on "Jesu." Settings of the English Te Deum regularly bring the words "thou art the king of glory O Christ" to a strong and often melismatic cadence on "Christ." The love and plangency with which composers treat these names lend a personal warmth to them in poetry. Herbert's poem *Jesu* and the savored phrase "*My Master*" in *The Odour* accomplish simplicity of tone but obtain richness of resonance from onomastic music, and in Milton's angelic anthems the plain style

Example 6. John Taverner, "Mater Christi," bars 24–31

of his language opens into a musical tradition of nominative expressiveness.

In twentieth-century American speech, pronouns are usually not much lingered over. Even in so feeling a phrase as "I love you," "love," not "you," usually gets the most space and highest pitch. More breath is spent on pronouns in English poetry and music. Byrd uses melismatic settings of "our" in his motet "Aspice Domine" (*BE* I), "Behold, O Lord, how the city filled with riches is made desolate. She sits in misery, and there is none to comfort her except thee, our God." The setting is primarily syllabic apart from moving notes on key words; but repetitions of "nisi tu, Deus noster" make up nearly a third of the motet, with the fullest elaboration on "noster": an outcry from the recusant church. Settings of English texts use such elaboration more moderately, but still notably. The "shee" of a madrigal or the "thee" of a prayer or canticle will often give the pronoun at least two beats instead of the one that we usually allot in reading, and remembering this emphasis on pronouns will help with more than meter. In Donne's *La Corona* the line "The ends crowne our workes, but thou crown'st our ends" works better metrically if we give slight emphasis to the first "our" and more to "thou" (not skimping "but"); and this emphasis both gives "our workes" more value and subordinates them to God's. Herbert's *Submission* becomes clearer if we give full measure (not stress) to the pronouns.

> But that thou art my wisdome, Lord,
>   And both mine eyes are thine,
> My minde would be extreamly stirr'd
>   For missing my designe.

I suspect that in "Who gave the eyes but I?" (*Love* III) the "the" is the indirect object of the verb; this common spelling of "thee" is found in the Coverdale Bible and occasionally retained well into the seventeenth century. When not skimped, but given full time within the gentle pulse of the monosyllabic line, "thee" and "I" encapsulate the intimate conjunction of Creator and creature, bridegroom and beloved, host and guest figured in the eucharistic poem. When we remember the mimetic and expressive treatment of words about seeing, the "eyes" that link the "thee" with the "I" receive an emphasis that, like Byrd's harmonic one on "regardeth" and "handmaiden," further joins the giver and the receiver. At the beginning of the poem, the speaker "dare[s] not look" on his Maker, who "sweetly questioning" replies that he gave the means of looking, implying that he is the object on which it is best to use them; the speaker replies that he has "mar'd them" – a dissonance – and Christ replies that he has born the blame – a resolution fully achieved when speaker, wanting to serve, understands that he must "sit and eat."

"A TRUE HYMNE": CONCINNITIES COMPOUNDED

As in musical composition, so in musically informed verbal composition, sound, structure, and expression join. In *A true Hymne*,[48] Herbert heeds St. Paul's exhortation to encourage one another in "psalms and hymns and spiritual songs" (Eph. 5.19, Col. 3.16). A hymn is a freely composed song of praise, not a scriptural text but what the heart "fain would say." The Greeks, Warren Anderson notes, "connected the term 'hymnos' with 'hyphainein,' meaning 'to weave' or 'to combine words artfully,'" a process Herbert's poem both abnegates and performs. From the late Middle Ages on, two trends in hymns emerged: toward through-composition and toward "the accord of particular texts with particular tunes."[49] In these ways, accounting Herbert's poems "musick" in their particular fit of form and sound to thought, Herbert's is "a hymne in kinde." Its genre or "kinde," a hymn that expresses a relation to Christ in the author's own words, was seldom used in the English Church, apart from the few non-scriptural poems, few of them hymns of praise, in *The Whole Book of Psalms*; anthems were most often based on scriptural texts, especially psalms. Even in secular books of devotional music, original expressions were comparatively rare. John Amner's *Sacred Hymns* of 1615, part-books for private use, included meditations on New Testament passages that sound unusually personal, though not artfully woven. Thomas Tomkins' setting of an anonymous text titled *An hymne* is another exception. Its text, though less crafted, and Tomkins' setting are close in spirit to Herbert's "true Hymne."[50]

Herbert's "hymne in kinde" is the right genre to express a desire to sing praise from the heart and the need and difficulty of doing so in perfect lines. Herbert takes the idea of through-composition to its ultimate end. Not only must the "soul" or message accord with the "lines" or verse-music, but the soul of the singer must be in tune with both: "The finenesse which a hymne or psalme affords, / Is, when the soul unto the lines accords." This accord will not occur if the words only *rhyme* (but are not the aptest ones for the sense), or if the words *only* rhyme (but do not stir the heart to rhyme with them), or if the *words* only rhyme (but the heart does not do its part in responding to them). A true hymn must be a repayment "in kinde" of the gifts of art to him who gave them. But the heart's rhyming is so much more important than all the rest that, given that alone, God will mend the song.

A true Hymne

My joy, my life, my crown!
My heart was meaning all the day,
Somewhat it fain would say:
And still it runneth mutt'ring up and down
With onely this, *My joy, my life, my crown.*

Yet slight not these few words:
If truly said, they may take part
Among the best in art.
The finenesse which a hymne or psalme affords,
Is, when the soul unto the lines accords.

He who craves all the minde,
And all the soul, and strength, and time,
If the words onely ryme,
Justly complains, that somewhat is behinde
To make his verse, or write a hymne in kind.

Whereas if th' heart be moved,
Although the verse be somewhat scant,
God doth supplie the want.
As when th' heart sayes (sighing to be approved)
O, could I love! and stops: God writeth, *Loved.*

The versification, though strophic, suggests through-composition by its fluidly changing rhythms and its word-coloring. In response to the words, the lines go rapidly ("And still it runneth mutt'ring up and down") or slow down ("Yet slight not these few words") or come to full stops (as at "stops"). The use of rhyme – the node of the theme – is itself mimetic. The identical rhyme of "crown" mimes the heart's poverty of words, while the circular stanza mimes "crown" by ending with the same words it began with. The off-rhyme of "behinde" with "time" suggests something musically out of step as well as ungenerously withheld. That the God who mends the rhyme "writeth, *Loved*," rather than saying it, perfects (literally, completes) the poem. The three voices – the heart, whose words are few but fine; the "I" who meditates on the heart's part in a true hymn; and God, for whom one word suffices – are tonally distinct, yet interwoven. In all these ways, the poem's verbal music formally presents "a true hymne" in the very process of subordinating art to the fineness of the accord between art and heart, and that accord to the heart's impulse of love, and that impulse to God's love; and this humility exalts art as bravely as in *Easter* Herbert asks God to "let thy blessed Spirit bear a part, / And make up our defects with his sweet art."

CHAPTER 2

The concinnity of the arts and the church music controversy

Poets and composers of the seventeenth century contended with religious and political controversy that raised questions about the relations among the arts, religion, secular power, civic life, and the creative self. Church music was at the heart of this controversy, fervently debated between those who favored an egalitarian plainness and saw elaborate ritual as human display and those who believed that God's service deserved the best expression human talent and divine inspiration could supply. These issues required poets to reflect on their own purposes, and some did so in elaborately crafted verse on sincerity and simplicity. Donne offers God a "crown of prayer and praise" in his circularly interlinked sonnet sequence *La Corona*, "Weav'd in my low devout melancholie," and adds,

> But doe not, with a vile crowne of fraile bayes,
> Reward my muses white sincerity,
> But what thy thorny crowne gain'd, that give mee,
> A crowne of glory.

Herbert pleads for simplicity in the hieroglyphical *A Wreath*, which structurally represents both his own "crooked winding wayes" and his hope that his work may become "a crown of praise." Marvell crafts poetic garlands, he says in *The Coronet*,

> Thinking (so I myself deceive)
> So rich a chaplet thence to weave
> As never yet the King of Glory wore:
> Alas, I find the serpent old
> That, twining in his speckled breast,
> About the flowers disquised does fold,
> With wreaths of fame and interest.

These wreaths concern crowns – of verse, praise, thorns, and glory – and recognize that human vanity can corrupt art just as it can crowned heads if they forget the crowns of thorns and glory.

53

This chapter considers the interrelations of the arts, some of their ethical and political implications, the continuities that link pre- and post-Reformation music, the changes the Reformation effected, and the quarrels that led to the iconoclasms of the 1640s. I have chosen the example of King's College Chapel – the center-piece of liturgical arts in the university most affected by religious radicalism – to represent the arts it joins and their relation to temporal and extemporal crowns. However, any liturgical community that employs the arts in its worship engages with their interrelations and with politically laden questions of continuity and invention and the reciprocities of human skill and divine grace.

The chapel of King's College, chartered as The College Royal of Our Lady and Saint Nicholas by Henry VI, combines architecture, decorations, pictorial windows, music, and liturgy into a nexus of history, politics, ethics, and the arts. The records of its choir go back to 1448. Its architecture, the kind of English Gothic known as Perpendicular, links it to the Middle Ages, while most of its windows and the organ screen between the ante-chapel and the chancel are of the Renaissance. Over all floats the fan-vaulted ceiling, gilded by light.

Perpendicular architecture, with its strong horizontal as well as vertical lines, represents the intersection of heaven and earth and the crossing of flesh and spirit which Herbert in *Man* describes architecturally: since a human being is "a stately habitation" that is "all symmetrie, / Full of proportions," he asks God to "dwell in it, / That it may dwell with thee." The chapel windows, low-arched English Gothic in shape but Renaissance in pictorial style, were glazed between 1515 and 1547 and form one of the world's fullest typological cycles of what Milton in *Il Penseroso* calls "Storied windows richly dight." The program depicts the two testaments, "the olde lawe and the new lawe," as confirmed in the contract of 1526; late fifteenth-century blockbooks, the *Biblia Pauperum* and the *Speculum Humanae Salvationis*, provided printed precedents.

Most typological pairs ("types" from the Hebrew Bible and their "antitypes" in the New Testament) are read as forerunners of Christ and their fulfillments. Arthur Lake, Bishop of Bath and Wells, preaching on the Psalms, taught that "*[A]ll things came to the Iewes in types*; therefore wee may not think that King *David*, had an eye onely to the corporall places, his eye pierced farther, even to that which was *figured* therein, hee looked to the *Kingdome of*

Christ."[1] The type may contrast with the antitype, for example the Fall of Eve with the Annunciation to Mary, or, more often, prefigure it, as the manna given to the Israelites does for the institution of the Communion at the Last Supper. As a secondary development, typology came to be applied to the individual believer, as in the representation of Solomon as Henry VIII in the chapel windows and in the spiritual experience related in typological poems by Herbert and by Henry Vaughan, who in *Trinity-Sunday* prays "So let the *Anti-types* in me / Elected, bought and sealed for free, / Be owned, saved, *Sainted* by you three!"[2]

The twelve bays between the columns of the vaults contain twelve windows on each side, each having ten vertical lights. Beginning at the northwest end, the lower lights contain the stories of the life of Christ, the Acts of the Apostles, and the career of St. Paul, framed by legends of the Virgin Mary, and most of the upper lights contain types of these events. Each window has two of these pairs; for example, the lower sections of window four depict the Circumcision of Christ and the Magi bringing gifts, while the matching upper sections depict the Circumcision of Isaac and the Queen of Sheba bringing gifts to Solomon. Between the pairs two central lights depict messengers, two angels and two men, probably biblical writers, bearing scrolls with explanatory scriptural texts. The east window contains the story of Christ's mock trial and his crucifixion.

Since their principal subjects are events celebrated through the liturgical year, these scenes correspond with the music and poems written for those celebrations. Donne's *La Corona* commemorates six events that the chapel windows also depict and adds the child Christ in the Temple. Herbert incorporates the major feasts and fasts into *The Church*. In the windows the Fall of the Idols is the antitype of the Worship of the Golden Calf and is followed by the Massacre of the Innocents; but in Milton's Nativity Ode the sacrifice of children to Moloch is halted by the fall of the pagan gods at the Incarnation. Of course, the poets obtain the narratives where the artists did, from the Bible. But knowledge of the program of the windows and the anthems sung surrounded by them helps the reader enter into the world of integrated arts the poets experienced and see new connections.

The chapel's history and iconography associate it with secular royalty as well as with the "King of Kings." After the defeat of Henry

VI in the Wars of the Roses, the building was continued with contributions from Edward IV and Richard III, interrupted after Richard's defeat at Bosworth, and resumed in 1506, when Henry VII came to Cambridge with his mother, Lady Margaret Beaufort, who took responsibility for completing her husband's projects and was foundress and benefactress of Christ's and St. John's Colleges. The directions of Henry VI required that the chapel be "in large fourme clene and substantial, but settyng a parte too gret curious workes of entaille and besy moldyng";[3] as if in anticipation of the Reformation, it was not to be over-decorated. While the chapel fulfills the requirements of substantiality and clarity of design, it is finely decorated with royal emblems: the Beaufort greyhound and portcullis; the Arms of Henry VII supported by dragon and greyhound; the portcullis, crown, and Tudor Rose in finely crafted stonework covering the interior walls of the ante-chapel; and royal cognizances filling the high window traceries. These symbols remind the viewer of the alliance of religion and the arts with royal power and patronage, for better and for worse, which was one of the issues of the Reformation and the Civil Wars.

The resplendent windows are, acceptably to the more moderate Reformers, mainly based on Scripture apart from the legendary Life of Mary, to whom the chapel is dedicated. The architecture and the windows invite the meditative worshipper to apply form and story to the relation of the soul to God and history and to the ethical choices of daily life. Richard Hooker says of the house of prayer, "the very glory of the place it self," even "the outward form thereof . . . hath moment to help devotion" (*Lawes* v.25). George Herbert begins *The Church-floore* "Mark you the floore?" and notes the symbolic value of each part; at the end we discover that these are types: "Blest be the *Architect*, whose art / Could build so strong in a weak heart."

The windows' typological program incorporates monarchs both sacred and profane: the Queen of Sheba bringing gifts to King Solomon as a type of the Three Kings; Queen Athalia as the type of King Herod in the Massacre of the Innocents; Solomon as the opposing type of King Herod judging Christ; the crowning of Solomon as the ironic type of Christ Crowned with Thorns. This visual commentary on just and unjust uses of power culminates in the east window where, below the Crucifixion, a portly Pontius Pilate, the imperial governor, relinquishes responsibility. "What is truth?" he asks (John 18.38) and, Bacon adds, "would not stay for an Answer."[4] Christ stands before him being tried and hangs above him on the cross, with its mocking inscription "King of the Jews,"[5] the two thieves on either side making their respective choices. The window tells all who enter that life is a matter of moral choice, and contrasts a ruler who refuses to see justice through with the "King" who gave his life not only for his friends but for his enemies.

The window before the east window on the north side aligns the Scourging of Christ with the Torments of Job, who did stay for an answer (Job 20.16, "the cause which I knew not I searched out"), and Christ Crowned with Thorns with the Crowning of Solomon, who in his famous Judgment also stayed for an answer, again represented as Henry VIII. The story of Paul, whose ship resembles the flagship of Henry VIII, includes the Apostle's appeal to Nero, known for justice early in his reign, garbed as a Tudor monarch holding the Sword of Justice; later, Paul was probably executed in the Neronian persecutions. Along with its devotional uses, the program contains a political message that might serve as praise, warning, and education for the two princes known as "England's Solomon," Henry VIII and James I, the latter with particular reference to the peacemaking inscribed in Solomon's name. Similarly, Orlando Gibbons' full anthem "Hosanna to the Son of David" (*EECM* XXI) might tempt James to compare himself with both Sons of David and teach him to recognize the ironies and responsibilities of that comparison.

The Book of Common Prayer and many anthems have texts concerning the themes of kingship discernible in the chapel decorations and windows, both honoring kings as God's vicars and praying for justice while declaring God's sovereignty. The Magnificat, said or sung daily at Evening Prayer, also contains commentary on power that might warn the overweening, and these verses were regularly set with expressive word-painting, especially "[The Lord] hath showed strength with his arm," often in strong homophony; "He hath scattered the proude in the imagination of their hearts," scattering voices in broken polyphonic phrases; and "He hath put down the mighty from their seats: and hath exalted the humble and meeke" falling and rising accordingly.[6] Royal anthems in the Loosemore Organ Book (NY Drexel 5469) include Byrd's "O Lord make thy servant," Tomkins' *Prince Henryes Funerall Anthem,* and Weelkes' "O Lord grant the king a long life"; Tomkins'

"Thou art my king O God" offers, perhaps, a correction to any idol-
atrous patriotism. The Ely books contain Amner's "O God my
king" (Ps. 145.1, 3, 8, 21) and Child's settings of "Thou art my
king," "Give the king thy judgments,"[7] and the prayer for the King
of England.[8] The prayerbook (I quote from a 1607 issue of the
1604 version) contains numerous prayers for the sovereign including two at communion, the first asking that God's "chosen seruant
James . . . (knowing whose minister he is) may aboue all things
seeke thy honour and glory, and that we his subjects (duely considering whose authority he hath) may faithfully serue, honour,
and humbly obey him"; and the second that since "we be taught by
thy holy Word, that the hearts of kings are in thy rule and gouer-
nance, and that thou doest dispose & turne them as it seemeth best
to thy godly wisdome," God should so "dispose and gouerne the
heart of James, thy seruant our King & gouernour, that in all his
thoughts, words, and workes, he may euer seeke thy honour and
glory, and studie to preserue the people committed to his charge,
in wealth, peace, & godliness" (Sig. C3). James himself, as king of
Scotland, supposes in the verse "argument" to *Basilikon Doron*
(1599) that kings sway God's scepter, and so must "Walke alwayes
so, as euer in his sight, / Who guardes the godly, plaguing the
profane."[9] The prayer "for the whole state of Christs Church militant here in earth" asks that under James "we may be godly and
quietly gouerned" (C3v), and the litany asks the "King of Kings"
and "onely ruler of Princes" to replenish the sovereign "with the
grace of thy holy Spirit, that he may alway incline to thy will, and
walke in thy way," with strength "to vanquish and ouercome all his
enemies," and with attainment of "euerlasting joy and felicity."
Whether these verses pray for continuance or amendment, and
whether the enemies are without or within, would depend on the
political viewpoint of each beseecher. Prayers for reciprocal justice
and obedience cut two ways, upholding authority while admon-
ishing the powerful of their responsibilities. The petitions' potentially subversive edge implies that, in words from Donne's *Satyre* III,
souls perish "which more chuse mens unjust / Power from God
claym'd, then God himselfe to trust."

The constellation of the chapel's windows, music, and liturgy
invites meditation on the relations between the life of each worshipper and the life of the King of Kings and his precursors, on the
relations between human and divine kingship, and on the

responsibility, power for good, fallibility, and mischief of rulers. Since kings of England and youths being prepared for administrative and clerical offices were among the worshippers, ideally the meditations offered by these arts and heartened by the moving power of music would affect the course of justice. In Shakespeare's words, "The man that hath no music in himself, / Nor is not moved with concord of sweet sounds, / Is fit for treasons, stratagems, and spoils" (*Merchant of Venice* 5.1.83–85). Unfortunately the ethical offerings of the arts do not always penetrate the breasts of their witnesses.

That the chapel was open to both university and townspeople may be gathered from the Jacobean edict, "We do forbid that women of the town be permitted to repair to the chappell of any college, to common places, or other exercises of divinity, unless it be in the case of an English sermon ad populum, for which the bells of such college is rung, or to the ordinary prayers in Kings College chappell."[10] Given its tradition of open services, it seems likely that much poetry was conceived, shaped, or indited beneath the storied windows of the chapel and within the textures of its fabric and its music. Poets had other sources of musical experience at Cambridge as well; Trinity College had its own choir from 1554, Peterhouse had a thriving musical life in the 1630s, other colleges had more modest sung services, and the university community attended the University Church, Great St. Mary's, on Sundays and ceremonial occasions. But King's offered a meeting-house of many arts that epitomizes, and perhaps helps to explain, the extraordinary meeting of structure, image, and music in their poems.

Edmund Spenser, at Pembroke College during the years 1569 to 1576, may have found the model for Archimago in the depiction of Satan in the window of the Temptation of Christ, musical bejewelment for Gloriana in settings of prayers for Queen Elizabeth, and inspiration for his *Fowre Hymnes* in music by Thomas Tallis, John Sheppard, Christopher Tye, and Robert White. Giles Fletcher no doubt heard music by Dr. John Bull, recently of King's; by Orlando Gibbons, whose tenure as chorister and organist at King's overlapped Fletcher's residence at Trinity; and by John Amner, at Ely from 1610. All of these composers would be known to Fletcher's younger contemporary, George Herbert, who matriculated at Trinity in 1609 and stayed as Fellow, Reader in Rhetoric, and University Orator until 1628. Edmund Waller was briefly at

King's in 1620. Milton was at Christ's College (1625–32) when Henry Loosemore became organist at King's. Richard Crashaw was at Pembroke and Peterhouse and Andrew Marvell and Abraham Cowley at Trinity during the height of the Laudian revival; the music they heard is represented in the Peterhouse "Caroline" part-books.

The music seventeenth-century poets heard at King's and other chapels cannot be fully documented because of the ravages of time and the more thorough ones of the Civil Wars, but surviving manuscripts give evidence of widespread use of work by the composers of the Chapel Royal and of cathedral and collegiate churches, and some indicate the special traditions of the Cambridge chapel and Ely Cathedral choirs. The manuscript identified by Thurston Dart as belonging to Henry Loosemore[11] – organist at King's College Chapel from 1627 until the Revolution put a stop to his services and again after the Restoration – contains compositions, many of them verse anthems, going back to *Prince Henryes Funerall Anthem* (1612), and many of the same composers and works are found in the Peterhouse books, compiled from about 1634 but also containing earlier compositions.[12] These, and manuscripts from Ely Cathedral,[13] contain works of Tallis, Byrd, Gibbons, and other members of the Chapel Royal as well as local composers. The Ely collection, though mostly copied after the Restoration, holds a preponderance of pre-Revolutionary works going back to the mid-sixteenth century, suggesting that successive copyists preserved the contents of previous manuscripts.[14] Many are by Ely organists. The collection contains service music by Tallis, Sheppard, Tye, Farrant, Barcrofte, Byrd, Johnson, Stroger, Morley, Portman, Gibbons, and Amner and anthems by these composers and others including White, Hooper, Mundy, Wilkinson, Child, Mudd, Ramsey, Henry and William Lawes, Tomkins, and Loosemore.

These manuscripts are rich in festive psalms and anthems exhorting all to praise God in music, an act the stricter reformers sought to restrict. Examples in the Loosemore Organ Book include Byrd's "Sing Joyfully unto God our strength," Tomkins' "Sing unto God," Amner's "I will sing unto the Lord," and Loosemore's "O Sing unto the Lord New Song" and "O God my Heart is Ready . . . Awake awake my lute," as well as his setting of Herbert's *Antiphon* (I), "Let all the world in ev'ry corner sing"; in the Ely book, Amner's "I will sing unto the Lord," Ramsey's "My song shall be alway," Henry Lawes' "My song shall be of mercy," and Child's "O sing unto the Lord"; in the Peterhouse part-books, Amner's "O sing unto the Lord" and "Hear O Lord, I will sing unto the Lord." These anthems, mostly on psalm texts, proclaim God's praise and, against a rising tide of musical iconoclasm, the right to praise skillfully.

The poet whose work most clearly resembles the arts combined in the chapel – the typology of its windows, the symbolism of its architecture, and the sounds and significances of its music – is George Herbert. In *The H. Scriptures* (II) Herbert exclaims,

> Oh that I knew how all thy lights combine,
>   And the configurations of their glorie!
> Seeing not onely how each verse doth shine,
> But all the constellations of the storie.

The sonnet addresses the Bible and the starry metaphor concerns the cosmos. But "lights" is also a word for the sections of a window, and just as in the Bible "This verse marks that," the lights of Scripture's story in the lights of the chapel windows comment on each other.

Although Herbert was a student at Trinity, an orator at Great St. Mary's, a rector at Bemerton, and a worshipper at Salisbury Cathedral, none of these had storied windows. The likeliest place for him to have seen windows in which, as he says to Christ metaphorically in *The Windows*, "thou dost anneal in glasse thy storie" is at King's. The chapel offers integrated visible, audible, intelligible, and expressive configurations such as Herbert achieved in poems, strove for in his vocation as priest, and calls in *The Windows* "Doctrine and life, colours and light, in one." But the window in which that story is annealed in the poem is the "Brittle crazie glasse" of the preacher as mere man, who becomes a window by grace yet cannot win souls by speech unless Christ makes his own life shine within his priest's. The story annealed in the glass of King's College Chapel is the story Herbert anneals in his life and in his poems.

In *Praise* (I) Herbert writes, "Man is all weaknesse; there is no such thing / As Prince or King." In *Peace* he looks for "Sweet Peace" in all the wrong places first, including the court:

> Then went I to a garden, and did spy
>   A gallant flower,

> The crown Imperiall: Sure, said I,
> Peace at the root must dwell.
> But when I digg'd, I saw a worm devoure
> What show'd so well.

The "Crowne Imperiall," according to John Gerard's *Herball*, is a lily of great beauty, but "The whole plant as well rootes as flowers do sauour or smell verie loathsomly like the fox." As if addressing a warning to would-be courtiers seeking employment, Gerard adds, "The vertues of this admirable plant is not yet knowne, neither his faculties or temperature in working."[15] After, perhaps, contemplating in these windows the life, trial, and death of the "King of grief" who became "King of Glorie, King of Peace," and at the same time being carried to heaven's door on music's wings by the chapel choir, it is no wonder that Herbert and church music together "say sometimes, *God help poore Kings.*"[16]

An anthem in the King's, Peterhouse, and Ely manuscripts by Orlando Gibbons, organist of the Chapel Royal of James I, represents an attitude toward worship that corresponds with typological and architectural poems in *The Temple*, especially *The Altar* and *Sion*. The text is, unusually for an English anthem, an original poem, as Herbert suggests (in *A true Hymne*) a true hymn should be. The first stanza seems to answer concerns that led to iconoclasm against temples of Anglicanism:

> Glorious and powerful God, we understand
> Thy dwelling is on high,
> Above the starry sky.
> Thou dwell'st not in stone temples made with hands,
> But in the flesh hearts of the sons of men
> To dwell is thy delight,
> Near hand though out of sight.

Its second and third stanzas avow that all offerings (including, one supposes, music and verse) are returns of God's gifts, given life by his "acceptation," and ask for God's presence "Whenever here or hence our supplication / From pure and unfeigned hearts to thee ascend," ending

> Arise, O Lord, and come into thy rest.
> Both now and evermore thy name be blest:
> Founder and foundation
> Of endless habitation.

The work is a through-composed verse anthem for countertenor and bass with five-part choir and organ, its text declaimed by the soloists with repetitions in polyphony and with moderate word-painting: upward motion of both notes and mode on "Above the starry sky," organ runs on "hearts," quickened notes to enliven delight, falling phrases on "O down on us fall showers" and rising ones on "Arise." These are carefully unified in the clean and substantial form of an anthem that is "all symmetrie, / Full of proportions," suitable for God's stately habitations "here or hence."

Herbert is of course strongly conscious, like Gibbons, that God dwells "not in stone temples made with hands" but in "flesh hearts" on earth and "Above the starry sky." In *Sion*, Solomon's Temple is the type of the temple of the heart, and the glory of outward edifices is of value only insofar as it aids inward edification. In Solomon's temple, as in the choir of King's, "The wood was all embellished," and everything "show'd the builders, crav'd the seers care." Words like "flourish," "brass," "embellished," and "pomp" fill this temple, C. A. Patrides suggests, with "musical overtones."[17] The proportions of Solomon's Temple were shown by seventeenth-century music theorists to match the mathematical proportions of harmony. Marin Mersenne writes that "The Holy of Holies represented the perfect unison . . . . The Temple was 60 cubits long, 20 cubits wide, and 30 cubits high [1 Kings 6]. Thus, 20 and 30 make the perfect fifth, 20 and 60 make the perfect twelfth, and 30 and 60 form the perfect octave . . . . the dimensions of the porch . . . also represent the perfect octave, for it was 20 cubits long and 10 cubits wide." These and other proportions show "that the disposition of the Temple . . . represents the perfect harmony of the city of peace, Jerusalem. Harmony is the mother of peace."[18]

King's College Chapel resembles Solomon's Temple in several particulars: made of stone "brought hither," with "windows of narrow lights," "chambers round about, against the wall of the house," and "without in the wall of the house . . . narrowed rests . . . that the beams should not be fastened in the walls" (1 Kings 6). But the temple of "the old lawe" with its "pomp and state," Herbert says, "sow'd debate" – as church music was doing – and God found out a remedy: "now thy Architecture meets with sinne; / For all thy frame and fabrick is within." There, life is a struggle between God and a "peevish heart," with the object of the battle to extract "one good grone" more dear than all "Solomons sea of brasse and world of stone." And here Herbert generously dismisses artful fabricks and musicks, including by implication his poems, as worthless by comparison with a contrite heart:

> And truly brasse and stones are heavie things,
> Tombes for the dead, not temples fit for thee:
>   But grones are quick, and full of wings,
>   And all their motions upward be;
> And ever as they mount, like larks they sing;
> The note is sad, yet musick for a King.

There is much comfort for an afflicted conscience in the thought that groans of shame and sorrow mount like larks, singing as they rise, however heavy they may feel, and that repentance is the music that best pleases God's ears; God's "musick" is a consort which all hearts – common, noble, even royal, of commingled classes and sexes – may join. Yet the poem, for all its dismissal of outward frames, is itself a temple, a carefully constructed fabric in rectangular form having the same number of lines as the chapel has bays, and is filled with verbal music that expresses and can extract from the hearer those grones that are far more precious than it – and so give it incalculable value. In *The Temple*, all Herbert's lights combine in portable chapels made of the architecture, story, and music of language. His poems participate with King's College Chapel and other places of musical praise in the calling they proclaim and perform: "Let all the world in ev'ry corner sing, / My God and King."

CONTINUITIES AND DEVELOPMENTS IN ENGLISH CHURCH MUSIC

During the extraordinary flowering of late sixteenth- and early seventeenth-century English poetry, poets were discovering and increasing the richness of their own language partly because the liturgy was now in the vernacular. Composers who set canticles, anthems, and psalms helped nurse vernacular poetry to maturity by matching to language the structural, mimetic, and expressive properties of music. The Reformers' principle that one should sing from the heart, and the ways composers expressed the heart's and the mind's experience, reoriented sacred music to include human response within the music itself. Medieval liturgical music might indeed move the heart because it contemplated eternal glory, but, John Stevens writes, before the Reformation "it was never the first duty of music to express emotion" and "it was not humanism but the Reformation which brought about a revolution in the way English people thought about song."[19]

English poets absorbed settings of the liturgy in college chapels, cathedrals, and major parish churches: Herbert at Westminster Abbey while attending Westminster School, in Cambridge at Trinity and King's Colleges, and at Salisbury Cathedral; Donne at Oxford, Cambridge[20] and St. Paul's; Milton at St. Paul's, possibly, as a student at St. Paul's School, in Cambridge while at Christ's College, and briefly at Ludlow and perhaps other parish churches endowed with choirs; Marvell while at Trinity College. Although few complete sets of liturgical part-books survived the British Civil Wars,[21] enough copies remain, along with sacred music in secular books, to allow reconstruction of the music they probably heard. Part-books indicate that choirs usually sang services and anthems by their own organists and their contemporaries or by recent predecessors: we may be sure, for example, that Herbert heard works by Edmund Hooper at Westminster Abbey, Donne by Adrian Batten at St. Paul's, Herbert, Milton and Marvell by John Amner and Henry Loosemore in Cambridge. At the same time, works by composers attached to cathedrals and collegiate churches and to the Chapel Royal were copied into part-books all over England. While contemporary music will serve as the basis of most of my explications, manuscript history gives some warrant for using sixteenth-century examples as well. Works by some early Reformation composers were copied into part-books from the mid-sixteenth century to the end of the seventeenth and beyond. Some were composed for the Sarum rite before the English liturgy of 1549 and adapted to Henrican and Edwardian Protestant requirements, then Marian Catholic ones, then the Elizabethan prayer book. Composers whose collective lives spanned these periods and who set both English and Latin liturgical texts include Robert Johnson (*c.* 1490–*c.* 1560), Christopher Tye (*c.* 1500–*c.*73), Thomas Tallis (*c.* 1505–85), John Sheppard, or Shepherd (*c.* 1520–63), Robert White or Whyte (*c.* 1535–74), and William Byrd (1543–1623). Some of their works were translated into English, and Latin works based on biblical texts could be sung in chapel services not open to the public, since the Preface of the 1559 prayer book grants that

"Though it be appointed in the afore written Preface that all things shall be read and sung in the church in the English tongue, to the end that the congregation may be thereby edified, yet it is not meant but when men say Morning and Evening Prayer privately, they may say the same in any language that they themselves do understand" (*BCP* 17). This paragraph was reprinted in subsequent editions and after William Laud became Archbishop of Canterbury was printed in large italics. The works of Tallis and Byrd, both English and Latin, were printed as well as copied, and were available for familial and social gatherings. In musical households such as the Herberts' and the Miltons', it seems likely that whatever good music was available was sung without blame for its origins, since music is a "thing indifferent" to those who can tell the difference between idols and art.

The following brief historical account of the relations between words and music is intended to point out native English traditions and innovations that preceded and continued to live in partnership with the influences of continental musical humanism and Protestant reforms, and, I believe, contributed to the distinctive qualities of English poetry.

Plainsong, the established chant of the Christian church since the late sixth century, unified the voices of a liturgical community in serene freedom from individual earthly concerns. Even so, some chants included limited word-painting, exclamation, and expression of jubilation and sorrow.[22] By the tenth century, plainsong began to be troped, another voice singing a commentary on the text over the slower chant, possibly in a vernacular language. As medieval polyphony developed from two to up to forty parts, the listener heard increasingly exalting sounds, but not words. This opacity reached its summit in the isometric motets of Dunstable and Dufay, for example, in which two or more sections of text are sung simultaneously.

Fauxbourdon, the singing of responses in parallel harmonies, provided the beginnings of choral homophony. By the early fifteenth century, English choirs used faburden or English descant, a more complex kind of improvised parallel harmonization, and added triads, thirds, and sixths as acceptable consonances. These and the use of passing seconds and sevenths gave English music its distinctive full sonorities. English composers also used a "wandering" cantus firmus, with different segments of plainsong in different voice parts. The most notable source of motets by members of the Chapel Royal is the Old Hall Manuscript,[23] whose composers occasionally used expressive near-homophony.

During the fifteenth century the stream of innovation flowed from England to the continent; Joannes Tinctoris found the possibilities of music "so marvellously increased that there appears to be a new art . . . whose fount and origin is held to be among the English, of whom Dunstable stood forth as chief."[24] John Dunstable, astrologer and mathematician, exemplifies the use of number and proportion to imitate the beauty of the cosmos; his epitaph in St. Stephen's Walbrook calls him "he who enclosed Heaven in his breast . . . the confederate to the stars."[25] Yet in "Quam pulchra es" (*MB* viii), rhythmic unity with occasional melisma gives a foretaste of the intelligibility and expressiveness that became prominent two centuries later, especially at "Veni, dilecte me, egrediamur in agrum" (Come, my beloved, let us go forth into the field), where "Veni" is expressed on long, yearning chords, "dilecti" in rich thirds with melisma and suspensions, and "egrediamur" in quickened rhythmic simultaneity, while "agrum," with its cadential melisma, seems to flower. Walter Frye in his *Missa Flos Regalis* uses expressive treatment for non-Marian texts as well.

Early Tudor masses alternated plainsong with polyphonic verses, using chants from the office of the day; then came fully polyphonic settings, often based on plainsong melodies from the Sarum rite, which had slight variations from the Roman rite. Since votive masses could be sung at any time, those for the Virgin were popular. By the beginning of the sixteenth century, John Taverner and the composers of the Eton Choirbook were producing music of timeless glory. The Eton Choirbook (1490–1502), one of three surviving pre-Reformation manuscripts (the others being from Lambeth Palace and Caius College, Cambridge), contains an anthem of Dunstable and "the largest extant collection of antiphons of the early Tudor Period," all praising the Virgin Mary.[26] Its composers include John Browne, William Cornysh, Robert Fayrfax, and Robert Hacomplaynt, who as Provost of King's energetically supervised the completion of the fabric and the glazing of the windows of the chapel.[27] These composers' connections with the Chapel Royal and other major musical foundations and Eton's position as the preparatory school for King's[28] suggest that the music the Eton Choirbook preserves was widely performed before the Reformation and perhaps during Mary Tudor's restitution of the Latin rite.

Historians of music call this music insular and conservative, because it retains the cantus firmus and rarely uses the imitation that was becoming the characteristic structural principle of Renaissance music; they also characterize it as florid and ornamental, making it sound both stodgy and frivolous. Rather, for all its intricacy, like King's College Chapel, it has a kind of soaring clarity. In its flexible and richly harmonized voicing, single voices ring clearly. Its euphonious style is distinctively English, and its composers, especially Browne and Cornysh, were highly innovative. Frank Ll. Harrison compares it with Perpendicular architecture: "Each was the final phase of Gothic in its medium, and both expressed the late medieval trend towards the adornment of devotion by the most elaborate and decorative forms of art and craft."[29] At the same time, instead of having "the strict form of the isorhythmic motet" its music moves "towards a more intimate expression and a more varied treatment of plainsong . . . already seen in the work of Dunstable and his contemporaries." While its composers continued the medieval interest in symbolic numbers and structural proportion, some devoted attention to intelligibility, modest word-painting, and expressiveness, for which Dunstable and the composers of the Old Hall Manuscript had given precedent. As a collection of Marian Antiphons, it was prohibited in reformed services and according to the college accounts was replaced in 1563–64 by "8 bookes of spalmes [*sic*] in meeter."[30] Nevertheless, some pre-Reformation works survived with new texts, and the articulate beauty of the Eton Choirbook, the melodic and rhythmic freedom and varied voicing, and the euphonious consonances that freed dissonance to be used for expressive purposes, increased the stock of subsequent composers.

Henry VIII, Henry Peacham tells us on the testimony of Erasmus, "of himself composed a service of four, five, and six parts."[31] In 1544, however, Archbishop Cranmer sent a letter to that sovereign with his translations into English of some "processionals" asking that his majesty edit the manuscript and "command some devout and solemn note to be made thereunto" that it may "much excite and stir the hearts of all men unto devotion and godliness." He adds, "But in my opinion, the song that should be made thereunto would not be full of notes, but, as near as may be, for every syllable a note, so that it may be sung distinctly and devoutly," and specifies such settings for the office canticles, hymns, "and all the psalms and versicles; and in the mass Gloria in excelsis, Gloria Patri, the Creed, the Preface, the Pater Noster, and some of the Sanctus and Agnus."[32]

An Edwardian Injunction of 1548 required that choirs

shall from hensforthe synge or say no Anthemes off our lady or other saynts but onely of our lorde And them not in laten but choseyng owte the best and moste soundyng to cristen religion they shall turne the same into Englishe settying therunto a playn and distincte note, for every sillable one, they shall singe them and none other.[33]

Injunctions of 1550 for St. George's Chapel, Windsor, where John Merbecke was organist, reduced the choir, abolished organ music, and declared that

whereas heretofore, when descant, prick-song, and organs were too much used and had in price in the church, great search was made for cunning men in that faculty, among whom there were many that had joined with such cunning evil conditions, as pride, contention, railing, drunkenness, contempt of their superiors, or such-like vice, we now inteinding to have Almighty God praised with gentle and sober quiet minds and with honest hearts . . . do enjoin [that vacancies among the clerks should be filled with] quiet and honest men . . . having always more regard to their virtue and learning than to excellency in music.

The Archbishop of York was especially severe, decreeing in 1552 that at York Minster "none other note" should be sung "saving square note plain, so that every syllable may be plainly and distinctly pronounced" and that "there be no more playings of the organs" during any service.[34]

The official objectives of the Reformation were so radical a rejection of the kind of music that Taverner and the Eton Choirbook composers produced that one might suppose English Church music reduced to chant. But music is irrepressible. Merbecke's *Book of Common Prayer Noted* (1550) did retain modified chants from the Sarum Breviary. Anglicans both ancient and modern would recognize, and the latter will be able to supply as they read, his noting of many passages, such as the Kyrie, "Lorde, have mercy upon us"; the greeting exchanged by the priest and congregation, "The Lord be with you / And with thy spirit"; and the Sursum corda, "Lift up your hearts." The use of simple syllabic chant for the whole service did not catch on, however. The Wanley part-books (*c.* 1547–52) contain harmonized service music and anthems, all in English, including adaptations of two mass settings by Taverner and Sheppard's "I give you a new commandment, that ye love one another" and Tallis' "If ye love me," "This is my commandment," and "Hear the voice and prayer," anthems that have never gone out of style.[35]

The reign of Mary Tudor helped preserve Latin polyphonic music, and shortly after Elizabeth's accession a Latin translation of the Book of Common Prayer appeared (*Liber Precarum Publicarum . . . in Ecclesia Anglicana,* 1560) for use in the royal and college chapels, where an international language was needed, giving opportunity for Latin anthems though not Marian antiphons. The Injunctions (1559) of Elizabeth I, a monarch of moderate views in liturgical matters, enjoins that

because in divers Collegiate, and also some Parish-Churches heretofore, there have been Livings appointed for the maintenance of men and children to use singing in the Church, by means whereof the laudable service of Musick hath been had in estimation, and preserved in knowledge: the Queens Majesty neither meaning in any wise the decay of any thing that might conveniently tend to the use and continuance of the said Science, neither to have the same in any part so abused in the Church, that thereby the Common-prayer should be the worse understood of the hearers, willeth and commandeth . . . that there be a modest distinct song so used in all parts of the Common-prayers in the Church, that the same may be as plainly understood, as if it were read without singing, and yet nevertheless for the comforting of such that delight in Musick, it may be permitted, that in the beginning, or in the end of Common-prayers, either at Morning or Evening, there may be sung an Hymn, or such like song, to the praise of Almighty God, in the best sort of melody and musick that may be conveniently devised, having respect that the sentence of the Hymn may be understood and perceived.[36]

For anthems, this formulation provided considerable leeway as to music "best" for God's praises. For service music – following a tentative period of primarily homophonic settings – English composers continued to use moderate polyphony, and, rather than suppressing pre-Reformation developments, modified them to respond to words.[37]

The Nunc Dimittis from Robert Parsons' First Service[38] shows some of the expressive possibilities of Elizabethan service music. It begins mainly homophonically in full choir, with "Lord, now lettest thou thy servant depart in peace" moving through several harmonic changes before subsiding to a satisfying triad on "peace." The two sides of the choir sing the next two verses antiphonally, rejoining for "To be a light to lighten the Gentiles," usually the climax of this canticle in which each composer illuminates "light" with rhythmic and harmonic brilliance. Parsons sets "light" with bass and treble doubled by the altos and the treble raised to the third, covering the unusual span of nearly two and a half octaves, on what would be another triad, except that the expected fifth in the tenor is replaced by a passing sixth. "Lighten," in a double musical pun, receives the lightness of shorter moving notes and a suspension. "And to be the glory of thy people Israel" is intelligibly stated in reduced voicing, then breaks into double-choir polyphony for a suitable rendering of "glory," continued in the Gloria Patri and the melismatic Amen. The mainly syllabic notes, the relatively simple harmonies, and the shapes of the lines work for verbal clarity, yet polyphonic voicing still has its say.

Plainsong long continued to be used as the melodic base for polyphony, keeping its roots in the ancient feasts and fasts, but freely segmented and elaborated: a re-forming in Reformation arts comparable to the reworking of scriptural iconography. Morley published his four-part homophonic harmonization of the Sarum chants, with the plainsong in the tenor, in his *Plain and Easy Introduction*. In his discourse on descant, Morley recommends looking at works by earlier sixteenth-century composers "where you shall find such variety of breaking of plainsongs as one not very well skilled in music should scant discern any plainsong at all, whereby you may learn to break any plainsong whatsoever." He gives the example of Osbert Parsley's "Salvator mundi," "broken in division, and brought in a canon three parts in one," and gives the plainsong melody "that you may perceive the breaking of every note and not that you should sing it for a part with the rest, for the rest are made of it and not upon it."[39] John Playford provided a comprehensive guide to English chant in his *Introduction to the Skill of Music* (1673).[40]

Many works by early and middle sixteenth-century composers continued to be known in the seventeenth century.[41] The recusant music-lover Edward Paston (1550–1630) owned works by Taverner, Sheppard, and Fayrfax as well as Byrd and Tallis and con-

tinental composers including Palestrina and Lassus.[42] But
Protestants had access to polyphonic music, both Latin and
English, as well. Byrd published Marian Masses, motets, and anti-
phons in the *Gradualia* and in the Four Part Mass "openly acknowl-
edges his debt" to Taverner.[43] The largest printed collection of
English service music in the sixteenth century and the first printed
in four parts, John Day's *Certaine Notes* (1560, 1565),[44] contains
service music and anthems for men and children by Thomas
Caustun, Tallis, Sheppard, Taverner, and others, including Robert
Stone's pleasant syllabic setting of the Lord's Prayer.[45]

The music of John Taverner illustrates the continuity by which
seventeenth-century poets may have known earlier composers.
Taverner has the harmonic gift of making voices tender, intense,
plaintive, plangent, solemn – nakedly personal and deeply reverent – at once. Among works sung after the Reformation with
English words are his Mean Mass and "Christe Jesu, pastor bone,"
from an antiphon on St. William of York, which was altered to
include in its text first Wolsey, then Henry, then Elizabeth (*TCM*
III). His motet "Mater Christi sanctissimi" is found in Edwardian,
Elizabethan, and Jacobean manuscripts[46] and, along with his *Missa
Mater Christi*, in the Peterhouse "Caroline" part-books. The original Latin text invokes Mary to beseech her Son, addressed as "Jesu"
and "Jesu bone," to receive the eucharistic prayer that forms most
of the antiphon, which is mainly syllabic, alternating antiphonal
homophony with polyphony to highlight sections of the text.
Expressive treatment of words includes a melismatic dance on
"Maria," repeated by the tenor, and a more extended one on
"filium": the mother is honored, but the Son more. "Jesu, O Jesu"
and "Jesu bone" poignantly harmonized on longas (or double
whole notes) provide a pause for meditation on the name of Jesus
(example 6). After receiving "cibo," life-giving food, "corpora"
responds with lively motion, and "Gratia" is melismatically graced.
An Elizabethan version at King's College (C Rowe MS 316, fols.
1–5r) retains its Latin title but substitutes a Protestant English text
that omits the queen of heaven and includes a prayer for the
Queen of England, while firmly subordinating her power to God,
"owre onlie governoure." The whole composition, and especially
the "Amen," illustrates Herbert's feeling of "Rising and falling with
your wings" in his poem to *Church-musick*.

It is impossible to be sure that any particular poet heard

Taverner's *Missa Gloria Tibi Trinitas*, but a whole species of instrumental pieces, the "In Nomine," issued from it. Taverner uses fragments of the Sarum antiphon in the mean part throughout the mass but fully quotes and develops it in imitative voicing only in the Benedictus, on the words beginning "In nomine Domini": hence the name. In Day's *Certaine Notes*, the anthem "In trouble and adversity" (headed "Exaudiat te Dominus"), with the chant melody in the countertenor, is headed in the bassus part book "In nomine of Master Tauerners."[47] For over a hundred years, composers from Tallis to Purcell used this melody and emulated Taverner's exploration of its contrapuntal possibilities as the basis for consort music.[48] John Milton Senior composed one for accompanied tenor voice and another, it is said, in forty parts.

Morley's *Plain and Easy Introduction* indicates the extent to which earlier composers were known in England in 1597. In an annotation on note length he advises those who doubt him to "look in the Mass of Mr. Taverner called 'Gloria tibi trinitas'" and "in the works of our English Doctors of Music" including Fayrfax, Tallis, Tye, and many other late fifteenth- to mid-sixteenth-century composers. He mentions Dunstable as an example of what Milton in his sonnet to Lawes calls "committing short and long" – that is, putting together short syllables and long notes, or the reverse. He knew the work of continental composers including Palestrina, Josquin des Près, Croce, Ferrabosco, Lassus, Striggio, and Clemens non Papa and defends the equal excellence of "those famous Englishmen who have been nothing inferior in the art to any of the aforenamed, as Fayrfax, Taverner, Shepherd, Mundy, Whyte, Parsons, Mr. Byrd, and divers others."[49] Continued command of and homage to the style of these predecessors may be seen in occasional skilled and lovely Latin polyphonic motets, probably written to fulfill requirements for university degrees, by composers who otherwise wrote only English Church music, such as Weelkes' "Laboravi in gemitu meo" and Tomkins' "Domine, tu eruisti animam meam."

The two composers who most fully represent the continuity and innovation inherited by the seventeenth century were Tallis and Byrd, who were well known partly because of their excellence and partly because they published their work. Thomas Tallis, whose long life (*c.* 1505–85) spanned four reigns, wrote elaborate settings for Latin texts in the spirit of the Eton Choirbook and English anthems and service music thoroughly acceptable to

Reformation requirements. Syllabic settings of words could lead to drily formal chordal arrangements; but Tallis' melodic gifts allowed him innovation within simplicity, and Tallis and his pupil William Byrd animated English church music by what Peter Phillips calls their "exceptional grasp of harmony," using harmonic modulations as "a servant of melodic phrases" to shape cadences matching and expressing verbal phrases.[50] Byrd (1543–1623), Organist of Elizabeth's Chapel Royal, is both a confluence of previous developments and an innovative genius whose music for both communions, as well as his consort songs and keyboard music, opened new paths for his successors. His work epitomizes that ability to combine heritage with venture seen in English music since Dunstable. In addition, he naturalized the developments of European imitative polyphony. Though most acclaimed for his masterful shaping of musical form, he also possessed a fine sensitivity to words. In the dedicatory letter to Henry Howard, Earl of Northampton, in his *Gradualia* of 1605 he defends the craft of sacred art and gives "the sweetness of the words themselves" credit for his inspiration:

For even as among artisans it is shameful in a craftsman to make a rude piece of work for some precious material, so indeed to sacred words in which the praises of God and of the Heavenly host are sung, none but some celestial harmony (so far as our powers avail) will be proper. Moreover in these words, as I have learned by trial, there is such a profound and hidden power that to one thinking upon things divine and diligently and earnestly pondering them, all the fittest numbers occur as if of themselves and freely offer themselves to the mind which is not indolent or inert.[51]

In 1575, Tallis and Byrd obtained a Crown patent to print and sell music and music paper; by this means their work, much of it Latin service music for recusant worship, could become part of the private musical experience of poets and readers. Their first production, dedicated to Queen Elizabeth, was called *Cantiones, quae ab argumento sacrae vocantur*, which Joseph Kerman renders "Songs which are [strictly speaking not sacred but only] called sacred on account of their texts," implying that they may safely be used by anyone without imputation of recusancy. "Since Queen Elizabeth accepted the dedication of the *Cantiones*," Kerman continues, "it seems reasonable to suppose that the motets, or some of them, were sung in her Chapel Royal." Prefatory poems by Richard

Mulcaster and Sir Ferdinand Heybourne also express the motive of making English polyphony known abroad.[52] The publication includes Byrd's popular "Emendemus in melius" and other motets whose "variety of experimentation, novelty, and expressive range must have dazzled contemporary musicians"; along with those that "draw imaginatively on native traditions . . . is a newer group of penitential motets which show a significant foreign influence by way of Alfonso Ferrabosco, the prolific Italian composer (and, probably, spy) who was in England in Elizabeth's service intermittently between 1563 and 1578" and through whose acquaintance with the style of Lassus "Byrd came to understand – and became, it seems, the first English composer really to understand – classical Netherlands imitative polyphony."[53] Byrd pays explicit homage to Taverner in his four-part mass[54] and to Taverner and Fayrfax in the *Gradualia*; as a pupil of Tallis and a teacher of Tomkins, Morley, and perhaps Phillips, Weelkes, and Bull, he spans the music of an entire century.[55] As a recusant and a frequently resident friend of families that harbored Jesuit missionaries, and as a distant relative of John Donne's mother,[56] Byrd may have been acquainted with Donne, who would in any case have heard his music at St. Paul's, and whose penitential poems share "variety of experimentation, novelty, and expressive range" with Byrd's penitential motets; he is known to have been a guest in the family of George Herbert;[57] as a fellow-contributor with John Milton Senior to Leighton's *Teares* he was known to the young John Milton, whose later experience of "Solemn Musick" in both Cambridge and London would have included ample infusions of Byrd's.

Further links between past and present were provided by the Laudian Revival. Bound into a 1634 Book of Common Prayer at Peterhouse are manuscript versions of music by Byrd, Tallis, and Farrant and a Latin Mass (*Sine nomine*), used as a source of anthems.[58] The Peterhouse part-books of the 1630s contain contemporary Latin litanies by Molle and Loosemore, sixteenth-century masses by Fayrfax, Taverner, and Tye, and anthems by Fayrfax, Taverner, Tallis, Marbeck, Phillips, and Byrd along with numerous living composers.[59] Their titles map the phases of a spiritual life, and might also be read as the insistence upon singing the Lord's praises with free use of human talent by those who felt themselves embattled by reformers.

In 1641 John Barnard of St. Paul's (perhaps a minor canon during Donne's tenure as Dean) published *The First Book of Selected Church Musick*, "the only printed collection of English liturgical music to appear between Day's *Certaine notes* [of 1565] and the Civil War."[60] It contains ten part-books including separate decani and cantoris medius, first and second contratenor, tenor, and bassus parts. This printed anthology and Barnard's much larger manuscript collection (L RCM 1045–51) contain numerous works that might otherwise have been lost in the iconoclasm. Barnard apparently intended a second volume containing works by contemporary composers, but the war intervened. His dedication to Charles I stresses English roots, tracing them from "the time that the old primate of England, *Theodore* with his assistant *Adrian* the Monk first establisht the skilfull use of Musick, throughout all the Saxon-English Churches," and prefers post-Reformation music. The reign of Elizabeth "brought forth a noble birth, as of all learned men, so of Famous composers in Church-Musick," and it has been his labor to preserve "the choycest Master-peces left us in Hymnes, Anthems, and Seruices" since that time "from the danger of perishing or corruption," since "next to the religious end it hath[,] nothing can more auaile to mitigate and civilize the rough and boystrous fancie of a Nation, that is esteem'd of many, to be naturally somewhat of the sowrest." A handwritten note in an incomplete copy laments: "Of this noble, matchless, and judicious selection of our Church Music no perfect copy is known to exist in consequence of the total dispersion of choirs, and destruction not only of organs, but also of music books both in manuscripts and printed, by the Puritans in 1643."[61]

Publishing of music for private use proceeded apace during the Commonwealth, much of it trifling. Some of Playford's collections printed during the 1650s (and even after choirs had been restored) boldly began with a frontispiece of a bosomy personification of "Musick" playing a lute and an epigram frankly complaining that "the Cannon, and the Churlish Drum / Have strook the Quire mute, and the Organs Dumb." Nevertheless, a few choir part-books escaped the iconoclasts, and those retained by private houses typically contained both secular and devotional music. After the Restoration many works reappeared, as may be seen in the Norwich part-books and Clifford's *Divine Services and Anthems*. *A Collection of Anthems Daily Us'd . . . in King's College* (1706), also sung on Sundays and special occasions at other Cambridge colleges and Great St. Mary's, gives only texts but specifies settings, among them *An Anthem Compos'd first in Latin In the Reign of King Edward the Sixth. By Mr. Tho. Tallis* ("I call and cry to thee"), the English version of Byrd's "Ne irascaris Domine" ("Bow down thine ear"), Edmund Hooper's "Behold it is Christ," William Mundy's *The Prayer of Manasses*, Thomas Tomkins' collect "Almighty God the Fountain of all Wisdom," Adrian Batten's "Hast thee O God" (Ps. 70.1–4), and settings by Child and Loosemore including verses from Psalm 103. Works by newer composers form a larger part of the collection, but the transmission of works from before the Civil Wars shows how liturgical communities conserved favorite works by past composers while supporting new ones.

Thanks to the developments in English music contributed by Dunstable, Taverner, the Eton Choirbook composers, and Tallis, when Reformers proclaimed that intelligibility of words and singing from the heart should have first priority, church musicians had techniques ready to develop without abandoning the richness of polyphony: the use of alternating chant and polyphonic passages, of homophony in key portions of the liturgy for which hearers needed aids to memory rather than total legibility, and of expressive and structural emphasis that reinforced the shape of a familiar text. In his encyclopedic account, Peter Phillips provides numerous examples of characteristics that give the music of the English Reformation its particular identity. These include "antiphony between decani and cantoris; scoring with a preference for divided altos at the expense of the tenor voice; the ABB anthem form; the 'short,' what will be called 'middle,' and 'great' styles of Service; melodic tags like the English cadence and clash; the scalic 'amen'; consecutive 6/3 chords, quasi-canon and circular harmonic progressions," and numerous specific figures.[62] These conventions and innovations are employed by composers of great melodic and harmonic gifts whose particular genius breathes life and beauty into them as varied as human identity. The early seventeenth century may be considered the golden age of English Church music partly because, in spite of the political controversies and partly because of them, so many excellences, often pitted against each other in other times, concented together.

Some features of English style had, I believe, a profound effect on English poetry. Taverner and the composers of the Eton

Choirbook, while using cantus firmi, proportionally balanced sections, and numerological symbolism, employed considerable
freedom and variety of voicing. Ensuing Renaissance polyphony
increased unity by means of counterpoint or imitation, building
harmonies vertically as additional voices enter. Imitation, Benham
states, is the most powerful means to unified structure; "indeed,
this must be considered the key Renaissance technique."[63]
According to Peter le Huray, the fundamental change in the
process of composition was "from a primarily horizontal method
of working, in which the separate parts were composed one after
another, to a vertical method in which all parts were developed
simultaneously."[64] However, kinds of voicing that exposed individual parts continued, especially in the typically English verse service
and verse anthem. Like the music of this tradition, much seventeenth-century poetry is highly structured, yet voices emerge with
startling individuality. As English polyphony sought to retain
verbal intelligibility and melodic appeal to the heart within its rich
sonorities, English poetry kept its capacity for expressiveness and
directness within its finely tuned close-weaving of words. Its verbal
harmonies, both audible and cognitive, resemble the composition
of Renaissance polyphony; though reading linearly, one is conscious of an extraordinary density of verbal resonances that form
vertical harmonies. And, as pure intonation allows and gives clarity
to close harmony and expressive dissonance, precise diction
increases the interactions of words, because not only the sounds
and ideas but, as I hope to show in subsequent chapters, the partials of language are in tune.

THE CHURCH MUSIC CONTROVERSY AND
THE CIVIL WARS

Although the windows of King's College Chapel survived both the
Henrican and the Cromwellian iconoclasms, the arts that fuse in
such churches alarmed those reformers who thought images and
all ceremonies not prescribed by Scripture conducive to superstition. The English Church until the 1630s took a moderate position, forbidding icons, Marian antiphons, and rites or music that
obscured words, but retaining traditions deemed edifying and
expressed with moderation and clarity. "Christ's gospel," the
prayerbook's preface "Of Ceremonies" declares, "is not a ceremo-

nial law, as much of Moses' law was, but it is a religion to serve God not in bondage of the figure or shadow, but in the freedom of spirit": a succinct statement of the rejection of elaborate ritual and the affirmation of each believer's free access to God by which many Protestants defined themselves. However, those traditions that the English liturgy "retain[s] for a discipline and order" are "neither dark nor dumb ceremonies, but are so set forth that every man may understand what they do mean and to what use they do serve" (*BCP* 19–20). Even so, the radical faction objected to even moderate use of non-scriptural traditions in public worship, including artfully composed choral and instrumental music rather than congregational singing of psalms to familiar tunes, and these attacks provoked defenses of church music throughout the seventeenth century, summed up at its close in St. Cecilia's Day sermons.

For Protestants, human works were unworthy and unnecessary to offer as propitiation; Christ himself, in the words of the Book of Common Prayer, made on the cross "a full, perfect, and sufficient sacrifice, oblation, and satisfaction for the sins of the whole world." The idea, intolerable to reformers, that humans could placate God by their sacrifices, as if Christ's sacrifice were not "full, perfect, and sufficient," had produced many of the abuses, such as selling indulgences, against which the Reformation rose. Hence instead of making or re-enacting a propitiatory sacrifice, prayerbook communicants offer "ourselves, our souls and bodies, to be a reasonable, holy, and lively sacrifice unto thee" in response to the perfect sacrifice already made. For liturgical purists whose advocacy of literal adherence to the practices of the Apostolic church got them the name of "Puritans," the offering of "our souls and bodies" was an individual act, and no one could make a "sacrifice of praise and thanksgiving" on another's behalf; to set portions of the liturgy to complicated music for a trained choir was to obscure the words and rob the worshipper of his or her part in the praise.

In his Cambridge dissertation on the church music controversy, John Harley Shepherd connects it to the changing meaning of "sacrifice," collecting censures of church music as outward, not inward, worship, an offering of art instead of heart, and defenses that refute the necessity of splitting the two. Shepherd documents a shift in sixteenth-century definitions of its purpose, from a sacrifice pleasing to God to an art "able to inspire in the worshipper emotions which complemented and illuminated the sense of the words." [65] This change incorporates the primacy of the word in Reformation thought and its subordination of works to faith. However, the choral tradition continued through the Elizabethan and Stuart periods, aided first, Shepherd shows, by defenses of its ability to arouse a heartfelt response to the words, then increasingly by claims "that a spiritual sacrifice of praise and thanksgiving was incomplete without the physical offering of works and arts," which, however, must be clear to the hearer, until "the art of music was once again granted a function in liturgical worship on the basis of its ability to please God with the beauty of its sound."[66]

The earlier seventeenth century represents a careful integration of spiritual and physical worship in the Church of England. But the elaboration of liturgical ceremony encouraged in the 1630s by Charles I and Archbishop Laud contributed to tensions between reformers and the monarchy and prelates. To reformers, unscriptural elaborations were elitist innovations, and the idea that human works could please God invited pride. To defenders, the poverty of a "sacrifice of praise and thanksgiving" that omitted God's gifts of talents entrusted to skilled artists disregarded divine providence and human dignity. Laudian investment in "the beauty of holiness" led to the furious reaction of the 1640s and the banishment of choral and organ music from English Churches.

Defenses of church music are founded primarily on the practices of the Jewish church recorded in Scripture, read typologically as applicable to Christian worship, and on three New Testament passages: the account of the Last Supper (and first communion service) in Matthew 26.30 and Mark 14.26, where Jesus and the disciples go forth to the Mount of Olives "when they had sung an hymn" (or, in the Geneva Bible, "when they had sung a psalme"[67]); 1 Corinthians 14.15, "I will sing with the spirit, and I will sing with understanding also"; and Ephesians 5.18–19, ". . . be filled with the Spirit; Speaking to yourselves in psalms and hymns and spiritual songs, singing and making melody in your heart to the Lord." But for Calvinist reformers, these passages were not authorizations for church music; those from the "Old" Testament were part of the ceremonial law, abrogated by the Gospel, and those from the New concerned only private worship or congregational psalm-singing before and after a church service devoted to clear and sober reading and preaching of the Word. The many volumes of psalms

and spiritual songs published in the sixteenth and seventeenth
centuries encouraged singing "to [or among] yourselves."

Incorporation of Judaic ceremonies into the Christian liturgy
embodies a sense of continuity between the two testaments, seen
in the King's College Chapel windows and retained in the lectionary of the Book of Common Prayer, that remained a key argument
in Anglican apologies for music throughout the seventeenth
century. (I am using "Anglican" for the established church and
"puritan" for dissenters within and without.) Both sides cited the
Bible and non-biblical authorities, such as Augustine and
Athanasius, in opposite ways, the dissenters to denounce choral
singing and instrumental music altogether, defenders to urge
choirs to sing from their hearts and both choirs and composers to
make the words intelligible and the music a help to hearers to sing
in their hearts as well.

Curiously, an early English critic of church music was John
Marbeck, or Merbecke, layclerk and then organist at St. George's
Chapel, Windsor, who was the first composer to set the newly
Englished liturgy. Marbeck had narrowly escaped execution in
1542/43 for writing against the Six Articles of 1539, which preserved the doctrine of transubstantiation, clerical celibacy, private
Masses, and other practices the Reformers objected to, and for pos-
sessing materials for his *Concordance* to the whole English Bible
(published 1550) at a time when Latin was still the official language of the church. His *Booke of Notes and Common Places* is loaded
against choral and instrumental church music with arguments that
practices ordained in the Old Testament and not the New smack of
works instead of grace and that "singing in your hearts" means not
singing otherwise, at least in church. His entry on "Musicke" cites
Calvin's opinion concerning Psalm 150 that while David "express-
eth the vehemencie and earnestnesse of his affection in praising
God" and urges the use of instruments as "helpes wherewith the
faithfull are woont to stir vp themselues," neither instruments nor
choral singing are proper to Christian worship, since "we drawe not
to our selues, (without respect) whatsoeuer was commanded the
Jewes of olde time. And I am out of doubt for my parte, that the
plaieng of Cymballes, singing to the Harpe and Viall" and the like
were "a part of the lawe of schooling: I meane of the solempne fur-
niture of the Temple." Christians may use musical instruments privately in order "not to seuer their mirth from the praises of God.

But when they haunt their holy assemblies, I think that musicall instruments are no more meet for the setting forth of Gods praises, then if a man shall call againe sensing and lampes, and such other shadowes of the lawe. Foolishly therefore haue the Papists borowed this and many other things of the Jewes. Men that are giuen to outward pomps, delight in such noise, but God lyketh better the simplicitie" of public worship in "a knowne tongue" (1 Cor.1); "What shall we then saye of chauntinge, which onely feedeth the eares with a vaine sounde." He also quotes Peter Martyr, who holds that "singers of songes and Psalmes, hav their place in the Church," but compiles a history of contrary judgments concerning the lightness and vanity that music may induce, including Gregory, who found that certain deacons "set all their pleasure on pleasaunt singing, not caring how they liued afore God," and Erasmus, who called "the curious manner of singing vsed in Churches" a "confused noise" in which "the common people heare [only] voyces signifieng nothing."[68]

Heinrich Bullinger (1504–75), Zwingli's successor in Zurich and a reformer influential in England, also turns biblical passages against those who used them in defense of music, arguing that "the same cunning kind of musicke brought into the church of God by Dauid . . . was abolished together with the temple and the ceremonies." The accounts of Jesus and his disciples having sung a hymn ('υμνησαντ ες, from 'υμνεω, humneo, to praise) might be rendered either "when they had soung an Hymne" or "When they had saide an Hymne." The Vulgate uses the latter (*Et hymno dicto*), and Erasmus' Latin translation uses both (*Et cum hymnum cecinissent* in Matthew and *Et cum hymnum dixissent* in Mark). Paul did not rebuke the church at Corinth for singing psalms, since "Their maner of singing differed much from the olde," but meant the passage from Ephesians to pertain to private gatherings rather than public worship. Yet, since the Apostle's *In corde* may mean "ioyfully or from the hart," no one should forbid "moderate and godly singing of Psalmes, whether it be publiquelie vsed in holie assemblies, or at home in priuate houses." In brief, if the church had retained its early way of singing, as near to speech as possible and only to increase audibility, and if it had left singing a thing indifferent, not requiring it or scorning those who used only spoken prayer, there would be no controversy. But in the unreformed church, Bullinger complains, singing has come to supplant Scripture reading and preaching, non-canonical texts are interpolated, "Creatures and dead men are called vpon," hired clerks and clergymen eager for benefices sing for money, they sing "in a straunge tongue" and compete to display their voices, and "There is hearde a long sounde, quauered and streyned to and fro, backwarde and forewarde, whereof a man cannot understand one worde." In contrast, "they that beleeue the Gospell, doe neither vse such singing, neither suffer it in the Church of God."[69]

Richard Hooker and John Whitgift were major apologists for the prayerbook liturgy, and the "T. C." whom they both oppose is the learned dissenter Thomas Cartwright, Fellow of Trinity College and Professor of Divinity, whose many objections to the episcopal hierarchy and ceremonial practices of the English Church included opposition to fixed forms of prayer, such as the canticles of the daily offices, and to the use of bells, organs, or any sort of singing apart from unison psalm-singing to simple tunes by the whole congregation before and after services. Whitgift – Master of Trinity, University Preacher, Regius Professor of Divinity, Vice-Chancellor of the University, and Canon of Ely – was in sympathy with Calvinist doctrine but defended the hierarchical discipline and uniform liturgy of the recently reestablished English Church. While Lady Margaret Professor in the university, Cartwright attacked church hierarchy and discipline from the pulpit of St. Mary's and was answered there by Whitgift, who in 1570, as Vice-Chancellor, ejected Cartwright from his professorship and in 1571, as Master of Trinity, from his fellowship.

In 1572, John Field and Thomas Wilcox published a landmark of puritan criticism, *An Admonition to the Parliament*, seeking to replace the episcopal hierarchy with a presbyterian form of government, for which they were imprisoned. Cartwright supported their views in *A Second Admonition to the Parliament* (London, 1572), to which Whitgift replied, initiating a printed debate of which Whitgift's 1574 *Defense* recapitulates both sides.[70] Both address their remarks to the Church of England. Donald McGinn points out that literary scholars, supposing Cartwright to be "the good shepherd Thomalin" in the July eclogue of Spenser's *Shepherdes Calender* and Whitgift akin to the "proude and ambitious" pastor Morrell, have preferred Cartwright.[71] Musicians are apt to side with Whitgift.

In brief, Cartwright contends that the public worship of the

English Church departs from practices of the Apostles, by which it should be strictly bound, since traditions unauthorized in Scripture are superstitious and hamper the free and heartfelt worship that alone is pleasing to God. Whitgift holds that what Scripture prescribes must be followed and what it forbids forbidden, but that it is absurd to forbid everything that Scripture does not prescribe. Both Cartwright's strenuous restrictions on liturgy and Whitgift's defense of non-scriptural traditions within it are meant to preserve kinds of spiritual liberty, but differ according to whose liberty is at stake. The debate encapsulates puritan literalism and egalitarianism as opposed to the latitude of the established church and its respect for (or, in the puritan view, abuse of) human authority. Their seeming quibbles over such matters as antiphonal psalm-singing are comparable to the quarrels over vestments, gestures, and images that might, in the reformers' view, mislead the simple into an iconic rather than a participatory mode of worship; and those quarrels are analogues of political debates between monarchical and parliamentary factions. Music was a political issue.

Richard Hooker defends the Book of Common Prayer and the careful ordering of "all things . . . apperteininge" on the grounds that public worship should be performed "with the most sollemnitie and majestie that the wisest could devise," for "the howse of prayer is a court bewtified with the presence of coelestiall powers, that there we stand, we pray, we sound forth hymnes unto God, havinge his Angels intermingled as our associates . . . how can we come to the house of prayer, and not be moved with the verie glories of the place it selfe, so to frame our affections prayinge, as doth best beseeme them, whose sutes thalmightie doth there sitt to heare, and his angels attend to furder?" (*Lawes* ii: 113–14). Against Cartwright's opinion that the singing of the canticles is absurd because true prayer comes spontaneously from present experience and inspiration, he objects that if repetition of prayers is superstitious, and prayers must always "wast away them selves in the makinge," then

surelie we cannot excuse Moses, who gave such occasion of scandall to the world, by not beinge contented to praise the name of almightie God according to the usuall naked simplicitie of Gods Spirit for that admerable victorie given them against Pharao, unlesse [lest] so dangerous a precedent were left for the casting of prayers into certaine poeticall mouldes, and for the framinge of prayers which might be repeated often although they never had againe the same occasions which brought them forth at first. Nor onelie that, but sundrie other sithence invented.

These include both "hymnes taken out of holie scripture" and those penned later (such as the Te Deum) that have regular places in the liturgy, including "some interlacede betwene the divine readinges of the lawe and prophetes." The Evangelist alludes to "theire custome of finishinge the Passover with certaine psalmes" by saying that "after the cup delivered by our Savior unto his Apostles, *they sunge* and went forth to the mount of Olives."

As the Jewes had theire songes of Moses and David and the rest, so the Church of Christ from the verie beginninge hath both used the same and besides them other also of like nature, the songe of the Virgin Mary, the songe of Zacharie, the songe of Simeon, such hymns as thapostle doth often speake of sayinge *I will pray and singe with the spirit*; againe *In psalmes, hymnes, and songs makinge melodie unto the Lord and that hartely.* Hymnes and psalmes are such kindes of prayer as are not woont to be conceaved upon a suddaine, but are framed by meditation before hand, or els by propheticall illumination are inspired, as at that time it appeareth they were when God by extraordinarie guiftes of the spirit inabled men to all partes of service necessarie for the edifyinge of his Church (*Lawes* II: 113–19)

As to setting public prayers to music, Hooker argues that David was "the author of addinge unto poetrie melodie in publique prayer, melodie both vocall and instrumentall for the raysinge up of mens hartes and the sweetninge of theire affections towardes god"; while "curiosity and ostentation of arte" must be avoided, music that "fitlie suteth with matter altogether soundinge to the praise of God, is in truth most admirable, and doth much edifie if not the understandinge because it teacheth not, yeat surely thaffection because therein it worketh much" (*Lawes* II:152–53). Although he is upholding a fixed liturgy, Hooker's defense of liturgical poems meditatively framed or inspired by the Spirit might suggest that in parts of the liturgy not prescribed but allowed, such as the anthems "in the beginning, or in the end of common prayers," poets and musicians might continue to provide meditative or inspired works.

George Wither's *Hymnes and Songs of the Church* (1623, *EECM* XXI), with two-part settings (to be filled in by singers or players) by Orlando Gibbons, supplements metrical psalters with, as the title continues, *Canonicall Hymnes and Spirituall Songs, appropriated to the seuerall Times and Occasions obseruable in the Church of England:*

though, Wither's preface avows, "not for that I would haue it thought Part of the Churches Liturgies, but because they are made in the Person of all the Faithfull." He includes a song "For the Communion," however. Wither refutes reformers such as Calvin and Cartwright: "Plainely false is their supposition, who conceiue, that the Hymns, Songs, and Elegies of the Old Testament are impertinent to these later Ages of the Church"; and he provides notes to each song giving its scriptural context and applicability to present experience. Of the opening *First Song of Moses* (Exod. 15), Wither writes, reminiscently of Dante's letter to Can Grande:

This Song was composed and sung to praise the Lord for the Israelites miraculous passage through the Red Sea, and for their delivery from those Egyptians who were there drowned. It may (and should also) be sung in the Christian congregations, or by their particular members, both with respect to the historical and mystical senses thereof: Historically, in commemoration of that particular deliverance, which God had so long ago and so wondrously vouchsafed to his persecuted and afflicted church: Mystically, in acknowledgment of our own powerful deliverance from the bondage of those spiritual adversaries, whereof those were the types: for Pharoah (signifying Vengeance) typified our great enemy, who, with his host of temptations, afflictions, &c. pursueth us in our passage to the spiritual Canaan.

Wither prefaces *The Second Song of Moses* (Deut. 32), "This *Song* was giuen by *God* himselfe, to be taught the *Iewes*... For it appeares the Diuine Wisdome knew that when the *Law* would be lost and forgotten, a *Song* might be remembered to posterity": a statement much resembling Donne's verses at the end of *The First Anniversarie*, published in a second edition two years earlier. Like other devotional poets, Donne takes the songs of Moses and David as precedents for his own work.

Among the most eloquent voices in the church music contro-versy was church music itself. Composers set psalms that urge musical praise, such as Psalms 81, 96, 98 and especially, because of their clear call to music in public worship, Psalms 149 and 150 as enthusiastic demonstrations, and for the invocations to "sing unto the Lord a new song" invented fresh figures in individual styles. Thomas Tomkins' "Be strong and of a good courage," an anthem for the coronation of James I (*EECM* xxxix), gives the kind of advice to kings seen in music sung at King's College, continuing, "and observe the commandements of our God, to walk in his ways, and keep his ceremonies" (from Joshua 1.6–7). Tomkins clearly declaims "To walk in his ways" in rising repetitions and word-paints "keep his ceremonies" with striking syncopation and repetition in a higher mode. When parliamentary powers made it increasingly difficult to "keep his ceremonies," Tomkins moved from advice to distress. In "O God, the proud are risen against me, / and the assembly of violent men / which have thee not before their eyes seek after my soul," the "assembly of violent men" (a variation of Ps. 86. 14–15) receives heartfelt dissonance. In 1649, deprived of his vocation as church musician, he was to write a wordless *Sad Pavan for these Distracted Times* (*MB* v).

Musical settings of texts lamenting divisions in the church were set by adherents of both the Church of England and the Church of Rome. Motets concerning Jerusalem in tribulation include Byrd's "Tribulationes civitatum," "Ne irascaris Domine," and "Vide Domine afflictionem nostram." "O Pray for the Peace of Jerusalem" (Ps. 122.6) was set for reformed worship by Thomas Tomkins, among others, and the beginning of Lamentations by composers of both persuasions including the notable Protestant John Milton the Elder, whose version was included in Myriell's *Tristitiae remedium* of 1616: "How doth the holy city remain solitary (alas), that was full of people . . . Among her lovers she hath none to comfort her; all her friends have dealt unfaithfully with her, and are her enemies."[72] John Donne, a Catholic by upbringing and an Anglican by profession, treats Lamentations, in his metrical translation "according to Tremelius," in ways applicable to both communions. The fact that both churches used these texts to lament their dangers and divisions further sharpens their poignancy. William Byrd perhaps makes an ecumenical musical statement in *The Great Service* by his emphasis in the Magnificat on "all generations shall call me blessed," his repetition in the Te Deum of "all believers," and in the Benedictus both his strikingly expressive treatment of "That we being delivered out of the hands of our enemies might serve him without fear" and his lovely resolution on "And guide our feet into the way of peace": all appropriately expressive of the words, yet particularly so for a member of a persecuted church speaking musically to its persecutors, who are also his patrons and friends.

Arthur Lake mentions one of Byrd's most popular anthems, "Ne irascaris Domine," in a sermon on the penitential Psalm 51, verse

15, "Thou shalt open my lips, O Lord, and my mouth shall show thy praise." Lake supports the reading of the Hebrew Bible that makes its ceremonies apt for Christian use, and also alludes to the chief principle of reformed church music: "Though the instrument be the *Mouth*, yet the Musitian is the Heart, he causeth the tune of the voice to sound, and addeth the Dittie to the Tune; and certainly the Musicke will never be well-come to God should any part of man be wanting thereunto; therefore *David* thus vpon himselfe, *Blesse the Lord, O my Soule*, and all that is within me blesse his Holy name." Lake laments the church's divisions and dangers: "*Sion* is as a *wildernesse*, and *Ierusalem* a *desolation*, what with the Turke, and what with the Pope, euery where is the sword bathed in Christian bloud," and adds, "if euer, *Ne irascaris Domine* would now be a seasonable Antheme, wee should all pray, *Be not wrath very sore, O Lord, neither remember iniquity for euer. And I would there were that compassionate disposition in vs, which appeared in the captiue Iewes, when they said, If I forget thee O Ierusalem, let my right hand forget her cunning, if I doe not remember thee, let my tongue cleaue to the roofe of my mouth, if I prefere not Ierusalem before my chieftest ioy.*"[73] Byrd's "Ne irascaris Domine" (Isa. 64.9–10; *BE* II), published in the *Cantiones Sacrae* of 1589[74] and widely used in translation as an English anthem, was applicable to both Byrd's beseiged Catholics and Lake's embattled Anglicans. It is particularly expressive of this irony in its plea, "Ecce, respice, populus tuus omnes" (AV "Behold, see, we beseech thee, we are all thy people"), which the English translator renders (alluding to the Venite) "Look down O Lord with thy merciful eyes and see, we be thy people and thy pasture sheep."[75]

Some taste of the liturgical and political experience of the poets and musicians in this study and of the puritan reaction to Laudian practices may be gathered from events at Cambridge University. Although the universities were historically independent from royal and ecclesiastical jurisdiction, the seventeenth century saw increasing external attempts to control discipline, starting with the Prohibition of Idle Games and Plays, and particularly to eject both Popery and sectarian non-conformity from these "nurseries and fountains of our church and commonwealth."[76] In 1604 (the year Phineas Fletcher received his B. A. and Orlando Gibbons left King's for the Chapel Royal) Sir Robert Cecil ordered the vice-chancellor and heads to make "a vigilent survey of orderinge of every the colledges and halls in the University (*in divinis officiis*), accordinge to the statutes of the University, the constitution of the Church, and the orders prescribed in the booke of Common Prayer; and withall take present order for the repressinge of all libertyes heretofore to the contrary; certifieinge me of the delinquents, except they shall assure you of present reformation" (214–15). These officials were to "be very vigilant agaynst private conventicles" and unauthorized preaching and to enforce the king's command "that no man shall preach in St. Marys church except he first subscribe to the three articles": that is, to the supremacy of the English sovereign as head of church and state, to the lawfulness of the Book of Common Prayer, and to the thirty-nine Articles of Religion (216–17).[77] In 1613 and 1616 (the year Herbert became a Fellow of Trinity and Jonson published his *Works*) the requirement of subscription was extended to all degrees. Students were required to attend the official Sunday sermons at St. Mary's both morning and afternoon, and all college chapels must conform to the "laws, canons, and constitutions of this our church of England" (274); members must "take the communion kneeling" and wear surplices and hoods according to their degrees. Scholars must not absent themselves from "catechizing in their colleges" from three to four or "the common prayer" from four to five "on Sundays and holy days" to attend sermons in parish churches or for other pretexts (275). Moreover, "Any fancifull conceit, savouring of Judaism, popish superstition, or puritanism, disagreeing from the laudable and approved customes of our church of England" should be "speedily checked and reformed" (277).

In 1625 (the year Milton entered Christ's and Charles I granted liberty of worship to Catholics) the Chancellor, Thomas Suffolk, asked the heads "to bring home that long banisht pilgrim, discipline, by whose absence the famous nursery of literature and good manners is in the eye of the state much declined" (336–37), enclosing a letter from Charles I offering help with this task. The dissolution of Parliament in 1629 was followed by eleven years of monarchical rule, with the result that Parliament could no longer hear grievances. In Cambridge, preachers were tried for non-conformity. In 1633, the year Donne's *Poems*, Herbert's *The Temple*, and Cowley's *Poetical Blossoms* came forth and Andrew Marvell entered Trinity College, William Laud became Archbishop of Canterbury.

In 1635, Laud sought the right of visitation but was resisted by both universities; he petitioned and won in 1636. (This external supervision was not limited to the Anglican side; in 1654, Cromwell appointed commissioners, some of them members of colleges, to visit both universities.)

In 1637 (the year Cowley entered Trinity) three puritan dissidents (Prynne, Burton, and Bostwick) had their ears cropped and were perilously shipped into exile,[78] and Milton wrote *Lycidas* and published *A Mask at Ludlow*. In the headnote to *Lycidas* in his *Poems* of 1645 he would declare that the poem "foretels the ruine of our corrupted clergy then in their height."[79] In 1639, during the First Bishops' War against the Scots, Milton returned from abroad because "the sad tidings of civil war from England summoned me back. For I thought it base that I should travel abroad at my ease for the cultivation of my mind, while my fellow-citizens were fighting for their liberty."[80]

In 1640 the Long Parliament began, Cromwell was elected member from Cambridge, and the tables began to turn. In January of 1640/41 the House of Commons resolved that the statute of 1613 imposing subscription to the three articles "is against the law and liberty of the subject, and ought not to be pressed upon any student whatsoever." In 1641 Cromwell urged destruction of episcopacy "root and branch." One of the victims of the puritan backlash was music. During the 1640s organs were smashed, choirs disbanded, and bell-ringing stopped, especially in the puritan stronghold of Cambridge. Cromwell warned the Dean and Chapter at Ely, "Lest the soldiers should in any tumultuous or disorderly way attempt the reformation of your Catholic church I require you to forbear altogether your choir services so annoying and offensive."[81]

According to Walker's *Sufferings of the Clergy*, the Chancellor of the University obtained orders from Parliament that no violence should be done to colleges or their chapels "and that divine service should be quietly performed and exercised, according to the settlement of the church of England, without any trouble, let, or disturbance." Nevertheless, according to the *Querela Cantabrigiensis*, "under pretence of papists, malignants, etc., there was scarce a scholar in all the University" who escaped examination. In 1642 Cromwell was frustrated in an attempt to prevent contributions and silver plate being sent to Charles I and "comes down from London again in a terrible manner with what forces he could draw together, and surrounds divers colleges while they were at their devotions in their several chapels, taking away prisoners several doctors of divinity heads of colleges . . . At length the town of Cambridge was pitched on for the prime garrison and rendezvous of the seven associated counties" after which "for near two years together, the prophanations, violence, outrages, and wrongs done to their chapels, colleges, and persons, by the uncontrouled fury of rude soldiers, notwithstanding the fore-mentioned protections, were matter of unspeakable grief to any that considered it." Revolutionaries "made Kings College chapel a place to exercise their soldiers in; and one who called himself John Dowsing, and by virtue of a pretended commission went about the country to break windows, battered and beat down all the painted glass, not only in the chapels, but contrary to, or at least besides, their own order, in the public schools, colledges, halls, libraries, and chambers; mistaking, perhaps (saith the Querela), the liberal arts for saints, which they intended in time to pull down too."[82] Under parliamentary ordinance nearly two hundred masters and fellows were ejected with the intent "to plant a new University, for propagating at least, if not inventing, a new religion."[83]

As a result of this exchange of repressions, the choirs of England fell silent. In 1644 Milton published *Areopagitica*, and did not inveigh against the censorship of church music. Indeed, he ridiculed lists of imprimaturs as "the pretty responsories" and "dear antiphonies, that so bewitched of late our prelates and their chaplains, with the goodly echo they made," suggesting by analogy that the music of the Laudian revival was a self-congratulatory usurpation of conscience. At the same time, he ridiculed the notion of enforcing virtue by suppressing books or arts, since "If we think to regulate printing, thereby to rectify manners, we must regulate all recreations and pastimes, all that is delightful to man. No music must be set or sung, but what is grave and doric" (*SM* 736, 740). And in *Of Education* he recommends "the solemn and divine harmonies of music" to compose the spirits and temper the passions of young scholars and military exercises to make them commanders who would not suffer their men "to comply with all rapines and violences" (*SM* 730).

Two of the poets primarily studied here, Donne and Herbert, died just before the Laudian proliferations. Milton, and more ambiguously Marvell, supported the revolution and made no public protest about the silencing of the choirs, but also defended the arts and their capacity to regenerate a nation. All experienced English Church music in its golden age, and none promoted the ceremonialism of the 1630s. Part of the strength of their poetry and much English Church music is that they mediate between the dogmatic positions that drive factions apart but, nevertheless, provide productive tensions to the arts. Both the highly developed state of the arts and theologically based attacks on them contributed to poets' philosophical and linguistic maturity.

The question of whether contrived art "framed by meditation before hand," in Hooker's words, can also be true devotion "from the heart" troubled many poets, along with the question of whether their work, as well as the scriptural psalms and songs, could be true offerings to God. The three highly contrived verse-crowns of Donne's *La Corona*, Herbert's *The Wreath*, and Marvell's *The Coronet* fret this question either implicitly or explicitly, for, as Marvell finds, the old serpent of self-display winds its way even into garlands for God. Traherne, comparing his childhood work of praise to Adam's, declares in *Silence*,

> To see, Approve, take Pleasure, and rejoyce
> Within, is better than an Empty Voice:
> No Melody in Words can equal that;
> The sweetest Organ, Lute, or Harp, is flat,
> And Dull, compard therto.

Yet in *Thanksgivings for the Body* he cries,

> O that I were as David, the sweet Singer of Israel!
>   In meeter Psalms to set forth thy Praises.
> Thy Raptures ravish me, and turn my soul all into melody.
> Whose Kingdom is so glorious, that nothing in it shall at all
>   be unprofitable, mean, or idle.
> So constituted!
> That every one's Glory is beneficial unto all; and every one
>   magnified in his place by Service.

Among the poets whose specific responses to musical controversy are most "reformed" are those skilled performers, Donne and Marvell. The metrical psalms Donne commends, and perhaps his metrical Lamentations, are suited to be sung by all. Marvell questions the process of artistry in *The Coronet*, and in *A Dialogue of the Soul and Created Pleasure* music is the most tempting pleasure that Pleasure can offer, and Soul rejects it as a particular danger, while in *Bermudas* the congregation of an "English boat," escaped from "prelate's rage," sings God's praise to "An holy and a cheerful note" in more luscious language than ever swam into the ken of Sternhold and Hopkins.

Among the poets whose work praises choral music are Herbert, who strove, in the words of *Jordan* (I), to "plainly say, *My God, My King,*" and Milton, promoter and defender of the Revolution. Explicitly antiprelatical and parliamentarian, Milton celebrates in his poems, though not his prose, the kinds of music the puritans denounced. In *Paradise Lost* Adam and Eve sing more sweetly than needed lute or harp, but the unfallen angels use just the kinds of "singing, pyping" and other ceremonies that Cartwright thinks "sinfully mixed with mans inuentions and deuices."[84] Herbert, Milton's predecessor in the praise of "Solemn Musick," contemplates the relation of heart and art and offers a reconciliation of the controversy over liturgical art as a spiritual gift; the one "full, perfect, and sufficient sacrifice" is exactly what makes it possible for sinful but sorry humans to return thankful works of beauty. He commends choral and antiphonal singing in *Church-Musick* and in his *Antiphons*, provides an improved metrical version of *The 23. Psalm*, and exhorts his lute, or poesie, to "Struggle for thy part / With all thy art." In *Praise* (II) gratitude that "thou didst cleare me" is the cause of his whole book of psalms and songs:

> Thou hast granted my request,
>   Thou hast heard me:
> Thou didst note my working breast,
>   Thou hast spar'd me.
>
> Wherefore with my utmost art
>   I will sing thee,
> And the cream of all my heart
>   I will bring thee.

CHAPTER 3

Tuning the instrument: Donne's temporal and extemporal song

John Donne is not usually considered a musical poet. His complex syntax, angular prosody, and abstruse allusions are antipodal to the pastoral and courtly verse from which song and madrigal writers drew. His declamatory style, however passionate, is usually too cerebral to fit the affective resources of monody. Most of his divine poems, however deeply felt, are idiosyncratic, unlike the deliberately universal motets of his recusant family's tradition or the scriptural anthems of the English Church; and the exception, the unexceptionable *Hymne to God the Father*, puns on his own name. Yet that hymn and some of his *Songs and Sonets* were set by his contemporaries, and his poems recurrently remind one of much less interesting texts that first rate composers set to very good music. Many of the *Songs and Sonets* are perplexed or vivified versions of song and madrigal themes. Sometimes these simpler texts and their settings illuminate allusions, prosody, tone, and the vexed question of the speaking voice. Disputes about whether his amorous verses are personal lyrics from intimate experience or coterie imitations or dramatic monologues from urbane observation may be, if not solved, at least enlarged by the recognition that courts and houses through the realm resounded with the words of comparable first-person private declarations openly shared in sociable part-singing: comparable, but with differences that highlight Donne's distinctions.

Of Donne's poems that composers set in or near his lifetime,[1] we have printed versions of *The Expiration* (Alfonso Ferrabosco, *Ayres*, 1609, and again anonymously), *Breake of Day*, and *The Baite* (both by William Corkine, *Second Booke of Airs*, 1612); and several settings in manuscript: John Hilton's *Hymne to God the Father* and an anonymous "Go and catch a falling star" (L BL Egerton MS 2013); Thomas Ford's *Lamentations of Jeremy* for three voices (O Christ Church MSS 736–38); "Sweetest Love I do not go" (anony-

94

mous, L BL Add. MS 10337 and a variant in O B Tenbury MS 1018); and three of the *Songs and Sonets* by well-known composers: John Coprario's *The Message* (O B Tenbury MS 1019), William Lawes' *The Apparition* (E EU MS D. C. 1.69), and Martin Peerson's *The Primrose* (*Fitzwilliam Virginal Book*, without text). Orlando Gibbons in *The First Set Of Madrigals And Mottets*, (1612) set "Ah, dear heart, why do you rise?" – dubiously attributed to Donne – as a chromatically pleading madrigal.

Some of these seem odd choices: in *The Message* the vengeful complainant hopes to "laugh and joy, when thou / Art in anguish"; *The Apparition* is a curse, comparable to Campion's "When thou must home to shades of underground"; "Goe, and catche a falling star" perpetuates the adage debated in *The Courtyer* that no woman can be both true and fair; *The Primrose* claims that a woman is false by nature and worth half a man. The fact that such anti-Petrarchan and misogynous texts especially caught the fancy of composers shows that Donne was plying a popular genre that also includes, for example, Suckling's "Why so pale and wan" and madrigals, balletts, and songs such as Weelkes' "Mars in a fury" (1598) and "No, no!" which ends "Who dares trust women or hell? Fa la"; Wilbye's "Ay me, can every rumour"(1598), ending "For women be contrary"; and Dowland's "What poor astronomers are they / Take women's eyes for stars" (1603), in which "women's eyes and stars are odd, / And Love is but a feigned god." Some of Donne's poems join, but far more revise, this genre.

In *The triple Foole* Donne records the experience of having poems set and sung, perhaps playfully, but embedding a critique of their value. He alleges that the performance makes a third fool of him who was two already, "For loving, and for saying so / In whining Poëtry." But the first folly is foolish only because his love is refused: "But where's that wiseman, that would not be I, / If she would not deny?" And the second is therapy to purge the first by straining it through the intricacies of verse; grief can be numbed by numbers, fettered in feet:

> Then as th'earths inward narrow crooked lanes
> Do purge sea waters fretfull salt away,
> I thought, if I could draw my paines,
> Through Rimes vexation, I should them allay.
> Griefe brought to numbers cannot be so fierce,
> For, he tames it, that fetters it in verse.

But along comes a musician who appropriates his poem to show off, and by performing it stirs up again the feeling the speaker was trying to control.

> But when I have done so,
> Some man, his art and voice to show,
> Doth set and sing my paine,
> And by delighting many, frees againe
> Griefe, which verse did restraine.

Although love and grief require (as tyrants) and deserve (as subjects) poetic tributes, these should not give pleasure – the point is to purge, not enjoy these pains – and songs by making them delightful and increasing their audience amplify the love and grief the verse was supposed to allay, so that they defeat the poet who tried to subdue them:

> To Love and Griefe tribute of Verse belongs,
> But not of such as pleases when 'tis read,
>   Both are increased by such songs:
> For both their triumphs so are published,
> And I, which was two fooles, do so grow three;
> Who are a little wise, the best fooles be.

In his chapter on "Poeticall lamentations" in *The Arte of English Poesie*, Puttenham commends the poet as a physician who makes "the very greef it selfe (in part) cure of the disease," treating "the trauails and torments of loue forlorne or ill bestowed" by the Paracelsian or homeopathic cure of "making one dolour to expell another, and in this case, one short sorrowing the remedie of a long and grieuous sorrow."[2] In this way poetry can do what Dryden in his *Song for St. Cecilia's Day* says music can do: "What passion cannot MUSIC raise and quell!" But Donne's triple fool, having written as physician to himself, is further grieved by the use of his grief to delight others and thus liberate his pain from the restraints he had imposed by verse, so that the very cure itself becomes another of love's "travails."

Is the best fool the least foolish fool or the most foolish fool? The first two fools, the lover and the poet-therapist, *were* a little wise, and the third, by republishing yet again in this complaint the very folly of whose publication he complains, presents to readers a folly to make them wise, or at least more wisely foolish. In this rueful, artful little poem a fool in the court of the world lets us laugh at him, but exacts the price of a vexation-by-reading that is our own therapy: one that stirs up, rather than allaying, complications of thought and feeling in order to purge and reintegrate these faculties. Throughout the *Songs and Sonets*, by vexing the habits and expectations of reading derived from more conventional treatments of his themes, including those found in popular songs and madrigals, Donne's verses refine the instrument of language.

Donne's connections to music are not limited to his poems that were actually set and sung or to his complications of themes found in musical genres; there is also a kind of musicality in the forms and textures of some of his poems. Renaissance poetry, like Renaissance music, acknowleges an ordered cosmos in its construction. Some works, like Spenser's *Epithalamion*, specifically imitate the workings of the heavens in their numerology; but all "numbers" or mathematically describable verse forms are allied to the cosmos, as music is, by proportion. The poet, Sidney says in his *Apology*, "cometh to you with words set in delightful proportion, either accompanied with, or prepared for, the well-enchanting skill of music."[3] Many of Donne's conceits are cosmological, especially in poems of mutual love, displaying the *musica humana* of correspondence with the heavens; and these are cast in cosmological, hence musical, proportions.

In *A Valediction forbidding mourning*, the conceit of the "stiffe twin compasses" draws on the emblem of the hand of God circumscribing the cosmos with golden compasses, surrounded by the motto CONSTANTIA ET LABORE; the fixed foot represents "Constantia," signifying both constancy and harmony, or proportion, and the moving foot "Labore." John Shawcross points out that this emblem was used as device by the Antwerp printer Christopher Plantin and that a circle with a point in the middle, representing the fixed foot, was the alchemical symbol for gold, "the only metal that was indestructible."[4] The emblem also appears on the title page of Plantin's four-language *Biblia Sacra* (Antwerp, ?1637) along with a representation of the harmonious creatures of the peaceable kingdom (Isa. 11.6). Its origin is the words spoken by Wisdom in Proverbs 8.27, "When he prepared the heavens, I was there: when he set a compass upon the face of the depth"; Dante uses it in *Paradiso* 19. The "fixt foot," constancy, makes the work of the laboring foot "just": the circle it draws symbolizes the perfection of God's design and of the marriage of "two soules . . . which are one." When the laboring foot "comes home," the two feet of the compass configure the literal meaning of "Constantia": standing together.

Visually, the circle represents the Ptolemaic universe, but as a symbol of perfection it transcends it, figuring the supranatural heavens, the Trinity (three "which are one"), and "perfect" time. Like music that structurally imitates the subject of its text, the poem itself makes its circle just by numerous returnings. The analogy of the dying virtuous man to the lovers who "make no noise" corresponds with the innocent moving of the spheres, the circling compass foot, and the "fixt foot" that "makes no show / To move" but moves in accord with the travelling one, in contrast to the harmful "Moving of the earth" and the mutability of the sublunary lovers living under the ever-changing, not always circular moon. The refinement of the lovers' souls corresponds with the refined gold that, because of its purity and incorruptibility, can be beaten to "airy thinness" without a breach; and that conceit links to the golden compasses of creation and the incorruptibility of the golden bodies of the heavens. This circle of connections makes the speaker "end, where I begunne" formally, with the virtuous lover passing quietly away on the journey he "must" take, but with a promise to return faithfully to his beloved who keeps his circle just.

This close-woven tessitura of words imitates at once the harmony of the spheres with their harmless trepidations and the close interweaving of the lovers' "Inter-assurèd" minds.[5] The fixed foot of the octosyllabic line keeps this circle just; the eight syllables correspond with the octave of the seven planets and the sphere of the fixed stars; the nine stanzas add the *primum mobile*, which, moving in its encompassing circle, keeps the motions of the lower spheres "just," which in the language of music means perfectly in tune.

RIME'S VEXATION: DONNE'S PROSODY

Donne's prosody is rarely so carelessly rough as it appears to readers who have neoclassical tastes or are unpracticed in partsinging, which exercises the singers' capacity to make fine adjustments in midstream by coupling syllables alertly to rhythm and rhythm to sense. Like the music of his contemporaries, Donne's verse is syllabic, not metrical in the sense of having a regularly stressed beat. Scanning his poems relies on skills that part-singing gives practice in, since the joining of parts requires precise adherence to the rhythmic pulse, while the musical line requires matching the words to the lengths of notes and pauses.[6] Much of the alleged roughness of Donne's prosody unfrets itself – without betraying his refusal of mellifluous regularity – if readers fit word lengths and rests into lines as singers do. Most of Donne's prosodic difficulties can be solved in this way, and it often turns out that unusual stresses, gaps, or accelerations that result from accommodating words to the syllabic pulse contribute to the thought or tone.

Joseph Kerman suggests, "Certain technical features in English madrigal poems point strongly to Italian influence" including "the canzone stanza, freely combining 7- and 11-syllable lines," extra syllables, and elisions.[7] Donne commonly takes such liberties. Composers can deal with word length by means of note values, and singers learn to adjust speech rhythms to the musical pulse. Readers of poetry also need adaptable timing. Confronted with decasyllabic lines like "So whether my hymnes you admit or chuse, / In me you'have hallowed a Pagan Muse" (*To the Countesse of Bedford*: "T'have written then") the reader needs to set a steady pulse, give "my" and "me" full counts, elide "you'have, and pronounce the "-èd" of "hallowed."

Often giving each syllable full value renders vexed lines perfectly regular. The following decasyllabic lines from *To Mr. Roland Woodward* require equal time for pronouns, prepositions, conjunctions, and auxiliary verbs that readers may be inclined to skimp. Giving a full beat to "our" and "have" sets one on the right track and also adds precision:

> If our Soules have stain'd their first white, yet wee
> May cloth them with faith, and deare honestie,
> Which God imputes, as native puritie.

Thus read, "our" means "yours and mine" and also humanity's as opposed to good angels'. Light stress on "have" turns "if" into "even if" and emphasizes the pastness of the stain. Giving all syllables equal weight achieves not only metrical regularity but a mimesis of "justification," which is the theological term for the concept in them. The third line takes no effort to justify – grace having answered the effort of the first two.

The previous lines on vanity have prepared for this mimesis of weighing.

> For though to us it seeme,'and be light and thinne,
> Yet in those faithfull scales, where God throwes in
> Mens workes, vanity weighs as much as sinne.

Here the synaeresis in the first line throws more weight on "be" than "seeme" (unless one admits an eleven-syllable line). The caesura at "scales" makes the line mime a pair of scales, not quite balanced until the enjambment "throwes in" the weight of "Mens workes." The third line tempts us to make light of "vanity" by speeding up, but the syllabic line requires giving it three equal syllables, so that the word itself gains weight (which the syntax requires too, "van-it-y" being the subject of the sentence and the referent of "it"). On the other hand, "sinne" picks up emphasis from its connotative burdensomeness and its cadential position, so that the two words being weighed both sound weighty. By a process like conceptual word-painting, Donne's prosody redefines vanity as not light and thin after all.

Emphasis on pronouns is particularly helpful, and in the case of second person ones increases intimacy of tone. Composers often lengthened pronouns either melismatically or by allotting them two or more pulses, sometimes for expressive purposes. Dowland's lute song "Now, O now, I needs must part" (*First Booke*, 1597) gives two pulses to each "thee" and a melismatic one-and-a-half to "I" in "I loved thee and thee alone." His *Third Booke of Songs* (1603) provides a notable analogue for the repeated "Shee" of Donne's *Anniversaries* in a musical tribute possibly to Queen Elizabeth, cast as a dialogue between the speaker and the god frequently addressed in the *Songs and Sonets*:

> Say, Love, if ever thou didst find
> A woman with a constant mind?
> None but one.
> And what should that rare mirror be?
> Some goddess or some queen is she?
> She, she, she, and only she,
> She only Queen of love and beauty.

The setting of the refrain follows each of the first four *shes* with a rest, an expressive hint for reading the repeated *shees* of Donne's more solemn tributes to a less exalted Elizabeth.

Giving emphasis or musical length to personal pronouns bridles phrases and lines such as "Fate grudges ús áll, and doth subtly lay / A scourge" (*The Calme*) or "Zealously mý Múse doth salute áll thée" (*To Mr. R. W.*). Stressing adjectival, demonstrative (as their name suggests one should), and connective pronouns can also sort out the syntax, as in *The Second Anniversarie*:

> Are there not sóme Courts, (And then, no things bee
> So like as Courts) whích, in thís let us see,
> That wits and tongues of Libellars are weake,
> Because théy doe more ill, then thése can speake?

Apart from the Latinate use of "they" ("Courts") and "these" ("Libellars") to point to the furthest back and nearest antecedents, clarification comes from accenting "this," which refers ahead to the last line. Comparing false-speakers with both kinds of courts, Donne puts us on trial by syntax and scansion.

Some alleged roughnesses are simply a matter of changed pronunciation. "Kindly I envy thy songs perfection" accents "-vy" and thereby adds a pun; and "perfection," with two syllables on "-tion," rhymes with "sweetes are sown" (*To Mr. R. W.*, whom Donne apparently liked to exercise in scansion). The ending "-tion" usually has two syllables in singing.

I do not mean by these examples that Donne's lines should be relentlessly smoothed out, but that we can learn from singing to place accents appropriately and appreciate the uses of Donne's metrical variety. Verse with evenly flowing iambs and trochees lacks the resources for dramatic voicing of Donne's syllabic pulse over which words may splash and tumble. Susanne Woods acknowledges that Donne "created a dramatic lyricism more various than that of his predecessors in the art, Wyatt and Sidney" and "was able to create a variety of characters and moods, from the cynical young courtier of 'Goe and catch a falling star' through the witty lover of 'The Flea,' the metaphysical one of 'The Extasy,' and the loving husband . . . of the majority of his *Songs and Sonnets*"; she also finds that "virtually all of his verse was characteristically rougher than the verse of his contemporaries."[8] Louise Schleiner distinguishes among "song, declamatory, and speech modes of lyric verse" and uses *The good-morrow* as a "pure example" of the latter.[9] Yet after its speech-mode first stanza ("I wonder by my troth, what thou, and I / Did, till we lov'd?") Donne breaks, at daybreak, into song: "And now good morrow to our waking soules."

When Donne gives us prosodic difficulties, say on lines about perplexity or language, there is usually a reason. He indulges in an

Italianate eleven-syllable line, for example, to poke fun at *Satyre*
IV's conglomerate and professedly polyglot courtier:

> Made of th'Accents and best phrase of all these,
> He speaks no language.

By his masterful control of metrics, he gives the reader the sort of
exercise, by vexations of prosody and syntax, that Gibbons gives
the amateur singer in "O Lord, I lift my heart to thee" (example
2) on the words "O let me not confounded be."

  Part of Donne's serious vocation is the purgation and vivifica-
tion of language, which entails the creation of language that no
one has uttered before. Vexed and idiosyncratic verse, not made
of stock phrases, but through-composed, exercises "the mind's
endeavors," the going about and about (in *Satyre* III) to get to the
top of the cragged Hill of Truth. The easy line, the political slogan,
the mellifluous seduction invite the reader to "sleepe, or runne
wrong." Language that makes the mind work is the Needle's Eye
to freedom.

SONG AND MADRIGAL THEMES IN "SONGS AND SONETS"

Thomas Morley remarks in his *Plain and Easy Introduction* that
"light music hath been of late more deeply dived into so that there
is no vanity which in it hath not been followed to the full; but the
best kind of it is termed Madrigal . . . a kind of music made upon
songs and sonnets such as Petrarch and many poets of our time
have excelled in."[10] Donne's *Songs and Sonets*[11] follows this "kind"
to the full as deeper explorations or witty parodies of its themes,
compiling subgenres – complaints, laments, aubades, maledic-
tions, valedictions, compliments, and an array of other courtly
genres, along with songs of ardent and fulfilled love. Among the
courtly or "coterie" genres are vanities which Donne perfects to
death. It would be hard to compose a piece of misogyny better
than "Goe, and catche a falling starre" or utter a curse more utter
than *The Curse*.

  There is some debate about whether Donne's poems are expressions of personal experience. One may hear his poems about
mutual love, where Woods finds "the loving husband . . . of the
majority of his *Songs and Sonnets*," as "white sincerity" and the more
preposterously posturing personae as speakers of dramatic mono-

logues with potentially curative properties. Both draw from song and madrigal conventions and enhance or perplex their themes in more subtle and pyschologically complex language, whether for personal expression or for social enjoyment and edification. By comparison with most song and madrigal collections, Donne's poems of mutual love are much more numerous and far more serious, and I think often, even when playfully, sincere; even so crafted a metaphor as "one another's hermitage" seems to be one of those sudden looks by which a true lover reveals himself.

One way we can discriminate among Donne's lyric voices and follow the operations of his wit is by reading in the context of social singing at the Inns of Court and in such households as Egerton's and the Countess of Bedford's. A composer or singer is not necessarily speaking for himself or herself, but may be. Songs are appropriable by anyone whose feelings they express, or who just likes to sing. Many of the *Songs and Sonets* take their themes from these sociable kinds of music. Sometimes they need to be read lightly; but Donne was a serious though witty person, and his renovations of genres demolish vanities by their superiority, including superior vanity, and deepen sincerities by wit, toughness, and generic detachment through which real love breaks in.

Clusters of analogues appear in madrigal and song collections of the late 1590s and early 1600s which suggest that Donne incorporated musical experience from his stay in the Egerton household,[12] when he was courting Anne More, and the early years of their marriage. Particularly pertinent publications include John Dowland's three books of *Songes or Ayres* (1597, 1600, 1603); Thomas Weelkes' *Madrigals of 5. and 6. parts* (1600); and Robert Jones' two books of *Songs and Ayres* (1600 and 1601). Weelkes' are all part-songs, and Dowland's (1597 and 1600) and Jones' (1600) are arranged to be sung either as solo songs or as part-songs, with string accompaniment. Dowland, whom Fellowes calls "the greatest song-writer that this country has produced,"[13] expanded the expressive resources of lute songs with polyphonically conceived, highly chromatic accompaniments. Other composers provide occasional connections. A few of these follow, in which Donne moves from cynicism to impatient wooing to extraordinary mutuality.

The claim of "Goe, and catche a falling starre" that "No where / Lives a woman true, and faire" exacerbates Byrd's "If women could be fair and never fond" (1588) and Dowland's setting of a text by Campion (1603),

> I must complain, yet do enjoy my love.
>   She is too fair, too rich in beauty's parts.
> Thence is my grief; for Nature, while she strove
>   With all her graces and divinest arts
> To form her too, too beautiful of hue,
> She had no leisure time to make her true.

Donne extends Dowland's "Can she excuse my wrongs with Virtue's cloak?" (1597) when in *The Dampe* the speaker asks that before killing him by rejection the addressee should level the field by killing "th'enormous Gyant, your Disdaine, / And let th'enchantress Honor, next be slaine." *The Flea* complicates one of Giles Farnaby's *Canzonets* (1598), which pities the flea "small of stature" and concludes "Were I a flea in bed I would not bite you, / But search some other way for to delight you." With ebullient perversity, Donne turns the flea into a temple and a fleabite into a marriage.

One of Weelkes' *Madrigals* (1600) provides a gloss for *The Extasie*:

> Like two proud armies marching in the field,
> Joining a thund'ring fight, each scorns to yield;
> So in my heart your Beauty and my Reason,
> The one claims the crown, the other says 'tis treason.
> But O your Beauty shineth as the sun,
> And dazzled Reason yields as quite undone.

Donne (himself "undone" for a while by his marriage) uses the military conceit but undoes the two conventions in Weelkes' text: the conflict of beauty and reason and the corollary that beauty belongs to women and reason to men.

> As 'twixt two equall Armies, Fate
>   Suspends uncertaine victorie,
> Our soules, (which to advance their state,
>   Were gone out,) hung 'twixt her, and mee.

Solomon asks, "Who is she that looketh forth as the morning, fair as the moon, clear as the sun, and terrible as an army with banners?" (Song of Solomon 6.10). In *The Exstasie* both are like armies, not "proud" but equal, and not constituted by the woman's beauty versus the man's reason, but by two equal "soules," "gone out" to "advance their state" – increase their spiritual territory by

encompassing each other. Since the armies are equal, neither con-
quers; instead, in the next stanza, they "negotiate." The revision of
metaphors to express equality is the signature of Donne's true love
poems, and is revolutionary. If there is anything like it in contemporary song and madrigal texts I have not found it. Conventional
amorous verse, sung or not, is apt to divide attributes between the
woman's face, voice, charm, and, often, scornful or virtuous non-
compliance and the man's fidelity or captivity. At the same time,
The Exstasie demolishes the body-soul conflict; it proceeds neither
by conquest of the body, by either seduction or transcendence, nor
by conquest of soul over body or "Reason" over "Beauty." Reversing
the Platonic adage that the soul is a prince in the prison of the
body, Donne makes the soul an imprisoned "Prince" until the body
becomes the serviceable incarnation and sensible "booke" of love.
The "dialogue of one" records the speaking union of two whole
and equal persons whose bodies and souls are individually and
mutually integrated.

A conceit in the madrigal tradition that does admit at least emotional equality is the exchange of hearts. Sidney's poem from
Arcadia, "My true love hath my heart and I have his," was set anonymously as a sprightly song in triple time with syncopations (and
later by John Ward as a two-part madrigal for three voices, 1613;
in *EM* 19). Its words concern innocent and happy love, beginning:

> My true love hath my heart and I have his,
> By just exchange, one for the other given.
> I hold his dear, and mine he cannot miss,
> There never was a better bargain driven.
> His heart in me keeps me and him in one,
> My heart in him his thoughts and senses guides.
> He loves my heart, for once it was his own,
> I cherish his because in me it bides.

As the stanzas proceed, the lovers' hearts become more complicat-
edly mingled, tempting the irreverent wit to conceive a comically
physiological image. Thomas Weelkes *(Balletts and Madrigals,*
1598; *EM* 10) uses the theme for a grammatical jest:

> Give me my heart, and I will go,
> Or else forsake your wonted "no."
> No, no, no, no, no, no, no, no, no, no.
> But since my dear doth doubt me,
> With "no" I mean to flout thee.

> Now is there hope we shall agree,
> When double "no" imparteth "yea,"
> No, no, no, no, no, no, no, no, no, no.
> If that be so my dearest,
> With "no" my heart thou cheerest.

As part of the joke in the refrain of repeated negations, while the upper voices shrilly ascend (the cantus, as Lady, resolutely going up the Dorian scale), the lower ones, descending in parallel, redouble the tempo with their "double 'no.'" At the end, just before the Lady reaches her modal octave, all voices shift into D major, confirming the lovers' cheer. In 1600 Weelkes returns with a version about the contingency of faithful love (*Madrigals of 5. and 6. parts*; *EM* 11–12):

> Take here my heart, I give it thee forever;
> No better pledge can love to love deliver.
> Fear not, my dear, it will not fly away,
> For hope and love command my heart to stay;
> But if thou doubt, desire will make it range.
> Love but my heart, my heart will never change.

Lovers who give their hearts without a fair exchange must either retrieve them or do without them. John Bennett (*Madrigalls To Foure Voyces*, 1599) gives an unrequited version: "Cruel, unkind, my heart thou hast bereft me . . . And yet still will I love thee." Later, Henry Lawes will set Henry Hughes' "I prithee send me back my heart," in which the lady changes her mind and decides to believe she has the doubtful lover's heart whether she has or not, and let him keep hers. "White as lilies was her face" in Dowland's *Second Book* (1600), dedicated to the Countess of Bedford,[14] declares "For my heart, though set at naught, / Since you will it, / Spoil, and kill it, / I will never change my thoughts." "A shepherd in a shade" in the same collection begins by asking the lady to return his heart:

> Restore, restore my heart again,
> Which love by thy sweet looks hath slain,
> Lest that enforc'd by your disdain I sing
> Fie, fie on love, it is a foolish thing.

But the dead heart is not only not revived and returned to its right-ful owner but is desecrated, an abandoned corpse:

> My heart where you have laid,
>   O cruel maid,

> To kill when you might save,
> Why have ye cast it forth
> As nothing worth
> Without a tomb or grave.

In the end, the shepherd asks only for a decent burial:

> O let it be entomb'd and lie
> In your sweet mind and memory,
> Lest I resound on every warbling string
> Fie, fie on love, that is a foolish thing.

Donne takes up the misplaced heart motif in *The Broken Heart*: "I brought a heart into the roome, / But from the roome, I carried none with me." *The Message* mocks the capitulation of lovers like the "shepherd in shade," asking the lady to "Send home my harmlesse heart againe" unless it has been corrupted by its sojourn with hers. Dowland's sweet conceit of the dead heart's burial may have activated Donne's mordant wit in *The Legacie*, a *reductio ad absurdum*, or *ad litteram*, of this recurrent theme. It begins innocently enough but turns bitter. The argument is that having been killed by parting, the lover as executor of his own will intends to send the lady his heart, but when he searches his breast for it he finds hers, which is untrue, and therefore not his to send.

> When I dyed last, and, Deare, I dye
> As often as from thee I goe,
> Though it be but an houre agoe,
> And Lovers houres be full eternity,
> I can remember yet, that I
> Something did say, and something did bestow;
> Though I be dead, which sent mee, I should be
> Mine owne executor and Legacie.
>
> I heard mee say, Tell her anon,
> That my selfe, that is you, not I,
> Did kill me,'and when I felt mee dye,
> I bid mee send my heart, when I was gone,
> But I alas could there finde none,
> When I had ripp'd me,'and search'd where hearts should lye;
> It kill'd mee'againe, that I who still was true,
> In life, in my last Will should cozen you.
>
> Yet I found something like a heart,
> But colours it, and corners had,

It was not good, it was not bad,
It was intire to none, and few had part.
As good as could be made by art
   It seem'd, and therefore for our losses sad,
I meant to send this heart in stead of mine,
But oh, no man could hold it, for twas thine.

Hovering between personal pain and courtly jest, this poem incorporates the tones of the earlier versions – the serious, tender lightness of the Sidney song in the first stanza, and the reproach of Dowland's songs (but far more bitter, and without any abject pledges) along with the teasing jokiness of Weelkes' madrigal in the second – and adds the sad chastisement of the third. Donne may just be playfully entering a courtly game of composing lyrics on a shared conceit, and doing it with parodic glee. But as Arthur Marotti remarks of the epigrammists of the Inns of Court, "The witty poet and the witty reader were assumed to be capable of sustaining both an imaginative involvement and a critical attitude toward poems – that is, to write and to read both poetically and metapoetically."[15] Though parodic, *The Legacie* is also a serious meditation on the theme of what a heart is.

When it comes to poems of mutual love, though, Donne renovates the whole idea of the migratory heart and proclaims its true habitat. In *The good-morrow*, "My face in thine eye, thine in mine appeares, / And true plaine hearts doe in the faces rest." And in *Loves infinitenesse*,

Loves riddles are, that though thy heart depart,
It stayes at home, and thou with losing savest it:
But wee will have a way more liberall,
Then changing hearts, to joyne them, so wee shall
   Be one, and one anothers All.

Perhaps the greatest difficulty in Donne's poems is not his convoluted syntax or "metaphysical" conceits but his delicacy and complexity of tone. The *Songs and Sonets* deepen the themes and conceits found in the texts of songs and madrigals and, by combining lightness and seriousness, tenderness and tough wit, directness and ironic allusion, incorporate the expressiveness and dramatic tension supplied by multiple simultaneous musical lines in settings of those texts. Other conventional topics Donne deepens and complicates, in addition to the exchange of hearts, are kisses, tears at parting, and the fires of love.

Let us consider a musical kiss. The witty text of Thomas Tomkins' "How great delight" for three voices (example 7) plays on Bembo's speech about words and kisses in *The Courtyer* explaining that "a kisse is a knitting together both of body and soule" because "although the mouthe be a percell of the bodye, yet is it an issue for the wordes, that be the interpreters of the soule."[16]

> How great delight from those sweet lips I taste,
> Whether I hear them speak, or feel them kiss!
> Only this want I have, that being graced
> With one of them, the other straight I miss.
> Love since thou canst do wonders, heap my blisses
> And grant her kissing words, or speaking kisses.

Much of the time the two upper voices are either in canon or in parallel thirds. For the first line of text, syncopation, suspension, and D minor and A major tonalities resolve unexpectedly in C at the semi-cadence on "taste," giving an almost tactile sense of desire and delight. The setting of the second line rises through minor tonalities but sharpens briefly into A major on "kiss," after which "or feel them kiss" repeats in a sensuous little duet on "feel," which is again repeated in the tenor while the upper voices make their way together to D major for a third kissing-cadence. "Only this want I have" expresses its something wanting on "have" with a dis-related third. "That being graced with one of them" expresses grace in dancingly syncopated notes. "The other straight I miss" has assertive major harmonies, but none of the voices matches another in words or rhythm: the voices are "straight" but each straightway misses the other. "Love since thou canst do wonders" employs homophony for the direct address to the wonder-working god and harmony reminiscent of Monteverdi's sensuous apostrophes to that god on "wonders." "Heap my blisses" heaps up through repetitions to another resolution on A major. On "And grant her kissing words, or speaking kisses" the two upper voices are in canon, while the lower one sings more sustained notes, so that the syllables "kiss" and "words" come together in two voices in bars 34 and 35 and twice in 36, once with "grant" joining the two. "Speaking kisses" rejoins the two upper voices on the same words in parallel thirds, syllabically on "speaking" as is appropriate to the word, and melismatically to sensuously ornament "kisses" with an inversion of the ornament on "feel," while the lower one continues to match "kisses" with the others' "speaking" and "words" until

Example 7. Thomas Tomkins, "How great delight" bars 33–47

the last two repetitions of "speaking kisses," when all three voices mingle the two words. In effect, the paradoxical request is musically granted, since the expressiveness of the music provides the feeling of kissing even as the words are minglingly sung.

Comparable combinations of wit and intimacy, lightness and intensity are poignantly explored in Donne's poems. The *Songs and Sonets* contain few kisses; the nearest line to Tomkins' Castiglionean theme begins his verse letter to Henry Wotton, "Sir, more then kisses, letters mingle Soules." But they contain many minglings of tone that might be compared to Tomkins' minglings of minor and major tonalities. Two such poems do contain or imply kisses, both of them tributes of verse to the grief of parting, and their tone is deeply serious under a kind of painful lightsome-ness of witty intimacy that only makes the seriousness more acute.

A kiss of harmonic complexity, though in a different mode from Tomkins', occurs in Donne's *The Expiration*. Ferrabosco set this poem as a strophic song (*Ayres*, 1609) in which, as Hollander points out, "the second verse cannot under any circumstances be sung to the setting that should, ideally, do for both of them."[17] It would have done better as a through-composed madrigal, not only for this reason but because harmonized voices can express mingled feelings better than one (even accompanied) can do. Ferrabosco's rather beguiling harmonies of voice and accompaniment express the painfulness of "Turne thou ghost that way, and let mee turne this," but with a greater stress of length and modal incongruence on the first phrase that undoes the mutuality suggested by the balance of Donne's line.

In the poem, the lovers and their feelings are thoroughly mingled, so that the speaker has to perform a kind of violence to effect the separation.

> So, so, breake off this last lamenting kisse,
>   Which sucks two soules, and vapors Both away,
> Turne thou ghost that way, and let mee turne this,
>   And let ourselves benight our happiest day,
> We ask'd none leave to love; nor will we owe
>   Any, so cheape a death, as saying, Goe;
>
> Goe; and if that word have not quite kil'd thee,
>   Ease mee with death, by bidding me goe too.
> Oh, if it have, let my word worke on mee,
>   And a just office on a murderer doe.
> Except it be too late, to kill me so,
>   Being double dead, going, and bidding, goe.

Clearly and perhaps autobiographically, this love is mutual, and the need for parting comes from without, from that "Any" whose murder of them by commanding them to part the speaker says they should forfend by parting voluntarily, suicidally. He asks strength of his beloved while mourning the separation as a death for both of them. In this way Donne revises the Petrarchan conceit of dying from love: this love is not unrequited, and both lovers are to participate in the death of parting by bidding the other's departure.

Not only the metaphorical death, but the farewell kiss itself is an expiration, doubled as each breathes in the other's breathed-out soul and as each soul is vapored by it. Since they are bereft of their souls, both are ghosts; since their love is mutual their parting must "benight" their "happiest day"; they will not let anyone else kill them so cheaply as to command them to "Goe" and – in a wrenching shift to the imperative across the stanza break – the speaker exhales a "Goe" so painful that he asks his beloved, if the bodkin-word has not killed her, to make his quietus with it. If his word (such is the power of words) has killed her, he hopes it will be his executioner – except that he is twice dead already, "going, and bidding, goe."

The composer who sets such a song or the reader who reads it needs a delicate ear and must make choices. Is "So, so, breake off" one of Donne's abrupt beginnings? Not exactly, since it marks a lingering ending, a "last lamenting kisse"; probably the words are difficult, muffled, tender, perhaps with a parodic thread of mock-parental gruffness within the tenderness, painfully resolute, adamantly gentle. Perhaps the lovers fear they may not see each other again. At the same time there is the intellectual argument, the hard quibble on murder and justice, the wit, the craft, all subsumed under the love.

Another farewell poem, *Witchcraft by a picture*, also uses wit in intimacy and pain, not to make light of or assuage the pain but to strengthen the sufferers, and again complex tonalities issue. The conceit on which it turns is that of lovers mirrored in each other's eyes, and in this case in tears – those popular subjects of word-painting; Dowland's three books of airs are full of them, and Thomas Ford (*Music of Sundry Kinds*, 1607) affords this stanza:

> Of thine eye I made my mirror,
> From thy beauty came my error;
> All thy words I counted witty,
> All thy sighs I deemed pity;
> Thy false tears that me aggrieved
> First of all my trust deceived.
> > Siren pleasant, for to reason,
> > Cupid plague thee for thy treason!

Again Donne renovates the conceit with a combination of mutuality and steel. Tears, usually the property of rejected lovers, and bewitchment, usually the property of cruel mistresses, join. Witchcraft was still too serious a topic to appear often in songs, but Donne uses it playfully to give a strange twist to the observation that the lover's image is drowned in the beloved's tears.

> I fixe mine eye on thine, and there
>   Pitty my picture burning in thine eye,
> My picture drown'd in a transparent teare,
>   When I looke lower I espie;
>   Hadst thou the wicked skill
> By pictures made and mard, to kill,
> How many wayes mightst thou performe thy will?
>
> But now I've drunke thy sweet salt teares,
>   And though thou poure more I'll depart;
> My picture vanish'd, vanish feares,
>   That I can be endamaged by that art;
>   Though thou retaine of mee
> One picture more, yet that will bee,
> Being in thine owne heart, from all malice free.

This lover is not misled by beauty, nor are his lady's tears false. Yet the lover injects a speculation that would risk offending if their love were less than fully trusting – "Hadst thou the wicked skill" – and goes even further, "My picture vanish'd, vanish feares / That I can be endamagèd." Donne uses similar conceits in opposite ways in *The Dampe*, a poem of the murder-by-disdain species common in songs, where anatomizing friends will, the speaker alleges the scornful mistress supposes, find her picture in his dead heart and be killed by love-melancholy through it as he has been, thus promoting "Your murder, to the name of Massacre." In *Witchcraft by a picture* the teasing thought is fully retracted at the end, since her heart is "from all malice free." Then why interject it? I think it assures her of her power over him and (within the dramatic scene) allows the lover to depart in a non-sentimental, witty way even within the full pity for them both that he feels as he kisses – "I've drunke" – her "sweet salt teares." The sweet-and-salt of the poem is a kind of gustatory hieroglyph of those tears.

A profound difference between Donne's parting poems and those of the madrigal tradition may be seen in "Song: Sweetest love, I do not goe" and *A Valediction of weeping* set against songs of Ferrabosco and Dowland. Ferrabosco's "Drown not with tears," from the same volume as *The Expiration* (1609), has some affinity with Donne's poems but gives an easy consolation that seems almost frivolous next to his:

> Drown not with tears, my dearest love,
> Those eyes which my affections move

> . . . Time, that hath made us two of one,
> And forced thee now to live alone,
> Will once again us reunite
> To show how she can Fortune spite.
> Then will we our time redeem . . .
> And strive with many thousand kisses
> To multiply exchange of blisses.

In *A Valediction of weeping* both lovers are weeping, and the one about to embark asks the opposite: "Let me powre forth / My teares before thy face"; they are "Pregnant of thee," so that when each falls "that thou falls which it bore," dissolving them both; each tear, bearing her – like a globe on which a map is overlaid – is a world which her teares "mixed with mine doe overflow . . . by waters sent from thee, my heaven dissolved so."

Dowland's "I saw my lady weep"[18] is a song (in stanza form similar to Donne's though shorter) of much melodic beauty and shapeliness with complexly expressive chromatic accompaniments and much poetic sweetness; but the text concerns the speaker's own feelings, rather than the lady's, in response to her grief, which remains abstract, and the last line consoles triflingly:

> O fairer than aught else
> The world can show, leave off in time to grieve.
> Enough, enough your joyful looks excels;
> Tears kills the heart, believe.
> O strive not to be excellent in woe,
> Which only breeds your beauty's overthrow.

Both Ferrabosco and Dowland speak of the woman's physical attractions; Donne addresses the whole woman and her specific sorrow, not just her beauty, and his tone is one of tender toughening, an attempt to give comfort in its root sense of strengthening, yet without a display of superior wisdom. On the contrary, the cosmographical conceit, perfectly twining metaphor with occasion, issues in a loving cry:

> O more then Moone,
> Draw not up seas to drowne me in thy spheare,
> Weepe me not dead, in thine armes, but forbeare
> To teach the sea, what it may doe too soone;
> Let not the winde
> Example finde,

> To doe me more harme, then it purposeth;
> Since thou and I sigh one anothers breath,
> Who e'r sighes most, is cruellest, and hasts the others death.

The consolation of tender wit on a cosmological scale is again notable in *A Feaver*, one of Donne's emotionally delicate risks. Fire is a favorite madrigalian image, treated to word-painting of licking flames to describe the lover's torment, imported from Italy in Noel Faignient's contribution to Yonge's *Musica Transalpina* (1588):

> Fierce Love that burns my heart makes all this venting
> While with his wings the raging fire he bloweth.
> Say Love, with what device thou canst for ever
> Keep it in flames and yet consume it never.

Morley's *First Book of Ballets* (1595) offers an alarm signal in

> Fire! fire! my heart! Fa la.
> O help! Alas! Ay me! I sit and cry me,
> And call for help, alas, but none comes nigh me! Fa la.
>
> O, I burn me! alas! Fa la.
> I burn! Alas! Ay me! will none come quench me?
> O cast, cast water on, alas, and drench me. Fa la.

George Peele's list of replies to the question "What thing is love?" concludes "It is a fire, it is a coal / Whose flames creep in at every hole" (Bartlet, *Book of Airs*, 1606). Campion's "Fire, fire" grows cosmological; since all England's rivers and the world's oceans cannot put out the lover's flames, he invokes a return of the Flood: "Come, you that once the world did drowne, / Some then you spar'd, but now save all, / That else must burne, and with me fall."

Weelkes' musically witty "Thule, the period of cosmography" (*Madrigals of 5. and 6. parts*, 1600) concerns volcanoes: Hecla (the volcano in Iceland that changed the climate of Europe) in ultima Thule, the "period" or most distant place of geographical knowledge, along with Etna (and in stanza two the island mountain Fogo) are symbols of passion's tumults.

> Thule, the period of cosmography
>   Doth vaunt of Hecla, whose sulphurious fire
> Doth melt the frozen clime and thaw the sky;
>   Trinacrian Aetna's flames ascend not higher.
> These things seem wondrous, yet more wondrous I,
> Whose heart with fear doth freeze, with love doth fry.

Weelkes' word-painting mimes both geographical and amorous flames and puns on them on "sulphurious" by swelling, flickering runs on the last three syllables, producing repetitions of "furious." The parts congeal in homophony on "frozen clime," quicken in ascent on "thaw the sky," ascend higher on "ascend not higher," and modulate mysteriously on "wondrous," where in Wilfred Mellers' words, "that flat seventh which had frozen us [on "frozen"] comes back much more significantly, long sustained, relaxing gently to the sub-dominant major: but it is almost immediately contradicted by the sharp seventh as we swing to the relative minor. This initiates a musical synonym for the paradox of simultaneous freezing and frying."[19] In stanza two Weelkes provides chromatic strangeness on "how strangely Fogo burns" and turns the six parts into the contrarywise leaps of a swarm of "flying fishes." The madrigal is not as serious as Donne's poem is, but both of them hyperbolically yet credibly unite emotional experience with macrocosmic fires, and the music fuses earnest amazement with its relative jocularity, while the poem infuses jocularity into its fierce concern.

Instead of the typical Petrarchan lover's metaphorical fires, Donne confronts the literal fever of a woman he loves, a fever that is really apt to kill her. He compares it not with volcanic flames but with the final conflagration of the earth. It is a poem of deep anxiety tempered with the light teasing of a visitor at the sickbed of a much-loved person, intimately known and secure in assured love, but begins with a direct confrontation with death few would dare.

> Oh doe not die, for I shall hate
>   All women so, when thou art gone,
> That thee I shall not celebrate,
>   When I remember thou wast one.

The next stanzas adumbrate the *Anniversaries*, arguing that she cannot leave the world behind, because she is its soul and it must die with her. Then comes Donne's renovation of and by fire:

> O wrangling schooles, that search what fire
>   Shall burne this world, had none the wit
> Unto this knowledge to aspire,
>   That this her feaver might be it?

> And yet she cannot wast by this,
>   Nor long beare this torturing wrong,

> For much corruption needful is
> To fuell such a feaver long.

> These burning fits but meteors bee,
>   Whose matter in thee is soone spent.
> Thy beauty,'and all parts, which are thee,
>   Are unchangeable firmament.

In the final stanza, the speaker agrees with the fever that it is better to have her "one houre, then all else ever." Beside this poem the bare conceit of the lover's flames looks puerilely self-regarding. Weelkes' geography of the climes of passion improves the conceit with emotional complexity and humour(s) in both senses of the word. Donne brings tonal richness into the text itself and puts the self-inflating lover to shame. Here is the real fire of love.

Donne's conflagrant interchanges of sacred and profane love, as in *The Canonization* and the Holy Sonnets ("What if this present were the worlds last night," "Batter my heart," "Show me deare Christ, thy spouse") fit with addresses to the god of Love in popular music and with the fact that amorous, moral, and devotional texts are mixed freely in song- and part-books. The source-text of the connection of erotic and sacred love in Renaissance poetry is the Song of Solomon (for example in the blazon of the bride in Spenser's *Epithalamion*), among the first sacred texts to receive emotionally expressive settings. Gibbons composed a winningly melodic setting, suitable for a love song, for Wither's metrical text in *Hymnes and Songs of the Church*, 1623:

> Come kisse me with those lips of thine;
> For, better are thy *Loues* then wine;
>   And as the powred *Oyntments* be,
>   Such is the sauour of thy *Name*.
> And, for the sweetness of the same,
> The *Virgines* are in love with thee.

Similarly, one cannot draw a firm line between Donne's secular poems and his devotional verse; all are part of a process of fine-tuning the instrument of expressiveness in language. If, as in music-books, his love songs and his holy sonnets had been inter-mixed in the *Poems* of 1633, we might think of Donne less as a reformed rake than as a man who wrestled with and rejoiced in human and divine love in all their perplexities. The *Songs and Sonets* may be Jack Donne's temporal songs, but some cross over into Dr. Donne's "extemporall" psalms, lamentations, and hymns in ways that reveal a core of integrity in his energetically complicated character. *A Feaver* is akin to *The First Anniversarie*, and the short love lyric also called *The Anniversarie* forecasts the second, *Of the Progres of the Soule*. In this holy amorous meditation on love and death, the egotist of *The Sunne Rising*, who proclaimed "She'is all states, and all Princes I, / Nothing else is," is doubly transformed. Now "wee . . . Prince enough in one another bee"; and while on earth only they are "such Kings," in heaven "we shall be throughly blest, / But wee no more then all the rest." This mutuality and its ultimate admission of "all the rest" to bliss is love grown up.

EXTEMPORALL SONG

La Corona is perhaps Donne's most musically constructed poem, with its seven circling sonnets and finely crafted rhyme scheme celebrating the major feasts of the liturgical year. At the beginning of this coronal cycle, identified as the hymns sent to Magdalen Herbert in 1607,[20] Donne proclaims, "'Tis time that heart and voice be lifted high, Salvation to all that will is nigh." The lifting of heart and voice together echoes the psalms and the defense of church music and the coupled line affirms three things about salvation: it is nigh at hand; it is offered to all; and each must "will" to have it. This willing, as many biographers have noticed, is a struggle for Donne, but that is no reason to think that his devotional poems are not sincere; quite the contrary. *A Litanie*, probably written in 1608,[21] announces Donne's part in God's "Musick" and joins the church in one choir in a prayer "that none be lost," for (as in Herbert's "musick for a King") "to thee / A sinner is more musique, when he prayes, / Than spheares, or Angels praises bee, / In Panegyrique Alleluiaes." The prayer is not in itself efficacious – only God can save – but the church, as well as the sinner, must "pray, beare, and doe":

> And whil'st this universall Quire,
> That Church in triumph, this in warfare here,
>   Warm'd with one all-partaking fire
> Of love, that none be lost, which cost thee deare,
>   Pray ceaslesly, 'and thou hearken too,
>   (Since to be gratious
>   Our taske is treble, to pray, beare, and doe)

Heare this prayer Lord, O Lord deliver us
From trusting in those prayers, though powr'd out thus.

The prayer has in common with *La Corona* a new sense of poetic
calling and more modesty about its power; there Donne asks that
Christ will "*Deign at my hands this crown of prayer and praise*" but here
he is only one voice in a "universal choir." Many of his divine
poems join themselves to parts of the liturgy often set to music: the
psalms, the Litany, the Holy Week Responsories, and hymns or
anthems. These have ancient roots in the Latin liturgy and altered
manifestations in the English one; they were among the observances most connected with music and, apart from the psalms,
most controverted in the liturgical disputes. I believe that Donne
was converting to private use devotional forms from his Catholic
past that were altered by the English Church and further threat-
ened by its puritan faction, not because he objected to the reforms
– his own modifications mediate between Catholic traditions and
Protestant concerns – but in order that by the prayers of each for
all in both traditions "none be lost."

In this mediation Donne avoids icons and antiphons or prayers
to the Virgin Mary even while recalling them. *The Crosse* and *La
Corona* are perhaps Donne's most iconic poems, meditating upon
form itself; yet they are also iconoclastic in that the mind is not
allowed to rest upon one emblem or interpretation of these forms.
The cross is everywhere in nature and craft, in the flight of birds,
the motion of a swimmer, the mast of a ship, the human body itself,
the very parallels and meridians by which all location is identified
on the globe and in the astronomical heavens. The crowns of *La
Corona* are many, of thorns, of Glory, of circularly woven poems "of
prayer and praise." *La Corona* addresses the Virgin and *A Litanie*,
addressed to God, affirms that "As her deeds were / Our helpes,
so are her prayers"; but neither prays to her. Similarly, in *An hymne
to the Saints, and to Marquess Hamylton,* Donne does not ask the
saints for intercession on the dead man's behalf, but tells them
that he increases one of their orders, but decreases all of
England's; among them, "the Chappell wants an eare, Councell a
tongue; / Story a theame; and Musicke lacks a song." Donne walks
a fine ecumenical line, employing catholic customs in new ways
unimpeachable by Protestants, a private arbitration of border disputes between the two communions.

In the Book of Common Prayer the Litany is prescribed "To be used upon Sundays, Wednesdays, and Fridays, and at other times, when it shall be commanded by the ordinary," presumably the bishop in times of public anxiety or calamity. As Hooker explains in defending it, the Litany derives from public processions associated with the veneration of saints, with the addition of "supplications . . . for thappeasinge of Gods wrath and the averting of publique evels." Because of the superstitions and misuses that became attached to these processions, reformers thought it better "that these and all other supplications or processions should be no where used but onlie within the walles of the house of God, the place sanctified unto prayer." To Cartwright's objection that the prayerbook makes "perpetuall" a rite that was "ordayned but for a time" of particular calamity, Hooker replies, "Doth not true Christian charity require that whatsoever any parte of the world, yea anie one of all our brethren elswhere doth either suffer or feare, the same wee accompt as our own burden?" (*Lawes* v.41). Donne's employments of traditional liturgical genres are highly individual, and most of them unsuitable for liturgical use; but they tie together in the ligature of language powerfully original expressions of religious experience common to all Christians. Whatever his theological struggles, in this binding together of communal forms and individual conscience he is, as the church he finally came to serve defines itself, both catholic and reformed.

Litanies might be chanted occasionally in intramural processions, but psalms were chanted daily in the offices and psalm texts sung as anthems in the English Church and as part-songs for private devotions. For the latter, a group published as or included in part-books relates to Donne's Holy Sonnets: the Seven Penitential Psalms. These were also the subjects of many sermon series. The psychologizing reader may find Donne's penitential poems masochistic or abject because the "comfortableness" of repentance to a seventeenth-century conscience does not conform to modern thought, except perhaps to the talking cure.[22] For seventeenth-century Christians a troubled conscience is a sign of grace. The first of the opening sentences at Matins offers this consolation: "At whatsoever time a sinner doth repent him of his sin from the bottom of his heart: I will put all his wickedness out of my remembrance, saith the Lord [Ezek. 18]." Arthur Lake says of Psalm 51, "[W]e never please God better than when we please our selves least . . . we are forbidden to despaire of our owne unworthines, as to presume of our righteousness: this text doth warrant us this comfort, when in these fits wee seeme to be furthest from God, God bringeth us then nearest unto himselfe; for this pang is a forerunner of health; but senslesse sinners have no part in this consolation."[23] Donne, preaching to the Countess of Bedford, alludes to the same Psalm: "[If] I look upon sinne, as sinne is now, the misery and calamity of *man*, the greater the misery appears, the more hope of pardon I have . . . *David* presents the greatness of his sinnes, and then followes the *Miserere mei, have mercy upon me, according to the greatness of thy mercy*. Is there any *little mercy* in God?" (*Sermons* III:197).

In this spirit, versification and musical settings of the Seven Penitential Psalms formed a popular genre, and the singing of them a pastime that offered the combined consolations of group confession, spiritual healing, and musical mutuality. The group was usually comprised of Psalms 6, 32, 38, 51, 102, 130, and 143, most often only the first few verses, in a variety of translations and paraphrases. Their first lines in the prayerbook psalter are these:

Psalm 6.   O Lord, rebuke me not in thine indignation, neither chasten me in thy displeasure.
            Have mercy upon me, O Lord, for I am weak; Lord, heal me, for my bones are vexed.

Psalm 32.   Blessed is he whose unrighteousness is forgiven, and whose sin is covered.
            Blessed is the man unto whom the Lord imputeth no sin, and in whose spirit there is no guile.

Psalm 38.   Put me not to rebuke, O Lord, in thine anger; neither chasten me in thy displeasure.
            For thine arrows stick fast in me, and thy hand presseth me sore.

Psalm 51.   Have mercy upon me, O God, after thy great goodness; according to the multitude of thy mercies do away mine offences.
            Wash me throughly from my wickedness, and cleanse me from my sin.

Psalm 102. Hear my prayer, O Lord, and let my crying come unto thee.
            Hide not thy face from me in the time of my trouble; incline thine ear unto me when I call; O hear me, and that right soon.

Psalm 130. Out of the deep have I called unto thee, O Lord; Lord, hear my voice.
            O let thine ears consider well the voice of my complaint.

Psalm 143.   Hear my prayer, O Lord, and consider my desire; hearken
             unto me for thy truth and righteousness' sake.
             And enter not into judgment with thy servant; for in thy
             sight shall no man living be justified.

Donne's sonnets to Richard Sackville, Earl of Dorset (Holy
Sonnets 1–6 in Dame Helen Gardner's edition, 162–67 in
Shawcross), are akin to this genre. Whether or not he meant them
to be set to music, Donne calls them in the dedicatory sonnets
"songs" fathered by Sackville, "Seaven to be born at once," though
"I send / as yet but six . . . the seaventh hath still some maime." As
usual in his uses of conventional kinds, these sonnets simultaneously enter the genre and depart from it. Although they are in no
way paraphrases of these psalms, the sonnets meditate upon and
sometimes allude to themes in them, and the sociable penitence
of musical versions may contribute to their tone without detract-
ing from Donne's intense self-scrutiny and highly wrought language.

The possible allusions to the seven psalms receive a Donneian
twist that often Christianizes the psalm:

Blessed is the man unto whom the Lord imputeth no sin, and in whose
spirit there is no guile. (Psalm 32.2)
Impute me righteous, thus pur'g of evill, / For thus I leave the world,
the flesh, and devill. ("This is my playes last scene")
[T]hou shalt wash me, and I shall be whiter than snow. (Psalm 51.7b)
[W]ash thee in Christs blood, which hath this might / That being red,
it dyes red soules to white. ("O my blacke Soule!")
Blessed is he whose unrighteousness is forgiven, and whose sin is
covered. (Palm 32.1)
Turn thy face from my sins. (Psalm 51.9a)
That thou remember them, some claime as debt, / I thinke it mercy, if
thou wilt forget. ("If poysonous mineralls")

These last lines refer more explicitly to the opening sentence of
Matins and the petition from the Litany, "Remember not, Lord,
our offences, nor the offences of our forefathers," as well as Psalm
25.6. While some ask God to remember themselves, Donne's penitent thinks it mercy enough if God will forget his sins.

However, Donne's speaking "I" never shuns rebuke; and his
desire for purgation is a part of his boldness before God. The
strength of his penitential longing asserts itself fully in *Goodfriday
1613*:

O thinke mee worth thine anger, punish mee,
Burne off my rusts, and my deformity,
Restore thine Image, so much, by thy grace,
That thou may'st know mee, and I'll turne my face.

In the sonnets, he resigns himself to God "As due by many titles" but as "thy sonne, made with thy self to shine . . . a temple of thy Spirit divine"; he begs God not only to impute to him no sin, but to "impute me righteous"; he begs not only to be thoroughly washed, but that after death, "my ever-waking part shall see thy face"; he not only fears death before full repentance, but mocks death too: "Death thou shalt die."

As the seventh sonnet, unfinished when Donne sent off the first six, Shawcross nominates "Wilt thou love God, as he thee!" or "Father, part of his double interest." Another possibility, which responds to and departs from the genre, is "Batter my heart": like the psalms, it importunes God's attention and healing, but it reverses the plea "rebuke me not" and insists on being not only washed, as Psalm 51 does, but chastened "throughly." Never one to cower, this penitent bares his breast to corrective affliction and pleads for healing in a boldly paradoxical way that matches the composer's harmonic intensities: "for I / Except you'enthrall me, never shall be free, / Nor ever chast, except you ravish mee."

Perhaps the musical version of the seven penitential psalms closest to Donne's sonnets in their sonnet form and paraphrastic liberties is Giovanni Croce's *Mvsica Sacra*, published in English translation in 1608 (Sackville became third baron in 1609): six-part, largely homophonic settings of, in the words of the translator's preface, "*Sonnets, composed first most exquisitely in Italian by S^{ior} Francesco Bembo . . . (the Substance of them being drawen from those seauen notable Psalmes called Penetentials; indited by that Sweete Singer of Israel, inspired of the holie Spirit).*" The English version is not elevated. The First Sonnet ("Ex Psal. 6") asks on behalf of the vexed soul,

Saue it (O Lord) Almightie-most Supernall,
Saue it (alas) from the'uer-neuer Dying:
For who in deepe Hell (and fierce Torments frying)
Shall sing thy praise, or can extoll th'Eternall?

The experience of singing such texts might well arouse the productive indignation of Donne's Muse.

Other "Penitentials" in the musical background include sets by

Orlando di Lasso, well known in England; William Byrd (sometimes compared with Lassus as "our Roland"), who published his settings as numbers I–VII of his *Songs of Sundrie Natures* (1589); Dowland, in *Lachrimae, or Seaven Teares* (1604); and Thomas Tomkins, who sets "thine arrows stick fast" (Psalm 38) with pointed sharps and dotted rhythms, along with individual settings of the seven psalms by Tallis, Morley, Gibbons, and indeed most composers of Donne's time. To these should be added settings of the non-scriptural hymns titled in Sternhold and Hopkins *The humble suit of a sinner*, *The Lamentation of a Sinner*, and *The complaint of a sinner*. Dowland begins his seven *Lamentations* for his friend and fellow courtier Henry Nowell, probably composed for his funeral service in Westminster Abbey in 1597, with the second of these. These and many of Dowland's psalm settings are expressive harmonizations of the Sternhold and Hopkins tunes with added rhythmic interest. He also set Psalms 38 and 130 separately as well as penitential consort-songs containing notable word-painting.

It would be a mistake to suppose that settings of the Penitential Psalms and related texts are dour or supine. Often they are very beautiful, combining moments of pain and pleading with a profound trust expressed in unhurried rhythms and melodic grace. Psalm 6 is frequently set, and the capacity of modal music for harmonic retuning serves it well.[24] In Byrd's verse anthem version "O Lord Rebuke me not" (*BCP, BE* xi), the solo for mean alternating with full choir to repeat each plea, Byrd's ear for the music of the words finds rising intervals and runs on the urgently repeated "O Lord" and structures a pattern of swelling and subsiding like a heaving breast, ending with an Amen of confident supplication. "Vexèd" receives a complicated ten-pulse figure that the poet who drew his pain through vexations of verse would appreciate. Gibbons' version, "O Lord, in thy Wrath rebuke me not," combines simple melodic beauty with a rich six-part texture. "O save me" is a simple plea, antiphonally repeated in the two upper voices in a stepwise descent, but with each repetition rising to a higher level; meanwhile the four lower voices undergo this process of retuning in more complex harmony, all voices becoming unified for the final "O save me," then moving more freely toward the "English cadence" of a passing clash and a final major chord. This "tuning of the breast," as Donne's younger friend George Herbert describes it, leaves the heart strangely open to that work, however painful.

The sonnets to Sackville and the poems that became *Songs and Sonets* had been circulated only in manuscript, apart from *The Expiration* in Ferrabosco's *Ayres* (1609); by the publication of the *Anniversaries* in 1611 and 1612 Donne became widely known. The *Anniversaries* mark a change in his relation to music and expand his early exploration in the *Satyres* of poetry as a serious vocation, turning now from satire to praise as the vehicle of instruction through the regeneration of language.

Donne concludes his *First Anniversarie* with a compact defense of the arts, taking God as model artist and the Song of Moses as the root example of divine poetry:

> Vouchsafe to call to minde, that God did make
> A last, and lastingst peece, a song. He spake
> To *Moses* to deliver unto all,
> That song: because hee knew they would let fall
> The Law, the Prophets, and the History,
> But keep the song still in their memory.
> Such an opinion (in due measure) made
> Me this great Office boldly to invade.

Song, be it musical or poetical, adheres to the mind because of the beauty of its form: the "due measure" of the triple pun. Donne invades in his own modest proportion the scribal office God-the-poet gave to Moses. But also, God originally communicated his opinion of the usefulness of poetry by speaking, through Moses, in due measure: that is, appropriate poetic form. And Donne has now expressed that opinion in his own "due measure," by following the Mosaic calling with his own poetical numbers. Like Moses, he is God's amanuensis, or – he would conclude *The Second Anniversarie* – God's Trumpet.[25]

This defense of sacred art bears on the church music controversy only tangentially, since Donne is not claiming that innovations in the genres of biblical writers may be used in the liturgy. Like *La Corona* and *A Litanie*, *The First Anniversarie* shows tolerance for ceremonial arts without advocating them. But because the Song of Moses was used as warrant for liturgical arts, Donne's emulation of it puts him nearer the camp of Whitgift and Hooker than that of their opponents[26] and allowed him to practice innovation in religious arts, and even to have his own *Hymne to God the Father* sung at St. Paul's.

There are two "Songs of Moses," in Exodus 15 and Deuteronomy

32, and in Revelation 15.3 the saints sing "the song of Moses the servant of God, and the song of the Lamb." The song from Exodus became part of the Jewish liturgy and was among the songs cast into metrical verse and set to tunes along with the Psalms. Both Songs of Moses are among the scriptural songs in George Sandys' *Paraphrase vpon the Psalms of David. And vpon the Hymnes Dispersed throughout the Old and New Testaments* (1636), set by Henry Lawes, and in George Wither's *Hymnes and Songs of the Church* (1623), with settings by Orlando Gibbons. Wither's preface to "The Second Song of Moses" (Deut. 32) so closely resembles Donne's verses at the end of the recently republished *First Anniversarie* as to suggest that Wither is paraphrasing them: "This *Song* was giuen by *God* himselfe, to be taught the *Iewes* . . . For it appeares the Diuine Wisdome knew that when the *Law* would be lost and forgotten, a *Song* might be remembered to posterity."

The Second Anniversarie marks another change in Donne's relation to music, the incorporation of music itself – both the idea of music and a solemn musical language – into verse. At "Up, up my drowsie soule, where thy new eare / Shall in the Angels songs no discord heare" an energetic "ascension" occurs just where the music comes in. What follows is a hymn to essential joy, imitating in its swelling cadences the proclamation that "This kind of joy doth every day admit / Degrees of grouth, but none of loosing it."

Donne's one overt poem about church music concerns the metrical psalter, in *Upon the translation of the Psalmes by Sir Philip Sydney, and the Countesse of Pembroke his Sister*. Sternhold and Hopkins' *Whole Book of Psalmes*, the dominant collection of metrical psalms from 1549 until the end of the seventeenth century, left much to be desired in the quality of its language. Archbishop Parker's Psalter with four-part settings by Thomas Tallis was not so popular, but includes a comment from St. Basil linking "concord singing" to social concord that has bearing on both the church music controversy and Donne's poem:

who can long repute him as an enemy, with whom he ioyneth himselfe in lifting vppe hys voyce to God in prayer. So that the song of the Psalme worketh charitie, which is the greatest treasure of all goodnesse that can be, deuising by this inducement of concord singing the knot and bonde of vnitie, so ioyning the people together after the similitude of a quiere in their vnitie of singing.[27]

Donne declares that the Sidneys "tell us *why*, and teach us *how* to sing, / Make all this All, three Quires, heaven, earth, and sphears." Parker's Psalter includes collects, indicating a tradition of sung prayer, and like many other translators and compilers he adds an "Argument" and an original collect at the head of each psalm. Parker clearly meant his psalter for use in church; for "The Song of the Three Children" (the Benedicite) the choir sings the Argument, the "Rectors" sing the verses, and the choir sings the refrain. The Argument for Psalm 148 urges, "To prayse here all be byd, what heaven or earth contayne: / The Lord is hye: and sapyent: nothing he made in vayne." Donne's ending resembles Parker's collect for Psalm 150 asking God, "the swete Tenor of all our harmony," to grant "that after wee haue sone vp our temporall songes in praysing of thy name, wee may at last be associated to that heauenly quire aboue, to behold thy glorious maiestye wyth thy saintes."[28]

Sidney names Moses and Deborah among those poets "chief, both in antiquity and excellency" because they "did imitate the inconceivable excellencies of God."[29] Donne, in turn, calls the Sidneys "this *Moses* and this *Miriam*" in his praise of their psalms. Among the "three Quires, heaven, earth, and sphears," only earth's is audible to us, and David's heirs, the Sidneys, whom he deems inspired by the same Spirit who inspired the originals, make David's songs singable now:

> The songs are these, which heavens high holy Muse
> Whisper'd to *David, David* to the Jewes:
> And *Davids* Successors, in holy zeale,
> In formes of joy and art doe re-reveale.

It is not the prose psalms sung "in thy Church" by chapel and cathedral choirs that Donne finds unsatisfactory, but the Sternhold and Hopkins texts most people sang both in church and at home. "When I behold that these Psalmes are become / So well attyr'd abroad" (that is, on the Continent, but also outside the church, as in the homes where the Sidneys' Psalms are sung) and "so ill at home" (in God's English house), he wonders "And shall our Church, unto our Spouse and King / More hoarse, more harsh than any other, sing?" The indictment echoes many Anglican laments about the quality of metrical psalms and defenses of offering the most excellent works of men to God in the liturgy. After the Revolutionaries had ejected all music except the metrical psalms, Abraham Cowley satirically commented,

> The Bells ring, and againe to Church we goe.
> Foure Psalms are sung, (wise times no doubt they be,
> When *Hopkins* justles out the Liturgy)
> Psalms, which if *David* from his seat of blisse
> Did heare, he'd little think theyr meant for his.[30]

Donne's conclusion echoes a thought reechoed throughout the century, that earthly song is practice for the heavenly hymns humans and angels will sing together: the songs of "this *Moses* and this *Miriam*" will last,

> And, till we come th'Extemporall song to sing,
> (Learn'd the first hower, that we see the King,
> Who hath translated these translators) may
> These their sweet learned labours, all the way
> Be as our tuning, that, when hence we part
> We may fall in with them, and sing our part.

The "them" with whom Donne looks forward to singing are saints of song, the Sidneys. The song will then be extemporal, outside of time, and extemporaneous, immediately inspired, but until then "sweet learned labours" are what tunes us.

In addition to admiring the Sidneys' work, Donne perhaps attempted to carry it on by versifying the *Lamentations of Jeremy*. These reconstruct in metrical verse a series of readings that in the Roman Church constituted the texts of some of the most powerful music of the litugical year, the Holy Week Responsories. The Book of Common Prayer provides Epistles and Gospels for the Communion service for every day of Holy Week, but not the Lamentations, which however were part of the yearly reading-through of Scripture. Donne's addition to the title, *for the most part according to Tremelius,* declares Protestant sympathies, but the Lamentations were used by both Protestants and Catholics to lament the plight of a divided Jerusalem. Some of the expressive-ness of the "'dirge meter' . . . of Hebrew elegiac poetry," R. K. Harrison writes, survives in the Vulgate "and inspired more than usually dramatic treatment of the texts typologically associated, as planctus, with the Passion of Christ." Donne's version using "the improved Latin text of the converted Jewish scholar John Immanuel Tremellius, who had been, following Cranmer's invitation to come to England, made King's Reader of Hebrew at Cambridge (1549) . . . drops the typology, and makes of his free translation a faithful lamentation of and for a captive and desolate Jerusalem, bereft of her people."[31] Which church and people Donne had in mind is a subject of controversy.

One reason for metricizing biblical prophecy could be to produce pointed satire – in Donne's case, probably pointed two ways. Like *Satyre* III, Donne's version interrogates both sides of the wars of truth. John Klause argues that the known text is a rewriting done around 1608 of a lost version from perhaps as early as 1589–91, and gives a penetrating historical analysis of the applications of the text to the particular sufferings of English Catholics. He also points out that by announcing Tremellius' version as his main source, Donne may have wanted to "forestall . . . suspicions" by rejecting "Roman authority over Scripture." In keeping with the attitudes of recent biographers, he concludes after an otherwise even-handed account that "Donne took the bread of history, now largely emptied of its sacred character, and used it (without scruple?) as barter in his quest for patronage."[32]

It may be, however, that Donne's verses were not subversive of one side or the other, much less self-serving, but admonitory to both, corresponding with the (probably later) Authorized Version's caption, "The miserable state of Jerusalem by reason of her sin." As Klause notes, "Donne confided in a letter to Goodyer his opinion that both 'Roman' and 'Reformed' Churches were 'diseased.'"[33] Donne's paraphrase of Jeremiah's lament, "*Sions* feasts, and sabbaths are forgot; / Her King, her Priest, his wrath regardeth not" (lines 111–12), might be deemed sorrowful for the loss of Catholic observances, critical of corruption or inattention in church and court, dismayed at both recusants' and dissenters' withdrawal from common prayer, prophetic of rebellion against church discipline and liturgy controlled by overweening kings and bishops, or all of these. Like composers of opposed loyalties who set the Lamentations as descriptions and explanations of their own condition, he expresses concern for, in both senses, "the whole state of Christ's Church militant here in earth" (*BCP* 253).

English Protestants may have sung the settings of published motets on these texts by Byrd and Tallis with a fervor equal to that of the Catholics for whom they were written, as well as versions by staunch Protestants such as John Milton Senior. Catholics, on the other hand, might have attended English services in good conscience had not emissaries from Rome, by taking the attitude that the English liturgy and claims to apostolic sucession were heretical, turned them into recusants, or refusers, and Elizabethan fears of vengefulness turned them into martyrs, a situation Donne decries in *Pseudo-Martyr*. In *Satyre* III he teaches that one must climb the Hill of Truth oneself, and asks whether it will boot one's soul at the last day "To say a Philip, or a Gregory, / A Harry, or a Martin taught the this? . . . That thou mayest rightly'obey power, her bounds know." His *Lamentations* lament the state of the divided Jerusalem of the church on earth in ways pertinent to both sides and to the divided souls of her inhabitants.

Another possible, though not poetic, reason for metricizing the splendid prose of biblical prophecy is to make it singable by amateurs, like the metrical Psalms. Donne's version presumably preceded those in George Sandys' *A Paraphrase*, set by Lawes, and Wither's *Hymnes and Songs of the Church*, set by Gibbons. If his was similarly treated, however, no such manuscript has come to light. Thomas Ford (d. 1648) set the first two verses of it as a three-part anthem (O Christ Church MSS 736–38), syllabically and fairly simply, so that, depending on the date of composition, Donne might have heard it performed at St. Paul's or in private. If, as Klause thinks,[34] the earlier version was the lost translation Donne mentions having sent to the Countess of Bedford, he might have thought of it as performable in court circles and foreseen a setting like Dowland's *Lamentations* (from the Psalms, not Jeremiah) for Henry Nowell.

The *Lamentations* are, perhaps, political, but they share with the Holy Sonnets a lenten, penitential mode. As poetry, Donne's translation does not, to my ears, draw on settings of the Responsories by his great continental near-contemporaries, Lassus, Palestrina, Victoria, and Gesualdo, nor of the English composers Thomas Tallis, Robert White, and the Norwich composer Osbert Parsley. However, the context of these and other settings of verses from Lamentations gives any serious redaction an added poignant gravity.

The other of Donne's genres subject to musical settings is the hymn. At least one of Donne's, *A Hymne to God the Father*, enjoyed wide circulation in manuscript and was sung at St. Paul's, Walton says, where Donne as Dean enjoyed hearing the choir perform it.[35]

This hymn has been belabored by biographical critics for puns on "done" and "more," as if all of the sins enumerated sprang from his marriage, but these readings do not hinder those who still read or sing it from applying it to their own condition.[36]

The Book of Common Prayer contains no texts that Donne's hymn can well be compared to. In practice, non-prescribed hymns were added as anthems, in keeping with Elizabeth's permission "that in the beginning, or in the end of common prayers, either at morning or evening, there may be sung an Hymn"; and some, such as Tomkins' "Above the stars my Saviour dwells" and Amner's "A stranger here, as all my fathers were" sound like personal utterances. But apart from those based on the psalms and other passages of Scripture, only a few anthems spoke in the first person singular in Donne's time, and they still spoke chorally. Donne's *Hymnes* are composed in highly individual language and often for particular occasions where one might expect petitions rather than hymns – the death of a friend, embarking on a dangerous voyage, a serious illness – yet converted to the genre of praise.

Critics, David Novarr particularly,[37] make a case for Donne's *Lamentations, Hymne to Christ, at the Authors last going into Germany* and *Hymne to God the Father* being intended for liturgical use. The case rests largely on their strophic form, greater metrical regularity, and greater attention to assonance and consonance than in his more declamatory verse; but English anthems were almost always through-composed, whether the verse being set was strophic and metrical or not, and often set texts lacking fluent prosody. Since congregational hymn-singing had not yet been introduced into the English liturgy, Donne's hymns could only have been used as anthems after the liturgy. The Latin liturgy of Donne's recusant family did include strophic choral hymns, not cast in the first person singular but often in the first person plural, full of paradox and striking images, many of which survive in translation in modern hymnals: "Crux fidelis" and "Pange lingua" from the Good Friday liturgy and "Salve festa dies" from the liturgy for Pentecost are well-known examples.[38] So far as I know, although Donne's hymns all have universal application, nothing so personal or overtly connected to an author's life had entered either liturgy. On the continent, Lutheran churches used non-scriptural vernacular hymns, but Calvinist ones did not; in England some dissenting churches encouraged congregational hymn-singing in the late seventeenth-century but the established church did not fully accept it until the early nineteenth. If Donne (as seems improbable but not impossible) meant his hymns to be sung in church, he showed radical ecumenical and generic independence, perhaps exemplifies Cartwright's belief that prayers should arise spontaneously for particular occasions, and offers the congregation he addresses as "dearly beloved" in his sermons the fruits of his private meditations as he does in his sonnets and *Devotions*.

In the *Hymne to God my God, in my sicknesse* he writes,

> Since I am comming to that Holy roome,
>   Where, with thy Quire of Saints for evermore,
> I shall be made thy Musique; As I come
>   I tune the Instrument here at the dore,
>   And what I must doe then, thinke here before.

Although here he alludes specifically to his own death, all of his divine poems are tunings of the instrument of language, and thus soul-tuning, in preparation to become God's "Musique" now and hereafter. The royal instrumentalists of James and Charles were "the King's Musick"; and the analogy may remind us what King is at the "calme head" of Power's stream in *Satyre* III. At the same time, the kind of music the king's chapel disseminated, and the kind of language Donne wrote, should dispel any impression that to be a member of God's Musick is to lose one's voice in some vaporous euphony. The innovative vigor and varied voicing of music for English choirs must have entered Donne's conception of both temporal and extemporal choirs and the language of his hymns.

In *La Corona*, Donne asks of Christ, "*Deigne at my hands this crown of prayer and praise*... But doe not, with a vile crowne of fraile bayes, / Reward my muses white sincerity, / But what thy thorny crowne gain'd, that give mee, / A Crown of glory." Some uncharitable critics may bestow a vile crown of bays for his wit, but will not deign to accept his muse's sincerity at all. Recent biographical criticism has not only revised Walton's estimation of him as penitential saint but has denied him spiritual sincerity at all points by its insistence that Donne wrote poetry primarily for patronage and for alliance with the incorrect political power of the monarchy. Donne's power as poet-physician and poet-priest for both the political and the spiritual aid of perplexed human souls, however, is still available to any spiritual seeker. The sense of his vocation in God's garrison –

even if that garrison is a corrupt court or a limited coterie – expressed in *Satyre* III, worried in all the *Satyres*,[39] and practiced in the *Devotions*, the divine poems, some of the verse letters, and the sermons, issued in a radical language of the soul.

In the *Songs and Sonets* Donne examines the language of love and hate through a spectrum of voices that either cast off the conventions of courtly and Petrarchan love poetry or remodel them into means of direct and intimate expression. Many of these voices are far from admirable: whether parodic or experiential, they are mirrors for our vices and solipsisms. Others invent a language of bare and complex mutuality of both body and soul. In the divine poems, Donne often addresses God with an erotic intimacy that allows importunate wooing, and always offers the vigor and precision of his individual power of utterance to the reduction of unconsidered custom and hypocrisy and the addition of deeply personal expression to the language of faith. His hymns are hymns in the root sense expressed by George Herbert as what the heart "fain would say," however much the self may obstruct its own intent. The direct confrontation of this peculiar self with God and his own hyperconsciousness of that self's imperfections energize Donne's renewal of devotional language. And this language affirms the infinite value of each particular and faulty self: "*Salvation to all that will is nigh.*" The willing is the difficulty, and Donne's struggles with his own strong will, his pleadings with God to break and renew it, are part of his spiritual sacrifice. By offering his wrestlings to the reader, he shares his tributes of grief wittingly as the "Triple Fool" does unwittingly when his songs are set and sung.

In the midst of *La Corona*, Donne describes one scriptural scene that is not commemorated by a major Holy Day: the child Christ "blowing out those sparks of wit / Which himselfe on the Doctors did bestow." That scene discloses, I think, Donne's particular *imitatio Christi*, an offering of holy wit to the faulty and divisive "Doctors" of authority as well as "all that will." Whether writing satires or songs of profane or sacred love, Donne was always at work liberating language, throwing off the tyrannies of customary or unregenerated words, entering new verbal space. A poet of thresholds, he spent his life tuning the instrument of his soul and the instrument of our language "at the door."

CHAPTER 4

The choir in Herbert's temple

George Herbert's life, like his verse, was permeated with music. His mother nourished a musical home life: Amy Charles reports that during the few months in 1601 when John Gorse kept Magdalene Herbert's *Kitchin Booke*, William Byrd, John Bull, and William Heyther were frequent guests, and musicians and dancers came for various entertainments.[1] John Donne, a family friend, tells in his funeral sermon that she "her selfe, with her whole family . . . did, every Sabbath, shut up the day, at night, with a cheerful singing of Psalms" (*Sermons* VIII:86). Both George (who also played the viols) and his brother Edward, Lord Herbert of Cherbury, were lutenists, the latter's lute-book containing 242 works by English and French composers, including several of his own.[2] At Westminster School, Charles notes, pupils by statute included "ten singing boys," and "the grammar scholars were to be taught for an hour" on Wednesday and Friday afternoons "by the choristers' master."[3] Services at Westminster Abbey, where Edmund Hooper was organist, also gave Herbert early experience of the polyphonic church music that gave him lifelong pleasure. Hooper was a contributor to *The Whole Booke of Psalmes . . . composed into foure parts* published by Thomas Este in 1592 and 1604, which the Herbert family may have used, and was according to John Morehen "one of the most respected composers of his generation," neglected now partly because of "the poor quality of so many of the metrical texts he set."[4]

Ian Payne recounts the musical life of Trinity College, Cambridge, which has had a choral establishment since 1554, directed during Herbert's time there by the composer Thomas Wilkinson, who succeeded John Hilton the Elder the year Herbert arrived. Robert Ramsey was present in the college from about 1612 or 1615 and, according to his successor George Loosemore, composed the college's "Grace-songs, which wee vse vpon our Solemne Feast-daies."[5] With the encouragement of its Master, Thomas Nevile, Trinity was, Payne deduces from college archives, perhaps the only college owning a large supply of musical instruments, including a regularly maintained consort of viols used "almost certainly as a medium of domestic music-making and very probably . . . as a means of accompanying some of the verse music performed in the chapel." After about 1615 the popularity of viols diminished and records show organ- and sackbut-playing in the chapel and the frequent presence of the university waits, the king's trumpeters, and other musical groups at the college,[6] possibly in the handsome new gallery of the hall. Amy Charles gives evidence of regular music practice by Trinity pupils,[7] and a book of *Ayres* by Herbert's classmate George Handford (C Trinity MS R.16.29) suggests the kind of secular singing that moved Herbert to write sacred parodies. He probably heard choral music at King's and as University Orator he attended commencements and other musically adorned festivities at St. Mary's Church. Among the composers prominent in Cambridge was John Amner, organist of Ely, who like Hooper was an innovative composer only a few of whose anthems are now well known, perhaps for the same reason; the texts of his *Sacred Hymnes* (1615) are less well crafted than the music. Herbert wrote numerous poems on the same themes, whether with the intention of supplying composers' worthier texts or to incorporate verbal music into his own collection of "sacred hymnes."

As Rector of Bemerton, Isaak Walton recounts, Herbert "went usually twice a week . . . to the *Cathedral Church* in *Salisbury*" where after the service "he would usually sing and play his part, at an appointed private Musick-meeting," probably along with cathedral musicians. "His chieftest recreation was Musick, in which heavenly Art he was a most excellent Master, and did himself compose many *divine Hymns* and *Anthems*, which he set and sung to his *Lute* or *Viol*."[8] No settings survive. At his death, Aubrey notes, he "was buryed (according to his own desire) with the singing service for the buriall of dead, by the singing men of Sarum."[9]

Psalm-singing and "musick-meetings" seem to have been not only sociable but also democratic events. Magdalene Herbert's "whole family" would include servants, and at Cambridge "many lay clerks and university musicians also worked as, *inter alia*, scholars' servants," such as Stephen Willmott, "University 'Mussission'; scholars' servant; launderer at Trinity."[10] Herbert's definition of himself as God's servant is not surprising in a person of aristocratic connections and talents, but it is also socially congruous with his part in God's consort.

Helen Wilcox recounts seventeenth-century settings of Herbert's poems, or alterations of them, demonstrating that the subtle free counterpoint, shaped by the texts, of Herbert's contemporary John Jenkins (O Christ Church MSS 736–38), and to some extent settings by Henry Lawes and John Wilson, are nearer in spirit to Herbert's subtle tones than later baroque settings. Jenkins' settings are "parallel to Herbert's paradoxical difficulty and ease," having "a lyrical directness which is found within the tension of contrapuntal writing," and the singers' experience is "practical and intimate (in small group performance, probably by amateurs) and individual (each singer seeing only his own part)," in distinction to later works for dramatic soloist and continuo in which the text becomes a pretext for "new invention" (a shift characteristic of post-Restoration music). An exception is George Jeffrey's setting (1669) of *Easter* as a verse anthem, its structure and word-painting "responding sensitively to the metaphors of Herbert's text." Louise Schleiner reproduces and discusses Wilson's setting of *Content*.[11]

HERBERT'S WORD-TUNING

Herbert's poems are as thoroughly attentive to each word's tonal relation to each other word as a composer of part-music is to harmonic configurations and their fitness to texts. He practiced – perhaps invented – a form of language analogous to polyphonic music sung in pure intonation, in which linear arrangements of words form vertical consonances whose overtones, as well as fundamental meanings, are in tune. Although verse is necessarily linear, it has many features (as music does) that depend on remembered connections, rhyme being the simplest example. I would like to suggest some series of word associations (the polyphonic harmonies, so to speak) in which not only do thematically related concepts and images form vertical chords, but also the partials or secondary meanings – puns, etymologies, allusions, and the like – are in tune as the partials of natural tuning are.[12] And, as musical consonances make objects around them resonate sympathetically, each in its own timbre, so Herbert's diction suggests further chains of meaning by resonating with other poems in *The Temple* and with their cultural and especially their musical contexts. By many musical means, Herbert's poems create infinitely resounding chords in antiphonally responding souls.

In *Employment* (I) the poet[13] contemplates his calling and his unproductivity using the metaphor of a flower, a common figure of poesie as well as of accomplishment in general. Theologically, *Employment* concerns the relation between grace and individual creativity. In a God-filled world, can a singer of praise really offer anything? Is any of what the poet offers really his? Are his gifts to God really gifts if his talent and inspiration are God's gifts to him? Does his craft contribute something of his own? His answer is that if God would "extend to me some good,"

> The sweetnesse and the praise were thine;
> But the extension and the room,
> Which in thy garland I should fill, were mine
> At thy great doom.

Grace and works are reciprocal, and the title (from *implicare*, to involve or fold together) carries this implication. But rather than stating in conventionally Protestant terms that God's grace increases God's glory, Herbert asserts, "[A]s thou dost impart thy grace, / The greater shall *our* glorie be" (emphasis added). Perhaps he suggests that the line from the Gloria, "We give thanks to thee for thy great glory," means that when God's glory fills his creatures it truly becomes theirs as well as his. Yet he, bringing neither honey nor flowers nor husbandry in his present state, laments,

> I am no link of thy great chain,
> But all my companie is a weed.
> Lord place me in thy consort; give one strain
> To my poore reed.

An earlier version in the Williams manuscript ends the poem differently:

> Lord that I may the sunns perfection gaine,
> Give me his speed.

This version completes the thought by suggesting a natural relation between flower and sun often seen in emblems, sometimes representing the soul's relation to Christ,[14] and does so with a pun on "speed" (as swiftness and as success). "Flower" and "sun" are consonant, but without unusual resonance. The revision, asking to be a "reed" in God's consort, at first glance changes metaphors. But "place me in thy consort" relates Herbert's earthly employment as singer of praise to his eternal one – a consonance – and "reed" ties the musical and the vegetable figures together in ways that form a "chain" of linked and tuned associations that make the singer a part both of the "great chain" of nature and of music that can, in Thomas Morley's words, "draw the hearer in chains of gold by the ears to the consideration of holy things."[15] Herbert's rhyme-words "weed" and "reed" retain their connection as flora, but "reed" – though the poet asks for only "one strain" – takes on, like panpipes or the reed stops of an organ, full diapason. The end-word "reed" is the fundamental, the final word that, like the final note in an anthem, determines the key or mode; and it is in tune not only with other words, but with secondary meanings of other words. The other partials of his language are tuned by that fundamental.

The poem is about the metamorphosis of a flower. For anyone familiar with Ovid's *Metamorphoses*, "reed" suggests Syrinx, Pan, panpipes. "Pan" is etymologically linked to diapason – $\Pi \alpha \nu$ is the neutral form of $\pi \alpha \sigma$, all – and diapason, or octave, is figuratively linked to the eight cosmic spheres. Both Pan and Apollo, the musician-god whom Herbert lost when he erased "sun," are figures of Christ in Renaissance poetry, but given the common "sun/Son" pun, the abandoned lines sound overreaching and far less suitable to Herbert's humble suit than "give one strain / To my poore reed." Since Pan is the god of shepherds, who are the putative Arcadian inventors of poetry, and the Good Shepherd is the God of pastors, "reed" links Herbert's employments as poet and as priest. Like overtones, the allusion admits a slight dissonance, since Apollo defeated Pan in a music contest, but Herbert does not contest with Apollo Christ, but asks to be placed in his consort. Yet this humility exalts. Being placed in God's consort suggests (in place of a flower that spreads and dies) an *eternal* flower, the Rosa Mystica that, in Dante's *Paradiso*, is also a choir. Before the pilgrim can join that choir, he climbs the mount of Purgatory with a reed, representing humility,[16] tied around him; and after his purgation, he ascends through the spheres – the cosmic diapason.

"Companie" visually encloses Pan, but its etymological root is "panis," bread – companions are those who break bread together – keeping the link with Christ. Untuned, the whole "companie" of the poet's attributes is a solitary and unproductive weed. To be placed in God's consort (and here both Pan and Syrinx are meta-morphosed) is to be tuned, as for Plato the attributes of the just man are tuned. Because the physical, intellectual, and spiritual properties of such language are fully integrated, it reintegrates the body, mind, and soul and so, like music, heals the hearer.

Employment employs no pagan gods; they are subsumed in the simplicity of Christ the maker of sun and reed in which light shines and music sounds. No intellectual ramifications are required for readers to find spiritual friendship in the simplicity of Herbert's poems. The just concent of tuned overtones that I have described is something that happens in one reader's mind; another reader might hear different concords. Yet, like music, Herbert's simplest words, chosen with such a sense of tuning, have infinite particles that resonate with each other and with the matter of light and sound in a wonderful plenitude of concinnities.

Herbert's *Paradise,* a poem about God's pruning of redeemed souls, has no musical metaphors, but plenty of "partials." Its topos is the enclosed garden in which Christ the Gardener of souls "prunes" his plants to make them "more fruitful." The garden enclosed (which is what the word "paradise" means) reminds us of both Genesis and the Song of Solomon. As Gardener, Christ is the second Adam who appears to Mary Magdalen (John 20.15), who mistakes him for a gardener. It concludes,

> Such sharpnes shows the sweetest FREND:
> Such cuttings rather heal than REND:
> And such beginnings touch their END.

Visually, each rhyme-word is a part or partial of its predecessor. While the rhyme-words are successively "pruned" to expose new meanings, they are also "inclosures," each word enclosing the next until the pruning discloses it. Some critics have objected to the spelling of "FREND" as forced, but that was a normal seventeenth-century spelling.[17] By choosing this spelling, Herbert both prunes the "I" and removes the potential wolf-tone "fiend." These prunings are "cuttings," the cuttingly disciplinary but soul-healing words of a true friend (Prov. 27.6); and in Herbert's gardening metaphor, as in actual gardens, "cuttings" are ends which become beginnings. The pruned words are themselves "ends," both as ends of lines and as results of the pruning, so that they touch their beginnings in other words visibly. The "end" of the poem, its purpose of restoring to the trees in God's garden the fruitfulness lost in the first paradise, touches the poem's own beginning, which alludes to the beginning of beginnings in Genesis. The "end" or purpose of the pruning is fruit, which God's pruning of the soul produces, and the poem reproduces this process formally by pruning down to the word "end" at the end as the fundamental to which the other words are tuned. Just as prunings increase fruit both on the pruned branches and by providing cuttings, the word-decreasings increase their meanings.

Many such consonances also resonate with musical settings of analogous texts. *The Odour. 2. Cor. 2.15* has numerous concords within itself, and is also flavored by settings of texts that contain olfactory images and names of God. The poem extracts its theme from its biblical flower, "For we are a sweet savour unto Christ, in them that are saved, and in them that perish"; the thought follows the Apostle's statement of calling, in which God "maketh manifest the savour of his knowledge by us in every place," and continues in the next verse, "To the one [them that perish] we are the savour of death unto death; and to the other [them that are saved] the savour of life unto life." Herbert, though, says that Christ is a sweet savor unto him, and he longs to become one to him. He likens the sweetness of the words "*My Master*" to "Amber-greese" (ambergris) which "leaves a rich sent / Unto the taster," and wishes that the words "*My servant*" might grow to have "some degree of spicinesse to thee"; then it would "with gains by sweetning me / (As sweet things traffick when they meet) / Return to thee."

> How sweetly doth *My Master* sound! *My Master!*
> As Amber-greese leaves a rich sent
> Unto the taster:
> So do these words a sweet content,
> An orientall fragrancie, *My Master.*
>
> With these all day I do perfume my minde,
> My minde ev'n thrust into them both:
> That I might finde
> What cordials make this curious broth,
> This broth of smells, that feeds and fats my minde.

My Master, shall I speak? O that to thee
　　My servant were a little so,
　　　　As flesh may be;
　　That these two words might creep & grow
To some degree of spicinesse to thee!

Then should the Pomander, which was before
　　A speaking sweet, mend by reflection,
　　　　And tell me more:
　　For pardon of my imperfection
Would warm and work it sweeter then before.

For when *My Master*, which alone is sweet,
　　And ev'n in my unworthinesse pleasing,
　　　　Shall call and meet,
　　My servant, as thee not displeasing,
That call is but the breathing of the sweet.

This breathing would with gains by sweetning me
　　(As sweet things traffick when they meet)
　　　　Return to thee.
　　And so this new commerce and sweet
Should all my life employ, and busie me.

The word-tuning, or trafficking, includes as consonances numerous words for spice and trade. An etymological "partial" matches "Pomander" (from pomum de ambra, apple of amber) with "Amber-greese." (Curiously, "Master" comes from *magister*, teacher, guardian, guide, which visually enfolds or encloses those bringers of sweets, the magi; and the messenger's inscription for the Magi window at King's College is from 1 Kings 10.2, where the Queen of Sheba brings Solomon "aromata multa."[18]) "Gains," "traffick," "commerce," "employ," and "busie" form a metaphorical chord which, by virtue of "orientall fragrancie" and "spicinesse" distantly alludes to the spice trade, tuning with each other the partials of these two sets of related words. In "*My Master*, which alone is sweet," "alone" has the double meaning, a paradox in itself, of "only" (of all phrases) and "by itself" (sufficiently). But what left "a rich sent [a scent sent] / Unto the taster" becomes a richness sent back to the giver, with interest; when the two spices "meet" they become "meet." (I shall not insist that this pomander's or amber-apple's "meet help" has a certain reverse fitness with the "apple" in the primal paradise, but Herbert's diction often con-

tains such curious hints of unstoppable resonance.) The words
that had left the taster "a sweet content" – both contentment and
content – contain enough, alone, to "content" him, but when
master and servant "traffick" as sweet things do, enriching each
other, this new "commerce" would not only content but "employ"
and "busie" him: a resonance with *Employment,* where "All things
are busie; onely I / Neither bring hony with the bees, / Nor flowers
to make that." The words themselves of *The Odour* produce a mingling of "sweets" that "traffick" with and mutually enrich each
other as musical harmonies do.

   If we add to such examples analogues from music, we can hear
an influx of musical connotations into the poem from settings of
words about fragrance and of epithets by which Christ is
addressed. Sweet smells melodically rise in settings of verses from
the Song of Songs. Thomas Tomkins' setting of "My beloved
spake" (*EECM* xiv) expresses "give a sweet smell" with rich rising
harmonies. Orlando Gibbons' settings for Wither's *Hymnes and
Songs of the Church* (1623), made, Wither says in his preface, "in the
person of all the Faithful," are (therefore) relatively simple, but
the settings for the Song of Solomon follow in the tradition by
their melodic and harmonic beauty. For Song 14, "Arise thou
North wind," on the verse "Upon my garden breathe ye forth /
That so my spices there that grow / From thence abundantly may
flow," in an otherwise harmonically uncomplicated chordal
setting, Gibbons modulates richly while the singer's voice rises on
the words "That so my spices there that grow." Song 9, "Come, kiss
me with those lips of thine," a sacred song of much melodic beauty,
"trafficks" with Herbert's poem on the line "As the poured out
ointments be, / Such is the savour of thy name." On the following
line, "And for the sweetness of the same, / The virgins are in love
with thee," the lower voice (or viol) performs a modulating ascent
on "sweetness." The other often-set sacred text about sweet odours
is "Dum transisset Sabbatum," in which the word "aromata," the
aromatic spices brought by the three Marys to Christ's tomb, is
richly embellished. These two sets of musical analogues, the Easter
respond concerning Mary Magdalen and the Song of Songs, also
chime together typologically. In the *Biblia Pauperum* the meeting
of the Bridegroom and the Spouse is the type of the meeting of
Christ and Mary Magdalen that same morning in the Garden.

   Herbert includes a deliberate prosodic difficulty, a sort of catch of the breath, on "unworthinesse." The verse form gives eight syllables to all but two of the second lines of stanzas. In the fourth stanza's "Then should the Pomander, which was before / A speaking sweet, mend by reflection," the "feminine" rhyme of "reflection" adds an undisruptive syllable while giving a suitable extension to the word: a pause for reflection on the word's fundamental meaning, an exchange of light or heat. But the fifth stanza's syllabic and accentual irregularity in "unworthinesse" makes the word itself unworthy of the line, unless the reader mends the prosody by slowing down to give full value to each syllable of "unworthinesse" and a strong stress to "pleas" in "pleasing." The conversion from distress to pleasure is thus, as in a madrigal, mimetically achieved. When Herbert extends the trafficking metaphor in the sixth stanza with "this new commerce and sweet," one should give a full beat – not necessarily stress – to the iambic second syllable of "commerce," as is etymologically proper. Byrd gives this syllable a five-note run in the Nativity motet "O admirabile commercium" (*Gradualia*, 1607) to represent the wondrous commerce whereby the Creator took human flesh upon himself and thereby bestowed divinity upon humanity. Herbert's prosodic flexibilities find some of their power, and the reader finds the aural flexibility to perform them, by the experience of music which, remembered, pours a breathing sweetness into the poem.

The repeated address, "*My Master,*" gains tonal richness from the fact that in English music since Dunstable, the names and epithets of Jesus have been set apart from the polyphonic texture in long homophonic chords and expressed in poignant harmonies. Taverner and the composers of the Eton Choirbook set "Jesu" as a tender cry. In Taverner's "Mater Christi" (example 6), "Jesu" modulates to imitate the action of Philippians 2.10, in Herbert's time part of the Epistle for the Sunday before Easter, "At the name of Jesus every knee should bow." (Article XVIII of the Church of England's *Constitutions and Canons Ecclesiasticall, 1604* directs that "when in time of Diuine Seruice the Lord IESVS shalbe mentioned, due and lowly reuerence shall be done by all persons present as it hath bene accustomed.") The repetition of this word seven bars later has a similar modulation in the inner voices, but this time raising the treble. Herbert's savored and repeated words "*My Master,*" when read, one might say, in whole notes, also receive an inflexion that figuratively bends the knee while raising the heart. Thomas Tallis, in "Hear the voice and prayer of thy servants," gives harmonic sweetness to "servants" and the repeated phrase "my name shall be there" (1 Kings 8.27–30). His modulations on this phrase remind one of the modulations in settings of words for fragrance, suggesting a fragrant name – as Herbert does in his poem. Herbert's savored phrase "*My Master*" accomplishes simplicity of tone but vibrates with the personal warmth of onomastic music. He infuses fragrance and music into a word that might otherwise seem authoritarian and submissive, but that, like Christ rising in "I brought thee flowers," brings its own sweets along with it.

"How sweetly does *My Master* sound" also alludes to the "sweetness" that, in music, meant perfect tuning. The "speaking sweet" of richly mingled harmonies in settings of fragrances and of names of Christ that flows into the poem is the musical equivalent of Herbert's "Pomander," expressing the pardon that "Would warm and work it sweeter than before" and more particularly the statement that "sweet things traffick when they meet." What better description of harmony could one devise? Apparently, being a reed in God's consort not only enfolds the poet's voice into a choir but returns the whole harmony to his "one strain," giving it infinite employment.

Herbert tunes language, then, by tuning words to each other so exactly that their partials are in tune, as in pure intonation. In this process he validates language and music as possible, though risky, instruments for discovering coherence among God, mind, and cosmos. But a third kind of tuning has to occur if these instruments are to produce true hymns, which Herbert calls in *The Temper* (I) "the tuning of my breast" by purgative affliction. This experience is prior to poetry and yet occurs within it. Word-tuning and breast-tuning intervolve. And like English polyphony and pitches themselves, the process includes dissonance as part of its structure. For singers, the intervals of a major or minor second or seventh are salutary; they alert one's ears and test one's intonation. For Herbert, dissonant experience and clashing prosody temper heart and art.

In *The Temper* (I) the speaker begins by exclaiming that he could praise God splendidly if his exalted states would last, if he were not racked, if he could merely roost and nestle, like other songbirds; if God did not "stretch / A crumme of dust from heav'n to hell."

But he concedes that his suffering is what tempers or tunes him, like the string of a musical instrument, and so makes it possible for him to praise in tune:

> Yet take thy way, for sure thy way is best:
> Stretch or contract me, thy poore debter:
> This is but tuning of my breast,
> To make the musick better.

The syllable-count of these contracting stanzas is 10.8.8.6 except in this stanza, where the trochaic tension and the feminine rhyme stretching the second line, or string, mark the retuning. After it, the vast expanse between heaven and hell over which the sufferer has been racked is itself contracted to whatever place, or pitch, he rises or falls to. Because he is now tempered,

> Whether I flie with angels, fall with dust,
> Thy hands made both, and I am there:
> Thy power and love, my love and trust
> Make one place ev'ry where.

Deniall is a hierophonic emblem of this tuning process. The speaker's breast is disordered and his heart and verse both broken, in this case, because of – or, possibly, causing – God's lack of response to his prayers: an affirmation, however, that God does or may respond, since the soul that cries has not always been a "nipt blossom" – it must have begun to blossom first. In this case the tuning is formal and the prayer begins to be answered when in the resolution of the last two lines the mind chimes with God's favors and together they mend the rhyme. Word-tuning is also present throughout, beginning with that plangent word "pierce," which composers so poignantly set to represent the nailing to the cross or the sword that pierces Christ's side and his mother's heart. But here the speaker's devotions do not pierce God's "silent eares" – ears not filled with the devotions' music and not responding. Instead, the speaker's thoughts "like a brittle bow, / Did flie asunder."

What kind of bow? At first, because of the mention of wars in the same stanza, one may suppose a bow that shoots the arrows of devotion that fail to pierce God's ears: oddly violent, but, like the "Engine against th'Almightie" in *Prayer* (I), an expression of fervor. Were it in good repair that thought-bow would be the bow of the true Eros whose bowstring ("corda") binds and shoots all creatures to their true ports, whom Dante redeems from paganism in *Paradiso* (1.109–26) and identifies as the God of Love, who is also the shepherd of Herbert's *23d Psalme*. But in stanza five we learn that the bow that has flown asunder, which is the speaker's bent thoughts (both crooked and overplied in the effort to pierce God's ears) is, or is also, the bow of a musical instrument, his soul, which "lay out of sight, / Untun'd, unstrung." The bow/string metaphor shows that this instrument is not a lute but a consort instrument, the viol.

"Bow" under another signification and pronunciation enters through the allusion in stanza four, where the speaker laments,

> O that thou shouldst give dust a tongue
> To crie to thee,
> And then not heare it crying! all day long
> My heart was in my knee,
> But no hearing.

The striking idea of dust's tongue resonates with Genesis 3.19 ("dust thou art, and unto dust thou shalt return") and many of Herbert's poems including *Easter* and *The Temper* (I). "My heart was in my knee" is an inversion of a line from the apocryphal penitential plea for grace, *The Prayer of Manasses, King of Iuda, when he was holden captive in Babylon*, included in both Authorized and Geneva Bibles in the seventeenth century:[19] "Now therefore I bow the knee of mine heart, beseeching thee of grace: / I have sinned, O Lord, I have sinned, and I acknowledge my iniquities." Herbert's physiology of a migrating heart is not so odd if we consider the love-song motif of strayed hearts, the many emblems in which figures hold their hearts in their hands,[20] or the title engraving to the pictorial *Encomivm Musicae* published by Philippus Gallaeus (Antwerp, *c.* 1590) in which Harmonia holds a winged heart with a pair of ears. The allusion to Manasses adds another "partial" to "bow" and brings body (the bowed knee), mind (the broken but reparable bow), and soul (the bowed viol) together to be tuned. With his heart in his knee, kneeling with and upon it, the pleader finds his breast "heartless" and begs for God's immediate "favours" so that they and his mind "may chime." The ensuing rhyme not only rhymes, but rhymes with this "chime."

Mario Di Cesare observes that the ending should not be read too patly, however: the "manifest aim" of Herbert's revisions of it between the Williams (Jones B 62) and Bodleian (Tanner 307) manuscripts is "to fill out the harmony, to fuse all the local sounds, make them 'chime' completely . . . gathering together the various strands of the poem into a harmonious but placid movement that stills, momentarily, the turbulence created by all that intensity," but in full knowledge that spiritual dryness may return and "the hope that, even if he cannot avoid the chalice of suffering altogether, he can be allowed some measure of calm endurance."[21] This reading gains musical support from the "English cadence," that moment of dissonance that so often prevents even the alleluias and amens at the ends of anthems from lulling the soul into complacency. The still popular "Lord, for thy tender mercy's sake" by Trinity organist John Hilton[22] contains a flatted seventh in the next-to-last of its soaring amens, perhaps just the proportion of pain in the resolution of Herbert's "chime." By exaltation and dejection, joy and pain, fullness and lack, God does the stretching and contracting that temper the breast, but language and music themselves become both expressions and means of that process.

Church-musick, which participates obliquely in the seventeenth-century's vast literature in defense of that art, seems to separate body, mind, and soul, but is also a meditation on their relation. Its first stanza is about the healing properties of sacred music. Herbert thanks this "sweetest of sweets," the aural *aromata* that gratify God, because "when displeasure / Did through my bodie wound my minde, / You took me thence, and in your house of pleasure / A daintie lodging me assign'd." Like the amphibious human, music has both physical and spiritual properties, a body, or house, and a soul.[23] Herbert uses the possibly plural "you" in addressing music, perhaps acknowledging the company of actual musicians and compositions, rather than the abstract idea, or else the multiplicity of parts – pitches, rhythms, voices, melodies, harmonies, instruments – or the three parts of music that correspond with the three parts of the soul in Plato or of the creation in Boethius. Rescuing him from bodily pain, music frees the poet's mind to enter it and soar: "Now I in you without a bodie move, / Rising and falling with your wings: / We both together sweetly live and love." Music has wings – like birds and like the Holy Ghost descending as a dove – hence, as it must have to be audible, a body; in fact, it is a new lodging for the spirit of the hearer, free of the passible body's pain. The stanza's rhythms kinetically imitate the wings' motion, but come back to earth to pray for those unfortunate enough to be kings, and so for the peace of the rest of the world: "We both together sweetly live and love, / Yet say sometimes, *God help poore Kings.*" Perhaps the displeasure which has wounded the speaker's mind through his body is a political displeasure, causing him painful emotions, and healing music has turned his grief to prayer. Music did in fact, both in sacred anthems and in secular songs, pray for and pity rulers. Herbert's diction suggests a popular song, set by Byrd, that asks "What pleasure have great princes / more dainty to their choice, / Than herdmen wild, who careless / In quiet life rejoice? / And fortune's fate not fearing, / Sing sweet in Summer morning." The sweetest of sweets, though, is not wild or careless song, but "church-musick" that mends care by rising and falling with healing in its wings.

In the third stanza Herbert addresses music, with another allusion to the Holy Spirit, as "Comfort." Like Keats later, Herbert wants not to be rejected into the world again: "Comfort, I'le die; for if you poste from me, / Sure I shall do so, and much more." "Poste," to ride with haste, is one of those tuning-words that brings several significations together. It originates from its opposite, *ponere*, to place, from the practice of stationing mounted couriers along the route to carry the king's packet or letters (so they help poor kings too), and later other people's as well. Since these messengers rode horseback, music's wings take on some hint of Pegasus. Herbert will "die . . . and much more" if music posts to heaven without him like Job's days, which are "swifter than a post; they flee away, they see no good" (Job 9.25).

In the end Herbert defends church music with more vigour than most theological apologists would allow themselves, making it a help, nearly a means, comparable almost to grace itself, to salvation: "But if I travell in your companie, / You know the way to heavens doore." "Companie" again acknowledges the plurality of music, suggests a pilgrimage, and through its root in "panis," or bread, suggests communion. Music knows the way to heaven's door, but that other body, broken, opens it.

What music, specifically, may have taken Herbert to heaven's door? Many compositions come to mind with his description of rising and falling with music's wings, especially the whole history of alleluias. A likely example of English service music is the Nunc Dimittis of Byrd's Great Service, especially its Gloria patris and Amen. Its rising and falling, but more rising than falling, figures and harmonies, the polyphonic entrances alternating high and low voices, the serene building up of sonorities are like calm but energetic flight; and it sets words that Herbert experiences in his release from pain and his posting heavenward – "Lord, now lettest thou thy servant depart in peace" – and that he expresses not without dissonances in the wingbeats of the poem's rhythms and the calm of its ending.

CHORAL AND CONSORT POEMS

Readers often think of Herbert's as a solo voice, "playing and singing," John Hollander says, "in secluded retirement."[24] But much of Herbert's musical experience was of church music and "musick meetings," and in many of his poems the voicing is polyphonic and the occasion a feast or fast of the liturgical year. In *The Country Parson* Herbert stresses public worship. In *Providence* he admonishes that anyone who fails to praise God "Doth not refrain unto himself alone, / But robs a thousand who would praise thee fain" (lines 18–19) and in *The Church-porch* he urges "Though private prayer be a brave designe, / Yet publick hath more promises, more love: / . . . let us move / Where it is warmest. Leave thy six and seven; / Pray with the most: for where most pray, is heaven" (lines 397–402).

Although the poems in *The Temple* are, as the title adds, "Private Ejaculations," prayers not for liturgical use, many of them have choral voices and combine meditation with corporate celebration as in the body for which the central poems are named, the church. As secretaries of God's praise, human beings sing for the whole creation, joining "with Angels and Archangels, and with all the company of heaven" the voices of everything that hath breath.

Herbert's two *Antiphons* are explicitly composed in choral form. The first is a verse anthem with choral refrain, beginning with the refrain as a psalm antiphon does. By casting it as a verse anthem, Herbert chooses a form that evokes the multiple voices it invokes. It contains three choruses in common time (the fourteeners differently divided from the 8.6 "common meter" of most of the authorized metrical psalms) and two quatrains in triple time.

> *Cho.* Let all the world in ev'ry corner sing,
> *My God and King.*
> *Vers.* The heav'ns are not too high,

His praise may thither flie:
The earth is not too low,
His praises there may grow.

Cho. Let all the world in ev'ry corner sing,
        My God and King.
    Vers. The church with psalms must shout,
        No doore can keep them out:
        But above all, the heart
        Must bear the longest part.

Cho. Let all the world in ev'ry corner sing,
        My God and King.

The refrain alludes to the Venite, or invitatory canticle at Matins, which begins "O come let us sing unto the Lord" and includes the verse "In his hands are all the corners of the earth." Corners are nooks and crannies, but in a typical English choir, including the one Herbert redesigned at Leighton Bromswold, two sets of choristers face each other across the chancel aisle, so that voices from "ev'ry corner" of the choir fill the chancel, a pattern Herbert invokes from "all the world."

The poem's diction would offer a composer numerous opportunities for word-painting by means of pitch, vocal textures, rhythmic and harmonic changes, suspension, and melisma. The words "high," "low," "flies," "grow," "above all," and "longest part" invite such treatment. Whether or not Herbert set the poem or offered it to be set, as we read it these musical expectations add tonal color. "Shout" implies many voices; composers wrote in the dynamics by multiplying voice parts. The church's psalms will penetrate every door and beget singing within; but the heart "above all" – most vitally, but also descanting over the voices of "all the world" – must go on singing after the psalms are done.

Antiphon (II) formally represents two choirs, one of men and one of angels, dividing antiphonally and reuniting in full choir.

Cho. Praised be the God of love,
    Men. Here below,
    Ang. And here above:
Cho. Who hath dealt his mercies so,
    Ang. To his friend,
    Men. And to his foe;

Cho. That both grace and glorie tend
    Ang. Us of old,
    Men. And us in th'end.
Cho. The greatest shepherd of the fold
    Ang. Us did make,
    Men. For us was sold.

Cho. He our foes in pieces brake;
    Ang. Him we touch;
    Men. And him we take.
Cho. Wherefore since that he is such,
    Ang. We adore,
    Men. And we do crouch.

Cho. Lord, thy praises should be more.
    Men. We have none,
    Ang. And we no store.
Cho. Praised be the God alone
    Who hath made of two folds one.

Angelic and human voices are often joined in anthems and in the liturgy; the Sanctus, Te Deum, and Gloria contain angelic utterances to which composers give distinct voicing. Being about men and angels, *Antiphon* (II) firmly integrates earthly and heavenly numbers by disposing quatrains, as Helen Vendler has pointed out,[25] in *terza rima*. Moreover, the heavenly threes and earthly fours are combined in an octave of choruses: full diapason.

In her expert account of its "fierce principles of construction," Vendler remarks that this poem is strangely toneless, that "the meter is peculiarly heavy-footed in its trochaic insistence," and that "for once Herbert's euphony and gracefulness have deserted him, especially in lines like 'Wherefore since that he is such, / We adore, / And we do crouch.'"[26] I think that the poem's tones are supplied partly by the ways composers treated the voicing of human and angelic antiphony and painted the diction Herbert chooses. The trochees – followed by parallel iambs – give strength to "Praised be," "here," "wherefore," "Lord," and, especially, the pronouns, as musical settings would do. "Praise" and "glorie" suggest soaring melismata, "none" reduced voicing, "grace" an embellishment, "mercy" harmonic warmth, "break" and "crouch" dissonance, which often signifies reverent awe. "Crouch" is a particularly adept instance, being related to both "crook" (fitting the metaphor of

shepherd and fold) and "cross." Words having to do with the cross
or with supplication or holiness were often musically expressed by
such a "cross-relation" and cadences were often preceded by it.
"Crouch" fulfills this convention both thematically and formally. It
acknowledges not only the bodily form and the humility of the
kneeling worshippers but also the crucifixion, by which Christ
broke not only "our foes" but himself, and the breaking of bread by
which, kneeling, "him we take." (Kneeling to take communion was
a matter of controversy – another cause of dissonance – and
Herbert takes the broad Anglican rather than the Puritan side.)
Formally the passing dissonance makes way for a resolution in
which form and thought are again perfectly conjoined. The voicing
literally crosses, so that after the humble access represented by
"crouch," the last come first: men and angels reverse their order, as
they had done at the beginning, and thus return formally to the
keynote of this octave of choruses. Moreover, after the mutual
renunciation of "we have none" and "we no store" the two choirs
unite in one fold. "Fold" hearkens back to "shepherd" and even
"tend."[27] Musically it invites instrumental "doubling" of voice parts
for a richly textured conclusion and the homophonic union of
voices in harmony, especially on the last word, "one." We do not
need to hear an actual setting to let the words be enriched, the
trochees lightened and aerated, by these con-notations.

   In both *Antiphon* (I) and *The 23d Psalme* Herbert acknowledges
the psalm-singing movement in which his own family participated.[28] Psalm-singing by men, women, and children in churches,
homes, and public gatherings was characteristic of the
Reformation, beginning, Nicholas Temperley recounts, with great
enthusiasm but diminishing as a congregational activity in
Herbert's time and becoming a private one, for which printed editions appeared at various levels of difficulty and musical interest.[29]
The singing of the Sternhold and Hopkins psalms – which much
improves their pedestrian verse – "in every corner" of the land had
lasting effects on both music and poetry, Temperley and his
sources show, marshalling the march of English verse toward
iambic regularity and establishing ballad or "common" meter and
other simple strophic forms as the norm for participatory psalm-
and hymn-singing. Meanwhile, poets continued to versify psalms
and composers to set them in varied stanzas. Forty years after
Herbert's death, Thomas Mace was still urging that there should

"not be too great a variety of Poetical *forms* or *shapes* in the *Staves*" so that all the Psalms could be set to a few known tunes; "And doubtless he is to be looked upon as the most *exquisite Poet*, who is *thus* able to command his *Fancy*."[30]

Herbert's fancy commanded, rather, forms specifically cast for, or by, each poem, but they include a common-meter psalm, the twenty-third, modeled on Sternhold's translation. This most pastoral of psalms, in which the shepherd-psalmist becomes God's lamb, is perhaps the one most suited to this act of artistic humility, the conforming of his measure to another's staves. Yet, the singer says to God, it is "thy staffe" that bears the burden of his song; "thy rod" guides and measures his feet. He rhymes both the eight-syllable and the six-syllable lines in the manner of Hopkins, though not Sternhold, and without their strained diction and syntax. George Puttenham deplored this rhyme scheme as "trifling";[31] but Herbert, who does not leave English lines unrhymed except to express disjunction and who never trifles, casts the psalm into full rhyme while freeing the rhythms within their measure and weaving the syntax more connectedly, and so making the verse more musical. As is usual with Herbert, effects that may at first seem weak or jarring prove on further inspection to be apt. If "shadie black abode" sounds unwontedly Spenserian, it does so suitably in a pastoral poem; oddly, Henry Lawes included this poem in a manuscript collection of pastoral songs (BL Add. 53723) in which "the God of love" is elsewhere Eros. The uninspired-sounding "frame," which is Sternhold's word to start with, alludes both to the frame of mind God supplies and to that mind's "framing" of words to fit known tunes, reversing Morley's advice that "whatsoever matter it be which you have in hand such kind of music you must frame to it."[32] Since metrical versions do nothing for translations of Hebrew poetry apart from aiding memory and making them singable in strophes, his purpose seems to have been to sweeten and deepen lines that could still be sung to the familiar tunes. The "measure" in Herbert's much-loved closing stanza assents to the enterprise of metrical order. If Herbert can "measure" the psalm so sweetly with a mind God has brought in frame, "surely thy sweet and wondrous love" can compose his days in even meeter form.

Herbert's consciousness of the relations between words and musical genres is further revealed in *A true Hymne*[33] and several other poems. *A Dialogue-Antheme* contributes to a genre that may

have been invented by his colleague Robert Ramsey,[34] who also
wrote numerous dialogue consort-songs. In the first antiphonal
exchanges the interlocutors, *Christian* and *Death*, answer each
other in parallel points of imitation. But at the end the counterpoint is interrupted by a musical stretto: Death is cut off by
Christian rather than the other way around. *Heaven* is an echo-
song and, with typically multiple aptness, personifies Echo herself
("Wert thou not born among the trees and leaves?") and causes
her assent to metamorphose her into the "Echo then of blisse"
found in the "holy leaves" that alone abide.

  Dooms-day is one of Herbert's sacred parodies of secular genres.
"Come away" is the refrain of many madrigals and lute songs,
entreating the beloved do so for purposes usually left tacit; it can
imply either seduction or wooing. Dowland's "Come away, come
sweet love" lightly sets a lyrical carpe diem poem asking the
beloved to rise "like to the naked morn" and fly to the grove "To
entertain the stealth of love . . . Wing'd with sweet hopes and
heav'nly fire." His "Come again, sweet love doth now invite" is
more explicit in the rising climax of its setting than in its text. In
December of the year Herbert matriculated at Trinity, 1609,
another student there, George Handford, composed and dated a
manuscript of *Ayres to be sunge to the Lute and Base vyole* (C Trinity
College MS R.16.29) mostly about unrequited love. Handford
invokes various entities in these songs to "Come," beginning with
the fire of love as cruel mistress, or vice versa, which serves as a
general invocation:

> Come, come sweete fyre why stayest thou? alas,
>   Come quickly, quickly come,
> Consume me all at once and give me leave to try
> If lyfe be sweeter then a louers martyrdom,
> Or dye mye foe to live in love then liveing dye.
> Come come sweete fyre why stayst? Nay then I see
> That thou wilt yet alas in pitty cruell be.
>
> Come come away o sweete why doe you stay,
>   O come away sweete fyre,
> And let me prove yf rest to love my death can giue
> Or yf my luke warme ashes haue not still desyre
> To kindl[e][35] heate of love wherein I dyeing live.
> Then come sweete fyre why stayst nay then I see
> That thou wilt yet alas in pitty cruell be.

It is easy to see why the piously bred George Herbert sent home to his mother from Trinity the sonnet asking "My God, where is that ancient heat towards thee, / Wherewith whole showls of *Martyrs* once did burn, / Besides their other flames? . . . Why are not *Sonnets* made of thee? . . . Why doth that fire, which by thy power and might / Each breast does feel, no braver fuel choose / Than that, which one day Worms may chance refuse?"

The phrase "Come away" with which each stanza of *Dooms-day* begins may allude specifically and urgently to Handford's use of it. It usually carries with it an echo of its origin in the Song of Solomon which, according the temperament of the reader, may add a touch of seriousness or irony, though Handford's text seems to expunge that echo.

Thomas Tomkins' anthem "Above the stars my saviour dwells" (example 8)[36] resacralizes the phrase by making Christ the soul's beloved as allegorical readings of the Song of Solomon do, in his setting of an anonymous text in which Christ is again the soul's Bridegroom:

> Above the stars my saviour dwells
> I love, I care for nothing else.
>
> There, there he sits and fills a place
> For the glorious heirs of grace.
>
> Dear saviour raise my duller eine,
> Let me but see thy beams divine.
>
> Ravish my soul with wonder and desire,
> Ere I enjoy, let me thy joys admire.
>
> And wond'ring let me say,
> Come Lord Jesu, come away.

Titled merely *An hymne*, the work was arranged both as a sacred madrigal for private use and as a verse anthem (combining passages for solo or single-part voices and full choir) for liturgical use, set for countertenor, six-part choir, and organ. It is unusual among seventeenth-century anthems in being what Herbert calls "A true Hymn," written from the heart rather than setting a prescribed text. By its desire for desire and the secular connotations of "ravish," "enjoy," and "Come away," *An hymne* becomes a sacred parody of those profane parodies. Tomkins' setting uses modal

Example 8. Thomas Tomkins, "Above the stars my saviour dwells," bars 31–40

modulations and occasional dissonance in the verse sections to express its personal quality as a love song, while affirmative tonal resolutions in the full-choir responses suggest the stability of the eternal "place" that the saviour "sits and fills." Word-painting on "raise" repeats in a rapturous instrumental flight in response to the solo voice's "ravish my soul," and the organ accompaniment engages in a rhapsody of its own to express the soul's "wonder and desire" in the "motions," or emotions, of harmonies, syncopations, and runs. "Come Lord Jesu, come away" takes a twelfth of the text but nearly a third of the anthem; Tomkins illustrates the saviour's answer to the soul's request to "let me say" by letting the singers say these words (counting by repetitions of the name "Jesu") thirty-eight times in antiphonal polyphony which grows from one voice to six voice parts, both intensifying the soul's plea and multiplying participants in it. Like many of Herbert's poems, *An hymne* is both deeply personal and expansively choral.

Herbert's *Dooms-day*,[37] by beginning each stanza with "Come away," is a sacred parody of profane parodies of a sacred text in an erotic genre. Henry Vaughan, in *The Feast*, addresses Christ as the "true bread" and pleads,

> O come away,
> Make no delay,
>   Come while my heart is clean & steady!
> While Faith and Grace
> Adorn the place,
>   Making dust and ashes ready.

Herbert urges the Bridegroom not only to renew his intimacy with the soul but to "Come away" from his dwelling above the stars and "Help our decay" by his Second Coming. Unlike Tomkins' anthem and Vaughan's eucharistic poem, *Dooms-day* presses the grimmer implications of the imperative, exploring the mortality and judgment through which all flesh must pass as a result of "Fleshes stubbornness." Its description of the "noisome vapours" of dead bodies gravely alters the expectations of a love song into a "cure of love" reminiscent of Burton as well as a cure of death. Even the image of the resurrection effected by the last trump is a little macabre:

> Come away,
> Make this the day.
> Dust, alas, no musick feels,
> But thy trumpet: then it kneels,
> As peculiar notes and strains
> Cure Tarantulas raging pains.

Finally, though, that trumpet ushers in the logos-music that made and remakes life:

> Come away,
> Help our decay.
> Man is out of order hurl'd,
> Parcel'd out to all the world.
> Lord, thy broken consort raise,
> And the musick shall be praise.

A "broken consort" is an ensemble of mixed instruments, so that, although its primary meaning here is one in need of repair, the plea to "raise" it also retains its meaning of diversity in unity. Again, both by association and by its own diction, the poem evokes an ensemble.

"TRUE HYMNES" FOR THE LITURGICAL YEAR

The structure of *The Temple* is complex, having many principles working at once.[38] One of these commemorates the feasts and fasts of the liturgical year in poems allied to the music of those seasons. Herbert begins not with Advent and Christmas, as the church year does, but with its central events, the Passion and Resurrection. In his dedicatory poem *The Altar*, he lays his heart, the broken altar presented in the praise-singing stones of his poems, before his maker and mender to be sanctified. The poems that immediately follow meditate upon the "full, perfect, and sufficient sacrifice" that makes possible the resurrection of a broken and contrite heart.

Arthur Lake, whose sermons contain diction akin to Herbert's, uses a metaphor of masonry that links *The Altar* with *Easter*, where the heart "calcined . . . to dust" by Christ's death is made just by his life:

[T]he Scripture doth often tell vs, that sinners have *stony hearts*, and therefore they must be *broken*, that they may be made *fleshy hearts*, as tender and soft as flesh. Now you know that when a Mason or Plaisterer will worke a rough stone into all kinde of shapes at his pleasure, he first breaketh him, (being calcined or otherwise prepared) all to pieces, and then those pieces he poundeth into dust, then that dust with liquor he can worke into a soft substance, which will receive any shape, according to the fancy of the Plaisterer. Even so must the Heart and Spirit of a man be hammered by Gods Word, broken and broken againe, so that it may be made plyable vnto the wil of God.[39]

Striving as he is to be "plyable," conscious that nothing good comes but with the help of grace, Herbert nonetheless also seeks not only "extension" but also "one strain," a personal part in God's consort, grace to make music. In *Submission*, where he gives his eyes, or human perspective, back to God, he also submits his desire for service as one submits a case, or a poem: "Onely do thou lend me a hand, / Since thou hast both mine eyes."

The Sacrifice is an example of liturgical continuity preserved in secular poetry. As Rosamond Tuve has pointed out,[40] it derives from the Improperia or Reproaches of Christ from the Cross sung during the Good Friday service in the Latin rite and more broadly from the Tenebrae Responsories for Holy Week. These meditative devotions were set to some of the most expressive music of the late Renaissance, notably by Palestrina, Victoria (who is represented in numerous English manuscripts), and Gesualdo. Although the Responsories were not included in the Book of Common Prayer, many English composers preserved the tradition by setting the passages from Lamentations in them, probably for Holy Week. Robert White set the Lamentations for five parts, as did Tallis and Byrd during the reign of Elizabeth I, and Protestants including Ferrabosco, Amner, and John Milton the Elder set verses in English. Thus this and other remnants of the Sarum liturgy, recast as anthems, were sung either privately or "in the beginning, or in the end of common prayers."

One of the verses from Lamentations repeatedly set in tones of compassion and grief is the second Responsory for Holy Saturday in the Roman and Sarum rites, "O vos omnes, qui transitis per viam, attendite et videte si est dolor similis sicut dolor meus," from Lamentations 1.12: ". . . all ye that pass by . . . behold, and see if there be any sorrow like unto my sorrow." By beginning *The Sacrifice* with "*Oh, all ye, who passe by*" and by the refrain "Was ever grief like mine?" Herbert evokes the intense suffering, loneliness, and love that the music given to these words expresses. I do not agree, on the basis of the text alone, with Helen Vendler's assessment that in the poem's "frigid ingenuity . . . Herbert's enjoyment of his own intellectuality reigns";[41] for a believing reader, an overload of feeling would be more of a hazard. But in addition, the music that saturates its bare words provides further expressiveness, so that Herbert's demanding rhymes and his reworking of the traditional paradoxes of the Improperia and the events of the Passion hold the acute pain of meditative passages in controlled intensity. The unusual roughness and grim drive of Herbert's diction are comparable to the startling melodic leaps and disrupted rhythms of Gesualdo's setting of the Responsories. The poem's sixty-three stanzas are the stones of an altar cemented, unsentimentally, with musical tears.

Amner's *Sacred Hymns* of 1615 (certainly known to Herbert in print, and perhaps as anthems earlier) contains an analogue to which Herbert's may be contrasted:

> Consider, all ye passers-by
> Regard ye not with pitying eye
> O see if ever grief or paine
> Were like the sorrow I sustaine.

Edmund Hooper, organist at Westminster Abbey when Herbert was at Westminster School, set another analogue as a verse anthem, with the stanza

Verse: His eyes wept teares of bloode to see thyre blindness,
          His heart was pierced with speare but more with griefe,
          In agony of soule for theyre unkindness
          That for they're Jesus they should choose a thief.
Chorus: Never was sorrow like his sorrow knowne,
          Never was love like his by mother shown.[42]

The more one reads Herbert's poems, the more actual music enters them, but the more one reads freely composed texts of English anthems – still a young genre – the more one suspects that Herbert saw a need for better ones.

Easter is a meditation in two parts[43] upon the Proper of the Easter liturgy, alluding to its lessons, psalms, collect, and "anthems" appointed for Easter Day. The first part is about heart-tuning and art-tuning, beginning with a Sursum corda, the call before the Sanctus to "lift up your hearts" in preparation for the Eucharist.

> Rise heart; thy Lord is risen. Sing his praise
>   Without delayes.
> Who takes thee by the hand, that thou likewise
>   With him mayst rise:
> That, as his death calcinèd thee to dust,
> His life may make thee gold, and much more, Just.
>
> Awake, my lute, and struggle for thy part
>   With all thy art.
> The crosse taught all wood to resound his name,
>   Who bore the same.
> His strechèd sinews taught all strings, what key
> Is best to celebrate this most high day.
>
> Consort both heart and lute, and twist a song
>   Pleasant and long:
> Or, since all musick is but three parts vied
>   And multiplied,
> O let thy blessed Spirit bear a part,
> And make up our defects with his sweet art.

Easter anthems, among others, were often composed, trinitarianly, in three voice parts or three structural parts or both. Herbert does both. The poem's central metaphor is the Latin pun on *chordae*, strings, and *corda*, hearts. Zarlino notes that Aurelius Cassadorius thought strings so named because they move our hearts.[44] Herbert alludes to the psalms appointed for Easter

Matins, which include the verses "My heart is fixed, O God, my heart is fixed: I will sing and give prayse. / Awake up my glory, awake Lute and harpe; I my selfe will awake right early" (Ps. 57.8–9). Orlando Gibbons set the latter verse by twisting a song of one voice, then two, then full consort.[45] Byrd's setting of "Haec dies" (*BE* III: "This is the day that the Lord hath made") has six (or three divided) antiphonal voice parts in three structural sections, the middle in triple time alternating long and short phrases as Herbert does lines. This alternation gives the poem a kinetic quickening mimetic of the resurrection and jubilant response. All the key words in the short lines – "delayes," "rise," "art," "bore," "same," "pleasant," "long," and "multiplied" – would often be word-painted with suspensions or melisma by contemporary composers; "Without delayes" would offer a pleasant challenge, since melisma would simultaneously delay and quicken the line. Further, the poem "twists a song" polyphonically. Its three parts enter imitatively, each an imperative, its closely spaced rhymes weave similar sounds like closely woven counterpoint, and its many enjambments carry the sense in varied, arching lines.

At the same time, the poem may be a hieroglyph of its metaphor for poesie, the lute, since its eighteen lines suggest the double strings of a nine-course lute, the long and half-lines representing courses tuned in octaves. Herbert's concern with "what key is best" may be illuminated by his brother Edward's lute book, in which the pieces are arranged by keys. As Iain Fenlon explains,

The music in Cherbury's book is for six-course lute with several diapasons, additional bass strings which (with the exception of the seventh course) were not stopped but rather tuned to the key of the piece to be attempted. Since retuning the diapasons was a tedious process which must often have required retuning all the courses – since their pitches would be affected by the change of tension on the lower strings – Cherbury's arrangement clearly facilitates performance.[46]

The second part of *Easter* (which is analogous in form to a two-part anthem) is made of tetrameter quatrains, the lines, with one appropriate exception, end-stopped, like the regular strophes of metrical psalm-singing.

> I got me flowers to straw thy way;
> I got me boughs off many a tree:
> But thou wast up by break of day,
> And brought'st thy sweets along with thee.

> The Sunne arising in the East,
> Though he give light, & th'East perfume;
> If they should offer to contest
> With thy arising, they presume.
>
> Can there be any day but this,
> Though many sunnes to shine endeavour?
> We count three hundred, but we misse:
> There is but one, and that one ever.

The two parts together form a verbal example of what Peter le Huray calls the fundamental change in Renaissance composition "to a vertical method in which all parts were developed simultaneously."[47] "Rise," "awake," and "consort" are linked to each other and to the daybreak imagery both by logical, linear progression and by a common tie, their echoes of the Song of Songs, also figured in the imagery of flowers, trees, perfumes, and "sweets." "Consort" by its reminiscence of "spouse" links to "takes thee by the hand" and by its primary meaning to "twist a song" and "bear a part," which also connects to "bore the same." "Twist" more remotely lines up with "key," etymologically connected with the "clue" that Herbert calls a "silk twist let down from heav'n" in *The Pearl*. "Contest" accords vertically with "struggle" and "vie" and "Our defects" with "we misse," mimed in the obviously (if biblically) inaccurate "we count three hundred." The "three" of the first part links to the "three" and the "one" of the second as well as to the three-in-one stanzaic form of each part.

"The Sunne arising" plays, by a familiar pun, on "thy Lord is risen" and the whole second part may be seen as parody in the musical sense, the use of a secular melody for a sacred song,[48] since its imagery commonly appears in poetic compliments to the beloved whose beauty outshines the sun and outspices the perfumes of the East – Donne's *The Sunne Rising*, for example. Through the "son" who comes forth as a bridegroom (like the sun in Psalm 19.5) bringing sweets, Herbert typologically conflates the Song of Solomon, the Entry into Jerusalem ("I got me boughs off many a tree"), and Mark 16.1, used as the Easter Gospel "for the second communion" in the Sarum rite and the 1549 Book of Common Prayer but not in subsequent editions,[49] in which "when the sabbath was past" the three Marys bring "swete odours" to the tomb of Christ only to find him already risen. Herbert may be acknowledging and supplying the omission of a reading that produced so many richly harmonized responds, beginning "Dum transisset sabbatum," in his aromatic meditation on the needlessness of burial spices.

The poem adds to the language of the Easter liturgy the quality that music adds to the liturgy itself; that is, sweetness: pure consonances in tune with the cosmos and the divine archetypes, giving the pleasure to the ear that Kepler and Galileo compare with the pleasure of "the business of generation"[50] and which Herbert, in keeping with his promise to make sonnets of God rather than Venus, attributes to the "sweet art" of the Spirit.

However, two lines in the first part may sound reductive or off-key: "His life may make thee gold, and much more, Just" and "all musick is but three parts vied / And multiplied." Why is the ethical "Just" much more than the gold into which, in *The Elixir*, God's touch transmutes all? Why is *all* music "but three parts"? Why, on Easter morning, his heart rising with his risen Lord, is Herbert so mathematical?

Herbert's "Just," though it may fall flat on the unprepared ear, is the perfect figure for tuning both heart and lute. It resonates with Plato's teaching (Republic 142.i) that the "just man" tunes "in the proportions of a musical scale" the three parts of his soul: reason, appetite, and a mediating spirit we might call "heart." "Just" is therefore consonant with both "key" in the second stanza and "three parts" in the third. "Proportion," as Orlando Gibbons argued, "beautifies everything, this whole Universe consists of it, and Musick is measured by it."[51] Thus music can, in Morley's words, "draw the hearer in chains of gold by the ears to the consideration of holy things."[52] The word "just" in music, astronomy, and mathematics means "exact." Morley speaks of "just Diatonicum" and Peacham of "just Diapason."[53] Herbert's "Just" is therefore *le mot juste* for a poem about heart-tuning. And the word receives musical treatment that reinforces its significance. The fact that "gold" is a noun in relation to "dust" but an adjective in relation to "Just," and spans the phrase "and much more," provides a suspension that strengthens the resolution on "Just." Christopher Tye gives a musical equivalent in his setting of "I lift my heart to thee, O God most just" (*EECM* xix), working up through long polyphonic phrases to near homophony on the last three words (bars 10–11) and intensifying "just" by suspension and resolution. Gibbons sets "O Lord I lift my heart to thee" (example 2) so that the final word "just" is the only word sung by all voices at once. In Byrd's "Justorum animae" (*BF* iv) the title words are set homophonically, the rest mainly polyphonically. These composers treat the word mimetically, as Herbert does by his prosody.

The Williams manuscript justifies the short lines on both sides, capitalizes "Just," and puts a large comma before it. Following the Bodleian and 1633 versions, some editors omit the comma, but it is important because "much more just" is not compact enough to be good poetic diction and because "just" is not properly comparative. It means "exact," as musical pitches have to be and as scales of justice have to be. Christ's rising, Herbert suggests, not only transmutes the heart to a golden instrument (like heavenly harps or Musica's golden lyre in Monteverdi's *Orfeo*) but tunes it.

Herbert's concern for tuning touches on the permutations in astronomical and musical thought from Pythagoras to Kepler, and particularly on musical temperament. Duckworth and Brown comment that "because in meantone temperament the pattern of just and tempered intervals is different for each key, each key possesses its own distinctive coloration": an observation pertinent to Herbert's search for "what key is best."[54] As D. P. Walker explains, for monody "Pythagorean intonation [in which thirds are dissonant] is more suitable than just . . . For polyphonic music . . . in which the major triad occupies a dominating and central position, just intonation has the advantage of making this chord as sweet as possible and in general of making all chords, both major and minor, more consonant." Kepler's music of the spheres, he points out, unlike Pythagoras', is polyphonic and in just intonation, having consonant thirds and sixths. But he was not able empirically to "find these ratios in the heavens" until "he placed himself in the sun and looked at the angular speeds of the planets from there."[55] For Herbert there is "but one" sun to teach "what key / Is best." Kepler, incidentally, finds the major and minor third to be derived from the golden section.[56] If one's heart is "gold," and much more, "Just," it is put in tune with a triune Creator and a sun- and Son-centered creation by the risen Lord "whose stretched sinews taught all strings what key / Is best."

A musical analogue for this poem is Thomas Weelkes' "Gloria in excelsis Deo" (example 9),[57] an anthem in three sections vied in six antiphonal voice parts (high, middle, and low, each divided) and multiplied both in the polyphonic imitations of the angelic *gloria* that begins and ends it and in the multiple modulations of its central English verse.

> Sing, my soul, to God thy Lord,
> All in glory's highest key;
> Lay the Angels' choir abroad,
> In their highest holy day.
> Crave thy God to tune thy heart
> Unto praises highest part.

Like Herbert's poem, and sharing diction and a six-line stanza, but without verbal craft and emotional complexity, the anthem is a mimesis of heart-tuning. At "Crave thy God to tune thy heart" Weelkes takes the choristers through a difficult pattern of chordal changes that provides a mimetic experience of what Herbert in *The Temper* (I) calls the tuning of the breast: from C minor to G major to C major, and then, on the word *tune*, to intervals so unexpected that each singer, looking at his separate part-book, must feel that he is about to sing a discordant note. Instead, they produce the brilliant chord of A major. They have had to make a leap of faith; it has felt wrong; and they have arrived at a new and higher harmony: a mimetic conversion experience. On "heart" they return to the chord on which "God" was first sung, so that the heart is now literally in tune with God. The chord progression resembles Herbert's second stanza, in which the process of tuning taught by Christ's "strechèd sinews" is painful, yet issues in joy. Each section of the anthem, moreoever, begins in what Plato might have thought the "slack" key of C minor and ends in C major. The third section returns to the polyphonic *gloria* of the first, but with cantoris and decani parts reversed. The Amen recapitulates the movement from minor to major, from passion to affirmation.

Why, given the wonderful variety of harmonic expression, does Herbert say that "all musick is but three parts vied / And multiplied"?

All consonances, as music theorists repeatedly pointed out, can be produced by three voices. But Herbert's phrase is characteristic in its multiple relations. Writers have vied since antiquity to multiply variations on the three parts of music. For Plato they were "words, musical mode, and rhythm," for Boethius the concords of the cosmos, of human faculties, and of audible music.[58] Herbert's "heart," "lute," and "spirit" varies and christens these. In the

Example 9. Thomas Weelkes, "Gloria in excelsis Deo," bars 40–52

Middle Ages, the three mathematically simple consonances of octaves, fourths, and fifths were thought necessities of a cosmos created by a three-personed God. In the *Ars novae musicae* of 1319, Jean de Muris says that "all perfection is implicit in the ternary number," and Mersenne's compendious *Harmonie universelle* collects much similar numerology. But in the spirit of empiricism and Reformation thought, Kepler detaches the three parts of music from iconic applications and gives a pristinely mathematical account of the fact that "all harmonies can be accomplished in

Example 9. (*cont.*)

three notes," concluding, "The cause of this fact different people seek vainly in different ways ... For ... this threefold number ... does not give form to the harmonies, but is a splendour of their form ... But since the Threefold is common to divine and worldly things, whenever it occurs the human mind intervenes and knowing nothing of the causes marvels at this coincidence."[59] The statement corresponds with the disciplined musical freedom of Renaissance composers and the disciplined verbal freedom of Herbert's poem, whose structures are not icons but splendors.

According to Johannes Lippius, defining the triad in 1612, "this harmonic Trinity is ... twofold. One [the major triad] is perfect, noble, and suave ... The other [the minor triad] is imperfect and soft."[60] Each has its "species" through chromatic notes.[61] Lippius' wording suggests traditional descriptions of the sexes, as musical ratios did for Galileo and Kepler: and so to the business of vying and multiplying. Mersenne says that "One of the principal reasons why three parts suffice in music" is that "they can make all the variety of consonances" so that further voices "only redouble and multiply the same harmony."[62] But Herbert's "vied" is more inclusive than Mersenne's "redouble" because it suggests dissonance as well as consonance. And since "vying" means matching "by way of return, rivalry, or comparison,"[63] it may refer to musical counterpoint and to matched and countered antiphonal choirs. The word resonates with both "likewise" and "contest." For the religious poet

or composer, vying and multiplying must seem the right way of creating, since the triune Maker of that maker, having created "the
three parts of the soul" in His image, vied it in counterparts, male
and female (one noble, one soft, some said) and told them to
multiply. All creation is thus vied and multiplied, and for Herbert
creation is God's music.

Christmas, like *Easter*, is a double poem, but with the forms
reversed and varied, *Christmas* beginning with quatrains (and an
added couplet) and the succeeding hymn alternating long and
short lines until the final couplet. It starts with a hunting scene, the
pleasure-seeking rider and his horse, or body, tired and led astray
by the "full crie" of the hounds, his emotions, and desires. Taking
up "in the next inne I could finde" the rider discovers "My dearest
Lord" waiting "till the grief / Of pleasures brought me to him,
readie there / To be all passengers most sweet relief." He addresses
him who had no inn, but the "rack" of the cross instead:

> O Thou, whose glorious, yet contracted light,
>> Wrapt in nights mantle, stole into a manger;
> Since my dark soul and brutish is thy right,
>> To Man of all beasts be not thou a stranger:
>
>> Furnish & deck my soul, that thou mayst have
>> A better lodging, then a rack, or grave.

Amner's *Sacred Hymns* (1615) provides an analogue for this "*prima
pars*":

> A stranger here, as all my fathers were,
> That went before, I wander to and fro.
> From earth to heav'n is my pilgrimage,
> A tedious way for flesh and blood to go.
>
> O thou that are the way, pity the blind,
> And teach me how I may thy dwelling find.

In Amner's four-part setting, highly chromatic writing for the quatrain expresses the strangeness and dissonance of the tedious way,
with restless polyphonic rhythms miming "I wander to and fro"
and with rising runs on the "to" (since the pilgrim is not yet there)
of "to heav'n." In the couplet, "O thou" is preceded by a rest in
each part and lengthened on whole notes for "O" and dotted
whole notes for "thou." The final line has few chromatic accidentals as it approaches its harmonic "dwelling." Amner subscribes a

New Testament quotation to each hymn, which for this one is "*Ego sum via, veritas, et vita*," a text upon which Herbert meditates in *The Call.*

Herbert weaves the dissonance and relief Amner's music supplies into the words. The rhythms of wandering astray enter his broken first lines, along with the horse's limping gait. His "O Thou" is set off by stanza break and comma and invites the lengthening and tender intensity centuries of musical settings had given those words. Amner's stranger is a simple pilgrim to heaven; Herbert's hunter hunts the wrong things and does not ask the way to Christ's dwelling, yet finds him at "the next inne" waiting for him. Rather than asking to dwell with him, he asks Christ, who at his incarnation contracted his glorious light and wrapped it in night's and flesh's mantles, to dwell in his dark and brutish soul – his ironic "right" – and make it a "Better lodging" than the cross and grave. The tension between the speaker's sense of utter unfitness and his compassionate desire to give his lord a better inn than the world did, which only Christ can furnish, furnishes the poignancies of suspension and dissonance. "To Man of all beasts be not thou a stranger" recalls the Christmas motet "O magnum mysterium," set by Victoria and Byrd, "O great mystery and marvelous sacrament, that animals should see the newborn Lord lying in a manger."

The hymn or *secondo pars* of Herbert's poem also has a distant analogue in Amner's "O ye little flock," a calmly spectacular through-composed verse anthem with organ or string accompaniment, the text paraphrased from Luke 2 and the Sanctus (Isa. 6.3) with introduction: "O ye little flock, O ye faithful shepherds, / O ye hosts of heav'n, give ear unto my song."[64] Apart from the surprising address to the "little flock," the hymn is pertinent to *Christmas* by the contrast between the text's conventional paraphrase and Herbert's innovative reworking of the story, and the innovative tones of Herbert's poem and Amner's music. The intimate voicing for the verse sections combines with an astonishing array of dissonances and complex harmonies in the choral ones. Herbert's voicing is also surprising: the shepherds, rather than the angels, are doing the singing; the soul, rather than the Lord, is the shepherd; the flock is those affections that had been astray, a flock "Of thoughts, and words, and deeds" echoing Sidney's "My sheep are thoughts" in *Arcadia*[65] and the prayerbook confessions of sins "committed by thought, word, and deed" (Communion) and by which "we have erred and strayed from thy ways, like lost sheep" (Morning Prayer). However, this shepherd and His sheep have obtained "sweet relief." God's word is their pasture and His grace their stream, so that the psalmist-shepherd and all the flock "shall sing" and chide the sun for not giving them more daylight hours to sing in. And now the new sun, the Apollo-Christ whose nativity is the subject of the poem, becomes the object of the singer's search, with whom he hopes to twine so thoroughly that light and song merge:

> We sing one common Lord; wherefore he should
>   Himself the candle hold.
> I will go searching, till I finde a sunne
>   Shall stay, till we have done;
> A willing shiner, that shall shine as gladly,
>   As frost-nipt sunnes look sadly.
> Then we will sing, and shine all our own day,
>   And one another pay:
> His beams shall cheer my breast, and both so twine,
> Till ev'n his beams sing, and my musick shine.

Critics who find Herbert obsessed with his own sinfulness might heed the bold cheerfulness of this extraordinary merger, or "admirabile commercium." Herbert's eucharistic poems, including *Love-joy*, *The Agonie*, and *The Bunch of Grapes*, incorporate the joy and pain embodied in the communion service and heard in musical settings such as Byrd's and Tallis' of "O sacrum convivium,"[66] an antiphon from the Corpus Christi liturgy of the Latin rite, which also contains the hymns "Ave verum corpus" and "O salutaris hostia."[67] Because of disputes over the nature of the sacrament and reformers' fears of idolatry of the host, this feast with its hymns and processions was not included in the reformed liturgy, but Byrd's settings of its hymns and antiphons were published in the *Gradualia* of 1605 and Tallis' settings of "O sacrum convivium" and "O salutaris hostia" in the *Cantiones Sacrae* of 1575. Benham believes that Tallis may have written them for the Latin version of the reformed liturgy as communion motets.[68] Both were given English texts, Tallis' preserving its original subject in "O sacred and holy banquet." This banquet and its host occupy the communion poem with which Herbert concludes *The Church*, *Love* (III).

Tallis' gift for replenishing a simple text with sumptuous

harmony is replete in his antiphon or anthem. The Latin text is "O sacrum convivium in quo Christus sumitur, recolitur memoria passionis eius: mens implétur grátia, et futurae glóriae nobis pignus datur," "O sacred banquet in which Christ is received, the memory of his passion is renewed, the mind is filled with grace, and the pledge of future glory is given to us."[69] Tallis' swelling harmonies and freely composed imitative setting, not based on plainchant, express words with special emphases, especially dissonance. Many of these come conventionally at cadences, but the cadences match the emphases of the syntax, so that both text and setting are climactic in the rhetorical sense of a rising series. Short runs in the middle voices on "Christus" create a complex dissonance against sustained notes above and below them, expressing the "memoria" of his passion in the uttering of his name. "Sumitur" is the passive of *sumo*, to take up, to put on or wear, to eat, to exact, to buy. It is related to *sumptus*, expenditure, and is the root of assume, consume, sumptuous, assumption, and consummation. Tallis moves this word from minor to major, with an A♯ in the Superius while the A of the tenor still sounds, marking the host's expense; at the moment of consuming, the partakers assume a new concord. The setting of "mens impletur gloriae" is especially gracious, with a longer dissonance on "gloriae." In the last, much-repeated phrase, "Datur" receives extension and dissonance, the highest note and the greatest tension, released in a conclusion of serene plenitude.

Love (III), too, not only describes a banquet, but is one. Its balance of generosity – "Love bade me welcome" – and reticence – "yet my soul drew back" – resembles the fullness and tensions of Tallis' music. The banquet's host is the *salutaris hostia*, the sacrificial victim who feeds and heals what he has made – "Who made the[e] eyes but I?" This Love is courteously solicitous, "sweetly questioning," and intimately gracious: "Love took my hand." The guest feels dissonant, "Guiltie" and "slack," like the modes Plato thought unworthy; he has "marred" what God has made. When reminded "who bore the blame" he offers, then, to serve. Love, however, produces in person the pattern the antiphon attributes to the memorial feast, and the soul who says "My deare, then I will serve" must sit and be served the "sacrum convivium in quo Christus sumitur." The last words of the poem and of *The Church*, "so I did sit and eat," express with simplicity and confidence the soul's amazed gratitude for Love's supplying of her most basic need.

"MY MUSIC SHALL FIND THEE": LANGUAGE AS DISCOVERY

"Truth" and "meaning" are scarcely acceptable words in the post-modern world, and all language is suspect, loaded with culturally constructed assignations of power. As courtier to the Christian God, Herbert is vulnerable to such a critique. Reading his poems, though, one may feel that his language is not a manipulation of words to express a preconceived idea or control another's thoughts but a way of finding connections, much as music for the music theorists whose work was circulating among students of the quadrivium was a way of searching the cosmos and finding relations between mind and matter, or among various kinds of consciousness. Music offered proof that the human intellect can know something of the intelligible world's invisible forms of which the perceptible world gives evidence. For, as D. P. Walker explains, the harmonies of music were empirically discovered. Men first noticed that certain musical intervals please the ear and move the soul. Only later did they measure their harpstrings and discover that these consonances could be mathematically expressed by simple and commensurate ratios. Latin *ratio* and Greek *logos* mean, among other things, relation and reason.[70] Similarly, in Herbert's language the way of discovery is the way of concinnity – finding "how all thy lights combine." It cannot usurp, because it is always searching. Relations between words, with their entwining over-tone-chains of association, and music, with its partials that can be put in tune with each other when notes are sung together, are "clues" through the labyrinth of phenomena, a "silk twist let down from heav'n." The fact that so many connections felicitously, but not adventitiously, occur in the process of composing a poem and resonate together, adding insight on insight and proliferating connections, hints that language is more than an autonomous system constructed by a precarious consensus; it means more than a writer can plan for. While any art can be manipulated to seduce and deceive, language is the most corruptible. But the more "musical" it is, the less closed-minded it can be and less propaganda it can impose. Although musical proportions may be mathematically expressed, they have no fixed agendas. The purest consonances in music are not without partials, including dissonant ones; but the more the partials in a relationship of pitches are in tune with each other, the "truer" the relation is to the ear. Like pitches, words are complex and mutually responsive. The work of a poem is to unlock perception by finding out at each moment within its form "what key is best." When Herbert's diction finds its key, all the poem's words ring true.

Herbert often says that he seeks simplicity, and he found it to such an extent that his poems have been widely loved and sung as hymns by people of no literary pretensions. At the same time, his simplicity is like the simplicity of Copernicus, Galileo, Kepler, Einstein, and Hawking, whose descriptions of the universe are more economical than those of their predecessors because they pack more information into fewer terms. As for Kepler the concords of music display the design of the cosmos to the marveling mind, so for Herbert the art of the Creator Spiritus and the uprisen hearts and arts of his creatures entwine in mutual and responsive song. The discipline of exact tuning leads to both simplicity and plenitude. By composing words that resonate together to produce both musical sounds and multiple meanings precisely tuned, Herbert makes his poems "gold, and much more, Just."

In the midst of *The Thanksgiving* – the poet's response to the Reproaches and the grief expressed by Christ in *The Sacrifice* – Herbert gives up on any verbal attempt to respond adequately to the Passion. Could he, he says in one of those moments when grief defeats language and the attempt to speak seems vain, make Christ's scourging (and his own) into verse? – "Thy rod, my posie?" In the renunciation itself, he does; the rod, like Aaron's, blooms.[71] The numerous sacrifices of thanksgiving he promises to make in the course of the poem include the promise of poetry that will "find" God: arrive or make its way by sending up the sweet savor of praise, but also discover him; and "ev'ry string / Shall have his attribute to sing." Arthur Lake again provides a homiletic gloss, using the place of the solo voice within choral singing as metaphor:

The mentioning of one form of God excludeth not the rest, but teacheth us rather, that God will manifest that attribute specially which then he names. Even as in a consort, though many sing, the rest favour their voices, that some one which may best affect, may most be heard; so from

God some one Attribute, but in concert with the rest, sounds out his glory, to make the deeper impression thereof in our hearts.[72]

In Herbert's poems, each string or line and each of those strings of association that keep resonating sympathetically among them has his – the string's – attribute to sing; all of these strings will "accord," string with string, attribute with attribute, heart with heart, "in thee" and "prove" by experience the God by whose attributes music and poetry are in turn found and tested:

> My musick shall finde thee, and ev'ry string
>   Shall have his attribute to sing;
> That all together may accord in thee,
>   And prove one God, one harmonie.

At the same time, Herbert's work of language-tuning is still "My musick" and proves a harmony in which there is always more to find.

CHAPTER 5

"Sole, or responsive": voices in Milton's choirs

Milton's imagination is essentially musical. Visual contexts help us perceive his innovations and distinctions, but music enters intimately into the workings of his thought. He has the ability to think in sound and in precise diction simultaneously. The sound does not choose the words, nor the diction sacrifice the sound. Like Herbert, he draws words from that mysterious source of both music and language whence precision, relation of sound to signification, and resonance among parts spring forth inseparable. His architectonics combine massiveness, unity, balance, and symmetry with beauty of detail and sublime flights, like the figural diversity within structural unity of the works of Taverner, Tallis, or Byrd. His early poems incorporate his musical experience at home, at Cambridge, and in collaboration with Lawes. The textures of his epic, like the English verse anthem and the Italian *stile concertante*, combine solo and choral voices, and the polyphonic church music, madrigals, consort songs, and keyboard music he knew pattern forth the richness of multiple relations in his language. His prosody is both mimetic and expressive. As in monody, his characters express powerful feelings through sound as well as signification; as in part-music, each line of thought has its linear energy and goal and at the same time forms consonances and dissonances with other simultaneous lines of thought. Though Milton scoffs at the music of the prelates and praises Henry Lawes for subordinating music to words, *Paradise Lost* is full of polyphony, and the way we hear it affects our response to his representation of goodness, of the politics of heaven, and of a God who shall be "All in All."

Sanford Budick writes that Milton's "half-interdicted images . . . point to his abstractive goals."[1] If Milton's imagery transmutes the visible into the visionary – or enables the imagination to see the visionary in the visible, rather than disabling itself by creating fixed icons – his music gives the visionary immediate emotive power. Like light that is itself invisible, Milton's music lets us see.

BRIGHT EFFLUENCE OF BRIGHT ESSENCE

The invocation to light beginning Book 3 of *Paradise Lost* greets eternal light with balanced structure in something like isometric proportions.

> Hail holy Light, offspring of Heav'n first born,
> Or of th' Eternal Coeternal beam
> May I express thee unblam'd? since God is Light,
> And never but in unapproached Light
> Dwelt from Eternity, dwelt then in thee,
> Bright effluence of bright essence increate.

These lines have musical power beyond their cognitive content to draw the listener into the suprarational moment. Their intense serenity, produced partly by the alliteration of vowels and aspirates, draws also from musical proportions. If one emphasizes the pronouns in the third line and speeds up "express," and if one reads "effluence" flowingly as two syllables, these lines are syllabically regular. At the same time, like an isometric motet, or like the Agnus Dei of Taverner's *Missa Gloria Tibi Trinitas*, they give an impression of acceleration. If one keeps a steady pulse and pauses at the commas, "Hail holy Light" has fewer syllables but as many pulses – technically, three stresses and a rest, though like polyphony they have no "beat," only length – and takes as much aural time as "óffspring of Héav'n first bórn," which, slowed down by its fricatives, can use almost as much time as "Or of th'Etérnal Coetérnal béam." The ensuing line, still decasyllabic if we compress "I express" by syneresis, is visibly longer and audibly swifter, and this acceleration is sustained by enjambed flow and a preponderance of accents on first syllables of words, phrases, and lines – apart from a suitable halt for the repeated "dwelt." By enjambing every other line, Milton structures the passage to contrast, yet join, the hesitant human questioning with the flow of light, culminating with the mimetic out-flowing of effluence in the strongly impelled swift flow of the sixth line.

At the same time, these six lines are balanced, like musical building-blocks, with the next six, linked by the even-handed "Or," each asking a question. The first, "may I express thee," both raises the problem of expressibility in language and points to the musical expressiveness of this passage of language itself. The second, "Or hear'st thou rather pure Ethereal stream, / Whose Fountain who can tell?" continues to express inexpressibility while descending to "the rising world of waters dark and deep" that light invests at the first creation. Thus, the rhythms of the first three lines enter the serenity of a light-filled eternity and mirror a cosmos of lights by making portions into proportions, while the form of the two balanced questions in twelve lines suggests the twelve divisions of the lunar year and the division into light and darkness of the solar day, and at the same time insert a personal voice, human singularity penetrating the cosmic dance and with bold humility approaching the throne of light. Like unbroken polyphony, the passage participates in eternity; like *musica espressiva* it joins heaven and earth through the disciplined yet deeply engaged and virtuosic voice of a human "I."

Meanwhile, by allusive parallels, Milton causes this and other passages on light to trope each other in the larger harmonic structure of the poem. The light in Milton's twelve lines is spiritual light "expressed" as phenomenal light – not a division, but a proceeding, the "bright effluence of bright essence increate" – to which the blind bard with imagination's eyes returns from the "*Stygian* pool." The "coeternal beam" has many meanings,[2] among them the relation of the Son to the Father as "Light of Light . . . By whom all things were made" in the Nicene Creed, the "lumen de lumine" that Byrd, for example, in his Mass for Five Voices sets with homophonic clarity and a harmonic radiance that spreads over the ensuing phrase. Milton's first six lines express the birth of phenomenal light or the effluence of preternatural light in which God dwells, and the second six, optatively yet processively, express the natural light which invested the world before the creation of the sun which it later fills; the stars, like virtuous virgins with "golden Urns" draw light to fill their lesser lamps from the sun (7.354–69), who comes forth from the east "jocund to run / His Longitude" like the sun in Psalm 19.5 "which cometh forth as a bridegroom out of his chamber, and rejoiceth as a giant to run his race." The virgins in the parable (Matt. 25.1–13) prepare for the bridegroom who, both there and in Christian allegorizations of the Song of Songs, is Christ, who in the creed is the "Light of Light." The invocation to Book 3 and the creation of the sun and stars on the fourth day in Book 7 are part of a leitmotiv that guides the epic's figural connections like a varied theme within a musical structure. Indeed, the whole poem might be compared with that "Mystical dance, which yonder starry Sphere . . . Resembles nearest, mazes intricate, / Eccentric, intervolv'd, yet regular / Then most, when most irregular they seem" (5.621–24). It would be hard to find a better definition of English polyphonic music from the Eton Choirbook ("intricate," "eccentric," "intervolved") to the variously expressive but masterfully controlled structures of William Byrd and his successors.

Phenomenal light in *Paradise Lost* also receives some madrigal-like imitation in sound. The beginning of Guarini's "A un giro sol de'begl'occhi," from Monteverdi's *Quatro libro dei madrigali*, is a thematic analogue of Eve's "With thee conversing I forget all time" (4.639–56), in which the presence of the beloved makes nature "sweet" as right tuning does music. Monteverdi sets the brightening sky ("E si fa il ciel d'un altro lum'adorno") on quick, spreading points of imitation like emerging stars; the alliterations of Milton's "silent Night," "starry train," and "glittering Star-light" also suit points of light. But Guarini's poem is the complaint of a sad lover smitten by a cruel lady, a genre Milton never meddled in, and Eve's is the symmetrically balanced, gracious nocturn of a happy spouse. The varied circularity of her love song imitates the "starry Sphere" and corresponds with the invocation in the morning hymn (5.166–79) to the sun, moon, and stars in their circular rounds whose "mystic Dance not without Song" this bridegroom and spouse – who have just met spiritual darkness in the dream Satan pours into Eve's ear – call upon to "resound / His praise, who out of darkness call'd up Light." Thus the invocation to Light in Book 3, Eve's nocturn, her following question about the stars, and Adam's musical answer in Book 4, the morning prayer and the "Mystical dance" that follows the Son's appointment as Vicegerent to the angels in Book 5, the creation of light and heavenly lights in Book 7, and Raphael's astronomical consideration of "Male and Female light" in Book 8 all constellate with grateful unity and vicissitude and resonate with increasing consonance in a structure that admits dissonance and darkness and out of them calls up light.

VOCATION AND SOLEMN MUSIC IN MILTON'S
EARLY POEMS

Milton's father, though he gave up his inheritance for his Protestant convictions, composed not only Reformation-style English anthems and psalm settings but also polyphonic settings of Latin religious texts. As a child he was probably a chorister at Christ Church, Oxford, the church of Taverner, some of whose works he might possibly have sung. He later wrote *In Nomines*, those secular links to the past. The composers among whom he is included in manuscript part-books indicate the company he kept, and the texts he set in addition to his instrumental music indicate the variety of his interests. The fact that Morley invited him to contribute to the *Triumphs of Oriana* and Leighton included him along with Dowland, Hooper, Bull, Byrd, Pilkington, Peerson, Gibbons, Weelkes, and Ferrabosco in his *Teares* confirms his place in a community of prominent musicians associated with both church and court. His works in Thomas Myriell's manuscript of many genres, *tristitiae remedia*, are "Faire ORIAN," seven anthems, and a Latin motet in six parts, its text an evening prayer set also by Byrd in plainer style (*TCM* IX).

Precamur Sancte Domine	Deo patri sit gloria
Defende nos in hac nocte	Eiusque soli filio,
Sit nobis in te requies	Cum spiritu Paracleto
Quietam noctem tribue;	Et nunc et in perpetuum.

As Ernest Brennecke, Jr., describes it, Milton's setting, "in his favorite mode, the Aeolian, which is distinguished by a very flexible system of harmonies," is harmonically "of the purest mid-sixteenth-century type; it exploits no emotional clashes and could readily pass as the work of Tallis or even of Palestrina." At the same time it is complicated by "a deliberate system of contrast and clash between the harmonic and time framework and the accents in the individual parts . . . [like] blank verse, following the dictates of an underlying regular quantity upon which is erected an endless variety of accentual stresses."[3] Readers of Milton the younger will recognize this pattern.

The elder Milton's English anthems or sacred part-songs are "O Lord behold my miseries," "If that a sinner's sighs," "Thou God of might hast chastened me," "When David heard," "O woe is me for thee, my brother Jonathan," "I am the resurrection," and "How

doth the holy City remaine solitary" with "She weepeth continually." The last pair, associated with the laments of recusants when
set by Byrd or Dering, shows that texts mourning the division of
the city of God were adopted by both factions.[4] "If that a sinner's
sighs" is an *In Nomine* for tenor and strings. Several works contain
moderate word-painting; in "I am the resurrection" all parts
ascend, and in the lament for Jonathan "Woe is me for thee" shows
the shape of wailing.

Three of these works set texts of a kind whose popularity as
tristitiae remedia is likely to perplex a modern audience unused to
finding consolation in the wounds of repentence and merciful
chastisement:

> O Lord behold my miseries
> My paine and deadly greife
> No help but in thy mercies
> to yeald my soule releife.
> I hate my selfe, and loath my sinne,
> My hart is rent with feare
> To think what state I have liv'd in
> My wits with torment teare.

If that a sinners sighs sent from a soule with griefe opprest may thee O
lord to mercy move and to compassion then pity me, and ease my misery.

> Thou God of might hast chastened me
> and me corrected with thy rod
> wounded my soul with misery
> and humbled me to know my God.

Like the Prayer Book's opening sentences for Morning Prayer and
the Seven Penitential Psalms, such sinners' sighs, part-sung and so
public, give relief to careful consciences.

Other Latin texts in Myriell's collection are set by Alfonso
Ferrabosco, Morley (including the still popular macaronic anthem
"Nolo mortem peccatoris"), Wilby, Ravenscroft, Lupo, Damon,
and Byrd. Other English anthems and sacred part-songs include
Tallis' "O Sacred and Holy Banket" and "With all our heart and
mouth," Byrd's prayerbook anthems "Christ rising" with "Christ is
risen" and his and many others' settings of Psalm 81, "Sing ioyfully
vnto God our strength," Weelkes' two laments for Absalom and
one for Jonathan, Gibbons' "See, see the Word is incarnate,"
Ferrabosco's setting of Ben Jonson's "Heare me, O God, / A

broken heart is my best part," and other works by these composers as well as Ravenscroft, Martin Peerson, East, John Munday, Parsons, Philips, George Handford (Herbert's contemporary at Trinity), Thomas Tomkins, Hooper, and many others. Croce (who set the Seven Penitential Psalms) is represented, as are other continental composers, most abundantly Marenzio.

Milton's use of Latin and of elaborate polyphony – most lavishly in a legendary forty-part *In Nomine* – shows his link with tradition, while his metrical psalms and his setting, similar to Tallis', of "If ye love me" show his Protestant interest in intelligibility and accessibility. His metrical psalm settings are found in Thomas Ravenscroft's *Whole Book of Psalmes* (1621 and 1633) in which various composers set the texts from Sternhold and Hopkins to four-part harmonies on the tenors or tunes "usually sung" in Britain and on the continent. Again, Milton is in good company, with Tallis, Dowland, Morley, and Tomkins among the contributors. Milton's settings are of Psalms 5, 27, 55, 66, 102 and 138 and the "Prayer to the holy Ghost" (example 10), which may have sung before sermons after the liturgy:

> Come holy spirit the God of might
> comforter of us all,
> teach us to know thy word aright
> that we do never fall.

(As is often the case, "spirit" is pronounced as one syllable, "spir't" or possibly "spright.") Like others in the collection, Milton's setting, based on the "Yorke" tune in the tenor, is mainly syllabic and easily singable but it is not without interest. Its eight- and six-syllable common meter lines are disposed on ten- and eight-pulse musical lines, with rests at the beginnings of the short lines and moving notes in the alto or medius part. Whether or not Ravenscroft collaborated with his composers in fitting tune to text, the first verse has some felicitous features. Beginning in the tonic, the harmony changes to a minor chord on "spirit" and moves to the dominant on "might." "That we do never fall" has an inverted minor chord and a suspension; the tenor moves downward toward "fall" and the bass falls twice in wide intervals, but cantus and medius are caught up. The accessibility of this hymn may affect one's response to the younger Milton's more exalted invocations of the Holy Spirit – the action is homely and familiar to him. Other

Example 10. John Milton, "A prayer to the holy Ghost"

verses have a more ironic relation to his life and work: "Lorde keepe our King and his Counsell . . . send preachers plenteously . . . Depart not from those Pastors pure . . . Keepe vs from sects and errours all . . . O Lord increase our faith in vs, / and loue so to abound: / That man and wife be void of strife, / and neighbors about vs round."

One of Milton's harmonizations of the York tune is included in *The Psalmes of David in 4 Languages and in 4 Parts Set to the Tunes of our Church* (1643) by William Slatyer, who had also provided tetraglottal captions for a large series of Bible illustrations pertinent to *Paradise Lost.*[5] In his preface Slatyer says, in ways that bring to mind more powerful expressions from Milton's poems, that "the sweet singer of Israel" provides an epitome of all poetry "besides such spirituall raptures as shall carry the soule with Angels wings to heaven, both to behold the wondrous workes, and as far as possible for humane frailty almost . . . to gaze at the glorious face of the Creator," while saints and angels joyfully "behold the singers here of these, thus ravished not . . . to mount Parnassus, but even unto mount Sion."[6]

The two English psalm paraphrases that Milton included in his *Poems* of 1645, "done by the Author at fifteen years old," are of Psalm 114, which he also translated into Greek, and of Psalm 136. Both of these commemorate the Exodus. They supply a need, since the *Fifti Select Psalms* of Edwin Sandys (1615) did not include either of them. Psalm 114, "In exitu Israel," is an interesting choice for literary and musical reasons; the boatful of souls arriving at the shore of Dante's Purgatory (*Purgatorio*, Canto 2) are singing it, and in a famous collaboration John Sheppard, Thomas Mundy, and perhaps William Byrd each set a segment of its Latin text.[7] Cowley includes a metrical translation in *Davideis* just after his account of the musical properties of creation and the healing power of music.[8] Although metrical psalms do not improve on Coverdale, Edwin and George Sandys and the very young Milton do improve on Sternhold and Hopkins. If in Milton's Psalm 114 the sea that "shivering fled, / And sought to hide his froth-becurled head" is a boyish personification, it is less awkward than "The sea it saw and suddenly / as all amaz'd did die: / The roaring streames of Iordan's flood, reculed backwardly"; and Milton's last lines are pictorially onomatopoetic as they invoke earth's awe of the strength of him "That glassy flouds from rugged rocks can crush, / And make soft rills from fiery flint-stones gush." Milton's Psalm 136, on the other hand, provides rhymed couplets of more grace-ful simplicity – apart from a few showy phrases – than the two Sternhold and Hopkins versions. In these psalms, perhaps meant to be sung to his father's harmonized tunes, the boy is father of the man: in Psalm 114 the seascape and landscape of Canaan respond to the arrival of those who "After long toil their liberty had won," and in Psalm 136 Milton enjoins, "O let us his praises tell, / That doth the wrathfull tyrants quell."

Milton was to translate another set of psalms in 1648, the year the *Choice Psalmes* of William and Henry Lawes was published with Milton's commendatory sonnet. These too are in the common meter of approved psalm-singing and his father's psalms, with all words that are not "the very words of the text" scrupulously put into "a different Character." In Psalm 81 these underscored addi-tions give emphasis both to intelligibility (sing loud, *and clear . . . that all may hear*) and to the ordinance of joyous singing and instru-mental music on feast days, and tell an England that thought of itself as a new Israel,

> This was a Statute *giv'n of old*
> For Israel *to observe*
> A Law of Jacobs God, *to hold*
> *From whence they might not swerve.*

The rest has to do with the liberation of the Hebrews "*from slavish toyle*" and the present need to "walk [God's] *righteous* ways," suggesting that Israel under Pharaoh is the type of England under Charles; but with regard to music, it would seem to be the revolutionaries who are the oppressors.

In a letter prefixed to *A Mask* in the 1645 *Poems,* Henry Wotton praises Milton as a writer of song texts:

I should much commend the tragical part, if the lyrical did not ravish me with a certain Doric delicacy in your Songs and Odes, whereunto I must plainly confess to have seen yet nothing parallel in our language.

Milton's early poems encompass not only "delicacy" but also the "prophetick strain" sought in *Il Penseroso.* Cedric Brown has shown with great sensitivity the sense of vocation as both pastor and artist that Milton expresses in *Arcades, A Mask at Ludlow,* and *Lycidas.* Brown's discussion of the Sabrina section of *A Mask,* "rich in song," and of the Attendant Spirit as pastor and singer in the tradition of David compared with the same vocational coupling in *Lycidas,* shows how indivisible these callings were for Milton and how consistently he fulfills the office of pastor and prophet to a nation in his art.[9]

ON THE MORNING OF CHRIST'S NATIVITY

Just after his twenty-first birthday Milton wrote the poem he placed first in the *Poems* of 1645 and titled *On the morning of* CHRISTS *Nativity. Compos'd 1629.* In it the "new-enlighten'd world" receives its Maker accompanied by an infusion of heaven's music. Its opening stanzas on the paradoxical grace of the Incarnation urge the Muse to present a gift to the new child before the Magi arrive at Epiphany and to "joyn thy voice unto the Angel Quire, / From out his secret Altar toucht with hallow'd fire," making the calling of Isaiah the type of his own. The poem relates the preparation of Nature for renewal by the entry of her creator; the music that announces this birth; and the silencing and deposition of "each peculiar power," those gods who divided the world by claiming dominion over particular aspects of nature and particular peoples, the worst requiring child sacrifice, and from whose tyrannies this Child's sacrifice would offer to liberate both Nature and nations.

The poem's verbal music, an introit or prelude and "The Hymn," represents the re-creation in poetic "numbers" that, like the structure and form of much polyphony, participate in the orderly variety of the creation itself. As Alan Rudrum remarks, "Milton's language is much more complex, and so are his rhythms and his rhymes, than those of an ordinary hymn . . . Milton *writes his music into the words themselves.*"[10]

Milton's lifelong project of joining *musica humana* to the music of heaven appears in the humble boldness of dispatching his muse to join to the angel choir. When that choir appears in the Hymn, their audience is "Shepherds . . . simply chatting in a rustick row,"

> When such musick sweet
> Their hearts and ears did greet,
>   As never was by mortall finger strook,
> Divinely-warbled voice
> Answering the stringed noise,
>   As all their souls in blisfull rapture took:
> The Air such pleasure loth to lose,
> With thousand echo's still prolongs each heav'nly close.

This music is both traditional and reformed. Like the poem as a whole, it combines formal beauty with the Protestant message discernible in the fall of the idols. The singular "voice" implies intelligibility of words and greets both the shepherds' ears and their hearts. The vocal music, "answering" instrumental passages as in a verse anthem, is warbled, or melismatic, as befits jubilant tidings, and each prolonged cadence reverberates: the sonorities are not seamless but have "closes" fitting the musical structure to the structure of words. After this announcement, heaven opens and a "Globe of circular light . . . surrounds their sight" displaying ranks of Cherubim and Seraphim harping with "unexpressive notes" – that is, unexpressible, but perhaps also suprapersonal – "to Heav'n's new-born Heir." Milton does not describe the Gloria in excelsis that everyone knows the angels are singing, but the instrumental music that reformers thought had no place in earthly sabbaths, for a day the puritan Parliament in 1644 – the year before the poem's publication – would forbid celebrating by "any merriment or religious services."[11]

The angelic choirs had produced such "holy Song" once before, "when of old the sons of morning sung" (as they do in *Paradise Lost*) and brings "rustick" shepherds, devotees of Pan, the news that the Lord of Nature is among them. This music can raise fallen Nature nearer her original intimacy with Heaven, for Nature "knew such harmony alone / Could hold all Heav'n and Earth in happier union."

The "Hymn" furthers this union by invoking the nine spheres to join the nine angelic choirs and heaven's organ to keep them in time and tune:

> Ring out ye Chrystall sphears,
> Once bless our human ears,
>   (If ye have power to touch our senses so)
> And let your silver chime
> Move in melodious time;
>   And let the Base of Heav'ns deep Organ blow,
> And with your ninefold harmony
> Make up full consort to th'Angelike symphony.

Although the music of the spheres might be supposed Pythagorean, Pythagorean music was not "symphonic" and counted only fourths, fifths, and octaves as consonant intervals, making an eighteen-part consort supernumerary. (In Kepler's sun-centered universe, on the other hand, the intervals of the third and the sixth matched his measurements of the intervals between the planets, so that theoretically the consonances of polyphonic music *were* in tune with the spheres.[12]) For Milton, the "full consort" of universal and supernal music has healing power to melt "leprous sin" from "earthly mould." But "not yet"; the Babe who "lies yet in smiling infancy" (that is, silence) first "on the bitter cross / Must redeem our loss" and finally act as the "dreadfull Judge" at his second advent to complete the work of ridding the world of "Th'old Dragon."[13]

Milton incorporates and expands liturgical and pictorial contexts. The readings for the communion service on Christmas Day, Hebrews 1 and John 1, concern the identity, exaltation, and kingship of the Son as creating Word and Redeemer. The collect asks "that we being regenerate and made thy children by adoption and grace, may daily be renewed by thy Holy Spirit." The Ode's acknowledgment that "speckl'd vanity" is not yet overcome accords with the observation of John 1, the Gospel reading for

Christmas Day, that "He was in the world, and the world was made by him, and the world knew him not." Contemporary paintings, unlike modern Christmas cards, contain sober symbols: the shepherds bring lambs to the sacrificial lamb in the crib; the ox and ass recall the Lord's complaint in Isaiah 1.3, "The ox knoweth his owner, and the ass his master's crib: but . . . my people doth not consider." The event is joyous indeed, the hinge of history on which heaven opens, but the suffering to come to the child is not evaded.

With its demanding rhyme scheme, varied line length, complex structure, and numerical symbolism, Milton's poem is as diversely voiced and proportionally cadenced as a verse anthem, and its central stanzas about music are the wellspring of its form. The combination of couplets, suspended rhyme, and final alexandrines in its eight-line stanza (the full diapason of an octave) provides both close concords of sound and delayed cadences that ask the ear to hold these sounds in unity. Stanza 9, the first about holy song, with singular "voice" of the angel in Luke 2.9, intensifies the relation of words and music: "sweet" and "greet" greet each other sweetly, "voice" and "noise" are "answering" in the close rhyme of the couplet, the longer-awaited, end-stopped rhyme "took" has the effect of taking up (the "raptus" of "rapture") the expectant listener, and the alexandrine "prolongs" the stanza's own "close." In stanza 10 the sounds hollow the mouth and round the lips in "sound" and "hollow round"; the delayed rhyme for "thrilling" does not attain fulfillment until "fulfilling," as Nature herself must wait for hers. "Alone" is matched with "union," oppositely denoting oneness, and the alexandrine expresses the plenitude of the union of "Heav'n and Earth" which it holds in one extended line. The rhymes in stanza 11 continue a close-chiming of sounds with each other and with their meanings, "sight" with "light," "array'd" with "displaid," "Cherubim" with "Seraphim," "quire" (the musicians) with "Heir" (the audience for whom their music is a gift, as Milton's is). The alliterations of stanza 12 and its many consonances and assonances also have an effect of sonorous binding together, while, as H. Neville Davies notes, this "central stanza of the Ode . . . is also marked by a pivotal image: 'the well-balanced world on hinges hung.'"[14] Stanza 13, "Ring out ye Chrystall sphears," culminates this demonstration of "melodious time," marshalling sounds to which Milton has sensitized and thus blessed "our human ears." The address to the turning spheres is especially rich in round sounds and sibilants. The rhyme of "chime and time" links the harmony and measure of the cosmos with the music of language, while the identical rhyme of the final syllables of "Harmony" and "symphony," with their root meanings of agreement together, functions as tonal resolution.

The poem's construction has been described in various ways that attend to number and proportion, hence to musical structure, and to music itself as its brilliant center. Arthur E. Barker locates in it a poetic conversion experience which "crystallized Milton's conviction of special poetical calling and provided him with a definition of his function."[15] He describes the "Hymn," consisting of three balanced movements, as Milton's "first achievement of composition in pattern in the full Miltonic sense . . . resulting from his recognition of the significance of the Incarnation" in both the pattern of his life and vocation and the pattern of his poem. Maren-Sofie Røstvig shows that "Milton's gift to the child [constitutes] an image of his acts as Creator and Redeemer . . . The creative Word imposes order on chaos, and hence the words of praise offered to Christ in celebration of his Nativity must themselves be highly ordered . . . Such is the beauty and the theological appropriateness of this structure that it becomes an object of contemplation in its own right." Sanford Budick states, "The poet's aim is the location and mimetic stationing of the central, all-organizing, all-dividing entity within the totally divided and ordered cosmos. By Milton and the tradition behind him, this enthroned entity is called Mercy." C. W. R. D. Moseley discerns detailed numerical symbolism in the "Triumph" of the King of Kings.[16]

In addition to its prosodic and formal music and its links to speculative music, the Nativity Ode has connections with the practical music found in the Church of England. Lancelot Andrewes' collected sermons were published in 1629, the year of the Nativity Ode and three years after his death, for which Milton had written *Elegia Tertia (On the Death of the Bishop of Winchester)*; he had become Dean of the Chapel Royal in 1618. His sermons on the Nativity, full of musical references and explicatory Latin phrases that are also titles of well-known anthems and carols, sometimes read like a gloss on the Nativity Ode as both contemplate the tidings of the *Angeles ad pastores*. "[I]t is not enough Christ is born,

but to take benefit by His birth we are to find Him . . . For to find
Christ is all, all in all." That is the angel's sermon, and "A sermon
would have an anthem of course . . . *Gloria in excelsis*, all the
Fathers call it *hymnum Angelicum*" with "the whole choir of Angels
to make Him melody." The angel's sermon begins with a sign, that
of the humble "cratch," which foretells the cross. If Christ had
come in glory, that would be no sign, because a sign must be "contrary to the course of nature . . . The sun eclipsed, the sun in sack-
cloth . . . that is the sign here." Milton uses the eclipse to a
different purpose; the natural sun hides his head as if "his infe-
riour flame, / The new-enlightn'd world no more should need."
The lowly sign of the manger, Andrewes continues, is balanced by
"a glorious song," and "If the sign mislike you, ye cannot but like
the song, and the choir that sing it. The song I shall not be able
to reach to; will ye but see the choir?" Milton makes us see them
helmed and sworded "in glittering ranks with wings displaid, /
Harping in loud and solemn choir." The song, Andrewes
explains, comes from angels "said to be soldiers" (Luke 2.15:
"cum Angelo multitudo militiae Coelestis laudantium Deum");
"They are not in the habit of choir-men, yet they sing; they are in
the habit of men of war, yet sing of peace." And they sing part-
music, for a reason: "The choir of Heaven did it, but to set us in;
we to bear a part, and it should be a chief part, since the best part
of it is ours."[17]

If in imagination we attempt to hear as well as see Milton's angel
choir, we need to heed Andrewes' caveat, "The song I shall not be
able to reach to," and Milton's that its "inexpressive" music is such
as "never was by mortall finger strook." However, what a contemporary audience might have heard on Christmas Day can help us
not to imagine too feebly. Lively anthems in Milton's musical
environment include Byrd's "This Day was Christ Born" and
"Laetentur coeli" (to which Andrewes alludes in the 1619 Nativity
sermon), Weelkes' macaronic "Gloria in excelsis Deo," and
Tomkins' "Behold I bring you glad tidings" (*EECM* IX) with the
pattern of solo tidings and choral response as in Luke and in
Milton's Ode.

Amner's "O Ye little Flock"[18] illustrates the way that individual
voices emerge in the verse anthem, this one composed for six
voices with organ or string accompaniment – "divinely-warbled
voice / Answering the stringed noise."

(Verse, medius 2)	O ye little flock, O ye faithful shepherds, O ye hosts of heav'n, give ear unto my song.
(Verse, MMAATB)	The shepherds were a-watching of their flocks by night, and behold an angel. And the glory of the Lord shone round about them, and they all quaked for fear.
(Full choir)	And the glory of the Lord shone round about them, and they all quaked for fear.
(Verse, medius 2)	Fear not, for unto you is born a saviour,
(Verse, MMA)	and not to you alone, but to all people, which is Christ our Lord.
(Full choir)	And suddenly an host of heav'nly angels sung and praised God, and said: Glory be to God on high, peace be on earth, good-will to men. Alleluia.
(Verse, medius 1 and 2, antiphonally)	And they cry one to another, holy, holy, holy
(MMA)	holy is the Lord of hosts:
(Full choir)	All the World is full of his glory, holy, holy, holy is the Lord of hosts: all the world is full of his glory. Alleluia.

The text contains two features pertinent to Milton, its bold summons to the "hosts of heav'n" along with the shepherds to "give ear unto my song" and the paraphrase of the Sanctus from the passage in Isaiah 6 that Milton also alludes to. The setting accords with Milton in a cross-relation recalling Christ's piercing on "which is Christ our Lord," a reminder that the new-born Babe "on the bitter cross / Must redeem our loss," and in an almost Monteverdian Alleluia for part two and an almost Handelian chorus for part three, like the bursts of brilliant music in Milton's poem.

Sacred Hymns also includes a double consort anthem (that is, two texts with different music joined together) for six voices with viols, "Lo, how from heav'n like stars" and "I bring you tiding." The text begins with a striking metaphor of light, summons the shepherds, and brings together the music of the spheres with the angelic Gloria.

> Lo, how from heav'n like stars the angels flying
> bring back the day to earth in midnight lying.
> Up shepherds up, this night is born your King,
> you never heard the spheres such music sing.

I bring you tiding, of joy abiding.
The Prince of Light, is born this night.
So up he sprang, and all heav'n sang.
Joy to the sorry, to God be glory. Alleluia.

Amner's highly chromatic, rhythmically free style sounds astonishingly modern. On the words "The Prince of Light is born this night" the unexpected accidentals and unprepared modulations cause harmonic instability that makes the resolutions particularly bright and reassuring, yet these are brief; just when you might expect the music to rise to a core key or mode and rest there, it chromatically veers elsewhere. The music, like Milton's words, does not allow us to think that night has been entirely vanquished yet, but rather unsettles any rest we might imagine that stable offers where angels stand in servicable order.

Milton's poem also has a musical analogue in Orlando Gibbons' "See, See the Word is incarnate" (*EECM* iii[19]), a through-composed verse anthem for five solo voice parts (MAATB) and six-part chorus (the parts variously divided), with organ or strings, composed when Milton was about eight years old. Like his poem, it incorporates qualities of light and shadow, brilliant joy and sober prophecy, flexible but controlled proportions, varied voicing, spatial and temporal synthesis, and temporal and eternal interfusion. The prose text attributed to Dr. Goodman, Dean of Rochester, is about the Incarnation in particular but incorporates Christ's ministry, mission, passion, resurrection, ascension, and enthronement "where all the choir of heaven all jointly sing," and enjoins human hosannas, for "the serpent's head is bruised, Christ's kingdom exalted, and heaven laid open to sinners."

Both anthem and poem begin with a sense of immediacy, proceed to the Virgin birth, the Magi, the angel choir, the shepherds, the Gloria and the proclamation of peace. Peter le Huray points out that Gibbons manages the long text within only three strong cadences.[20] Milton's "Hymn," too, has three marked sections or movements. The anthem begins, like the poem's "hymn," in a subdued tone with an alto or tenor solo or section (editions vary) and adds a voice or voice part for each verse until the fifth, which returns to single voicing. The five narrative sections, mainly for lower parts with a muted effect, are followed by contrastingly brilliant choral responses. The first entry of the full choir, for the Gloria, modulates from B flat minor to F major to produce a burst of aural light. While the narrative continues through the life and passion of Christ, the chorus still responds to the birth: "Let us welcome such a guest with Hosanna"; Milton calls his Muse "To welcome him." The anthem concludes with "a glorious ascension . . . where all the choir of heav'n all jointly sing: Glory be to the Lamb that sitteth on the throne . . . we triumph in victory, the serpent's head bruised [though not broken], Christ's Kingdom exalted, and heav'n laid open to sinners."[21] Milton, also referring to Revelation, is more cautious: full triumph will delay until the "terrour" of the "trump of doom" and the Last Judgement. Our bliss "But now begins" – it only begins, but it does so now, at this birth, from which time "Th'old Dragon under ground / In straiter limits bound" still, but "Not half so far . . . Swindges the scaly Horrour of his foulded tail."

SOLEMN MUSICK

At a Solemn Musick encapsulates in twenty-eight lines (a perfect number, as Moseley observes, equalling the sum of its divisors[22]) a history of the world from creation to apocalypse, a recognition of the union of words and music, a reaffirmation of Milton's vocation, and an apologia for the arts. It describes an eternity of harmony among diverse beings, out of which human ones and the world in their charge have fallen, and into which they can reenter when they choose. "Solemn" has no gloomy or lugubrious connotations; its roots connect it to occasions of serious joy, as in the "Solemnization of Matrimony." "Wed your divine sounds" invokes the reunion of music and texts by composers who did not follow the letter of Cranmer's proscription of sacred polyphony but made words intelligible by both baring and enacting them. For the worship of "all creatures," polyphony is the most expressive form. Since Milton had not yet been to Italy, we may hear in the mind's ear the moderate polyphony of English sacred music in which the musical lines and the words are twin-born.

Milton wrote this poem sometime in the early 1630s, perhaps after listening to the choir of Westminster Abbey or St. Paul's during one of his trips to London "for learning music and mathematics" (*SM* xvii), or, since "a . . . Musick" suggests occasional rather than service music, of an ensemble such as "the King's musitians" or "the Duke's musit[ians]" whose visit is recorded in the Christ's College account books for 1628–29. What the poem tells us is that the music was vocal and that as in *Il Penseroso* it could "bring all heav'n before mine eyes" and ears. The poet invokes the combined power of words and music to present to our upraised imaginations (and we have a part in the upraising) the "undisturbèd song of pure concent" sung by angels and saints before God's throne, so that "we on Earth," who have been thrown temporarily out of step and off pitch by "Man's First Disobedience" and its effects, may "keep in tune with heav'n" not only after but "till" God unites us to his "celestial consort." In theme and form the poem combines a sense of serene and timeless plenitude in heaven with a concern (like Andrewes') for the part of human voices in the harmony. The word that most does the knitting is the humble "till" of the third to last line.

Milton's intention in this respect may be gathered from his revisions. The Trinity College manuscript[23] has, scored out, "that wee below may learn with hart & voice . . . rightly to answer . . . & in our lives & in our song may keepe in tune with heaven," a thought not revoked but made more concise and original ("With hart & voice" is a standard phrase) in the final version. He does, however, revoke a pair of lines in which he asks the spheare-borne sisters[24] to "snatch us from the earth a while, us of our selves and home bred woes beguile": earth and home-bred woes are not to be escaped through art but regenerated and repaired by it. And he omits the injunction to leave out "those harsh chromatick jarres / of clamourous sin that all our musick marres," first changing "chromatick" to "ill-sounding" and then excising the line: a recognition that chromaticism was an expressive part of "solemn musick." The contrast between these revisions and more transcendent treatments of the Court of Heaven indicate Milton's concern with keeping "in tune with heav'n" in the present world.

Milton treats the Apocalypse historically and typologically (rather than only eschatologically), as did the medieval commentary of Berengaudis, often included in Anglo-Norman manuscripts of the Apocalypse, which says that "the beauty of the saints begins in this life and is made perfect in everlasting blessedness,"[25] and *The Lamb of God* (the "Ghent Altarpiece") of Jan and Hubert Van Eyck, which puts the history of the world from Adam and Eve to the Adoration of the Lamb within one's view, as Milton puts it within one sentence, and places contemporary people among the great multitude with recognizable buildings behind them. When the panels are closed, on ferial days, we see the Annunciation taking place in the city of Ghent. When they are open, on feast days, beneath the heavenly realms humans and angels worship the Lamb, and identifiable kings approach who are actually at war, but who, if they behaved as they do in the painting, would answer with "undiscording voice" rather than "harsh din."

Since "pure concent" means pitches tuned as nearly as possible to the intervals of earthly physics and eternal numbers, keeping "in tune with Heav'n" is a literal as well as a spiritual act. It requires celestial singing lessons, and Milton gives one. Form and prosody suggest the kind of music composed by William Byrd, for example, who employs textural richness while letting words shape the musical lines. Byrd writes in the dedication of his *Gradualia* of 1605 that sacred words have "such a profound and hidden power that to one thinking upon things divine and diligently and earnestly pondering them, all the fittest numbers occur as if of themselves."[26] Milton says in *Paradise Lost*: "I . . . feed on thoughts, that voluntary move / Harmonious numbers" (3.37–38). The Te Deum from Byrd's Great Service of 1600 (example 11) illustrates the rhythmic freedom and varied voicing of "fittest numbers" that change fluidly over the steady pulse. On "Holy, Lord God of Sabaoth" comes a marked shift to triple rhythm; "All the earth doth worship thee" is fittingly homophonic, with held notes emphasizing *all, worship,* and *thee*; the cry of the angels is antiphonal in response to Isaiah 6, "one cried to another"; yet the whole canticle is an unbroken, interwoven concent of many voices.

Milton presents the apocalyptic vision in one unbroken sentence of twenty-four lines,[27] with a half cadence at "everlastingly." The long-suspended rhyme with "Jubily" overarches and unites the individual phrases as the "undisturbed song" of polyphonic voicing does. At "To him that sits thereon" there is a marked shift to a three-beat line. After the half cadence, "all creatures" enter this paradisal syntax. After the full cadence, the final quatrain (necessary both formally and thematically to complete the "perfect number") imitates the metrical psalmody of congregational singing by its end-stopped lines and march-like rhythms, suitable to two-footed beings. But the iambic beat subsides at "celestial consort" and the closing hexameter reaches back toward the seamless polyphony of heavenly "concent."

Example 11. William Byrd, Te Deum from the Great Service, bars 22–32

The scriptural and liturgical texts behind the poem were set with special zest by Renaissance composers because they are about music and challenge innovative word-painting: particularly the many psalm verses about singing (among which Psalms 95, 100, and 98 are a part of the daily office in the Book of Common Prayer) and the angelic Sanctus from the visions of Isaiah and St. John, incorporated into the Communion service and the Te Deum. In addition, Milton was surely thinking of the readings in the prayerbook lectionary (which retains portions of the Apocrypha) for All Saints Day and familiar with their settings.

The first lesson for Matins is Wisdom 3. Byrd's motet on Wisdom 3.1–3 (*BE* vIa, from *Gradualia*, 1605) is comparable with the music of Milton's "just spirits": "Justorum animae in manu Dei sunt, et

Example 11. (*cont.*)

non tanget illos tormentum mortis: visi sunt oculis insipientium mori: illi autem sunt in pace"; the Authorized Version reads, in part, "But the souls of the righteous are in the hand of God, and there shall no torment touch them. In the sight of the unwise they seem to die: and their departure is taken for misery . . . but they are in peace." Byrd "justifies" or makes straight the words "Justorum animae" in nearly homophonic chords. Suspensions and ascending voice parts on "in manu Dei" provide a kinesthetic experience of shared and upheld poise, while divided entrances at "non tanget illos" provide motion and texture for the word "touch." "Tormentum mortis" moves into what we would now call a minor key, and at "insipientium" the moving parts restlessly contradict each other. "Illi autem sunt in pace" uses gently subsiding imitative phrases, free of metrical stress and responsive to each other, not only to express peace, but to create mimetically the experience of making peace.

The readings for Evensong are Wisdom 5 and Apocalypse 19, in which John hears "a great voice of much people in heaven, saying, Alleluja." Thomas Weelkes' "Alleluia. I heard a voice,"[28] its text surrounded and pierced by alleluias and its five-part texture making unusual use of high trebles, is appropriate to Milton's diction of upliftedness by music "able to pierce" dead things and present to our "high-rais'd phantasie" a universal song through "perfect Diapason." The Communion begins with the collect asking God who has "knit together thy elect in one Communion and fellowship" for "grace so to follow thy holy Saints in all virtuous and godly living that wee may come to those vnspeakable ioyes, which thou hast prepared for them that vnfainedly loue thee." Thomas Tomkins' setting (*EECM* v) gradually "knit[s] together" polyphonic voices, reaching homophony at "fellowship" and ending in eight-part antiphonal polyphony. The Gospel is Matthew 5, the Beatitudes, a text that also "knits" heaven and earth. The epistle, Apocalypse 7, includes the passage "[L]oe, a great multitude . . . of all nations, and people, and tongues stood before the Seat, and before the Lambe, clothed with long white garments, and palmes in their hands . . . And all the Angels stood in the compasse of the Seate . . . and worshipped God." Amner provides a double verse anthem that contrasts to Milton's poem by its much simpler text:

> Thus sings the heav'nly choir
> With zeal burning like fire,
> Alleluia.
> And all the saints with purest robes attending
> Upon the Lamb, their knees full lowly bending.
> Alleluia.
>
> The heav'ns stood all amazed,
> The earth upon them gazed.
> Alleluia.
> At length both heav'n and earth for joy confounded
> With voice as loud as thunder sweetly resounded.
> Alleluia.

Amner's setting,[29] in five-part polyphony but with considerable use of parallel duets and trios, declaims the text in largely stepwise and syllabic tunes, with long notes on stressed syllables such as Milton commended in Lawes;[30] but it admits melisma on the alleluias, rolling runs on "thunder," and a series of melismatic modulations on "gazed" that represent the changes within the amazed watchers. Other "madrigalisms" occur with intensifying accidentals on "zeal" and "amazed," agitated rhythms on "burning like fire," and descending whole notes on "bending." The penultimate verse line enacts a polyphonic mingling of heaven and earth in which three voices sing the words "heaven" and "earth" together, then "at length" confound them, the alto singing "earth" while the other four parts sing "heaven" and all five voices coming solidly down on "earth" before breaking into overlapped polyphony on "for joy confounded." The phrase "Sweetly resounded" literally re-sounds within the polyphonic texture twenty-three times, sweetly sharpened by accidentals.

At a Solemn Musick responds to contemporary anthems in its word-painting as well as its rhythms and syntax. The first line of simple iambic pentameter is "Their loud up-lifted Angel trumpets blow," which by its metrical regularity imitates a trumpet fanfare as vocal composers would do. "Touch their immortal harps of golden wires" shifts the accent to the first syllable, giving it a tactile, plucking quality. Byrd and his contemporaries could hardly set the words "rising" or "falling" without ascending or descending notes, "rejoice" without syncopation or melisma, "sin" without dissonance, or "everlastingly" without prolongation. Milton incorporates such mimesis into prosody. "Disproportion'd sin," with its plosives and clashing consonants, and the syntactic tensions at "sin / Jarr'd" and "harsh din / Broke" contrast with the suavity of "whose love their motion sway'd / In perfect Diapason": a musical concept that means, appropriately, more than one thing. First, it means a perfect octave, for Pythagoras the purest consonance: earth should be in tune with heaven a well-tuned octave of spheres below it. Byrd illustrates this concept musically in the Te Deum by descending an octave from "Heav'n" to "earth" in five voice parts (beginning at example 11, bar 30). Second, it means all the consonances of a scale or mode: Greek *dia*, through, and *pason*, all. An octave is not a very interesting consonance, and all the notes sounded together are not consonant at all, but the two meanings work together in the poem. Within the pure concent of heaven and earth when they are in tune, all sing their parts justly, using all the combinations of notes their diversity allows, kept harmonious and commensurate by the sway of their great choirmaster. Milton's phrase "those just Spirits," like Byrd's setting of the words "justorum animae," is a mimesis of justification. One can not articulate it clearly without accenting each word equally. "O may we soon again renew that song" probably causes most readers to raise the pitch of their voices, and "To live with him, and sing in endless morn of light" suggests a melismatic suspension ending on a brilliant chord. In these ways, Milton demonstrates the observation of Jacopo Mazzoni, one of the literary theorists he recommends in *Of Education*, that "Poetry takes its instruments entirely from music, since in that art there is the greatest power to bring the greatest delight to the human soul."[31]

Reading Milton's solemn music is an exercise in multiple responsiveness that tropes its tenor, which *is* responsiveness: of voice to verse; of the listener to both; of all creatures to each other's voices and to the Maestro whose love makes them a choir; to the just measure and just relations of which music is experience and metaphor. By a mimesis of retuning according to musical principles, Milton exercises his readers' capacities to keep in tune with heaven "here on earth."

MILTON AND ITALY

Milton became acquainted with Italian music theory through reading and with Italian music both through Henry Lawes and during his travels in Italy in 1638–39.[32] He may have met visiting Italian composers in his father's music circle, and long before his trip to Italy he wrote love sonnets in Italian to a lady who was named for her native Emilia in northern Italy and who sang.[33] They praise the "Donna leggiadra il cui bel nome honora / L'herbosa val di Rheno," the lovely lady whose name honors her country. In "Qual in colle aspro," Love draws from the poet's lips the new flower of a foreign language, summoning the image of Flora in Botticelli's *Primavera*. "Diodati, e te'l dirò con maraviglio" praises the lady's speech and her singing that could divert the laboring moon from the midst of the sky. Unlike Petrarchan lute song and madrigal texts on the cruelty of unresponsive women, Milton's sonnets emulate those "who never wrote but honour of them to whom they devote their verse."[34]

According to his nephew and pupil Edward Philips, while in

Venice Milton "shipped up a parcel of curious and rare books which he had picked up in his travels . . . particularly a chest or two of choice music-books of the best masters flourishing about that time in Italy, namely, Luca Marenzio, Monte Verde, Horatio Vecchi, Cif[r]a, the Prince of Venosa, and several others" (*SM* xxxv). These composers are now known chiefly for madrigals and theatre music, and in the case of Monteverdi dramatic monodies such as the *Lamento d'Arianna* and operas that combine monody with madrigal choruses. All were connected to church or court or both, and all wrote both madrigals and motets, in most cases for the entire church year, many of them polychoral or *concertato*, as well as sacred song and instrumental music for private use. It seems probable that Milton's two chests contained monodies, madrigals, keyboard music, and sacred music, and that he sang and played from them insofar as domestic and civil disorders and, after his blindness, memory allowed.[35]

Speculative connections between Milton and these composers may be adduced, some pertaining to poems written before the Italian journey. Luca Marenzio wrote eighteen books of madrigals, sensitively setting texts by Sannazaro, Petrarch, Tasso, and Guarini. Raymond Waddington points out similarities between Orazio Vecchi's *Mascherata della Malinconia* (from *Dialoghi da Cantarsi et Concertarsi*, Venice, 1608) and Milton's *L'Allegro*.[36] His published books of motets and *Sacrae Cantiones* include "Euge serue bone" (possibly pertinent to Abdiel, along with Tye's Mass *Euge bone*), an interesting "Cantate Domino canticum novum," "Per feminam mors" (Eve, of course, with Mary as antitype), and a setting of the Benedicite Omnia Opera Domini that might suggest an antiphonal structure, though with more voices, for the morning prayer of Adam and Eve.[37] Carlo Gesualdo's *Sacrae Cantiones* for five, six, and seven voices of 1603 include "Sancti Spiritus," "Venit lumen tuum," "Illumina nos," and others with texts pertinent to Milton's invocations. Although the least known of these composers today, Antonio Cifra was the most prolific choral composer of the Roman school and also, like Monteverdi, a writer of monodic arias. His cantata-like *Angeles ad Pastores* contains dialogue between solo voices and choir. Henry Lawes playfully set the table of contents from Cifra's *Scerzi et Arie* (Venice, 1614), which his countrymen proclaimed "'a rare Italian Song.'"[38] His *Sacrae Cantiones* for two to eight voices was published in Rome in 1638, the year of Milton's sojourn.

Monteverdi's concertante psalms fit Adam's description of angelic music in *Paradise Lost* 4.677–89. Milton's identification of himself with Orpheus in early poems may have spiced an interest in *Orfeo*, in which Musica sings the prologue and Orpheus reclaims his bride from death by charming Charon, Pluto, and Proserpina by his singing, only to lose her again. The story has many parallels and contrasts pertinent to the story of Adam and Eve, but an ending in which Orpheus is deified and Eurydice must remain in the underworld forever: an outcome that may profitably be contrasted with the conclusion of *Paradise Lost.*

In Rome Milton heard the celebrated Neapolitan singer Leonora Baroni, whom he praised in three epigrams. In 1638, the year of his journey, Monteverdi published in Venice his eighth book of madrigals, *Madrigali Guerrieri, et Amorosi*, in which the sensuous close harmonies of earlier books have given way to more virtuosic singing by smaller forces, some with solo parts similar to monody. It includes several epigrams by Giambattista Guarini and others, and it seems possible that Milton chose this genre partly because such epigrams were among the works that he heard Leonora sing.[39]

Guarini's "Mentre vaga Angioletta," set as a virtuoso duet for two tenors with instrumental accompaniment, resembles and contrasts with *Ad Leonoram Romae Canentem* (*CM* 1:228). Its speaker says that while Angioletta's singing allures all gentle souls, he wonders how the Spirit of Music catches and shapes her throat and makes of it, in no customary way, a fountain of exquisite harmony: "Musico spirto prende / Fauci canore, e seco forma, e finge / Per non usata vita / Garula, e maistrevol armonia." A description follows of the many virtuosities of singers, set to music that demonstrates those agilities, and the ending evokes Milton's "O Nightingale": thus by singing and singing again, the heart – miracle of love! – is made a nightingale, and, not to stay sad, takes flight.

The epigram to Leonora is a more serious matter, and I have discussed it at length elsewhere.[40] In lines slightly reminiscent of Guarini Milton writes

> Quid mirum? Leonora tibi si gloria major,
> Nam tua præsentem vox sonat ipsa Deum.
> Aut Deus, aut vacui certè mens tertia cœli
> Per tua secretò guttura serpit agens;

Serpit agens, facilisque docet mortalia corda
Sensim immortali assuescere posse sono.

[What wonder, Leonora, if to you comes greater glory: your voice itself expresses God among us. God, or at least a third mind leaving heaven, steals on his own through your throat and works his way; works his way, gently leading mortal hearts sensibly to grow used to immortal sounds.]

The epigram says very little about Leonora's singing – she is Art, raising our phantasies – but the poet's own language ranges the cosmos and returns to a single voice because it is often through single voices that God speaks: "Quòd si cuncta quidem Deus est, per cunctaque fusus, / In te una loquitur, caetera mutus habet." In William Shullenberger's translation, "If God, through all things fused, himself is ᴀll, / In just one, you, he speaks; all else turns still."[41]

CREATION MUSIC: "PARADISE LOST"

Milton's epic develops the themes condensed in *At a Solemn Musick*. It sings of "the fair musick that all creatures made" *in principio*, the jar of "disproportion'd sin," and ways human beings and "the Quire / Of Creatures wanting voice" (9.198–99) can rejoin the song. Its prosody pays a musician's attention to the relations of sound and sense. Although most good poets use mimetic sound, the joining of "voice and vers" in contemporary music surely contributes to the extraordinary awareness of prosodic opportunities that invests each line and the extraordinary resonance among them.

Milton imitates the sounds of war naturalistically, as when "to confirm his words, out-flew / Millions of flaming swords, drawn from the thighs / Of mighty Cherubim" who "fierce with grasped Arms / Clashd on thir sounding shields the din of war, / Hurling defiance toward the Vault of Heav'n" (1. 663–69). He renders Satan's "remorse and passion" as composers render sighs, in broken lines, when he addresses his troops – who have also, militarily speaking, broken lines – and his grammatical confusion expresses both his state and theirs: "O Myriads of immortal Spirits, O powers / Matchless, but with th' Almighty, and that strife / Was not inglorious, though the event was dire, / As this place testifies, and this dire change Hateful to utter"(1.622–26). When Adam becomes conscious of being alive, even the most sedentary reader can be caught up in his kinetic vigor as

> Straight toward Heav'n my wond'ring Eyes I turn'd,
> And gaz'd a while the ample Sky, till rais'd
> By quick instinctive motion up I sprung,
> As thitherward endeavoring, and upright
> Stood on my feet.   (8.257–61)

No singer of madrigals would miss the slow open vowels as Adam contemplates the heavens, the doubling of vowels at "Eyes I" like a lover's two-note gaze, the turn of the line at "turn'd," the suspension at "rais'd," the quickening of rhythm as Adam springs, and the way he lands on his feet – and the two feet of trochee and iamb – at the caesura.

When Raphael, whom God has sent to warn Adam and Eve after the petition in their morning hymn, has concluded his narrative of the War in Heaven, Adam asks for an account of the creation which he calls "thy Song" (7.72, 107). Creation brings number and proportion to the elements of chaos in a fabric woven of many lines, each day's work evoking a choral response "When the morning stars sang together, and all the sons of God shouted for joy" (Job 38.7). Raphael's account is, line for line, perhaps the richest collection of mimetic prosody in English, in which every act and living thing is described in words whose sounds imitate that act or life.

Many madrigals and psalm settings contain imitations of nature's voices. William Byrd's birds warble imitatively (in both senses) and beasts play rhythmically in "This sweet and merry month of May." Not only birds (enabling him to pun on his own name) and beasts but worms and dolphins romp in his setting of Thomas Watson's "Let others praise," written "In gratification unto Master John Case, for his learned book lately made in praise of Music" (1589; *BE* XVI):

> [H]e wrytes of sweetly turning Sphaeres,
> how Byrds, & Beasts & wormes reioyce,
> how Dolphyns lou'd Arions voice,
> he makes a frame for Midas eares.

Byrd gives the dolphins a playful leap, especially in the treble II and bass parts, and decoratively dots Arion's name in arched curves – like Milton's "bended dolphins" – with a reharmonization at the cadence on "eares."

Of course, imitative prosody is not dependent on word-setting. Vergil's *Georgics* and Ovid's *Metamorphoses* sometimes imitate the gaits, flights, and voices of the creatures. But Milton uses several kinds of prosodic mimesis that singing madrigals would make audiences more aware of and some kinds that neither poet nor reader would have been likely to think of without it. For example, madrigal composers were apt to ornament words having to do with the senses to alert the hearers'. Milton's Raphael alerts the senses by such words even when they do *not* refer to sense experience; he extracts double meanings from their positions in the passage. At the creation of the fish (7.309–416), "Forthwith the Sounds and Seas, each Creek and Bay / With Fry innumerable swarm," Milton calls attention to Raphael's virtuosic display of sounds by the word "Sounds," though it turns out to mean something else. He calls attention to sight as fish "sporting with quick glance / Show to the Sun thir wav'd coats dropt with Gold"; the glance is of light, not sight, but the quick succession of single syllables and the enjambment mime both kinds of glancing. At "Sea: part" the caesura mimes "part" meaning separate, while the sense is "a portion." By these syntactic puns he alerts both the senses and the wits; by his displays of mimetic sounds he connects our senses and wits empathetically with the creatures and their elements.

Milton's attention to the relation of image and sound, I believe, was nurtured by his musical experience. But the actual performance of music enters the prayers of Adam and Eve and fills the angelic anthems that provide the chorus of *Paradise Lost*. Two problems about Milton's choral Heaven persistently arise: the problem of interest and the problem of monotheism.

The anthems of Milton's angels have been imagined in ways that make Heaven seem uninteresting. Compared with the drama and profusion of other passages, their language is relatively abstract and serene. Thomas Greene remarks that in his epic Milton

> had not . . . lost his conservative distrust of language, which had rather
> been deepening with the years. It affects both that style Milton
> accommodated to heaven and the other he accommodated to hell. In
> heaven it is reflected in the abstract and colorless speeches of God and
> the decorous choral hymns of the angels which aim at stark simplicity.[42]

Milton does not attempt to depict heavenly utterance by baroque display, but his attitude towards the elements of his own act of creation in "Harmonious numbers" does not seem governed by distrust of the heavenly Muse. He distrusted the malicious abuse and the pusillanimous misuse of language, and represents them in Hell, but his primary interest, judging from the illimitable richness of his own, was in regenerating as much as possible of the beauty and utility of the original gift of language under the direction of "that eternal Spirit who can enrich with all utterance."

For angelic anthems Milton frequently defers to biblical and liturgical language; and they are porous to the music of the psalms and canticles to which they allude, as his sun is to light. In them he demonstrates the premise of the young Christ in *Paradise Regain'd* that "*Sion's* songs" are all the music and poetry one needs by showing them seminal of the new songs Psalms 98 and 149 exhort congregations to sing. The biblical pretexts may provide a sense of plainness by their familiarity and unembellished style, but they are astonishing texts, and Milton sang them and heard them sung to astonishing music.

The problem of monotheism is more acute because of the easy equation between monotheism and monarchy and because of the violence that has been done to life and conscience in its name. In spite of Milton's arguments for religious and political liberty, or because they promote a Christian republic, to many readers the "pure concent" with which the saints and angels and all creatures sing "To their great Lord, whose love their motion sway'd" in *At a Solemn Musick* and the hosannas with which faithful angels greet divine acts and announcements in *Paradise Lost* suggest an authoritarian political theology. Stanley Fish appears to think that the heavenly choirs sing in unison when he worries that the prophecy that "God shall be All in All" (3.331–41) opens "the prospect of merging in an undifferentiated union" that "turns into the horror of a uni-verse in which all distinctions will have been effaced."[43] Marshall Grossman calls the harmony of the angels in response to this prophecy "a final, implicit metaphor for the dialectic of the individual and the community to which he or she is joined by the measured rule of an internal law ('Umpire Conscience') and the shared 'light after light' in which that law is read." But he also finds that "The ultimate resolution of the historical process is understood as the abolition of all difference."[44]

If the harmony of Milton's angels is a metaphor for the kind of earthly or heavenly community he hopes for, we need to consider what kind of voicing produces that harmony.

"No voice exempt" is the narrator's political comment on the first angelic anthem, "no voice but well could join / Melodious part, such concord is in Heav'n." "Melodious part" implies not unison chant but distinct voice parts, and the phrase's musical contexts suggest the diverse voicing, the interplay of solo and ensemble passages, and the alternations, tensions, supensions, and resolutions that constitute a "dialectic of the individual and the community" in English music from Taverner to Amner and in the *stile concertato* and the *stile concertante* that Milton heard in Italy. In this music all lines have equal interest and importance; as David Wulstan says of even so complex a work as Tallis' forty-voice *Spem in alium*, "[I]t is possible for each singer to imagine that he has been given the most telling part of the texture."[45] In addition, each voice has its own timbre and in verse anthems and services its moments of singularity. These diverse voices carefully balanced in response to each other represent what Milton calls "the fair musick that all creatures made" before "disproportion'd sin" broke its beauty and that he thinks inspired human art can help "all creatures" make again; and it implies a style of government admitting dissonance in which "no voice but well could join" in a variously concenting commonwealth.

When Milton's angels sing on earth they employ both solo and choral voicing, for both antiphonal and full choir, as Adam reminds Eve,

> Sole, or responsive each to other's note,
> Singing thir great Creator: oft in bands
> While they keep watch, or nightly rounding walk,
> With Heav'nly touch of instrumental sounds
> In full harmonic number join'd, thir songs
> Divide the night, and lift our thoughts to Heaven.
>   (4.683–88)

Milton's well-known distrust of high-church ritual (*Of Reformation, CM* iii:20, 74; *Of Prelatical Episcopacy, CM* iii:87–88) does not apply in heaven, where the angels raise their hymns in impromptu jubilation. They have no written notes and no choral director – their "motion" is "sway'd" by "love" that apparently, like the author's thoughts, "voluntary move / Harmonious numbers" (3.37–38). Yet their music resembles the music of the English

Church, the multichoral polyphony of the Roman one, and the *concertato* and *concertante* styles of Monteverdi, whose *Selva morale et spirituale*, largely psalm settings, printed in 1640, was probably being sung while he was in Venice and does not confuse piety with austerity. It is the kind of music the puritan reformers proscribed; Cromwell banned it at Ely and let his army destroy part-books and organs. Such prohibitions applied only to the church – other gatherings could sing as they chose – but since both Paradise and Heaven are models of the worshipping community, Milton's angels seem oddly unreformed. The question arises whether Mammon's allegation of "Forc'd Halleluiahs" (2.243) is a critique of the Laudian church. Mammon is no austere reformer, however, but the advocate of conspicuous, self-glorifying consumption, of art gone wrong. Doctrinal objections to high Anglican ceremonies do not pertain in Paradise or Heaven, where "the beauty of holiness" is innocent of snobbery or manipulation, no one is deceived by iconic symbols, no one sings only to show off, and no one is unable to join in. In their prayers, Adam and Eve are the whole congregation and contain the whole human race. They sing, so far, without instrumental accompaniment, their voices "More tunable than needed Lute or Harp / To add more sweetness" (5.151–52). The angels use all kinds of instruments, and all voices "join / Melodious part." Milton leaves each reader free to imagine the angels' music, but his descriptions of their performances, the materiality of his heaven, and the pleasures of angelic companionship and embraces give every encouragement to imagine all the kinds of choral music Milton knew by those who compose, as Byrd says, by "diligently and earnestly pondering" the words.

Chronologically, the first music in *Paradise Lost* is not a hymn but "song and dance" in response to the appointment of the Son as "Head" of the gathered Hierarchies with "Holy Memorials, acts of Zeal and Love" emblazoned on their banners. This announcement provokes one archangel's rebellion and initiates the epic action. But the response of the angelic orders is curiously usual. Their dance and song and the suggestion that the angels have been occupied with memorable "acts" tell us much about angelic life.

> That day, as other solemn days, they spent
> In song and dance about the sacred Hill,
> Mystical dance, which yonder starry Sphere

Of Planets and of fixt in all her Wheels
Resembles nearest, mazes intricate,
Eccentric, intervolv'd, yet regular
Then most, when most irregular they seem:
And in thir motions harmony Divine
So smooths her charming notes, that God's own ear
Listens delighted.   (5.618–27)

Milton's syntax wheels through the enjambments of "Sphere" and "Wheels," and his prosody breaks into intricate sound-figures at "mazes intricate" to stabilize on the spondee of "Then most," then spins off this momentary irregularity to regularize the line about seeming irregularity while playing against the more halting "yet regular" the more lightly running "most irregular." The syntactical energy of the whole passage pours into "Listens," which is what not only God's ear but also the reader's does, not only to that day's dance but to the whole poem. The universe, created later, imitates this dance; Raphael, gestures toward it "yonder" and uses astronomical terms to show Adam what the angelic dance is like. His tone of seraphic pleasure is also Milton's pleasure in describing the art of poetry he is exercising as, itself, dance and music as intervolved and vagarious, yet ordered, as the starry wheels.

After dance and song, evening comes ("for change delectable") and the angels, with the good appetites of dancers, "turn / Desirous" to their feast and "rubied Nectar" in a symposium of "communion sweet," while God watches "rejoicing in their joy." When "ambrosial Night" springs from God's mountain, the angels sleep, "save those who in thir course / Melodious Hymns about the sovran Throne / Alternate all night long." "Alternate" has, as is appropriate to the word itself, two meanings. The angels take turns, and they sing antiphonally.

Readers for whom dancing and singing are not great pleasures, or who simply want to get on with the story, may not stop to imagine the implications of this description of heavenly life. Like the creation, and like the eminent acts that issue out of the angelic Orders, the dances can be intricate because the dancers participate in an underlying pattern. More freedom would be chaos, which is not freedom at all. The art that most perfectly expresses the varied abundance that issues out of order and degree is music. However, the angels do not dance perpetually, as the stars do; the dance is their way of expressing communal joy in the Center to which they may move eccentrically.

Are we to suppose God tyrannical in his announcement of the Son's vicegerency and the loyal angels indifferent in their diurnal song and dance? Milton offers the reader the same political choice God offers the angels. Satan (as he will come to be called) claims that the angels' "Imperial Titles . . . assert / Our being ordain'd to govern, not to serve." (Govern whom?) Abdiel protests his assumption of equality with the Son "by whom, / As by his Word the mighty Father made / All things, ev'n thee," and asserts that the angels' glory is not "by his Reign obscur'd, / But more illustrious made, since he the Head / One of our number thus reduc't becomes" (5.835–43). The rebel angel disputes this point and claims that they are "self-begot, self-rais'd / By our own quick'ning power," in "fatal course . . . the birth mature / Of this our native Heav'n," contradictorily denying a prior cause and ascribing it to fate. Later Raphael will describe Earth generating the animals as part of the Creator's providential (if Lucretian) method of bringing forth; here the Adversary supposes that Heaven generated the angels but begs the question of the first cause that Abdiel has just so confidently proclaimed. Since Abdiel's version, already given credence by his fearless solitary truth-telling, is confirmed by Raphael's affirmation that the creating Word is omnific (7.217), either Satan's dimming mind has forgotten this intuitive knowledge or he is deliberately substituting a new creation myth of his own for the purpose of gaining a kind of political power whose manifestations in the world are entirely unmusical.

When the Son is about to go forth in the Chariot of Paternal Deity to quell the rebels, he obediently assumes "Sceptre and Power," which he "gladlier shall resign, when in the end / Thou shalt be All in All" and he, the Son, will become principal singer in the choir of the blessed:

> Then shall thy Saints unmixt, and from th'impure
> Far separate, circling thy holy Mount
> Unfeigned *Halleluiahs* to thee sing,
> Hymns of high praise, and I among them chief.
> (6.742–45)

The Messiah will sing with his disciples after the Passover meal, perhaps the "Halleluiah" Psalms, before going forth to a different kind of victory.

In order of appearance in the text, the first angelic anthem in *Paradise Lost* is the hymn (3.374–82) with which the victorious

angels respond to the Father's acceptance of the Son's offer to die
to redeem mankind, which ends with the salutation and proclamation,

> Hail Son of God, Saviour of Men, thy Name
> Shall be the copious matter of my Song
> Henceforth, and never shall my Harp thy praise
> Forget, nor from thy Father's praise disjoin.
>
> (3.412–15)

The angels then recount the Son's agency in divine acts: the
creation of the "Heav'n of Heavens and all the Powers therein,"
including themselves, and the defeat of the rebel faction. When
they come to the immediate topic of their song, the Son becomes
more than an agent by his "unexampl'd love." Perceiving the
Father inclined to pity sinful Man, he "to appease thy wrath, and
end the strife / Of Mercy and Justice in thy face discern'd . . .
offer'd himself to die." This act of celeritous discernment, compassion, and sacrifice elicits from the angels their remarkable salutation and promise that his Name will provide the matter of their
song not only now but "Henceforth."

Considering the vision, drama, and theodicy packed into these
lines, they seem, on contemplation, less and less stark and simple.
They become even richer and more complex if we recall that they
are sung.

Liturgical texts were sometimes stark enough. The Nicene
Creed, though astonishing, is not great poetry, yet musicians
express its words in great music. Milton models his redemption
hymn, beginning "Thee Father," on the Te Deum laudamus,[46] a
prose poem nearly as matter-of-fact as the creed, but makes it far
more poetic; and he tells us enough about how the angels perform
it to summon remembered music:

>   thir gold'n Harps they took,
> Harps ever tun'd, that glittering by thir side
> Like Quivers hung, and with Preamble sweet
> Of charming symphony they introduce
> Thir sacred Song, and waken raptures high;
> No voice exempt, no voice but well could join
> Melodious part, such concord is in Heav'n.
>
> (3.365–71)

The Te Deum, the only non-biblical canticle in the office of the
Book of Common Prayer (the Benedicite, though Apocryphal, was

bound into English bibles as "The Song of the Three Children" until the 1640s), is appointed to be said or sung "After the first lesson . . . in English, daily through the whole year" (*BCP* 53). It is an appropriate source of resonance since it sums up the process of salvation that the angels are praising. Their warm exclamation, with or without music, is not stark: "O unexampl'd love, / Love nowhere to be found less than Divine!" (3.410–11).

The Te Deum ends with a brief litany, including the line "And we worship thy name, ever world without end." Milton's angels, too, end by magnifying "thy Name" which will be, day by day, "the copious matter of my Song / Henceforth." The sudden change to the singular "my" has been thought a departure from genre and decorum. John Leonard points out that Richard Bentley changed the pronouns to the plural and also thinks this passage a temporary interruption of Milton's "sense of exclusion from prelapsarian language."[47] But the final line of the Te Deum also changes from "we" and "us" to "in thee have I trusted: let me never be confounded." Choral voices often use singular pronouns in settings of psalms and canticles, and in the Te Deum composers traditionally imitate the experience of not being confounded by taking the choir through a many-voiced canon or fugue. The recognition of each singular voice within the harmony is suitable for a Protestant poet highly conscious of individual choice concerning participation in the ties or ligaments from which the word "religion" comes, whose own voice perhaps joins the angels' as each chorally hails the Son whose "Name / Shall be the copious matter of my Song."

Since the name is the matter of song, we might consider ways the names of the Son are sung in sixteenth- and seventeenth-century music. Music added to the name of the Logos unifies the logos of language and the logos of mathematical proportion. The angels do not actually utter a name, only a series of epithets, but allusion to the Te Deum brings to mind a line that received emphatic expressive treatment from composers: "Thou art the king of glory, O Christ." The angels do not know this future eponym, but they have seen him "annointed," and Satan therefore calls him (ironically) "our King / The great Messiah" (5.690–91), of which Khristos is the Greek form. Even though in the Te Deum "Christ" appears at the beginning of the section on the Son, composers bring the music to a major cadence on it, usually with extended repetition, melisma, and modulation before the final acclamatory chord. William Byrd in his "Great Service" sets the eight-word sentence for ten-part choir with seventeen contrapuntal entrances and twenty-one repetitions of "Christ." Later he changes to syllabic homophony for clear articulation on "And we worship thy Name." It would be difficult for a seventeenth-century reader of an anthem modeled on the Te Deum not to hear onomastic music when "Name" and "Song" conjoin. The beings that issue from divine Being are part of the "copious matter" summed up in the unnamed Name, which is copious matter for the arts because its bearer speaks into being all living things, by his incarnation joins their lives, and by atonement redeems them so that no entity need be lost when "God shall be All in All" (3.341).

The angel choirs sing many times during the creation story. The first choral response comes after the Father's declaration that, having cast out the rebels, he can "repair / That detriment" and "create / Another world" and a Race to dwell there

> till by degrees of merit rais'd
> They open to themselves at length the way
> Up hither, under long obedience tri'd
> And Earth be chang'd to Heav'n, and Heav'n to Earth,
> One Kingdom, Joy and Union without end (7.157–61)

The angels receive this unusual statement (the idea of changing Heaven to Earth suggests not only the monism of "one first matter" [5.472] but continuing and processively integrated creation) with a three-part Gloria (7.182–91), beginning like the annunciation to the shepherds of the Son's human birth – "Glory they sung to the most High, good will / To future men, and in thir dwellings peace" – but also praising "just avenging ire" for expelling the ungodly from "the habitations of the just" and the wisdom that "had ordain'd / Good out of evil to create." They recognize, also, that God's creativity is limitless – from this new world he will "diffuse / His good to Worlds and Ages infinite" – and unlike Satan they do not resent it. By incorporating the Gloria in excelsis, Milton summons many jubilant settings for the Nativity and for the Gloria (set for example by Amner, Jeffreys, Loosemore, and Thomas Tomkins, whose verse version combines solo and choral voices) sung in the liturgy just after the communion because, Lancelot Andrewes says, "it behoves to be in or as near the state of the Angels as we can" when we join their song "to make but one choir."[48]

The first day of creation does not pass unsung, Raphael says,

> By the Celestial Choirs, when Orient Light
> Exhaling first from Darkness they beheld;
> Birth-day of Heav'n and Earth; with joy and shout
> The hollow Universal Orb they fill'd,
> And touch'd thir Golden harps, and hymning prais'd
> God and his works, Creator him they sung,
> Both when first Ev'ning was and when first Morn.
>
> (7.253–60)

Milton again alludes to the liturgical daily offices and forefends archetypal and binary oppositions of day and night when "Ev'n / And Morning *Chorus* sang the second Day" (7.274–75). He does not tell us with what hymns the angels "solemniz'd" (7.48) the second through fifth days, but they are jubilant after the sixth. When the Creator has finished his work, "Answering his great Idea," and returns to heaven to view it, Raphael reports,

> Up he rode
> Follow'd with acclamation and the sound
> Symphonious of ten thousand Harps that tun'd
> Angelic harmonies: The Earth, the Air
> Resounded (thou remember'st, for thou heard'st)
> The Heav'ns and all the Constellations rung,
> The Planets in thir station list'ning stood,
> While the bright Pomp ascended jubilant.

What they sing alludes to Psalm 24, one of the proper Psalms for Ascension Day; as echoes of the Gloria compare the birth of the world with his nativity, this hymn parallels the ascension of the Son after the creation to his ascension after the resurrection.

> Open, ye everlasting Gates, they sung,
> Open, ye Heav'ns, your living doors; let in
> The great Creator from his work return'd
> Magnificent, his Six days' work, a World.
>
> (7.557–68)

Byrd set the Latin version of Psalm 24.7, "Attolite portas," in the *Sacrae Cantiones* of 1575 (*BE* 1); it was adapted to English words, as "Lift up your heads, O ye gates." Although it is an early work and in imitative polyphony, Byrd's setting is revolutionary, Craig Monson states, because its exuberant text had not traditionally been set but was among those "picked for their expressive potential," a motive that "represents the birth of a new aesthetic stance among English composers."[49] Byrd's six-part texture doubles the upper parts, and the high voices along with the repeated leap of a fifth on "Lift up your heads" express not only the raising of the gates but also the jubilation of the welcomers. At the question "Who is this king of glory?" and the answer "The Lord strong and mighty in battle" (as the Son has been in the War in Heaven) each pair of voices asks and answers in duets descending from highest to lowest, so that the identity of the king of glory spreads in a series of echoes from voice to voice and from heaven to earth. Amner, Gibbons, and Weelkes also wrote jubilant settings of this psalm text, and since the psalm is associated with Ascensiontide, other exultant anthems written for that season, such as Gibbons' "O Clap your hands" and "The Lord is gone up with a merry shout" come to mind.

But again, Milton emphasizes that the way to heaven is also the way to earth, and the gates emit as well as admit; the angels, generous of spirit and in utter opposition to Satan, quickly turn their thoughts from ascent to descent and the expansion of their own field of active charity.

> Open, and henceforth oft; for God will deign
> To visit oft the dwellings of just Men
> Delighted, and with frequent intercourse
> Thither will send his winged Messengers
> On errands of supernal Grace. So sung
> The glorious Train ascending.   (7.569–74)

On the first Sabbath, God does not keep his day of rest "in silence holy":

> the Harp
> Had work and rested not, the solemn Pipe,
> And Dulcimer, all Organs of sweet stop,
> All sounds on Fret by String or Golden Wire
> Temper'd soft Tunings, intermixt with Voice
> Choral or Unison; of incense Clouds
> Fuming from Golden Censers hid the Mount.
>   (7.594–600)

"Hid" of course does not conceal the danger that elaborate liturgy can obscure truth when practiced by and for fallible human beings; and even "fuming" and, by its sound, "Censers" might be thought cautionary. But primarily the passage recalls Psalm 150,

"Praise God in his sanctuary," the sonorous conclusion and epitome of the whole Book of Psalms, with its invocations of trumpet, lute, harp, timbrels, strings, pipe, cymbals, voices, and dance and a jovial assertion of their rightful place "in his sanctuary," set mimetically with special zest by many composers, including Byrd in *Cantiones Sacrae* (1591). The diversity of instruments recalls visual representations of angelic consorts as actually and symbolically a harmony composed of every sort of voice and timbre.

Milton's diction in the rest of this anthem encourages vigorous musical imagining with its mentions of measure, numerousness, lessening and diminishing, might and thunder, the "amplitude almost immense" (immeasurable) of the starry universe, the clash of good and evil resolving in hallelujahs. Like Milton's sonnets to Cromwell and Fairfax, the angels commend avenging thunder, but laud creativity more: the Son is "greater now in thy return / Than from the Giant Angels; thee that day / Thy Thunders magnifi'd" – and thunder might roll in a bass solo as in Weelkes' "Alleluiah. I heard a voice as of strong thund'rings" – "But," the angels continue, "to create / Is greater than created to destroy." Like the Nativity Ode, their hymn is shaded with the knowledge of suffering to come but praises God for using Satan's evil to create "more good" and again shows pleasure in the closeness of heaven and earth and the prolificacy of potential life: "Witness this new-made World, another Heav'n / From Heaven Gate not far . . . and every Star perhaps a World / Of destin'd habitation" (7.615–22). The angels are optimistic about "Thrice happy men . . . Created in his Image" but understand that this happiness is contingent: "thrice happy if they know / Thir happiness, and persevere upright" (7.625–32). As with each anthem, "the Empyrean rung, / With *Halleluiahs*" (7.633–34), which in contemporary music received daring and innovative settings. As Milton alludes to the church music controversy in 1648 in his translation of Psalm 81, so Raphael ends his creation song: "Thus was Sabbath kept."

In *Paradise Regained*, Satan offers Jesus the "schools of antient Sages" wherein "thou shalt hear and learn the secret power / Of harmony in tones and numbers hit / By voice or hand, and various measur'd verse, / *Aeolian* charms and *Dorian Lyric* Odes" and all poetry and philosophy. "Secret power" suggests art used to subdue and manipulate when "with Empire joyn'd" (*SM* 4.251–57, 4.284).

The Son replies that Greece derived and badly imitated these arts from Hebrew song and story; no other music is worthy "to compare / With *Sion's* songs . . . Where God is prais'd aright" (4.346–48). Does Milton, reacting to the pomp, circumstance, and improbity of restored royalism, finally renounce the instrumental and choral music that had so often resounded in his Heaven?

Like other poets who wove poetic crowns, Milton was aware that into the artist's *imitatio* of the Creator the serpent tries to work his way. He had elaborated Sion's songs beyond what Hooker with regard to the Song of Moses called "the usuall naked simplicitie of Gods Spirit." But *Paradise Regained* does not renounce the Muse who inspired "That Shepherd, who first taught the chosen Seed" and still inspires from "*Sion* Hill." At the end, Satan has tried to find out who Christ is ("Who is this King of glory?") and been found unable to receive the answer.[50] As Satan falls and Christ stands on the pinnacle, the "fiery Globe / Of Angels" that sang his birth bear him up and polychoral "Angelic Quires" sing "Heavenly Anthems of his victory." The anthem we hear lauds the Son "whether thron'd / In the bosom of bliss and light of light / Conceiving" or "enshrin'd / In fleshly Tabernacle," an echo of the deposit of light in the sun. Again a conjunction of divine and human occurs; heavenly light enters flesh and makes flesh a temple of light.

Will the choirs of creatures that the Son creates and joins lose their distinct voices when "God shall be All in All"? Will the "grateful vicissitude, and eccentric regularity" of the created world turn "into the horror of a uni-verse in which all distinctions will have been effaced"?[51] The God of Book 7, and of Genesis and Job, delights in differentiation.[52] The choral music Milton describes, in which the angels rejoice that "God shall be All in All," suggests that the unity of the God-filled or God-reentering congregation of creatures is not limited to, though it may include, the unity of chant, but is a polyphonic web of being in which each voice is distinct, and made distinct by being part of the unity. Members of choirs feel the process of mutual tuning to achieve beauty as a liberating experience, in which one's voice enters into a wholeness out of which is born its own particular meaning. In God's consort this mutuality and distinctness would, according to Milton's poetic principles, be improvised, a miracle made possible by the unifying integer of the "All" that the other "All" is "in." One of those *Alls* consists of Heaven and Earth and all those creatures in both. The fear that the "All" of beatitude might lack scope for individuality is allayed by the kind of music Milton heard and Milton's choirs sing. Hearing that music behind and within his verse, both as actual music and as metaphor, might help dispel the idea that, as R. J. Z. Werblowsky thinks, "Satan's grandeur and magnificence . . . [are] not matched poetically by God, his angels, and the Messiah himself," or that, as Thomas Greene thinks, "the dramatization of goodness fails."[53] Grandeur and drama are not essential to goodness, but the music of Paradise and Heaven shows goodness as a boundless source of creativity and the unmusical heart of Satan fit for "stratagems and spoils."

Does Milton distrust language? Unlike music, language cannot be tuned mathematically. But like music, it is made of the elements of creation. In a world of complexity, the more polysemous language is – the more concinnities, including dissonances, it has, and the less Satanic reductivity it can support – the more precise it can be. Milton's poetic "numbers" are neither unfallen nor fallen, but language in the continuing process of creation and recreation. He attributes its regenerative power to "that eternal Spirit who can enrich with all utterance" and presents it as a "full-voic'd Quire" whose voices are "Sole, or responsive to each other's note." Milton's verse incorporates such music to express a polyphonic creation and a trust that the God who made these voices will enhance, not erase, their unions and distinctions when "th'old Dragon" no longer swinges his venomous tail.

CHAPTER 6

Empire of the ear: the praise of music

English poetry and music in the early seventeenth century had a special genius for integrating the human and the holy. But in Restoration and especially Georgian society, according to Nicholas Temperley, "worldly and superficial attitudes to church music, and to religious worship in general, were the prevailing ones," though these attitudes were opposed by the high-church movement on the one hand and evangelical societies on the other.[1] Correspondingly greater distance arose between the speakers of poems and God and between words and music. Music became more regular of key and beat, and poets took up the metrical reins of the neoclassical couplet and the pursuit of grammatical regularity and conceptual clarity. Abstract universality, rather than resonant literality, became the ideal. By the middle of the next century, in an excess of rational principles, Friedrich II of Prussia could command his musicians to obey despotic musical rules, not on religious grounds but on grounds of correct taste.[2] With the neoclassical reduction of the particular came a reduction of the connectedness of music to particular words. Eighteenth-century composers who most skillfully continued to heed literal meanings in through-composed settings of English words were inspired to do so by seventeenth-century poets: Handel by Milton's *L'Allegro* and *Il Penseroso* and by Dryden's *Song for St. Cecilia's Day* and *Alexander's Feast*, and Haydn in *The Creation* by *Paradise Lost*.[3]

Much baroque music required, and the basso continuo supported, a virtuosity that transported musical experience into the concert hall. Roger North contrasts this change to music-making in the house of his grandfather, who employed John Jenkins and Henry Loosemore: "And the servants of parade, [such] as gentlemen ushers, and the steward, and clerck of the kitchen also play'd; which with the yong ladys my sisters singing, made a society of musick, such as was well esteemed in those times . . . And on Sunday night voices to the organ were a constant practise, and at other times symphony intermixt with instruments." But after the Restoration, concerts by professional virtuosi in London replaced music-making at home, with the result that "When wee know not how to pass the time, we fall to drink . . . Now when music was . . . practible to moderate and imperfect hands, who for the most part are more earnest upon it than the most adept, it might be reteined in the country. But since it is arrived to such a pitch of perfection, that even masters, unless of the prime, cannot entertain us, the plain way becomes contemptible and rediculous, therfor must be lay'd aside."[4] Musical performance was becoming institutionalized and commodified. As secular music moved from private to public performance and religious arts moved from the sacred to the sublime, the intimate colloquy of words and music waned.

Shortly after the Restoration, when church music had just burst its Interregnum bonds, Samuel Pepys wrote in his diary, "Thence to Whitehall Chapel, where sermon almost done and I heard Captain Cookes new musique," in which "vialls and other instruments play a symphony between every verse of the anthem . . . and very fine it is."[5] Pepys' response to the new music also expresses a new attitude; he has dropped in at the Chapel expressly to hear the anthem and has revelled in its splendor. The preachers at the St. Cecilia's Day services at the end of the century were still reminding their listeners, like their predecessors during the church music debates, that music is only an aid to the worship of God in the heart; and the Dean of St. Paul's on St. Cecilia's day of 1699, while heartily endorsing both vocal and instrumental music, was annoyed by those who, like Pepys thirty-six years earlier, came to cathedral services only "to hear Better Voices, and more Curious Compositions, and more Artful Singing than we can meet with in other places," who "Crowd into the Church to hear the Anthem and when that is over, to the great Disturbance of the Worship of God, and the Scandal of all good Christians, Crowd as fast out again" – not lending ear to the Dean's sermon.[6]

Not surprisingly, during and after the Interregnum poems and music, like Pepys, turned from the music of praise to the praise of music – primarily instrumental music. Three such poems, by Andrew Marvell, John Dryden, and Nicholas Brady, illustrate the process of change. Marvell's *Musick's Empire*, published in 1681 but probably written three decades earlier, retains the principles of musical language and was not, apparently, set to music. Dryden's *A Song for St. Cecilia's Day, 1687* was intended to be set and uses language to imitate musical sounds, but not to create reverberating verbal chords in the antiphonally responding soul. Henry Purcell's setting of Brady's text for St. Cecilia's Day, 1692, with which we end as we began, is the swan song of the close embrace of English words and music, though sometimes the swan revives.

THE EMPIRE OF THE EAR

Marvell was at Trinity College during the Laudian revival, supported the revolution, and wrote *Musick's Empire* after the silencing of the choirs. His poems about singing – by a fair singer, a boatful of psalm-singers, and a singer of hallelujahs – sometimes join together the sacred and the secular, but not as musical genres. Both *A Fair Singer*, though a graceful compliment to both the singer and music, full of madrigalian thought, and *A Dialogue, between the Resolved Soul and Created Pleasure* are suspicious of the "sweet chordage" of "fatal harmony." *Musick's Empire* exhibits the polysemous literality of earlier seventeenth-century verse, but with a kind of ambiguity that marks the times; it too contains virtuosic flights of word and sound association like the consonances between justly tuned harmonic series, yet in its very exactness it begins to crumble into uncertainty. Marvell's virtuosity signals a change, even as he wraps up the tradition of cosmic music within it.

Rather than praising God directly, *Musicks Empire* praises music to praise a human hero who praises God. Oliver Cromwell and Thomas Fairfax, military leaders and musicians of whom Marvell wrote other poems, have been nominated as the recipients of this ambiguous honor.[7] I shall favor Fairfax, Marvell's employer at Nunappleton – who, like music, had retired from the public scene – as the gentle conqueror who renounces "feats of arms," rather than Cromwell, whose capability for "martial rage" Marvell includes in *The First Anniversary* while comparing Cromwell to Amphion and whom he treats in the *Horatian Ode* with an ambivalence no Irish reader would be likely to miss. If *Musick's Empire* was meant for Cromwell, the destruction of church music by the revolutionaries would give it an ironic dimension for many readers including Fairfax, who opposed Kirkrapine.

Musick's Empire is a short history and defense of music touched
so lightly that it might melt "into thin air," like Prospero's masque,
if it did not recall to us that the element we breathe – Satan's putative realm, the stuff of ayres, the irreducible necessity of life – is the
body of music. Everything in nature has the capacity to make it
into sound. A musical word-painter would enjoy the poem's opportunities to imitate these sounds, its genealogical proliferation of
musical instruments, and its concluding hallelujah chorus. If in
accord with Charles Butler's descriptions of the modes, it would be
set in the "Dorick Moode" which is that of both "the Psalms in
Meeter" and "those sober feast hymns, wont to be sung in the praiz
of honorable men."[8]

Cromwell's puritans encouraged psalm-singing and other
sacred music outside church; "Thus sang they, in the English boat,
/ An holy and a cheerful note," Marvell writes of the escape of dissenters from Laudian persecutions in *Bermudas*; they sing to the
stroke of their own oars, not in the nave of a church but in a "small
boat" safe from "Prelates rage" in the temple of nature filled with
listening winds.[9] With his frequent equipoise for taking both sides
of a question, Marvell in *Musick's Empire* writes a defense of music
which does not explicitly lament the loss of church music, instead
addressing music's highest secular use, the praise of a good man –
but one who sings "Heavens Hallelujahs."[10]

The more in tune words are, the more language connects us to
"holy Mathematicks" and "Heavens Hallelujahs." Like Herbert's,
Marvell's words have fundamentals – or literal significations – and
partials, so that the most exact phrase also has the most power of
suggestion. Numerous words form chords with other words: not
only obvious ones like "sound," "echoes," "consort," and
"numbers," but also words linked by root or allusion: like "sullen"
in "sullen Cell," which comes from the same root as "solitary" and
may echo the "sullen bell" of Shakespeare's Sonnet 71. The root
of "Colonies" is *colonus*, cultivator, which is what the gentle conqueror became when he gave up feats of arms. "Gentler" relates to
Genesis, progeny, and general (as in the Lord General Fairfax).

Musick's Empire is like music in another way: it evanesces. He has
built into his "subtle cells" such teasing partials that rigid reading
simply will not fit into his "cases fit," fabricated of multiple meanings that seem constantly about to deconstruct themselves were
they not founded on fundamentals of irreducible literality. A

deconstructionist could leave it in shambles by pointing out the disappearing referents.

> First was the World as one great Cymbal made,
> Where Jarring Windes to infant Nature plaid.
> All Musick was a solitary sound,
> To hollow Rocks and murm'ring Fountains bound.

Cowley's *Davideis* makes a similar point in a more neoclassical way:

> Such w   God's Poem, this *World's* new *Essay*;
> So wild and rude in its first Draught it lay;
> Th' ungovern'd Parts no *Correspondence* knew,
> An artless *War* from thwarting *Motions* grew;
> Till they to *Number*, and fixt Rules were brought
> By the *eternal Mind's Poetick Thought*.[11]

Marvell's statements, in contrast, call themselves into question. The world is "one great Cymbal," but cymbals usually come in pairs.[12] (To revise a classic Zen question, what is the sound of one cymbal clapping?) Nature is infant, which is to say speechless, yet winds jar, rocks reverberate, fountains complain; three of Nature's four elements, in the musical sense, speak. "All Musick was a solitary sound": if that means only one sound, how can it be music? If it means alone, with no eardrum to strike, can it be sound at all? The clause adumbrates Bishop Berkeley's famous question.

Rock music comes back in stanza five:

> Then Musick, the Mosaique of the Air,
> Did of all these a solemn noise prepare
> With which She gain'd the Empire of the Ear,
> Including all between the Earth and Sphear.

What could be more unanalogous than air and cemented bits of stone? What does Marvell mean by having music's mastery suddenly contract into so small an organ – or does the ear expand? If music's dominion is over the ear, how does it include "all between the Earth and Sphear" and why "between," as if earth and sphere were themselves unmusical?

But having undone themselves as they fly, Marvell's words, like music heard again, come back to mean more. "First was the World as one great Cymbal made"; the pun on "symbol" alerts us to double meanings in the very moment that onefoldness is so peculiarly used, and we see that the world-cymbal is instrumental and needs to be interpreted and tuned. Most cymbals, like Marvell's, have no particular pitch, but small "*cymbles antiques* or crotales" come in various sizes and pitches,[13] hence the "well-tuned cymbals" of Psalm 150. Within this one-handed engine, all music was at first a solitary sound: both one undifferentiated chaos of noise, out of which creation will come by separation and ordered union, and alone, not able to increase and multiply until differentiation occurs; bound – on its way and confined – to empty rocks and mumbling water. Marvell is recounting the Genesis creation story in musical terms. He leaves out the next four days of creation, however, and moves straight to humanity.

The history of audible music involves tuning instruments, ordering pitches into scales, making pleasing intervals into melodies, and the discovery of harmony, inventions that may exceed the wheel in importance to the human spirit.[14] Jubal, "the father of all such as handle the harp and the organ" in Genesis 4.22, brings musical order out of chaos and calls solitary echoes out of their monkish cells to couple and propagate: the birth of earthly harmony.[15] But Jubal is an odd creator-figure, because the first biblically recorded use of earthly music is distinctly fallen; as Milton says, the Sons of Cain appear "studious / Of Arts that polish Life" but are "Unmindful of thir Maker, though his Spirit Taught them," and they yield up their virtue seduced by the "Soft amorous Ditties" of "fair Atheists" (*PL* 11. 609–12, 11.584, 11.625). Music can become a "vanitas" like the obscene musical instruments in Bosch's Hell. Marvell acknowledges this fallen potentiality only prosodically: in "And *Jubal* tuned musicks first jubilee" one has to give full length to "tuned" in order to tune the line.[16] But the allusion prepares for Marvell's gentle conqueror, a regenerate Jubal who flees vain uses of good art. At "*Jubilee*" the puns thicken. Jubal gives to the unhoused sounds the organ's city, where each seeks a consort and which "the Progeny of numbers" overpopulates, withdrawing into families of musical instruments Marvell calls "harmonious Colonies" – inviting, perhaps, a musical critique of the colonies of once overpopulated England.

Musical instruments are either wind or wire, "to sing Mens Triumphs, or in Heavens quire." Trumpets and harps are the only angelic instruments mentioned in the Bible; in illuminated apocalypses they are painted in real gold. That heaven's choir should have winds and wire is perhaps not only metaphorical but monistic, like Milton's "golden wires," and shares Milton's heavenly materialism; musical instruments, and music being made of air, are among the evidence that both heaven and earth are composed of "one first matter."

The comparison of music to mosaics of stone is breathtakingly complicated. "Mosaique" comes from the Greek word for muses and music and also alludes to the Mosaic account of creation and the beginning of the arts, of which Marvell's history of music is an epitome. The "light *Mosaic*" of the "*Sibyls* leaves" in the grove at Nunappleton makes "the Mosaique of the air" another page in "*Natures mystic Book.*"[17] Mosaics are among the most fixed and durable forms of art, and music is the most ephemeral; yet music once "noted," or preserved in symbols, can outlast even mosaics in stone. Actual mosaics of Jubal's invention of music would display a topos of which the poem is a word-mosaic. Music is the mosaic of the air in the sense that its composite bits are made of air, and the musical pitches made of that air are framed in the law of nature and incipient in natural objects – even stones, of which mosaic is made, respond to song, as Herbert says[18] – and so those pitches are as fixed and timeless as (or perhaps more so than) the Law of Moses, which was written in stone and meant to penetrate hearts of stone and become inscribed in flesh. Music too is said to move and reform our stony hearts; here, homeopathically. Since a melody is called an aire and is literally made of air, the mosaic of music is made of aires made out of air. Part-music is made of different airs, as mosaic is made of different colored stones, mixed and patterned. Language, hence Marvell's poem, is, like music and mosaic, put together of many minute parts and like music transmitted through vibrating air to the ear, which, like the poem, is music's empire. Just as the phrase "Mosaique of the air" is a reversible metaphor – the music is a mosaic made of air, and the air[e] is a mosaic made of music – so is the genre: a *laudes musicae*, praise of music and praise made of music, the music of the poem whose praise the gentle conqueror it praises – like music – flies.

Not until its dispersal into individual instruments and voices, Marvell has it, does music "prepare" a "solemn noise" (alluding to the Psalms) and gain "the Empire of the Ear, / Including all between the Earth and Sphear" – Milton's "high first-moving Spheare,"[19] the primum mobile, one supposes. How marvellous that the words "Earth" and "Sphear" both include "ear" – which is shared "between" the two of them and which they are orthographically between – and "Sphear" also includes "hear." But why "between"? That leaves music nothing but air (Milton's "terrae . . . et coelo interfluus aer"[20]) to rule. But that is what music is made of; and besides, "between" is as in "a marriage between," not just betwixt; music connects Earth and the prime-moving Sphear. And the sounds victorious over this empire are all summoned to praise a particular human being – perhaps Thomas Fairfax, a military conqueror who renounced power and wrote metrical psalms[21] – who flies that music to join heaven's choir, the purpose of music's heart-tuning here on earth. Like Dylan Thomas' "sullen art," Marvell's musical encomium is ignored by its subject, leaving us its outer audience to reap its benefits.[22]

The subject of the poem's praise is a gentler conqueror than music because music has conquered him; but that is exactly why he is a conquerer, even of music: a well-tuned soul, conqueror of itself, makes music and is music, and is therefore fit for public office. Marvell's just man joins heaven's choir by his humility as music does him homage, each made victorious by service to the other, and Marvell's verbal music does homage to a conqueror who, having conquered himself, flees that music, because it praises him, but joins it to raise hallelujahs, which the poem is doing too. Thus music and poetry, those gentle conquerors, offer to contribute to the concord of public life. A mind working harmonically is conscious of multiple relations, listens to many different voices, puts itself in tune with them, and sustains a long-term melody and harmony through its separate mosaic-moments. A fine-tuned poem, charting *"Paradices only Map,"*[23] connects the mind with all creation and so represents the kind of mind it praises.

The fine-tuning of Marvell's resonances may be seen by comparison with the more obvious puns of another lyric in the *laudes musicae* tradition by Katherine Phillips, from Playford's edition of Henry Lawes' *Second Book of Ayres* (1655), which has a pleasant but less layered kind of word play:

> Nature which is the vast Creation's Soul,
> That steady curious Agent in the whole,
> The Art of Heaven, the order of this frame,
> Is only Musick in another name.
> And as some King conquering what was his own,
> Hath choice of several Titles to his Crown;
> So Harmony on this score now, that then,

> Yet still is all that takes and Governs Men.
> Beauty is but Composure, and we find,
> Content is but the Concord of the Mind;
> Friendship the Unison of well tun'd Hearts;
> Honour's the Chorus of the Noblest parts:
> And all the World, on which we can reflect,
> Musick to the Ear, or to the Intellect.

Phillips' poem is not so much discovery as display; and in that respect it adumbrates the spirit of musical encomia to come. It tells us that all the world "is but" music, and its key-signature is "Intellect." It versifies, with double meanings, a conventional philosophy of music that Marvell's modulates by showing that human art is needed to make both music and its ethical uses audible and by making ethical music – and its frailty – audible in his poem.

WONDROUS MACHINE

Both Dryden in *A Song for St. Cecilia's Day, 1687* and Brady in the poem set as *Ode on St. Cecilia's Day 1692* consider the ethics of music on the level of psychology, displaying ways that music can create and soothe emotions. This concern is partly a political one. Looking back on foreign and civil wars at a *fin de siècle* of relative peace, they deploy art (like Rubens earlier in the Banqueting House) against the personal and national passions that promote turmoil.

Like Marvell's, Dryden's encomium to music begins at the beginning, with harmony calling order out of chaos at the creation of the world, but it then moves immediately to the emotional power of music:

> What Passion cannot MUSICK raise and quell!
> When *Jubal* struck the corded Shell,
> His list'ning brethren stood around,
> And wond'ring, on their Faces fell
> To worship that Celestial Sound.
> Less than a God they thought there cou'd not dwell
> Within the hollow of that Shell
> That spoke so sweetly and so well.
> What Passion cannot MUSICK raise and quell!

"Corded Shell" is a punning epitome that makes one think of the binding of the "universal Frame" in stanza one; but while Marvell's stanza on Jubal invokes sacred history (from "Jubilee" to celestial "City"), Dryden's recounts a pagan response, like the satyrs worshipping Una. The poem proceeds onomatopoetically to represent the various passions that various instruments "raise and quell": trumpet and drum arouse to arms, flute and lute lament the woes of love's victims, "Sharp VIOLINS proclaim" the pains and rages of disdained lovers. Some of these are not very desirable passions, though perhaps "quelled" by, as Puttenham says, "making one dolour to expell another"; but the instruments that rouse them are dismissed and subsumed by the "sacred ORGAN" which produces "Notes inspiring holy Love, / Notes that wing their heav'nly ways / To mend the Choires above." The theme of Cecilia's great invention improving or at least matching heaven continues:

> *Orpheus* cou'd lead the savage race;
> And Trees unrooted left their place,
>   Sequacious of the Lyre;
> But bright CECILIA rais'd the wonder high'r:
> When to her ORGAN vocal breath was given,
> An angel heard, and straight appeared,
>   Mistaking Earth for Heaven.

In the St. Cecilia legend, as Hollander points out, it is Cecilia's prayers, not her music, that draw an angel down;[24] and in the many paintings of St. Cecilia and the Angel from the Ghent Altarpiece to Gentileschi, tradition might lead the viewer to suppose that the angel is inspiring Cecilia. In Brady's ode, where "Cäcilia oft convers'd with Heaven," "Some Angel of the Sacred Choir / Did with his Breath the pipes inspire: / And of their Notes above the just Resemblance gave." Dryden pleasantly reverses, in fact, the whole convention of heavenly music inspiring human hearts, but was not the first to do so; Donne (alluding to 1 Peter 1.12) says with regard to the Sidney Psalms that "Angels lerne by what the Church does here." As Hollander observes of Dryden's final chorus, his is "praise of a practical music that is mundane rather than *mundana*, worldly rather than universal. The second member of this pair has become merely a term with which to exalt the other."[25]

Dryden's "Grand chorus" comes to a surprising conclusion: just as in the beginning sacred music set the spheres in motion to praise their creator,

So when the last and dreadful hour
This crumbling Pageant shall devour,
The TRUMPET shall be heard on high,
The Dead shall live, the Living die,
And music shall untune the Sky.

The conceit is skillful: music tuned the visible, audible world in the beginning and will unmake it in the end; only heavenly music will last. But the stanza is oddly disturbing for its occasion. In *Dooms-day*, "Dust, alas, no musick feels, / But thy trumpet: then it kneels"; Herbert calls on Christ to "Help our decay" and "thy broken consort raise." Milton hoped for the sin-flawed creation to be retuned, not untuned: Nature in the Nativity Ode "knew such harmony alone / Could hold all Heav'n and Earth in happier union"; in *Paradise Lost* the final conflagration will renew, not consume, and God will receive the faithful "into bliss, / Whether in Heav'n or Earth, for then the Earth / Shall all be Paradise" (12.463–64). Dryden's dissolution by unstringing the chorded shell of the world splits matter from spirit at a time in poetic history when faith and intellect were going separate ways, as were words and music. Perhaps part of the explanation of this separation lies in the fact that of the poets studied here, only Dryden was at Cambridge while the choirs were bare of choristers.

The occasion for Dryden's poem was the St. Cecilia's Day celebration of November 22, 1687.[26] This yearly festival, composed of a feast at Stationers' Hall, preceded (sensibly) by a concert featuring an ode to the patroness of music by a noted composer, was instituted by the Musical Society of London in 1683, having earlier precedents on the continent; it spread to Oxford, Salisbury, and Dublin, and expanded in 1693 to include a church service, at St. Bride's Church in the case of the London meetings, with specially composed service settings and a sermon in defense of church music which, like Dryden's and Brady's poems, codified musical wisdom. These sermons rehearse, from a more secure position, the scriptural authority used by earlier defenders, but emphasize two features in common with the poems and music for these occasions: they particularly defend the use of instrumental music in worship services and stress the effects of music on the passions, which, as some pointed out, music can affect without the necessity of words. These effects are natural, for, as the chaplain of Christ Church tells Oxford music-lovers anatomically in 1696, "By the Frame of our Nature we may perceive ourselves fitted and prepar'd for the Reception of Harmonious Sounds; as we are fenc'd about with Nerves, we find ourselves already strung, and most of us tun'd for this heavenly Entertainment."[27] "Reception" marks a notable change, however, from earlier ideas of human beings as a singing species, secretaries of praise joining all creation by the verbal articulation of nature's voice.

The first of these sermons, on *The Lawfulness and Expediency of Church-Musick*, was preached at St. Bride's Church to "The Anniversary Meeting of Gentlemen, Lovers of Musick" on November 22, 1693 by Ralph Battell, "Sub-Dean of Their Majesties Chapel-Royal." Battell proclaims, "That none may therefore henceforth go about to separate those two things which agree so very well together, I will assert the Lawfulness, yea the Fitness and great Expediency of both Vocal and Instrumental Musick in the Church, during the solemn Worship of God there." He justifies this practice from that of "the Heathen" and the Levites, exactly those whom puritan detractors had used against it, points out that church music was not part of the ceremonial law of Moses but instituted by David, adds New Testament examples including the heavenly songs in Revelation, and argues that the reason "the Primitive Christians" did not use instrumental music was that they met in secrecy and besides "had not wherewithall to be at the charge of these Aids and Ornaments to their Religious Worship," which the church added as soon as it was able. He adds another reason that sums up what happened to devotional music and poetry in his own time, as well: "As Inspiration in singing Psalms (which was doubtless an extraordinary Gift common to the Primitive Christians), began to cease, Instruments and Skill were brought in its Room, even as Learning and ordinary means took place instead of extraordinary Gifts."

Against the scruples of the Geneva Bible, Battell adduces "the Authority of the Assembly-Divines" and of "Mr. *Baxter*, much esteemed among the Separatists," who supported instrumental church music "in his cases of Conscience, annexed to his Christian Directory,"[28] and lauds it as "conducing toward the more magnificent and solemn Worship of God." And he quotes numerous witnesses to the good effects of music on the soul, such as David's cure of Saul attributable "only to the Notes of Musick [that is, without words, in sharp contrast to earlier opinion], and their natural

Efficacy in the subduing of all black Melancholy and Despair; all Anger, Malice, and Envy, or the like foul Passions," and his Psalms, in which he was "the Author of adding Melody, both Vocal and Instrumental, for the raising up of mens Hearts, and moving their Affections towards God." Of course, "the Heart is the best Psalmist, and the inward Affection of the Soul is the best Musick in God's ear, and it is purely for the sake of this, that the other is used."[29] But what is defended is again not the musical expression of words, no longer under attack, but instrumental music.

Nicholas Brady, "Chaplain in Ordinary to His Majesty," who in addition to the 1692 *Ode* produced with Nahum Tate *A New Version of Psalms*, gave a particularly impassioned defense, choosing as his text for the 1697 sermon the verses from The Second Book of the Chronicles describing the music used at the dedication of Solomon's Temple:

13. It came even to pass, as the Trumpeters and Singers were as one, to make one Sound to be heard in Praising and Thanking the Lord; And when they lift up their Voice, with the Trumpets and Cymbals, and Instruments of Musick and praised the Lord, saying, for he is good, for his Mercy endureth for ever: That then the House was filled with a Cloud, even the House of the Lord;

14. So that the Priests could not stand to Minister by reason of the Cloud; For the Glory of the Lord had filled the House of God.

This manifestation of divine approval "by God's Vouchsafement of the Shekinah, or Divine Presence," shows that although other sacrifices "are swallowed up, in that great Oblation which *Christ* offered once for all," and the Temple of Solomon "Superseded by the *Temple* of his Body," praise and thanksgiving "with the joynt Melody of *Voices* and *Instruments of Musick*" will continue to the end of the world and "make a considerable part of [Heaven's] infinite Felicity." Therefore "God here distinguish'd it, by vouchsafing his Presence at that particular juncture."[30]

Purcell's concertante Te Deum and Jubilate for the St. Cecilia's Day service of 1694 were repeated at the service at which Brady preached and triumphantly carry out the program of these sermons. The Te Deum begins with a trumpet flourish, the brass joining the chorus on "the Father everlasting" and returning for other expressions of praise, while deferring to the viols and to meditative solo melodies for the more solemn and prayerful verses. On "heav'n and earth are full of the majesty of thy glory" Purcell playfully inserts a brief bass solo on "and earth"; but he minimizes word-painting and uses his expressive gifts, particularly on such prayers as "O Lord, have mercy upon us," imbuing the words "O Lord" with an affective reverence that musically bends the knees of the heart. The Jubilate continues trumpet announcings and echoings of the voices. Both are dramatic and virtuosic examples of the "magnificent and solemn Worship" to which Brady's sermon gives so appropriate a gloss that listeners may have felt that they too had been given a glimpse of the Presence. The musical entertainment for the same day was Dryden's *Alexander's Feast, or the Power of Music*, with a lost setting by Jeremiah Clark; Handel's is the one that now lets us hear Alexander's musician Timotheus lead him and us through all the passions of the human soul only to be superseded by Cecilia.

Purcell's setting of Brady's *Ode on Saint Cecilia's Day* is a sprightly secular work but retains a literal relation (as seen in chapter 1 above) between words and music. It depicts the soul of the world bringing the "jarring Seeds of Matter" into "one perfect Harmony" in ways that show what a composer might do with Marvell's poem. The ode begins:

> Hail! Bright *Cecilia*, fill ev'ry heart
> With love of thee and thy Celestial Art,
>   That thine, and Musick's Sacred Love
>   May make the British Forest prove
> As famous as *Dodona's* Vocal Grove:
>   Hark! hark! each Tree its silence breaks,
>   The Box and Fir to talk begin!
>   This [in] the sprightly VIOLIN,
>   That in the Flute distinctly speaks!
>   'Twas Sympathy their list'ning Brethren drew,
> When to the *Thracian* Lyre with leafy Wings they flew.

Purcell sets the first five lines for declamatory bass and chorus, with homophonic hails and sinuous polyphonic intertwining to represent the double reciprocity of "thine, and Musick's Sacred Love": our love of them can create a harmonious world. In the instrumental accompaniment to the duet for bass and soprano that follows, Purcell makes England's forests vocal in the most literal way. The oracle of Zeus in Dodona published its tidings through the sounds of the woods, including the rustling of oak leaves. Now British trees literally "speak" as flutes (recorders), made of box, and violins, made of fir. To the suggestion that a natural woody sympathy drew trees to Orpheus' lyre, Purcell supplies musical word-painting of "leafy Wings," performed on instruments made of those very trees. One may recall that Marvell's *Garden* would have trees labelled, if at all, not with lovers' names but with their own; and that in *Easter* Herbert tells his lute (often of yew) "The crosse taught all wood to resound his name, / Who bore the same." Cowley in *The Garden* is more explicit: not only do birds, winds, and fountains give natural music, but trees make possible the music of art:

> But to our Plants Arts Musick too,
> The Pipe, Theorbo, and Guitarr we owe.
> The Lute it self, which once was Green and Mute,
> When *Orpheus* strook th'inspired Lute,
> The Trees danc'd round, and understood
> By Sympathy the Voice of Wood.[31]

In performing Purcell's Ode, England's forests literally become music and so enter a universal harmony infinitely – and resinously – resonant.

The trees that speak in Purcell's orchestra understand Orpheus' music as a "Universal Tongue," transcending Babel and incorporating all creatures in its language: "'Tis Nature's Voice; by all the moving Wood / Of Creatures understood: / The Universal Tongue, to none / Of all her num'rous Race unknown." From Nature music learned

> At once the Passions to express or move;
> We hear, and straight We grieve or hate, rejoice or love:
> In unseen Chains it does the Fancy bind;
> At once it charms the Sense and captivates the Mind.

"Her num'rous Race" is both all creatures and Marvell's "progeny of numbers." But the text being sung by human voices is about instrumental music. It is instruments that "to talk begin" and speak the "Universal Tongue" which, as Battell affirms, may be attributed to the notes alone.

Dryden's stanzas incorporate imitative sounds and rhythms into the words; we hear the leafy rustlings in "Sequacious," trumpet fanfare in the changed rhythms of "The TRUMPET'S loud clangour / excites us to arms," and the friction of "Sharp violins" that proclaim "Fury, frantic indignation." Brady's stanza includes some mimetic prosody, especially the fluttering glide of leafy wings in the last two lines. But on the whole, Dryden's and Brady's words, while delightful, are not in themselves musical; they depend on their musical settings in a way that Herbert's, Milton's, and Marvell's do not. In these, music is intrinsic in the words; in those later poems, the intrinsic music is about extrinsic music, and both words and music serve music. Though they praise music as a creative principle, they also move away from the relation between words and music conceptually. Marvell's culminates in a single human voice, Dryden's "diapason clos[es] full in man," Brady's eulogizes *musica speculativa*, and the latter two were set for human soloists and choirs, but all three texts mainly concern the development and effects of musical instruments, and only Marvell's mentions a human voice at all. Cowley suppresses Orpheus' voice – he only strikes his instrument, which is also what the sequacious trees follow in Dryden's ode – and Brady suppresses even his name, metonymizing him into a "Thracian Lyre."

After its apostrophe to the "Soul of the World" who tunes the "Heavenly Round," Brady's *Ode* makes the organ the culmination of human musical culture.

> With that sublime Celestial lay
> Can any Earthly Sounds compare?
> If any Earthly Music dare,
>   The noble ORGAN may.
> From Heav'n its wondrous notes were giv'n,
> (*Cecilia* oft convers'd with Heav'n,)
> Some Angel of the Sacred Choire
> Did with his Breath the Pipes inspire;
> And of the Notes above the just Resemblance gave,
>   Brisk without Lightness, without Dullness Grave.

The section concludes (in some versions) with an organ solo, and the poem continues, like Dryden's, with praise of the organ, which masters those secular instruments that stir and quell passions:

> Wondrous Machine!
> To thee the Warbling Lute,
> Though us'd to Conquest, must be forc'd to yield:
> With thee unable to dispute,
> The Airy VIOLIN
> And lofty VIOL quit the field;

> In vain they tune their speaking Strings
> To court the Fair, or, praise Victorious Kings,
>   Whilst all thy consecrated Lays
>   Are to more noble Uses bent;
> And every gratefull Note to Heav'n repays
>   The Melody it lent.
>
> In vain the Am'rous FLUTE and soft GUITARR
>   Jointly labour to inspire
>   Wanton Heat and loose Desire;
>   Whilst thy chaste Airs do gently move
>   Seraphic Flame and Heav'nly Love.
> The FIFE and all the Harmony of War
>   In vain attempt the Passions to alarm,
>   Which thy commanding Sounds compose and charm.
>   Let these among themselves contest
>   Which can discharge its single Duty best.
>   Thou summ'st their diff'ring Graces up in One,
> And art a Consort of them All within thy Self alone.

Purcell sets "Warbling" lyrically and "must be forc'd" heavy-handedly. "Unable" affords a virtuoso passage to the bass; only a really good bass is "able" to do this line. Fittingly, the last two lines are more sensuously concenting than "Wanton Heat," which has a sort of tyrannous repetition heard in "must be forc'd to yield"; seraphic ardor, in contrast, expresses insatiable satisfaction.

Organs – until they were dismantled or destroyed – had long been part of cathedral and some parish worship; larger parishes such as Ludlow had them in the fifteenth century (the Ludlow account books for 1472/73 record a payment "to Sir Edm'd White for mendyng of ye organs ij s. vj. d"[32]). Knowing a little about what is happening inside an organ, the spooky materiality of this "wondrous machine" and the work of filling its lungs and shaping its many voices, gives its sonic splendors an intense reality.

A pipe organ begins as trees made into lumber, ores made into ingots, and a designer's plan for a particular space, style, and sound. A cathedral organ may have as many as eight thousand pipes, from the smallness of a human finger to the largeness of a guided missile. Those who make them cut, plane, and join the lumber and press and roll the ingots into sheets and cut them into strips and fans which they thin down by hand, then roll into cylinders and cones that contain the speaking parts. They make wooden trunking to carry the air from the organ's sheep-skin

bellows, or lungs, to the windpipes in its chests; these wind chan-
nels are square to make straight the ways of the organ's breath and
keep its pitches true. If you blow into the small end of a formed
pipe it will squeal or croak in the general vicinity of some pitch and
timbre, but its true tone must be found by the voicer, who makes
its pitch "just" by precise adjustments to its mouth and ears – its
whistle-opening and the small flaps beside it. If you blow into the
end of a tuned pipe it will speak true. When the whole organ has
been assembled in a church, the voicer will adjust the pipes again
within their acoustical home.

In operation, an organ respirates, taking air into its bellows and
returning it laden with sound, and thus, as Brady says, "every grateful Note to Heav'n repays." As the wind from the bellows flows
through the trunking it is admitted to the pipes, which the organist selects by pressing their keys, attached to the pipes (in a non-
electronic organ) by long, lithe strips of wood called trackers.
These frail wands, guided by delicate carved bearings, lead from
the keyboard down to the base of the console and then up to particular pipes. When the player touches a key, its tracker opens a
pallet, allowing the organ's breath to enter the pipe and make it
speak. Each tracker provides a direct connection between the
musician's finger and the pipe's voice, evoking the strength of all
the slender means on which beauty depends, like the nerves that
transmit energy from the musician's mind to his fingers and
thence to them. These slender ribbons are the tensile attachment
between skillful flesh, controlled by the console of a disciplined
and attentive mind filled with the music of a master voyager in the
mathematical registers of light, and the skillfully wrought and
pierced hollow rods that give voice to this collusion of spirit, air,
and ear. A tracker organ is "perpendicular" in its interplay of
matter and spirit.

Organs speak, but unless they join a choir they speak without
words. In these poems, the organ takes the prize for sublimity and
for combining all instruments, as its generic name implies. Marvell
takes the "organ" of Genesis to be a pipe organ and other instruments to issue from it, while the others use the new invention of
crediting that invention to Cecilia and the organ as a consort of all
the rest. The conceptions of the organ as a recapitulation of creation and as a city are illustrated in seventeenth-century engravings.
Robert Fludd's many-turreted temple of music in *Utriusque Cosmi*

Historia (1617) incorporates organ pipes,[33] and Athanasius Kircher's *Harmonia Nascentis Mvndi* in *Musurgia Universalis* (1650) represents an organ whose registers are the days of creation. On the continent such conceptions evoked baroque visual splendors. The castle organ built in 1658 which Johann Sebastian Bach played as organist to the Court of Weimar (1708–17) occupied a special room built into the high ceiling, the "Himmelsburg," so that one looked up through a balustraded rectangular opening at the organ's gold-festooned pipes with a background of clouds and angels as if one were looking up into the celestial city, whence the music poured. Baroque organ music, along with other music, became more "lofty" than its pre-war predecessors.

Like this "Wondrous Machine," musical society as represented by the St. Cecilia's Day celebrations was organized, virtuosic, and civic, and spread, like Marvell's "organ's city," forming "colonies." Music became more iconic than it had been during church-music disputes. The addresses to St. Cecilia herself in the Odes were not religious – she is an allegorical figure for music as a channel to the divine rather than a person with intercessory powers. But, like the worship of saints, the worship of music put some distance between the worshipper and the Creator. Milton's Adam and Eve heard angels all around; Cecilia's performance "brought an angel down." The change was perhaps not so much from a sacred to a secular aesthetic as from "Heaven in ordinarie" (Herbert's *Prayer* I) to "the religious sublime." Alexander Shapiro, tracing this conception from the St. Cecilia's Day festivities through the early oratorios of Handel, argues that musicologists have created an artificial "dichotomy between devotion and drama" and "have tended to ignore the integral role of religion in eighteenth-century culture . . . The critical elements of Handel's early English oratorios – ceremonial music and biblical paraphrase – emerged from an indigenous English tradition of sublime art and hence owed much of their contemporary significance to this religious aesthetic."[34] Music and poetry of city and court provided liturgy and art far above daily life – and, as Pepys said, "very fine it is."

Nevertheless, participation in church choirs and the building and playing of organs burgeoned as more parish churches developed voluntary choirs.[35] Nor have close connections between words and music entirely disappeared. In the twentieth century Ralph Vaughan Williams, Benjamin Britten, and Gerald Finzi are among those who have found natural relations between them. In addition, technology allows composers to add the voices of creatures not "wanting voice" after all: Henry Purcell gives voice to box and fir, but Alan Hovhaness incorporates the voices of live whales. The connection of words and music has never entirely disappeared from poetry either, and it too may be resurging among contemporary poets who find a numinous connection to "nature's voice" in their verbal music. Poets and choirs still sing, in a world increasingly conscious that it must become more choir-like to live.

Appendix 1: music, poems, and iconography for the liturgical year

The following lists selected music and poems corresponding with the feasts and fasts of the church and with topics in the King's College Chapel windows and the *Biblia Pauperum*. In each window, A and C are the lower lights, containing the antitypes, and B and D the upper ones, depicting the corresponding types. Descriptions of the *Biblia*, cited by opening, are from Henry, *Biblia Pauperum*. Descriptions of the windows are supplemented from Wayment, *The Windows of King's College Chapel* and *King's College Chapel, Cambridge: The Great Windows*. The *Biblia* has two types for each antitype, the windows one. In some cases I have taken titles of topics from these books. Local manuscripts are cited parenthetically: the organ book attributed to Henry Loosemore as (L), the Peterhouse part-books as (P), and the Ely Organ Book as (E). Some Latin motets are included, since Latin could be used in college chapels.

Annunciation

[This topic follows the order of the windows here rather than the liturgical calendar.]

Window 3A–B: The Annunciation; The Temptation of Eve.

Biblia 2a: The Annunciation; The Temptation of Eve; Gideon's Fleece.

Music: Parsons, "Ave Maria."

Poem: Donne, "The Annunciation and Passion."

Christmas Day

Window 3C–D: The Nativity; Moses and the Burning Bush.

Biblia 2b: The Nativity; Moses and the Burning Bush; Aaron's Rod.

Music: Sheppard, "Verbum caro factum est"; Byrd, "Laetentur coeli," "O magnum misterium," "This Day was Christ Born," "Rejoice, rejoice with heart and voice"; Gibbons, "See, see the Word is incarnate"; Weelkes, "Gloria in excelsis Deo"; Amner, "O

ye little flock" (E, P), "Rejoice, rejoice with heart and voice" (E);
"Lo, how from heav'n like stars"; "I bring you tiding" (*Sacred
Hymns*).
Poems: Herbert, *Christmas*; Crashaw, *In the holy nativity*; Vaughan,
Christ's Nativity, *The Shepherds*; Milton, *On the Morning of Christ's
Nativity*.
The Circumcision
Window 4A–B: The Circumcision of Christ; The Circumcision of
Isaac.
Poems: Crashaw, *An Himne for the Circumcision day of our Lord*, *To the
Name above Every Name*.
Epiphany
Window 4C–D: The Visitation of the Magi; The Visitation of the
Queen of Sheba bringing gifts to Solomon, portrayed as Henry
VIII.
Biblia 3a: The Magi; Abner before David; Sheba before Solomon.
Music: Sheppard, "Regis Tarsis"; Bull, "Almighty God which by the
Leading of a Star."
Poem: Crashaw, *In the Glorious Epiphanie*.
The Presentation
Window 5 A–B: The Presentation of Christ at the Temple; The
Dedication of the Firstborn (Exod. 13.2).
Window: C–D: The Flight into Egypt (with falling idol); The Story
of Jacob and Esau.
Biblia 3b: The Presentation; The Presentation of the Firstborn
(Lev. 12); Anna Presents Samuel.
Music: Tallis, "Videte miraculum."
Innocents' Day
Window 6A–B: The Fall of the Idols; The Worship of the Golden
Calf.
Biblia 4a: The Flight into Egypt; Jacob Flees Esau; David Flees Saul.
4b: The Fall of the Egyptian Idols; The Worship of the Golden
Calf; The Fall of Dagon.
Window 6C–D: The Massacre of the Innocents by King Herod; The
Massacre of the Royal Children by Queen Athalia.
Biblia 5a: The Massacre of the Innocents; Saul has the priests slain;
Athalia has the princes slain.
Poems: Crashaw, *Upon the Infant Martyrs*; Milton, *On the Morning of
Christ's Nativity*.
Baptism of Christ

[The Gospel narrative, Matt. 3, is read at Matins on St. John the Baptist's Day in the 1559 BCP.]

Window 7A–B: The Baptism of Christ; Naaman washed in the Jordan.

Biblia 6a: The Baptism of Christ; Crossing the Red Sea; the Bunch of Grapes, or the Great Cluster.

Music: Gibbons, "This is the Record of John" (P). (However, the text, John 1, is the Gospel for the Fourth Sunday of Advent in the 1559 BCP.)

Poem: Herbert, *The Bunch of Grapes.*

Lent

Window 7C–D: Satan Tempts Christ; Jacob tempts Esau to sell his birthright.

Biblia 6b: The Temptation of Christ; Esau sells his birthright; the Fall.

Music: Tye, "Miserere mei Domine" (P); Tallis, "Wipe away my sins" (L); Mundy, "O Lord I bow the knees of my heart" (L); Byrd, "O God whom our offenses" (L) and "Ne irascaris" (L, P); Hilton, "Lord, for thy tender mercy's sake" (formerly attributed to Farrant); Barcroft, "O Lord, we beseech thee" (L); Morley, "Nolo mortem peccatoris" and "Laboravi in gemitu"; Batten, "Haste thee, O God"; Amner, "Remember not, Lord, our offenses" (L), "Lord, in thy Wrath" (E), and "Woe is me" (P); Morley, Batten, Giles, and Amner, "Out of the Deep" (P).

Poems: Donne, Holy Sonnets; Giles Fletcher, *Christ's Victory and Triumph*; Herbert, *Lent*; Milton, *Paradise Regain'd.*

Window 8A–B: The Raising of Lazarus; Elisha Raises the Shunammite's Son.

Biblia 7a: The Raising of Lazarus; Elias Raises the Sarephtan; Elisha Raises the Shunammite.

Passion Sunday

[Called the Sunday Next before Easter (BCP, 1559); called "Palm Sunday" in Lake's sermons and by Wither, who pointedly defends the designation.]

Window 8C–D: Triumphal Entry into Jerusalem; The Triumph of David.

Biblia 8b: The Entry into Jerusalem; The Triumph of David; Elisha is Greeted.

Music: Tallis, Mundy, "Salvator mundi"; Gibbons, Weelkes, "Hosanna to the Son of David."

Poems: Herbert, *Antiphon* I (L), *Praise* I; Vaughan, *Palm-Sunday.*
Thursday before Easter
Window 9A–B: The Last Supper; The Israelites gather manna
(bread from heaven).
Biblia 10b: The Last Supper; Melchisedech Offers Bread and
Wine; Moses and the Manna.
Window 9C–D: The Agony in the Garden; The Fall of the Rebel
Angels.
Biblia 11b: The meeting of Jesus with Judas and the officers (John
18.4–6) conflated with The Agony in the Garden; The Foolish
Virgins; The Fall of the Rebel Angels.
Music: Tallis, Byrd, "O sacrum convivium"; Tallis, "If ye love me."
Poems: Herbert, *The Agonie; The Banquet; Love* (III); Vaughan,
Mount of Olives (I).
Window 10A–B: Judas Betrays Christ with a Kiss; Cain and Abel.
Good Friday
Window 11A–B: Christ before the High Priest Caiaphas; Jeremiah
tried and imprisoned for treason.
Window 11C–D: Christ before Herod; Noah mocked by Ham.
Window 12A–B: The Scourging of Christ; The Torments of Job.
Window C–D: Christ Crowned with Thorns; The Crowning of
Solomon.
Music: Weelkes, "Give the king thy judgments"; Tomkins, "O God,
the proud are risen against me"; Peerson, *The Passion.*
Poems: Donne, *La Corona*; Marvell, *The Coronet.*
East Window, lower range: Christ Shown to the People (Ecce
Homo), left; Pilate Washing his Hands, center; Christ Carrying
his Cross, right. Upper range: Christ nailed to the cross; The
Crucifixion; Christ taken down from the cross.
Biblia 12b: Pilate Washing his Hands. 13b: Christ Carrying his
Cross. 14b: The Crucifixion; Christ's side pierced. The Creation
of Eve. Moses strikes the Rock.
Music: Tallis, White, Byrd, Parsley, *Lamentations;* Amner, "Consider
all ye passers-by."
Poems: Donne, Holy Sonnets; *Good Friday 1613, Riding Westward,
The Crosse, A Litanie;* Herbert, *The Sacrifice, The Thanksgiving,
Good Friday, Sighs & Grones, The Jews, The Bag, Self-Condemnation;*
Crashaw, *To Pontius washing his hands*; Vaughan, *The Passion, The
Incarnation, and Passion.*

Easter

Window 16A–B: Christ Rising from the Dead; Jonah cast up by the whale.

Window 16C–D: Christ Appears to his Mother; Tobias Returns to his Mother.

Biblia 16a: The Resurrection; Samson removes the gates of Gaza; Jonah cast up by the whale.

Window 17A–B: The three Marys at the Empty Tomb; Reuben at the Empty Pit (finding Joseph gone).

Biblia 16b: The Three Marys at the Tomb; Reuben at the Pit: The Betrothed Seeks the Beloved (from the Song of Solomon).

Window 17C–D: Mary Magdalene finds Christ alive in the Garden (Nolo me Tangere); Darius finds Daniel alive in the lions' den.

Biblia 17a: Mary Magdalene finds Christ; Daniel found alive in the lions' den; The Betrothed finds the Beloved.

Music: Taverner, Tallis, Robert Johnson, "Dum transisset Sabbatum"; Byrd, "Haec dies"; Tallis, Tye, Byrd (L), Amner (L), Batten (P), "Christ rising"; Byrd, Gibbons, "If [then] ye be risen again with Christ"; Amner, "My Lord is hence removed" (L), "St. Mary now, but erst the worst of many"; Portman (P) and Loosemore, "O God my Heart is Ready" (L, P); "Tomkins, My beloved spake."

Poems: Herbert, *Easter, Easter Wings, Sunday* ("A Samson bore the doors away"); Vaughan, *Easter-Day, Easter-Hymn*.

Ascension

Window 20A–B: The Ascension of Christ; Elijah taken up into Heaven.

Biblia 18b: The Ascension of Christ; Enoch Ascends to Heaven; Elisha recovers Elijah's mantle.

Music: Gibbons, "O Clap your hands"; Byrd, Gibbons, Amner (L), "Lift up your heads, O ye gates"; Amner, "He that descended man to be"; Tomkins, "Arise, O Lord."

Poems: Vaughan, *Ascension-Day, Ascension-Hymn*.

Whitsunday (Pentecost)

Window 20C–D: The Holy Spirit given to the Apostles; Moses Receives the Two Tables of the Law.

Biblia 19a: Pentecost; Moses Receives the Law on Sinai; Elijah's Sacrifice is accepted.

Music: Sheppard, "Spiritus Sanctus"; Tallis, "O Lord, give thy Holy Spirit," "If ye love me," "Loquebantur variis linguis."

Poems: Vaughan, *White Sunday*.

Holy Days not represented in the windows

Trinity Sunday

Music: Sheppard, "Libera nos"; Byrd, "O lux beata Trinitas"; Weelkes, "Alleluia, I heard a voice."

Poems: Herbert, *Trinitie Sunday*; Vaughan, *Trinity-Sunday*.

St. Michael and All Angels

Music: Dering, "Factum est silentium."

Poems: Herbert, *To All Angels and Saints*; Milton, *A Mask at Ludlow*, *Paradise Lost*.

All Saints

Music: Taverner, Tallis, "Audivi: media nocte"; Byrd, "O quam gloriosam," "Justorum animae"; Ward, "I heard the voice of a great multitude"; Tomkins, "I heard a voice from heaven" (text from funeral rite), "Almighty God, which hast knit together."

Appendix 2: chronology

1515–47	Completion of the fabric and making of the windows of King's College Chapel.
1516	Thomas Wyatt (1503–42) enters St. John's College.
1534	Act of Supremacy: Henry VIII (1491–1547) becomes supreme head on earth of the Church of England.
1543	Thomas Tallis, c. 1505–85, becomes organist and probably choirmaster of the Chapel Royal. William Byrd born (d. 1623).
1547–53	Edward VI (b. 1537).
1549	Book of Common Prayer.
1553–58	Mary Tudor (b. 1516), Catholic ruler.
1556	Sternhold and Hopkins, *One and fiftie Psalms of David* (Geneva); later editions called *The Whole Book of Psalms*.
1557	"Tottel's Miscellany": *Songes and Sonnettes*.
1558–1603	Elizabeth I (b. 1533).
1569–76	Edmund Spenser (1552–99) at Pembroke College.
1574–76	Francis Bacon at Trinity.
1583–87	Thomas Morley choirmaster at Norwich.
1587	Christopher Marlowe (1564–93) M. A., Corpus Christi.
1588	William Byrd, *Psalmes, Sonets, and Songs*. *Musica Transalpina* published by Nicholas Yonge.
1590	Thomas Watson's *Italian Madrigalls Englished*.
1590, 1593	Spenser, *The Faerie Queene*.
1590, 1596	Sidney, *Arcadia*.
1591	John Fletcher enters Cambridge University.
1594–97	Richard Hooker (c. 1554–1600), *Lawes*.
1595	Sidney, *An Apology for Poetry*.

1596–1606?	Orlando Gibbons chorister and organist at King's.
1597	Thomas Morley, *A Plain and Easy Introduction to Practicall Musicke.*
	Thomas Weelkes, *Madrigals to 3. 4. 5. and 6. Voyces.*
1598	Henry Peacham, M. A., Trinity. Friend of Dowland.
1600	Byrd, *The Great Service.*
	Morley et al., *Triumphes of Oriana.*
	John Dowland's *Second Book of Songs.*
1601–11	Shakespeare's major tragedies and romantic comedies.
1603–25	James I (b. 1566).
1604	Hampton Court Conference.
	Prohibition of Idle Games and Plays.
1604–25	Orlando Gibbons organist of the Chapel Royal.
1609	George Herbert (1593–1633) enters Trinity College.
	Lancelot Andrewes Bishop of Ely.
1610–41	John Amner organist at Ely.
1615	Amner's *Sacred Hymns.*
1616	Death of Shakespeare and Cervantes.
	Ben Jonson's *Works* published in folio.
	Order for Subscriptions, before taking University degrees, to the Act of Supremacy and the liturgy and doctrine of the Church of England.
1619	Kepler, *De harmonice mundi.*
1621	John Donne Dean of St. Paul's; Milton at St. Paul's school.
1623	Shakespeare's First Folio.
	Sir John Suckling (b. Norfolk) matriculates at Trinity College.
1625	Death of James I; Accession of Charles I, m. Henrietta Maria of France. Liberty of worship granted to Catholics.
1625–32	John Milton at Christ's College.
1627–70	Henry Loosemore organist at King's College (interrupted).
1629–40	Parliament dissolved. Personal rule of Charles I.
1633	Donne's *Poems* and Herbert's *The Temple* (posthumous); Cowley's *Poetical Blossoms.*

	William Laud becomes Archbishop of Canterbury.
1633–41	Andrew Marvell (1621–78) at Trinity College.
1635–43	Richard Crashaw Fellow of Peterhouse; ejected by revolutionaries.
1637	Milton's *Mask* published; music by Henry Lawes.
1637–42	Abraham Cowley at Trinity College.
1640	Long Parliament begins. Oliver Cromwell warns against choral services at Ely.
1640–41	House of Commons declares Order for Subscriptions unlawful. Cromwell urges destruction of episcopacy "root and branch."
	John Barnard, *The First Book of Selected Church Musick.*
1642–52	British Civil Wars.
1644	Milton, *Areopagitica* and *Of Education.*
	Royalists defeated at Marston Moor.
1645/46	Milton's *Poems.*
	Laud executed, episcopacy abolished.
1649	Charles I executed. Council of State and Republic.
1653–58	Commonwealth; Oliver Cromwell, Lord Protector; Milton, Latin Secretary; Marvell, assistant (1657).
1654	John Dryden B. A., Trinity College.
1659–95	Life of Henry Purcell.
1660	Restoration of Charles II.
1667	Milton, *Paradise Lost. A Poem Written in Ten Books.*
1674	Milton, *Paradise Lost. A Poem in Twelve Books.*
1680	Newton, *Principia.*
1681	Marvell's *Miscellaneous Poems* (posthumous).
1688	James II exiled; end of religious uniformity and of monarchical power independent of Parliament.
1736–40	Handel's settings of Dryden's *Alexander's Feast* and *Ode for St. Cecilia* and Milton's *L'Allegro* and *Il Penseroso.*

Appendix 3: glossary of musical and liturgical terms

These simple definitions indicate my principal uses of these words. For fuller definitions and histories see *Grove*.

Equivalent note and rest values:

British	US
breve	double whole note
semibreve	whole note
minim	half note
crotchet	quarter note
quaver	eighth note
semiquaver	sixteenth note

Agnus Dei: section of the Mass following the Sanctus and Benedictus: "Lamb of God, who takest away the sins of the world, have mercy upon us."

Air, ayre: a song usually for accompanied solo voice, though accompaniments are sometimes used as vocal parts.

Altus, alto: the voice part above the tenor.

Anglican chant: harmonized homophonic singing of psalms and other portions of the liturgy.

Anthem: a short choral work, added at the end of the liturgy in pre-Restoration services.

Antiphon: chant sung before and after a psalm or canticle.

Antiphonally: sung responsively from side to side.

Bar (US "measure"): a segment of musical notation marked off by bar lines.

Bassus, bass: the lowest voice or instrumental part.

Benedicite: Morning canticle from the Apocryphal part of the Book of Daniel, beginning "Benedicite omnia opera Domini Domino"; "O all the works of the Lord, bless ye the Lord."

Benedictus: Morning canticle (Luke 1.68–79), "Blessed be the Lord God of Israel."

Benedictus qui venit: passage (Matt. 21.9) following the Sanctus in the Roman rite (and modern Anglican rite), "Blessed is he that cometh in the name of the Lord."

Book of Common Prayer: the official liturgy of the Church of England since 1549, in various editions.

Broken consort: an ensemble of diverse kinds of instruments.

Cadence: the conclusion of a section of a work, or a point where all or most parts of a polyphonic texture come together on one chord.

Canon: (1) the portion of the Mass or Holy Communion containing the consecration of the sacrament. (2) Cleric attached to a cathedral or collegiate church. (3) A musical work in which the voices sing the same melody, entering at different times so that they overlap; a round is a circular (repeatable) canon.

Canticle: verses sung or said in Roman and Anglican daily offices: their titles in the Book of Common Prayer are Venite exultemus domino, Te Deum laudamus, Benedicite, Benedictus, Jubilate Deo, Magnificat, Cantate domino, Deus misereatur, Nunc dimittis. See "Incipit."

Cantoris: the north or Gospel side of the choir, were the cantor is seated, and the choristers who sit on that side. See also "Decani."

Cantus: upper voice part.

Cantus firmus: the plainsong or other tune on which a polyphonic work is based.

Choir (also Quire): (1) group of singers; (2) the part of the church containing the choir stalls.

Choirbook: a single large book shared by choir members.

Chromaticism: the inclusion of accidentals or chromatic notes in a composition.

Collegiate Church: a large church, such as Westminster Abbey, that has a chapter, or body of officials, but is not the seat of a bishop.

Common meter: the meter most used in the metrical psalms, alternating four-beat and three-beat lines; ballad meter.

Common time: 4/4 time.

Communion: The Holy Communion, Lord's Supper, or Eucharist. Communion was commended to be received "oftentimes," at least "thrice a yeere" for parishioners and four times a year for students, according to the *Constitutions and Canons Ecclesiasticall, 1604,* XIII, XXI, XXIII. The Reformation BCP Communion service does not include the Kyrie, the Benedictus, or the Agnus Dei, and the Gloria is sung or said after the Communion. The Kyrie is included in the preces at Morning and Evening Prayer.

Concent: singing in harmony.

Concertante: having solo parts within an ensemble, usually an orchestra.

Concertato: having voices and instruments of different natures combined and set off against each other.

Consonance: notes sung or played simultaneously (or, in unharmonized melodies, consecutively) with intervals more than three half-steps apart. In Pythagorean tuning, only fourths, fifths, and octaves were considered consonant. In diatonic tuning, thirds and sixths are also consonant.

Consort: a small ensemble of instruments, voices, or both.

Continuo: instrumental accompaniment providing rhythmic and harmonic support.

Contrafactum: the replacement of the original text of a composition with alternative words, such as vernacular for Latin ones.

Counterpoint: the combining of several melodic lines to produce harmony.

Countertenor or contratenor: male voice part above the tenor; in early music, male altos.

Credo: The Nicene Creed, said after the Gospel in the BCP; see also "Mass."

Cross-relation: "[T]he relation set up when, for instance, the notes A♮ and A♭ occur simultaneously or in immediate succession in different PARTS – that is, a special effect of harmony in which the parts are not unanimous in whether they treat a particular note as sharp, natural, or flat. (*Cross-relation,* the standard American term is clearer than 'false relation,' more usual in Britain.)" Jacobs, *The Penguin Dictionary of Music,* 88.

Decani: the south or Epistle side of a choir, where, in a cathedral, the Dean (Decanus) is seated; the choristers who sit on the south side.

Diminished: having an interval smaller than that of the key or scale in use.

Dissonance: simultaneous sounding of intervals less than four half-steps apart on a diatonic scale.

Doxology: see "Gloria patri."

Duple time: rhythms divisible into groups of two beats or pulses.

Equal temperament: tuning in which the steps of the scale are divided by equal intervals, as on a piano keyboard, as distinguished from natural or mean-tone tuning.

Faburden: English harmonization in three parallel parts with the plainsong in the middle voice.

False relation: see "Cross-relation."

Fauxbourdon: continental form of faburden, with the plainsong in the top part.

Fundamental: (1) the root note of a mode or key. (2) The composite sound of an overtone series; sometimes, the first partial in the series.

Gloria: a part of the Mass or Communion beginning with the Gloria in excelsis Deo and glorifying Father, Son, and Holy Spirit.

Gloria in excelsis Deo: the song of the angels at the birth of Christ (Luke 2.14).

Gloria patri: verse said or sung after psalms and canticles and elsewhere in the liturgy: BCP "Glory be to the Father, and to the Son, and to the Holy Ghost. As it was in the beginning, is now, and ever shall be: world without end. Amen."

Great Service: an integrated setting of the sung portions of Morning and Evening Prayer, usually the Venite, Te Deum, Benedictus, Kyrie, and Creed of Matins and the Preces, Magnificat, and Nunc Dimittis of Evensong; distinguished from Short Service.

Hemiola: a rhythmic shift in which a group of two notes and a group of three notes occupy the same amount of time.

Homophony: music in which all voices produce the same rhythm at the same time; chordal composition.

Hymn: a song, anthem, or poem of praise.

Imitation: restatement of linear phrases by overlapping successive voices.

Improperia: the Reproaches of Christ on the Cross.

Incipit: words chanted by the cantor at the beginning of a liturgical text.

Intonation: singing in pure pitches. In the Pythagorean scale, thirds and sixths are not consonant; "just" intonation "was an attempt to overcome this problem by basing the tuning on both the pure fifth (3:2) and the pure major third (5:4)" (Duckworth and Brown, *Theoretical Foundations* 18).

Isorhythmic motet: a motet in which an extended rhythmic pattern in the cantus firmus repeats, either reiteratively or proportionally, through the whole piece.

Jubilate or Jubilate Deo: Morning canticle (Psalm 100) beginning "O be joyful in the Lord all ye lands."

Just intonation: see "Intonation."

Key: in tonal music, the primary tone center; the root pitch of the tonic chord.

Kyrie: the first section of the Mass, beginning Kyrie eleison, and the prayers in the BCP Morning and Evening Prayer beginning "Lord, have mercy."

Leading tone: the seventh step of the scale, leading to a return to the tonic.

Longa: a note whose value is longer (by various pulses) than a whole note.

Macaronic: having a mixture of Latin and vernacular words.

Madrigal: polyphonic part-song for unaccompanied voices, usually through-composed and "vocally conceived with correct verbal accentuation in all the parts" with "sound-unity of music and words" (Roche, *The Madrigal*, 3, 25).

Magnificat: Evening canticle, the words of Mary in Luke 1.46–54, beginning in the BCP "My soul doth magnify the Lord."

Mass: the Roman Catholic or high Anglican liturgy of the Eucharist. The parts of the Ordinary set to music as an integrated composition are the Kyrie, Gloria, Credo, Sanctus and Benedictus, and Agnus Dei (q. v.). In English Renaissance masses the Kyrie was troped, having words added fitting the proper of the day, and therefore was not part of the musical structure of a composed mass.

Mean: the voice part between (hence its name) trebles and altos; in seventeenth-century music, usually the upper part.

Measure: (1) (British "bar") a segment of music marked off by bar lines in modern scores, either metrically or, for early music, in rhythmic phrases. (2) rhythm.

Melisma: a group of notes (strictly, five or more) sung to one syllable.

Modality: the mode of a work or phrase, as distinguished from tonality.

Modes: the kind of scale used in the church modes, named for classical modes but not the same. They are roughly the scales produced by playing only the white keys on a piano, from D to D, E to E, and so forth.

Monody: music sung by one voice with instrumental accompaniment, especially in late sixteenth- and seventeenth-century Italy.

Monophony: unaccompanied and unharmonized melody sung by one or more voices.

Motet: a sacred choral work in Latin.

Musica espressiva: music in which the expression of emotion is the primary purpose.

Musica humana: the musical proportions of the human soul.

Natural tuning: tuning of voices or instruments as nearly as possible to the consonances found by the division of a monochord into simple mathematical proportions.

Nicene Creed: the creed of the Mass and of the BCP Communion service (erroneously named for the Council of Nicea in 325 AD).

Notation: figures representing pitch and time values placed on a stave (staff).

Nunc Dimittis: Evening canticle, the words of Simeon in Luke 2.29–32, beginning in the BCP "Lord, now lettest thou thy servant depart in peace."

Office: daily services, apart from Communion; in the Church of England, Matins and Evening Prayer.

Ordinary: parts of the liturgy used at all times, as distinguished from the Proper.

Overtones: see "Partials."

Parody: setting of a text to previously existing music, especially of a mass text to a secular tune.

Part-book: a book containing one voice part of a choral work or part-song.

Partial: "One of the component vibrations at a particular frequency in a complex mixture. It need not be harmonic. The fundamental and all overtones may be described as partials, but the term is most often used in referring to the components in the tone of a bell" (*Grove* XIV:254).

Partials: the vibrations that constitute a particular pitch. Since different segments of a vibrating bell, string, or column of air vibrate at different rates, the pitches they produce contain the fundamental, or the vibration of the whole, and partials, or the less audible vibrations of the segments. The closer to the fundamental, the most audible pitch, the overtones in the series are, the more consonant they are; the farther away, the more dissonant.

Passion Sunday: Palm Sunday, called in the Reformation BCP "The Sunday Next before Easter."

Plagal mode: "Any of the church modes whose [range of scale degrees] includes the octave lying between the 4th below and the 5th above the final of the mode" (*Grove* XIV: 800).

Plainchant or plainsong: a liturgical chant in which all voices sing the same notes in the same rhythm at the same time.

Polyphony: music produced by several voices or instruments, usually with different musical lines or entering at different times (though homophony may be included), as distinct from plainchant or monody.

Prayer of Consecration: the prayer before the Communion in which the bread and wine are consecrated with the words of Christ at the Last Supper.

Prayer of Humble Access: the prayer before the Communion in the BCP, beginning "We do not presume to come to this thy table (O merciful Lord) trusting in our own righteousness, but in thy manifold and great mercies."

Preces: the prayers between the Creed and the Collects at Morning and Evening Prayer.

Proper: portions of the liturgy designated for particular days of the liturgical calendar, as distinguished from the Ordinary, including Psalms, Gospels, Epistles, Proper Prefaces, Antiphons, and Responsories.

Responsory: a chant in which the priest or cantor and the choir sing alternate verses. In the Roman rite, these appear in the daily office; hence the Good Friday Responsories are the responsorial chants appointed for that day.

Rhythm: the temporal organization of music.

Sanctus: the fourth section of the ordinary of the Mass; in the BCP, "Holy, holy, holy, Lord God of hosts; heaven and earth are full of thy glory; glory be to thee, O Lord most high."

Sarum rite: the Catholic liturgy as practiced in Salisbury Cathedral and, with minor variations, elsewhere in England.

Short service: a setting of the most frequently sung canticles of the BCP, usually the Magnificat and the Nunc Dimittis.

Stave or staff: a set of parallel lines on which notation is placed to indicate pitch and time values.

Stile nuovo: in the seventeenth century, the *stile moderno* or *seconda prattica*, the use of freer harmonizations and melodic leaps, often with the support of a *basso continuo*, than in the stricter polyphony of the *stile antico* or *prima prattica* that preceded it.

Strophic: having stanzas of the same form, or having two or more verses set to the same music.

Sursum corda: verses and responses before the Proper Prefaces; in the BCP Holy Communion beginning "Lift up your hearts."

Suspension: the holding of a note while other voices proceed, producing a dissonance.

Syncopation: a change of rhythmic emphasis produced by stressing a beat that would usually be unstressed within a rhythmic pattern.

Te Deum: morning canticle beginning "We praise thee, O God."

Temperament: tuning of a scale that compromises intervals to avoid discords in instruments of fixed tuning.

Tenebrae Responsories: responses sung in the Roman rite after the readings from Lamentations during the Offices on Thursday, Friday, and Saturday of Holy Week, so called because of the gradual extinguishing of candles during these services.

Tenor: the voice between the contratenor and the bass that in most medieval polyphony sings the cantus firmus.

Tessitura: the vocal range in which a piece generally lies.

Texture: the relations between various voice parts: homophonic or polyphonic, many or few, relative spacing, and the like.

Theorbo: an instrument of the lute family with longer courses than the standard lute and with extra bass strings. Mary Sidney, Lady Wroth, is shown holding one in her portrait by John de Critz at Penshurst Place (illustration in *Grove* XVIII:740).

Through-composed: having non-strophic music, written to suit the words throughout, whether or not the text is strophic.

Tonality: the quality of music based on the major or minor scale, having a tonal center established by the tonic chord.

Treble: the voice part with the highest range. In seventeenth-century English music the treble voice was rare, the means having the highest part in the texture.

Triple time: rhythm perceived as divided into groups of three pulses.

Tritone: an interval formed by three whole steps (an augmented fourth), such as C against F♯. It was known as the devil's interval and forbidden in the Middle Ages.

Trope: words and music added to a liturgical chant.

Underlay: the arrangement of words beneath the notes of a musical score.

Veni Creator: a hymn beginning "Come, Holy Ghost."

Venite: morning canticle (Psalm 95) beginning "O come let us sing unto the Lord."

Verse anthem, verse service: anthem or service combining solo and choral voices and sometimes an organ or other instruments.

Versicle: a short sentence in the liturgy answered by a response (choral or congregational).

Vibrato: rapid fluctuations in pitch, used as an ornament or, in bel canto singing, for projection and expressiveness; distinguished from just intonation in part-singing.

Voicing: the distribution of notes among various voice parts in a choir.

Word-painting: use of music to imitate the images or ideas of a text.

Notes

1 NATURE'S VOICE: CONCENT OF WORDS AND MUSIC

1 Boethius' classic division in *De institutione musica* (Strunk, *Source Readings*, 1:84–85) into *musica mundana, musica humana*, and *musica instrumentalis* does not include the supracosmic music of Dante and Milton, but all share the idea of eternal numbers. Other definitions of "the three parts of music" are discussed in chapter 4.

2 In *Prolusion II*, "circumactos ad modulaminis dulcedinem coelos" (*SM* 1102); Milton's clause is conditional. M. N. K. Mander discusses the prolusion and its sources and analogues in "Milton and the Music of the Spheres."

3 D. P. Walker, *Studies in Musical Science*, ch. 4.

4 Clifford, *Divine Services*, sig. A6.

5 Donne, *A Valediction forbidding Mourning*; Milton, *PL* 7.351.

6 Browne, *Religio Medici*, in *Works*, 1:84. Among the declaimers against church music was William Prynne, who thought all music not wholly "grave, and serious" apt "to poast men on to sinfull actions" (*Histrio-Mastix*, 287, 289).

7 Donne, *Devotions*, 23.

8 Fludd, *Microcosmi historia*, title page to vol. II and 1:90; engravings by Jan Theodore de Brÿ. Many Ptolemaic maps add a ninth sphere, the *primum mobile*, to the spheres of the planets (including earth) and fixed stars; this one expands it to form nine more spheres representing the nine choirs of angels as classified by Dionysius the Pseudo-Areopagite, divided into three hierarchies corresponding with three parts of the soul designated Ratio, Intellectus, and Mens, ascending from the most discursive to the most intuitive faculties.

9 The relations of Renaissance cosmography to music and poetry are amply treated by S. K. Heninger in *Touches of Sweet Harmony*.

10 I use the term "Renaissance" broadly for arts that combine a rebirth of classical "humanistic" concerns with native English traditions. Usually I will not sort styles into the imposed categories of Renaissance, mannerist, and baroque but treat works individually.

11 On varieties of tuning see Mark Lindley, "Temperament," in *Grove* and

Duckworth and Brown, *Theoretical Foundations*, ch. 3. The differences are recorded in J. Murray Barbour and Fritz A. Kuttner, *The Theory and Practice of Just Intonation*. The simplest way of thinking about the relation of consonances to matter is to remember that when a string is divided exactly in half, the half produces a note an octave higher than the whole. Fourths and fifths may also be produced by simple proportions, and hence for Pythagoras were true consonances; thirds and sixths are more complex.

12 *BCP*, preface to the Sanctus.
13 De' Bardi, "Discourse on Ancient Music and Good Singing" (*c.* 1580), in Strunk, *Source Readings*, II:108–09.
14 Peter Phillips traces the beginnings of the verse anthem in *English Sacred Music*, 63–66.
15 Until the early sixteenth century, all members of English choirs, except boy choristers, were clerics, and could presumably understand Latin. The boys in the Chapel Royal and the college and cathedral choirs were supposed to be educated by the foundations.
16 Phillips, *English Sacred Music*, 41, 42.
17 These changes and continuities are traced in chapter 2.
18 For texts and scores of English madrigals and lute songs see *The English Madrigalists* [*EM*] and *English Lute-Songs* [*EL*]; texts may also be found in Fellowes, *English Madrigal Verse*. Most of the madrigals mentioned in this section are performed by the King's Singers on *All at once well met*.
19 Stevens, *Music and Poetry in the Early Tudor Court*, 12; Cornysh, Fayrfax L BL Add. MS 5465, fol. 33.
20 Benham, *Latin Church Music*, 61.
21 Morley, *A Plain and Easy Introduction*, 291
22 Amner, *Sacred Hymns*, titled "An Alleluia. In memorie of the Gunpowder day." A version is also in L BL Add. MS 17792–96.
23 Peacham, *Compleat Gentleman*, quoted in Strunk, *Source Readings*, II: 146.
24 "Reioyce, reioice with hart & voyes" in the Hammond part-books (O Bodleian MSS Mus. f. 11–15), song 24, which differs from the chorus of the same name in *BF* 13.
25 L BL Add. MS 17792–96, fol. 114v in cantus part-book. John Ward's "Downe, caytive wretch" (O Christ Church MSS 56–57) puns on "partes": the cantus sings "whilst heavenly thoughts doe descant on the ground," the contratenor "milde temperance the goulden meane must keepe," the tenor "And constant fayth the Tenor sweetly sounde."
26 O Tenbury MS 1382, 1617. Tomkins' *Musica Deo Sacra* was published in 1668.
27 *At a Solemn Musick*, Trinity MS, *Milton's Poetical Works*, ed. Fletcher, I: 390.

28 Peacham, *Compleat Gentleman*, quoted in Strunk, *Source Readings*, ii: 146.
29 On musical structure see John Aplin, "Structural Devices in English Liturgical Music, 1545–1570."
30 Kerman, *Masses and Motets*, 165–67.
31 Kepler, *Harmonice Mundi*, ch. 3.
32 From the contracts of 1626, in Wayment, *The Windows of King's College Chapel*. A fuller description of the chapel occurs in chapter 2.
33 Hugh Benham discusses this point in *Latin Church Music*, 137.
34 A *Salve Regina* by Robert Wylkynson, choirmaster at Eton from 1500 to 1515, is a nine-part anthem, each of the nine voice parts illuminated in the manuscript by an initial containing the name of one of the nine choirs of angels.
35 Peter Phillips, record notes to *Missa Gloria Tibi Trinitas*.
36 Plato, *Republic*, 142.
37 Plato, *Republic*, 86–87; compare *PL* 11.131–33.
38 Stevens, *Music and Poetry*, 35, 37.
39 Peter Phillips, record notes to *William Cornysh: Stabat Mater*.
40 Mellers, *Harmonious Meeting*, 24–25.
41 Raynor, *Music in England*, 65.
42 Zarlino, in Strunk, *Source Readings*, ii:40. This excerpt contains technical material on modal music and a section on adapting musical rhythms to verbal ones, which Morley freely appropriates (*Introduction*, 291–92).
43 Duckworth and Brown, *Theoretical Foundations* 36–37. The Pythagorean scale from which modes were derived did not have exactly the same intervals as the tempered keyboard.
44 Plato, *Republic*, 86–87.
45 For a seventeenth-century set of definitions sometimes at variance with Plato's – suggesting that, like modal music, definitions of modes were variable – see Butler, *The Principles of Musick*.
46 Winn, *Unsuspected Eloquence*, 35–36; 40 (with reference to Augustine, *Exposition of the Ninety-Ninth Psalm*); 58–59.
47 Peter Phillips discusses the range and arrangements of voice parts in *English Sacred Music*, 57–58.
48 Portions of this commentary are revised from my "Hierophons," 126–27.
49 Anderson, "Hymn: Ancient Greek," in *Grove* viii:836; Tom R. Ward and Nicholas Temperley "Hymn: Protestant," *Grove* viii:845–88. Even in secular books of devotional music, vernacular hymns to Christ and renderings of New Testament texts were relatively rare.
50 This anthem is described in chapter 5.

2 THE CONCINNITY OF THE ARTS AND THE CHURCH MUSIC CONTROVERSY

1 Lake, *Sermons*, 224.
2 By the time Herbert and Vaughan were writing poems, typology in the visual arts, suspect to those reformers who thought both images and "the olde lawe" should be dispensed with, had gone "into an eclipse," Wayment notes (*The Windows of King's College Chapel*, 7), the chapel at Hatfield House (1609) being among the few seventeenth-century works to employ it; but it survives in altered form in Protestant homiletics, music, and poetry. On Protestant uses of typology and their changes of emphasis see Lewalski, *Protestant Poetics*, ch. 4.
3 Quoted in Wayment, *The Windows of King's College Chapel*, 9.
4 Bacon, "Of Truth," in *Essayes*, 7.
5 I[esus] N[azarenus] R[ex] I[udaeorum], the ironic charge against him.
6 Monteverdi, *Magnificat a sei voce* (1609), puts a swagger and a bit of processional (or recessional) music into "Deposuit potentes de sede."
7 Also set by Weelkes "For the King's Day" (*MB* XXIII). The text, partly from the Litany, begins "Give the king thy judgments, O God, and thy righteousness unto the king's son. Then shall he judge the people according to the right, and defend the poor."
8 Anthems for November 5, commemorating the defeat of the Gunpowder Plot, might also fall into the category of national anthems, such as Hooper's "Hearken yee nations" in NY Drexel MS 5469 and Weelkes' "O Lord how joyful is the king," which has a vengeful text on the defeat of the plot (*MB* XXIII).
9 James I, *Workes*, 137. The epigraph on the title page is 1 Kings 3.12, "Loe I haue giuen thee a wise and an vnderstanding heart."
10 Heywood and Wright, *Cambridge University Transactions*, II:276.
11 NY Drexel MS 5469. See Thurston Dart, "Henry Loosemore's Organ Book." Part of this MS is missing, the dates of particular pieces uncertain, and the attribution based partly on the signature "Edward Tuck Chorister of Kings Colledge 1729" in a later hand on pages 38 and 104; but its 227 pages give a fair idea of the kind of music sung at King's during Herbert's, Milton's, and Marvell's residences in Cambridge.
12 Dom Anselm Hughes recounts the history and contents of the Peterhouse manuscripts in his *Catalogue*.
13 C CUL Ely MSS 1, 4, 28–29 (two organ books, tenor and bass partbooks), "possibly containing fragments of pre-Restoration books" (le Huray, *Music and the Reformation*, 95) and recording a long musical tradition at Ely.
14 Barnard's printed collection (1641) may also have been a source for subsequent part-books.
15 Gerard, *Herball*, I:153–54. My thanks to Jeremy Maule for calling my

attention to this emblematic flower. See also Sidney Gottlieb, "The Social and Political Backgrounds of George Herbert's Poetry," 110.

16 Herbert, *The Thanksgiving, Praise* (II), and *Church-musick.*

17 Patrides in Herbert, *The English Poems of George Herbert,* 129n.

18 Mersenne, *Traité de L'harmonie universelle,* Book 2, trans. John Bernhard Egan, 223–26.

19 Stephens, *Music and Poetry,* 59 and 68.

20 Donne received an honorary degree of Doctor of Divinity, as a royal chaplain, in 1615. Samuel Brooke, D. D., to whom he wrote the verse letter "O thou which to search out the secret parts / Of the'India, or rather Paradise of knowledge," was Master of Trinity.

21 However, the only known liturgical source of English Church music between Day's publications in the 1560s and 1617 (O B Tenbury MS 1382) is the fragmentary Ludlow part-books (le Huray, *Music and the Reformation* 93).

22 Examples may be found in Robertson and Stevens, *The Pelican History,* 191–94

23 Abraham, *Concise Oxford History,* 141–42. On the Old Hall Manuscript see Bukofzer, *Studies in Medieval and Renaissance Music,* ch. 2.

24 Tinctoris, *Proportionale musices* (*c.* 1476), in Strunk, *Source Readings,* II:5.

25 Quoted in Bent, *Dunstaple,* 2, trans. Charles Maclean.

26 Harrison, *The Eton Choirbook, MB* x:xiii.

27 Wayment, *The Windows of King's College Chapel,* 2.

28 Henry VI in the college charter of 1443 calls them "our Royal foundation of S. Mary of Eton" and "our College Royal of S. Mary and S. Nicholas" (Stubbs, *The Story of Cambridge,* 147).

29 Harrison, *New Oxford History of Music,* III:303; quoted in Abraham, *Concise Oxford History,* 186.

30 Harrison, *The Eton Choirbook, MB* x: xvi, xiii

31 Peacham, *The Compleat Gentleman,* quoted in Strunk, *Source Studies,* II: 143.

32 Cranmer, Letter to Henry VIII, quoted in Strunk, *Source Studies,* II: 160–61.

33 Lincoln Statutes, III:592–93, quoted in *EECM* XII: xii.

34 Windsor and York Injunctions, quoted in le Huray, *Music and the Reformation,* 24–25.

35 O B MSS Mus. Sch. e. 420–22; Fellowes, *English Cathedral Music,* 29, 42.

36 [Church of England,] *A Collection of Articles,* 79 (a copy with revised spelling of the *Iniunctions geuen by the Queenes Maiestie* published in English in 1559).

37 For a list of "Edwardian and Early Elizabethan Services and Anthems" see le Huray, *Music and the Reformation,* 183–85. Nicholas Temperley gives examples of early harmonizations of the Litany, Psalms, and

Canticles in *Music in the English Parish Church*, II:30–53 and also reproduces Marbeck's chants for the Lord's Prayer, Preces, and Venite and psalm tunes from Sternhold and Hopkins.

38 Parsons, transc. and ed. Peter le Huray in *The Treasury of English Church Music*, 33–44.

39 Morley, *A Plain and Easy Introduction*, 177–79.

40 Le Huray, *Anglican Chant*, Grove I:430–31. On other uses of chant see John Aplin's "Structural Devices in English Liturgical Music, 1545–1570."

41 Such as L BL Add. 30480–84; see Hughes-Hughes, *Catalogue*.

42 Charles Hamm and Jerry Call, "Sources, MS, IX.19: Renaissance polyphony, 16th-century English sacred," *Grove* XVII:695.

43 Philip Brett, *BE* v.iii; see also Brett, "Homage to Taverner in Byrd's Masses."

44 Day's publication contains music based on the *BCP* of 1549, thus preserving music of the very early English Reformation, and was probably delayed by the reign of Mary Tudor, as John Aplin explains in "The Origins of John Day's 'Certaine Notes.'" The first edition of all four parts is *Morning and Evening Prayer and Communion*, 1565, which historians call *Certaine Notes* as well.

45 Stone, ed. le Huray, *Treasury*, and Jackson, *Anthems for Choirs*.

46 C Peterhouse MS 40, probably before 1550; O Christ Church MSS 979–83, late sixteenth century; O B MSS Mus. Sch. e. 1–5, Latin and English, 1585; O B Tenbury MSS 34–41, *c.* 1600; L BL Add. MS 34049 (cantus), early seventeenth century (Fellowes, *TCM* I).

47 Attributed to Thomas Caustun, but according to Peter Phillips "an almost completely faithful transcription" of an *In Nomine* by Taverner (*English Sacred Music*, 24).

48 For a fuller account see Benham's chapter on Taverner and Aston in *Latin Church Music*; John Milson, "Music," 181–85; and *In Nomine* in the Discography.

49 Morley, *A Plain and Easy Introduction*, 123–25, 291, 35, 255.

50 Phillips, *English Sacred Music*, 35.

51 Byrd, *TCM* VII, facsimile facing p. 3; quoted in Strunk, *Source Readings*, II:137. Since *Gradualia* I sets primarily texts for masses devoted to the Virgin Mary, and since the dedicatee was a member of King James' privy council (and probably a Catholic), one sees both boldness and a degree of security in this declaration.

52 Harrison, *EECM*, II:vii.

53 Kerman, "William Byrd," in *The New Grove High Renaissance Masters*, 240–41.

54 Brett, "Homage to Taverner," 169.

55 Kerman, *New Grove High Renaissance Masters*, 266 and 267.

56 On the close relations of More's descendants see Bald, *John Donne*, 22–26.

57 Charles, *A Life of George Herbert*, 43.
58 Peterhouse Printed Book G.5.30; fully described in Hughes, *Catalogue of Musical Manuscripts at Peterhouse*, 49–51.
59 Among these are Taverner, *Jesu Christe Pastor Bone* and *Mater Christi* mass and motet; Fayrfax, *O bone Jesu* mass; Tomkins, "My beloved spake"; Loosemore and Portman, "My heart is ready" and Amner, Batten, Giles, and Morley, "Out of the Deep."
60 John Morehen in *Grove*, II:166.
61 From a ten-volume set of part-books made up in the Library of Hereford Cathedral; if the set originally contained an organ book, it is missing.
62 Phillips, *English Sacred Music*, 10–24.
63 Benham, *Latin Church Music*, 4.
64 Le Huray, *Music and the Reformation*, 135.
65 Shepherd, "The Changing Theological Concept of Sacrifice." I am indebted to Shepherd's dissertation for several quotations in this chapter.
66 Shepherd, "The Changing Theological Concept of Sacrifice," 313.
67 *The Bible and holy scriptvres* (London: C. Barker, 1576). Donne states that what Christ and the Apostles are said to have sung is "a Hymne composed of those six Psalmes, which we call the Allelujah Psalms, immediately preceding the hundred and nineteenth" (*Sermons* : VI. 293).
68 Marbeck, *Notes and Common Places*, 754, 1015–20.
69 Bullinger, *Fiftie godlie and learned sermons*, 932–35.
70 Whitgift, *An answere to a certen Libell* (1572); Cartwright, *A Replye to an Answere* (1574); Whitgift, *The Defense of the Aunswere* (1574); Cartwright, *The Second Replie . . . agaynst Master Doctor Whitgiftes second answere* (1575). Whitgift's 1572 tract quotes Cartwright's admonitions, and his 1574 tract quotes both sides of the previous debate.
71 McGinn, *The Admonition Controversy*, 29. McGinn finds that the writings of Whitgift, who scrupulously quotes his opponent throughout, "inspire nothing but confidence" (65).
72 Brennecke, in *John Mitton the Elder*, provides the text (89), describes the music (89–90), and quotes excerpts in score (192–95), noting that the words Milton chooses are from the Geneva Bible with the exception of "Lady" from the "Great" Bible. Brennecke, suggests that Milton's polyphonic setting of a text excluded from the English liturgy is an "illustration of his curiously divided enthusiasms," sympathetic artistically to tradition but politically to revolution (88–89).
73 Lake, *An Exposition of the one and fiftieth Psalme*, 1628, in *Sermons*, 1629, 197 and 232. The preface mentions that Lake gave the benediction at Wells "after the Sermon done, and the Psalme sung as the manner is" (x).

74 Joseph Kerman discusses the history and harmonic structure of this motet in *The Masses and Motets of William Byrd*, 162–67.

75 Both Latin and English words to the first part of this two-part anthem are found in le Huray, *The Treasury of English Church Music*, 87–95.

76 James I, in Heywood and Wright, *Cambridge University Transactions* II:254; further quotations will be cited parenthetically.

77 The "three articles" are in the 36th canon of the Ecclesiastical Constitutions and Canons of 1603–04, published in English in 1604; for a "virtual facsimile" see [Church of England:] *Constitutions and Canons Ecclesiastical, 1604*, XXXVI. They are quoted in Masson, *The Life of John Milton*, I:217.

78 On connections between this event and *Lycidas* see John Leonard, "'Trembling ears.'"

79 Cedric Brown illuminates the connections between these two poems in their political contexts in *Milton's Aristocratic Entertainments*, ch. 7.

80 *Defensio Secunda* (1654), *YP*, IV.1: 618–19.

81 Le Huray, *Music and the Reformation*, 30.

82 The author appends the note "Though I think I have heard the glass of Kings College was saved by being taken down; probably before this reformer came thither in his round."

83 Walker, *Sufferings of the Clergy* part i, quoted from Heywood and Wright, *Cambridge University Transactions*, 480–89.

84 Cartwright, in Whitgift, *Defense*, 605.

3 TUNING THE INSTRUMENT: DONNE'S TEMPORAL AND EXTEMPORAL SONG

1 Shawcross lists these and reproduces the tunes of some in Donne, *Complete Poetry*, and Ernest W. Sullivan II provides plates of the printed ones in *The Influence of John Donne*. On Donne's attitude towards these settings see Brian Morris, "'Not, Siren-like, to tempt': Donne and the Composers."

2 Puttenham, *Arte of English Poesie*, 62–63.

3 Sidney, *Apology*, 38.

4 Shawcross, in Donne, *Complete Poetry*, 400, n. 2. George Wesley Whiting provides background for the golden compasses in *This Pendant World*, 104–10. See also Graham Roebuck, "Donne's Visual Imagination and Compasses."

5 In Fludd's map (see ch. 1, n. 8) "Mens" is the most intuitive faculty of the soul, the level of epiphany.

6 Cf. Pattison, "Speech periods are freely counterpointed on the metrical base" (*Music and Poetry*, 199).

7 Kerman, *The Elizabethan Madrigal*, 28.

8 Woods, *Natural Emphasis*, 249–50.

9 Schleiner, *The Living Lyre*, 10–11.

10 Morley, *A Plain and Easy Introduction*, 294.

11 Donne's collection shares its title with "Tottel's Miscellany" (*Songes and Sonnettes*) and two collections of part-songs by William Byrd, *Psalmes, Sonets and Songs* (1588) and *Psalmes, Songs, and Sonnets* (1611).

12 The Egerton family was a musical one; the Earl of Bridgewater for whom Milton and Lawes composed *A Mask* made a copy "as a youth of Coprario's book of musical composition," SM Huntington Library MS EL 6863, *Rules how to compose* (Brown, *Milton's Aristocratic Entertainments*, 33 and 187 n. 81).

13 Fellowes, *English Madrigal Composers*, 313.

14 The Countess of Bedford's estate at Twickenham Park was a meeting place for poets and musicians, including Dowland and Donne (Parry, *Seventeenth-Century Poetry*, 60). Donne's relation with her began *c.* 1608 but he may have known Dowland's songs earlier.

15 Marotti, *Coterie Poet*, 69.

16 Castiglione, *The Courtyer*, trans. Hoby, 355.

17 Hollander, *The Untuning of the Sky*, 188. This setting for solo voice and lute is reproduced in Sullivan, *The Influence of John Donne*, 57.

18 Wilfred Mellers describes both poem and setting in *Harmonious Meeting*, 86–89, and comments, "Perhaps the third stanza is better omitted" (88).

19 Mellers, *Harmonious Meeting*, 44.

20 Donne, ed. Shawcross, *Complete Works*, 413.

21 See Donne, *Letters*, 32–33.

22 Elaine Perez Zickler compares Donne's case divinity to Freudian and post-Freudian approaches to subjectivity in "John Donne: The Subject of Casuistry."

23 Lake, *Sermons*, 220–21.

24 For example, Byrd, "Lord, in thy wrath" (*Psalmes, Sonets, and Songs*, 1588, *BF* xii), and "Lord in thy rage" (*Songs of Sundrie Natures*, 1589, *BF* xiii); Gibbons, "O Lord in thy wrath" (le Huray, *Treasury*, 191–97).

25 On uses of the trumpet see Numbers 10.1–10 and Exodus 19.13–19, 20.18.

26 Hooker's opinions and Wither's (below) are discussed more fully in chapter 2.

27 Parker, *The Whole Psalter translated into English Metre*, ?1567, sigs. E ii verso-E iii.

28 *Ibid.*, sig. RR iiii.

29 Sidney, *Apology*, 18.

30 Cowley, *The Puritans Lecture*, lines 80–84, in *Collected Works*, ed., Calhoun, 1:96.

31 Harrison, "Lamentations," in Jeffery, *A Dictionary of Biblical Tradition*, 433.

32 Klause, "Donne's Lamentations," 359.

33 Klause, "Donne's Lamentations," 357; Donne, *Letters*, 88.

34 Klause, "Donne's Lamentations," 342; Donne, *Letters,* 304.

35 Walton, *Lives:* "I have rather mentioned this *Hymn,* for that he caus'd it to be set to a most grave and solemn Tune, and to be often sung to the *Organ* by the *Choristers* of St. *Pauls* Church, in his own hearing; especially at the Evening Service, and at his return from his Customary Devotions in that place, did occasionally say to a friend, '*The words of this* Hymn *have restored to me the same thoughts of joy that possest my Soul in my sickness when I composed it*' (62).

36 Donne's *Hymne to God the Father* is included in the Episcopal Hymnal (1982), set by Donne's contemporary, the younger John Hilton, who also wrote one of the commendatory poems in Sandys' and Lawes' *A Paraphrase vpon the Psalms of David* (1638). Novarr agrees with Brian Morris that Donne is unlikely to have heard Hilton's setting (Morris, "'Not Siren-like to tempt,'" 238; Novarr, *The Disinterred Muse,* 173–74, n. 188), but I find the argument from Hilton's youth and secularity unpersuasive.

37 Novarr, *The Disinterred Muse,* 129–31, 142–50, 184–92.

38 Modern versions, including the extraordinary nineteenth-century translations of J. M. Neale, may be found in modern hymnals by their Latin titles in the Index of Tunes.

39 Camille Wells Slights discusses the regeneration of language as vocation in Donne's *Satyres* in *Casuistical Tradition,* ch. 4, and comments that "As a Christian poet, he must decide whether he ought to become involved in a shallow and sordid society . . . By showing the incipient recluse of 'Satyre I' developing into the dedicated public servant of 'Satyre V,' Donne provides a model of a man discovering how to act according to his conscience in a perplexing situation" (177).

4 THE CHOIR IN HERBERT'S TEMPLE

1 Charles, *A Life of George Herbert,* 42–43.

2 C Fitzwilliam MS Mu 689, described with bibliography in Fenlon, *Cambridge Music Manuscripts,* 155–59.

3 Charles, *A Life of George Herbert,* 50–51.

4 Morehen, "Hooper, Edmund," in *Grove* VIII:687.

5 George Loosemore, prefatory letter to Trinity MS R. 2. 58, *Graces . . . in Trinitie Colledge hall.*

6 Payne, "Instrumental Music at Trinity College," 128–29, 138; see also his "Musical Establishment at Trinity College."

7 Charles, *A Life of George Herbert,* 96.

8 Walton, *Lives,* 303.

9 Aubrey, *Brief Lives,* 310. Settings of the sung portions of the burial service by Thomas Morley may be found in *EECM* XXXVIII.

10 Payne, "Instrumental Music," 134n and 139.

11 Wilcox, "The Sweet Singer," 53–55; Schleiner, *The Living Lyre,* 64–70.

12 When two or more pitches are sounded together, the more partials are in tune, the more consonant the intervals. At the same time, partials far removed from the fundamental in an overtone series include dissonances. The harmonic series was not yet fully formulated in Herbert's lifetime, but the complexity of pitches can be deduced from the fact that when a bell, a string, or a column of air is vibrating at a particular pitch the segments that produce other pitches are vibrating also.

13 I find myself unwilling to fight off a strong inclination to call the speaker in Herbert's poems "Herbert."

14 Wither, *Emblemes*, interpreting the sun as "Him, that is the sunne of Righteousness," with the motto "Non Inferiora Secutus"; Heyns, *Emblemes Chrestiennes* (reproduced in Lewalski, *Protestant Poetics*, fig. 17), which has as its explication John 8.12, "I am the light of the world."

15 Morley, *A Plain and Easy Introduction*, 293.

16 Clearly I find anachronistic Janis Lull's assertion that the reed is a "symbol of male egotism – at once phallus, musical instrument, and pen" ("George Herbert's Revisions," 5; quoted with approval in Schoenfeldt, *Prayer and Power*, 241).

17 E.g. James Howel's title, *The Pre-eminence and Pedigree of Parlement* [rebutting a work of] *Mr. Prynne; wherein he stiles him No Frend to Parlements* (1649).

18 Wayment, *The Windows of King's College Chapel*, 57.

19 The 1640 Geneva-Tomson-Junius Bible is the first English Bible to deliberately omit the Apocrypha, with a note explaining the omission, but retains the Prayer of Manasses after Malachi (A. S. Herbert, *Historical Catalogue* #545). Weelkes' "If King Manasses" (*MB* XIII) is a penitential anthem responding to this text.

20 Lewalski discusses and reproduces heart emblems in *Protestant Poetics* and suggests that "Herbert's entire collection of religious lyrics . . . invites analysis as a kind of 'heart book'" (204).

21 Di Cesare, "God's Silence," 95, 98.

22 This anthem is ascribed to Richard Farrant in some manuscripts and in others to John Hilton the Elder, organist and choirmaster at Trinity from 1593 or 94 until his death on March 20, 1608/09 (Payne, 130–31). The Amens are found only in manuscripts attributed to Hilton and are included in Greening's edition in *The Oxford Book of Tudor Anthems*.

23 Spenser's Castle of Alma in Book 2 of *The Faerie Queene* is described in musical proportions analogous to the human body, as is the Temple of Solomon in Mersenne (*Traité de L'harmonie universelle*, Book 2).

24 Hollander, *The Untuning of the Sky*, 288. Parts of the ensuing observations appear in Maleski, ed., *A Fine Tuning*, 116–43. Joseph Summers in *George Herbert: His Religion and Art*, ch. 6, shows that Herbert creates

hieroglyphic forms (as distinguished from emblematic content) that "image the subject . . . for those who could 'spell'" (135); I am indebted to this insight for the recognition that Herbert also creates hierophonic forms for those who can sing. Related studies include Charles, "George Herbert: Priest, Poet, Musician"; Hayes, "Counterpoint in Herbert"; Low, *Love's Architecture*, chs. 2 and 4; Ostriker, "Song and Speech"; Schleiner, *The Living Lyre*, ch. 2; Stein, *George Herbert's Lyrics*.

25 Vendler, *The Poetry of George Herbert*, 210–11.

26 *Ibid.*, 212.

27 Heather Ross (Asals) says of "crouch" that "it is this gesture which finally makes one of the heaven and earth which the poem echoes between: 'Praised be the God alone, / Who hath made of *two folds one*' (*Equivocal Predications*, 31), perhaps suggesting that the literal "two folds" of the crouching bodies are an emblem of the union.

28 A full-length study of Herbert's knowledge and use of the Psalms may be found in Coburn Freer, *Music for a King*.

29 Temperley, *Music of the English Parish Church* I, chs. 2–4. Temperley supplies examples of early harmonizations in vol. II.

30 Mace, *Musick's Monument*, 2.

31 Puttenham, *The Arte of English poesie*, 96.

32 Morley, *A Plain and Easy Introduction*, 290.

33 Discussed in chapter 1.

34 Ramsey's "In guilty night" is "A Dialogue between Saul, the Witch of Endor, and the ghost of Samuel" (*EECM* VII).

35 MS has "kindly." I have also supplied lineation and punctuation for the first verse.

36 This popular work had several versions for both private and choral use, varying from solo or duet with strings to solo with four- or seven-part choral response. Liturgical sources include O B Tenbury MS 791, the "Batten Organ Book" (*c.* 1630), the Durham cathedral part-books (*c.* 1620–70), and York Minster MS M. 29 (s), 1640 (the absence of a manuscript before 1620 proves nothing, since few earlier church music manuscripts exist). An earlier secular version for voices and viols has been edited by John Milsom for Oxford University Press (1990).

37 Number 73 in the Williams MS. C. A. Patrides points out the similarity to the anonymous text of "Come away, come sweet love" in his edition of *The English Poems of George Herbert*, 212n.

38 Chana Bloch believes that "the random order of *The Temple* is deliberate," like the order of the Psalms; "If he regarded his poems as a kind of psalmody, it is entirely possible that he intended the fluctuation between sorrow and joy, doubt and answer": *Spelling the Word*, 240; cf. Coburn Freer, *Music for a King*, 140.

39 Lake, *Sermons*, 215.

40 Tuve, *A Reading of George Herbert*, 24.

41 Vendler, *The Poetry of George Herbert*, 137.

42 Hooper, in O Christ Church MS 56 (which also contains Amner's "Consider, all ye passers-by") and in O B MS Rawl. Poet 23, anthems from the Chapel Royal, 1635.

43 The two poems called *Easter* have separate titles in the Williams manuscript but are printed as one poem in subsequent editions. They appear to form a poem in two parts like a through-composed anthem divided into "prima pars" and "secunda pars" with different meters and musical treatments. I have retained the capital *J* of "Just" (as does Hutchinson) from the Williams manuscript and added accent marks on "calcined" and "streched."

44 Zarlino, *Istitu ione armoniche* (1558), in Strunk, *Source Readings*, II: 60.

45 Gibbons, "Psalm to the First Preces" (*TCM* IV). After the central section for full choir, partly antiphonal and largely homophonic, the psalm concludes "This is the day which the Lord hath made: we will rejoice and be glad in it" for three polyphonic voice parts. The Proper Psalms for Easter Day are Psalms 2, 57, 111, 113, 114, and 118.

46 Fenlon, *Cambridge Music Manuscripts*, 159. It is tempting to speculate whether the arrangement of *The Temple* is affected by keys in which Herbert set or intended to set his poems.

47 Le Huray, *Music and the Reformation*, 135.

48 On Herbert's use of parody see Tuve, *Essays*, 207–51. Sacred parodies of profane songs were common in Renaissance music; Taverner's *Western Wynde* Mass turns a secular tune into a sacred one. Conversely, the secular *In Nomine* and the use of polyphony based on a cantus firmus in secular music grew out of church music. Although historians tend to talk about the secularization of the arts in the Renaissance, many sacralized the secular as well.

49 The Palm Sunday liturgy was also omitted, though the Sunday before Easter was still alluded to by that name.

50 Kepler and Galileo, in D. P. Walker, *Studies in Musical Science*, 32 and 53–54.

51 Gibbons, preface to *First Set of Madrigals and Mottets of 5. Parts* (1612).

52 Morley, *A Plain and Easy Introduction*, 293.

53 Morley, *A Plain and Easy Introduction*, 103; Peacham, *Compleat Gentleman* (1622) quoted in Strunk, *Source Readings*, II:147.

54 Duckworth and Brown, *Theoretical Foundations*, 19.

55 Walker, *Studies in Musical Science*, 35–37.

56 *Ibid.*, 53.

57 Weelkes, ed. Collins, who notes, "Bar lines have been added, note values reduced by half, and the pitch raised a minor third . . . While performance without instrumental accompaniment would not be wrong, the composer probably would have expected the organ or other instruments to double the voices."

58 Plato, *Republic*, 86; Boethius, *De institutione musica*, in Strunk, *Source Readings*, I: 84–85; see also Finney, *Musical Backgrounds*, ch. 1.
59 De Muris, in Strunk, *Source Readings*, I: 173; Kepler, trans. Duncan, *Harmonice Mundi*, ch. 3: "On the Harmonic means, and the Trinity of Consonant Sounds," section 37. Walker explains that Kepler rejected number symbolism in favor of geometric analogies that correspond to "archetypes in the soul of man [and the] mind of God" (*Studies in Musical Science*, 44).
60 Easley Blackwood explains the physical reason for this impression in *The Structure of Recognizable Diatonic Tunings*.
61 Lippius, *Synopsis Musicae novae* (1612), quoted in *Grove*, "Polyphony," XII:417.
62 Mersenne, *Harmonie universelle* (1636) IV:213. All consonances may be accomplished by three notes in a diatonic scale because of inverted intervals.
63 OED "vie," 5.
64 See chapter 5 for full text. Settings in *Sacred Hymns* and the Peterhouse and Ely part-books have variants according with their respective uses as sacred madrigals or consort music and church music. An edition of *Sacred Hymns* by John Morehen is currently in progress.
65 Sidney, *Arcadia* (1590), Book 2: "My sheep are thoughts which I both guide and serve" (I: 163).
66 Ralph Vaughan Williams uses the plainchant of this communion hymn in his setting of *Love* (III) in *Five Mystical Songs*. Herbert's many uses of "taste" and "taster" in his Eucharistic poems are reminiscent of "Gustate et videte" (set for example by Gregorio Allegri, 1621), a text known to twentieth-century choirs from Vaughan Williams' "O taste and see."
67 Kerman discusses Byrd's related settings of the Corpus Christi liturgy in *The Masses and Motets of William Byrd*, ch. 5b.
68 Benham, *Latin Church Music*, 166.
69 Text and translation from *The Ninth Book of Chester Motets*, ed. Anthony G. Petti; my description relies on this partially reconstructed score.
70 Walker, *Studies in Musical Science*, 7.
71 Num. 17, Heb. 9.4.
72 Quoted in Shepherd, "The Changing Theological Concept of Sacrifice," 126–27.

5 "SOLE, OR RESPONSIVE": VOICES IN MILTON'S CHOIRS

1 Budick, *The Dividing Muse*, 7.
2 Hughes mentions several in his Introduction to *Paradise Lost*, section 56.
3 Brennecke (p. 85) speculatively reconstructs Milton's early musical experience in *John Milton the Elder and his Music*, bringing London's

chief musicians into the Milton household, and provides modern notation for several of his father's compositions.

4 For a fuller discussion of this piece see chapter 2.

5 I have reproduced the first twelve engravings in *A Gust for Paradise*, fig. 1–12.

6 Slatyer, sig. A4. Slatyer's idea is that if we sing twenty-two psalms each evening we can complete the psalter in a week. This publication provides the first "nocturn."

7 *EM* viii. Benham doubts Byrd's authorship (*Latin Church Music*, 25) but Kerman supports it (*High Renaissance Masters*, 232).

8 Cowley, *Davideis* (1. 483–515). See also Michael East's setting of the prayerbook version, example 1.

9 Brown, *Aristocratic Entertainments*, 111–12, 119, 125–31, 164–70, et passim. On Lawes' music see Evans, *Henry Lawes*, and Basile, "The Music of *A Maske*."

10 Rudrum, *A Critical Commentary*, 3.

11 *Ibid.*, 11.

12 D. P. Walker, *Studies in Musical Science*, ch. 4.

13 In *Christian Doctrine* Milton (if it was Milton) writes, "His kingdom of grace . . . began with his first advent . . . but his kingdom of glory will not commence until his second advent."

14 Davies, "'Laid artfully together,'" 105.

15 J. Martin Evans disagrees: "[T]he *Nativity Ode* is the most rigorously depersonalized of all Milton's nondramatic works," implying "a choric rather than an individual speaker" ("A Poem of Absence," 31). I am not sure that these views are incompatible, however.

16 Barker, "The Pattern of Milton's 'Nativity Ode'"; Røstvig, "Elaborate Song," 55, 59, 64, 65; Budick, *Dividing Muse*, 23–27; Moseley, *Poetic Birth*, 110–14.

17 Andrewes, *Sermons on the Nativity*, 193–95, 197–98, 206–07, 210.

18 My thanks to Jeremy Maule for a manuscript copy in score.

19 Also edited by John Morehen in le Huray, *Treasury*, 198–219.

20 Le Huray, *Music and the Reformation*, 315.

21 Changed to "believers" in some parts.

22 Moseley, *Milton's Poems of 1645*, 121.

23 Facsimile in *John Milton's Complete Poetical Works*, ed. Fletcher, 1:390.

24 Platonic sirens, *Republic*, 161–17.

25 Brieger, *The Trinity Apocalypse*, 20.

26 Byrd, in Strunk, *Source Readings*, ii: 138.

27 There are "four and twenty elders" seated around the throne in Revelation 4, represented with harps in illustrations.

28 Weelkes, "Alleluia, I heard a voice," ed. Townsend Warner, rev. Bray.

29 Amner, "Thus sings the heav'nly choir" (Part 1) and "The heav'ns stood all amazed" (Part 2), ed. Pilgrim.

30 In *To Mr. H. Lawes, on his Aires*, Milton contrasts Lawes to composers

who err by "committing short and long," literally putting together short syllables with long notes and long syllables with short notes. Cf. Morley, *A Plain and Easy Introduction*, 291.

31 *SM* 729; Mazzoni, *On the Defense of the Comedy of Dante*, 58.

32 Margaret Mather Byard recounts Milton's musical experience in Rome in "'Adventrous Song.'" M. N. K. Mander reads "The Music of *L'Allegro* and *Il Penseroso*," in the context of Italian theory and practice, with attention to moral and rhetorical concerns. Louise Schleiner comments on "Milton, Doni, and Italian Dramatic Song" in *The Living Lyre*, chapter 5, and imagines musical settings for monodic and choral passages. Sandra Corse traces Milton's interest in both monody and polyphony and the influence of the Florentine camerata on English music in "Old Music and New." Lee Jacobus argues that *Lycidas* is related to Italian monody through Lawes in "Milton Hero."

33 Anna Nardo discusses these sonnets in *Milton's Sonnets and the Ideal Community*, 32–37.

34 Milton, *An Apology for Smectymnuus, CM* iii:303.

35 Marenzio (1553–99) was introduced to England by Thomas Watson's *First sett, of Italian madrigalls englished* (1590). His sacred music includes service music, motets for the church year, *Sacrae cantiones*, and *Madrigali spirituali*. Vecchi (1550–1605) directed the choirs at the cathedrals of Reggio and Modena and at the court of Modena produced such entertainments as the madrigal comedy *L'Amfiparnaso* (1594). Carlo Gesualdo (*c*.1560–1613), most notorious for his assassination of his first wife and her lover, wrote intensely moving penitential music, the *Responsoria* of 1611, as well as many madrigals and motets. His later marriage to Leonora d'Este took him to the court of Ferrara, and afterwards, living in near-isolation at Gesualdo, he kept a consort of musicians and devoted himself to music. Title pages call him "Ill. et Ecc. D. D. Caroli Iesvaldi Compsanorum Comitis Venusinor Principis," hence "the Prince of Venosa" in Philips' list. Antonio Cifra (1584–1629) wrote madrigals, *scherzi*, masses after the style of Palestrina, more adventurous concertato motets, polychoral psalms and litanies, and *scherzi sacri*. Claudio Monteverdi (1567–1643) was at the court of Mantua and later the Basilica of San Marco in Venice, out of which polychoral music spread through Europe.

36 Waddington, "A Musical Source for L'Allegro?"

37 I have discussed this passage, with Praetorius' setting, in *A Gust for Paradise*, 138–44.

38 Lawes, preface to *Ayres and Dialogues* (1653); quoted by Ian Spink, *Grove* x: 557.

39 Gary Tomlinson discusses this genre and relationship in *Monteverdi*, ch. 4.

40 "'Tongues of men and Angels': Ad Leonoram Romae Canentem."

41 Unpublished at this writing.
42 Greene, *Descent from Heaven*, 383–84.
43 Fish, "Wanting a Supplement," 66.
44 Grossman, *Authors to Themselves*, 66 and 64.
45 Wulstan, *Tudor Music*, 307.
46 I have discussed the similarities in "The Copious Matter of My Song."
47 Leonard, *Naming in Paradise*, 240–42. Positive interpretations of the change are found in *The Poems of John Milton*, ed. Cary and Fowler, 585, and Lewalski, *Rhetoric of Literary Forms*, 166.
48 Andrewes, *Sermons on the Nativity*, 211. Cf. Herbert, *Antiphon* (II).
49 Monson, in *The Byrd Edition* vol. I, *Cantiones sacrae (1575)*: vii.
50 Marenzio set "Quem dicunt homines esse filium hominis" for four voices; Newberry Library, "An Ancient Manuscript from the Library of Dr. Pepusch."
51 Fish, "Wanting a Supplement," 66.
52 On the lack of entity in Hell, see also Rumrich, *Matter of Glory*, 86–93.
53 Greene, *Descent from Heaven*, 409; Werblowsky, *Lucifer and Prometheus*, 14.

6 EMPIRE OF THE EAR: THE PRAISE OF MUSIC

1 Temperley, *Music of the English Parish Church*, I: 103.
2 See Julianne Baird, *Art of Singing*, 13.
3 Dryden's poem was first set by Giovanni Battista Draghi, whose "poetic sensibilities and musical powers," Zimmerman says, "were not such as to enable him to take full and imaginative advantage of the opportunity Dryden had provided" (*Henry Purcell*, 152). Stella Revard discusses *The Creation* and other works inspired by Milton in "From the State of Innocence to the Fall of Man."
4 North, *Roger North on Music*, 10–12.
5 Pepys, *Diary*, III:197.
6 W. Sherlock, *A Sermon Preach'd at St. Paul's Cathedral*, 23–24.
7 Hollander (*Untuning of the Sky*, 309n) calls Fairfax and Cromwell "equiprobable" but chooses Cromwell. On the history and complexity of Marvell's political poems see Annabel Patterson, *Marvell and the Civic Crown*, especially chapter 2.
8 Butler, *Principles of Musick*, 4–5.
9 Graham Parry points out that in 1653, while tutor to a ward of Cromwell's, Marvell lived in the house of John Oxenbridge, a Puritan minister who had emigrated to Bermuda during the Laudian persecutions: *Seventeenth-Century Poetry*, 242.
10 Quotations from *Musick's Empire* are from *Poems and Letters*, ed. Margoliouth.
11 Cowley, *Davideis*, 1. 451–56.

12 "Assumed details: A pair of objects are struck together, with one part of the pair held in each hand; the objects are usually round." Brown and Lascelle, *Musical Iconography*, 82. A single cymbal may of course be struck with something else, here jarring winds.

13 Theodore Karp, *Dictionary of Music*, 120.

14 John Hollander finds that in this poem "*musica instrumentalis* is considered historically prior to celestial harmony" in *The Untuning of the Sky*, 310; but I think this statement is colored by Hollander's thesis that the sky is being "untuned" in the seventeenth century. That Jubal finds or "invents" practical music does not necessarily mean that celestial music did not already exist; but in Marvell's monistic poem, human beings discover music empirically.

15 Jubal (or Tubal) was said to have "inuented the science of Musick, by the stroke and noise of hammers of his brother Tubalkain, which was a Smith" (Marbeck, *Notes and Common Places*, 754); he observed that hammer strokes produced various pitches on the anvil according to their weight and realized that instruments could be made to do so in a controllable way. Heninger reproduces a woodcut of Jubal's discovery and Pythagoras' experiments proving the musical ratios from Franchino Gafori's *Theorica musice* (Milan, 1491), in *Touches of Sweet Harmony*, 102.

16 "First" does not appear in the 1681 folio, so that the line requires a disyllabic pronunciation of "tuned"; Donno supplies "first" from O B MS Eng. poet. d. 49.

17 *Upon Appleton House*, lines 77–84. Hollander, justifying the connection with Moses in both poems, notes that "the multiplicity of 'harmonious Colonies' is recalled by reference to the variegated tesserae of a mosaic which can merge, from any distant viewpoint, into an overwhelming unified figure" (313) and also that "light Mosaick" is "both an adjective-noun and noun-adjective qualification" (314).

18 Herbert, "Nam saxa mirantur canentes." *De Musica Sacra* in *Latin Poems*, 32.

19 Milton, *On the Death of a Fair Infant, SM* 13, line 39.

20 Milton, *Ad Patrem, SM* 140, line 87.

21 John Wilson in *Fairfax* mentions Fairfax's "metrical version of the psalms and Biblical songs" in the Bodleian Library. Jeremy Maule informs me that Fairfax was growing deaf when Marvell is thought to have composed the poem, a condition that would cast a poignant irony over Marvell's musical praise – which of course can be "heard" without sound.

22 Cedric Brown speaks of Marvell's "dextrous teasing of the Fairfax family," *Aristocratic Entertainments*, 155.

23 *Upon Appleton House*, line 768.

24 Hollander, *The Untuning of the Sky* 410

25 *Ibid.*, 410.

26 Richard Luckett and Thomas Connolly offer contending views on the St. Cecilia legend in the arts, Luckett in " St. Cecilia and Music" and Connolly in *Mourning into Joy.*

27 S[ampson] Estwick, *A Sermon Preach'd at Christ-Church*, 2.

28 Baxter, *Christian Directory.* Baxter himself wrote a notable hymn, "Ye holy angels bright," summoning angels, saints, blessed souls, and his own to join in song.

29 Battell, *Church-Musick*, 2, 12, 9–10, 14–15, 21–22. Andrew Willett had cautioned in 1607 that not the "Notes of Musick" but David's words healed Saul, since "spiritual euills are not chased away with carnall means . . . But Musicke hath a wonderfull force, in working vpon the affections" (*Harmonie vpon the First Booke of Samvel*, 33).

30 Brady, *Church-Musick Vindicated*, 19–21.

31 Cowley, *Several Discourses*, in *Works*, ii: 328.

32 Peter Klein, in Francis and Klein, *The Organs and Organists of Ludlow Parish Church*, 7.

33 See for example Hollander, *The Untuning of the Sky*, figure opposite page 242.

34 Shapiro, "'Drama of an Infinitely Superior Nature,'" 215–16. Thanks to Robert Ryan for this reference.

35 Nicholas Temperley traces the beginnings of the voluntary English parish choir to an anonymous publication, *A new and easie method to learn to sing by book* (1686) and the preface to Barber's *Book of psalme tunes in four parts* (1687), as well as controversy over degrees of congregational participation and separation from the choir, in *Music of the English Parish Church*, i: 141–42 and 344–48.

Discography

The performances listed follow Renaissance and early baroque performance practice apart from a few not available on recent recordings. Dates (when known) are both copyright and performance dates unless a separate performance date is specified as [P]. AC=audiocassette, LP= long playing record, CD=compact disc. Works itemized by individual composer are mentioned in the text. Several works by seventeenth-century English composers unavailable in other collections are included in the recent series *Ars Antiqua Choralis: Choral Masterworks from the 15th to 18th Centuries* by The Cathedral Singers, dir. Richard Proulx, GIA CD 299, 323, 290, and 334.

COLLECTIONS

All at once well met: English Madrigals. The King's Singers. EMI CDC 7 49265 2. 1987.

As I Went to Walsingham: Elizabethan Music. The Musicians of Swanne Alley, dir. Lyle Nordstrom and Paul O'Dette. Harmonia Mundi CD HMC 905192. 1987.

Barbour, J. Murray, and Fritz A. Kuttner. *The Theory and Practice of Just Intonation.* LP, Musurgia Records, Theory Series A, no. 3. Jackson Heights, N Y, 1958.

"Draw On Sweet Night": English Madrigals. The Hilliard Ensemble, dir. Paul Hillier. EMI CDC 7 49197 2. 1988.

English Madrigals. Quink Vocal Ensemble. Telarc CD-80328. 1993.

English Madrigals. The Tallis Scholars, dir. Peter Phillips. EMI AC 4AE-34483. 1982.

Eton Choirbook.

   The Crown of Thorns. The Sixteen, dir. Harry Christophers. Collins CD 1316 2. 1991, [P] 1990.

   The Pillars of Eternity. The Sixteen, dir. Harry Christophers. Collins CD 1342 2. 1992.

   The Rose and the Ostrich Feather. The Sixteen, dir. Harry Christophers. Collins CD 1314 2. 1991.

   Stabat Mater: Music from the Eton Choirbook. The Sixteen, dir. Harry Christophers. Meridian C D E 84174. (Undated; since 1982.)

Hail, Gladdening Light. Music of the English Church. The Cambridge
Singers, dir. John Rutter. Collegium COLCD 113. 1991.
*In Nomine: 16th C. English music for viols including the complete consort
music of Thomas Tallis.* On original instruments. Fretwork. Amon Ra
CD-SAR 29. 1987.
Madrigals and Wedding Songs for Diana. The Consort of Musicke, dir.
Anthony Rooley, with Emma Kirkby and David Thomas. Hyperion
CDA 66019. 988.
Morley, Parsley, a d Inglott. The Choir of Norwich Cathedral, dir.
Michael Nicholas, organ Neil Taylor. Priory PRCD 396. 1991.
Music from Walsingham. The Festival Choir of The National Shrine of
Our Lady, dir. Nigel Kerry. Herald AC HAVPC 149. 1992.
Old Hall Manuscript, The. The Hilliard Ensemble. EMI CDC 7 54111 2.
1991.
The Purcell Circle: The Mistress. Settings of poems by Abraham Cowley.
Musica Oscura CD 070986. 1994.
Songs to My Lady: English Songs and Lute Pieces. Paul Esswood and Jürgen
Hübscher. Harmonia Mundi, Quintana CD QUI 903012. 1991.
The Triumphs of Oriana: Madrigals. Pro Cantione Antiqua, dir. Ian
Partridge. Archiv CD 437 076–2. 1977.
Venetian Monody in the Age of Monteverdi. Ensemble Chanterelle, Sally
Sanford, soprano; Catherine Liddell, chitarrone, lute, baroque
guitar; Robert Strizich, lute, baroque guitar. MHS LP 7055T. 1984.
When David Heard . . . Anthems by Weelkes [and] Tomkins. The Choir of
Trinity College, Cambridge, dir. Richard Marlow. Conifer CDCF
216. 1993.

INDIVIDUAL COMPOSERS

Amner, John. *Cathedral Music by John Amner.* The Choir of Ely Cathedral,
dir. Paul Trepte, David Price, organ, and The Parley of
Instruments, dir. Peter Holman. Hyperion CDA66768. 1995.
Includes "Consider all ye passers by," "Gloria," "I will sing unto the
Lord" (the Song of Moses), "O ye little flock."
"Come, Let's Rejoice." On *Hail, Gladdening Light.*
Anon., "My true love hath my heart." On *As I Went to Walsingham.*
Byrd, William. *Ave Verum Corpus: Motets and Anthems.* The Cambridge
Singers, dir. John Rutter. Collegium AC and CD COLC 10. 1989.
Includes "Attolite portas," "Justorum animae," "Praise God in his
sanctuary."
Cantiones Sacrae. 1589. The Choir of New College, Oxford, dir.
Edward Higginbottom. CRD CD 3420. 1983.
Cantiones Sacrae. 1591. The Choir of New College, Oxford, dir.
Edward Higginbottom. CRD CD 3439. 1986.
"Come, woeful Orpheus." On *English Madrigals.*

Gradualia, vol. 1: *The Marian Masses.* The William Byrd Choir, dir.
  Gavin Turner. Hyperion CDA 66451. 1990.
The Great Service. The Choir of King's College, Cambridge, dir.
  Stephen Cleobury. EMI CDC 7 47771 2. 1987.
Magnificat from the Second Service. On *Music from Walsingham.*
Mass for Four Voices; Mass for Five Voices. Choir of St. John's College,
  Cambridge, dir. George Guest. EMI CD-EMX 9505. 1986.
Psalmes, Sonets & Songs, 1588. (Selections.) The Consort of Musicke,
  dir. Anthony Rooley. L'Oiseau-Lyre CD 443 187 2. 1994, [P] 1981.
"This sweet and merry month of May." On *All at Once Well Met.*
Campion, Thomas. *Ayres.* Drew Minter, contertenor; Paul O'Dette, lute.
  Harmonia Mundi CD HMU 907023. 1990.
Cornysh, William. *Stabat Mater.* The Tallis Scholars, dir. Peter Phillips.
  Gimell CDGIM 014, 1988. Includes "Salve Regina," "Woefully
  Arrayed," "Stabat Mater."
Dowland, John. *First Booke of Songes.* The Consort of Musicke, dir.
  Anthony Rooley. L'Oiseau-Lyre CD 421 653–2. 1989, [P] 1976.
Second Booke of Songes. The Consort of Musicke, dir. Anthony Rooley.
  L'Oiseau Lyre CD 425 889–2. 1990, [P] 1977.
Third Booke of Songes. The Consort of Musicke, dir. Anthony Rooley.
  L'Oiseau Lyre CD 430 284–2. 1991, [P] 1977.
Mr. Henry Noell Lamentations 1597: Psalmes & Sacred Songs. The
  Consort of Musicke, dir. Anthony Rooley. L'Oiseau-Lyre AC KDSLC
  551. 1979.
Dunstable, John. *Motets.* The Hilliard Ensemble, dir. Paul Hillier. EMI
  CDC 7 49002 2. 1984.
Fayrfax, Robert. "Aeternae laudis lilium." On *Aeternae Laudis Lilium.*
  Choir of Jesus College, Cambridge, dir. Geraint Bowen,
  Christopher Argent, organ. Cambridge, 1985. The Abbey
  Recording Company, Oxford, LP Alpha ACA 546.
Magnificat, "Regale." On Eton Choirbook: *The Rose and the Ostrich
  Feather.*
Gesualdo, Carlo. *Tenebrae Responsories for Holy Saturday.* The Tallis
  Scholars, dir. Peter Phillips. Gimell CDGIM 015, 1987.
Gibbons, Orlando. *Anthems and Songs of Praise.* The Clerkes of
  Oxenford, dir. David Wulstan. Nonesuch AC N5–71391. 1981.
  "Lord, grant grace."
Church Music. The Clerkes of Oxenford, dir. David Wulstan. Calliope
  CD CAL 9611. 1987; [P] 1975 and 1977. *Hymns and Songs* (from
  Wither); "Hosanna to the Son of David"; "O Lord, I lift my heart to
  thee."
Second Service and Anthems. The Choir of New College, Oxford, dir.
  Edward Higginbottom, with David Burchell, organ. CRD CD 3451.
  1988. "Glorious and Powerful God"; "O Clap your Hands"; "O
  Lord, in thy Wrath"; "See, see the Word is incarnate."

Handel, George Frideric. *L'Allegro, Il Penseroso, ed Il Moderato.* [Text by John Milton, rearranged.] Monteverdi Choir and English Baroque Soloists, dir. John Eliot Gardiner. Erato ECD 880752. 1981.

Ode for St. Cecilia's Day. Text by John Dryden. The English Concert and Choir, dir. Trevor Pinnock. Archiv CD 419 220–2. 1986.

Lawes, Henry. *Sitting by the Streams: Psalms, Ayres, and Dialogues.* The Consort of Musicke, dir. Anthony Rooley. Hyperion CDA66135. 1984.

Lawes, William, and Robert Johnson. *Orpheus I am.* [Settings of poems by Herrick, Jonson, Shakespeare, and others.] With Stephen Stubbs, *Tragicomedia.* EMI Classics CDC 7 54311 2. 1991.

Marenzio, Luca. *Madrigaux à 5 et 6 voix.* Concerto Vocale, dir. René Jacobs. Harmonia Mundi CD HMA 1901065. 1988, [P] 1982.

Milton, John, Sr. "Fair Orian, in the morn." On *The Triumphs of Oriana.* Works forthcoming by Fretwork.

Monteverdi, Claudio. *Mass of Thanksgiving* and *Venetian Vesper Music* (*Selva Morale e Spirituale,* 1641). Taverner Consort, Taverner Choir, and Taverner Players, dir. Andrew Parrott. EMI Classics CDS 7 54886 2 (USA CDCB 54886). [P] 1989, 1984. 1993.

L'Orfeo. The Monteverdi Choir, The English Baroque Soloists, His Majesties Sagbutts & Cornetts, dir. John Eliot Gardiner. 2 discs. Archiv CD 419 250–2. 1987.

L'Ottavo Libro de Madrigali: Madrigali amorosi 1638. Virgin Classics CD VC 7 91157–2. 1991.

Quattro Libro dei Madrigali. The Consort of Musicke, dir. Anthony Rooley. L'Oiseau-Lyre CD 414 148–2 1986.

Morley, Thomas. "Nolo mortem peccatoris." On *Hail, Gladdening Light* and *Morley, Parsley, and Inglott.*

Short Service. On *Morley, Parsley, and Inglott.*

Palestrina, Giovanni Pierluigi. *Canticum canticorum. Madrigali spirituali.* The Hilliard Ensemble, dir. Paul Hillier. EMI CDS 7 49010 8. 1987, [P] 1986.

Purcell, Henry. *Anthems for the Chapel Royal.* Choir of Trinity College, Cambridge, dir. Richard Marlow. Conifer AC MCFC 152. 1987.

Ode on St. Cecilia's Day 1692. [Text by Nicholas Brady.] Taverner Choir and Players, dir. Andrew Parrott. EMI CDC 7 47490. 1986.

Te Deum & Jubilate, Funeral Music, Anthems. Choir of St. John's College, Cambridge, dir. George Guest. London CD 430 263–2. 1991, [P] 1972.

Sheppard, John. *Church Music.* The Sixteen, dir. Harry Christophers. Hyperion AC KA66259. 1988.

English and Latin Church Music. Christ Church Cathedral Choir, Oxford, dir. Stephen Darlington. Nimbus CD NI 5480. 1996.

Sheryngham, *Ah, gentle Jesu.* On Eton Choirbook: *The Crown of Thorns.*

Stone, Robert. The Lord's Prayer. On *Hail, Gladdening Light.*

Tallis, Thomas. "Christe Jesu, pastor bone." On *Hail, Gladdening Light.*
The Complete English Anthems. The Tallis Scholars, dir. Peter Phillips.
Gimell CDGIM007; AC1585T-07.
Latin Church Music, I. Spem in Alium (a 40) and Complete Responds.
Taverner Consort, Taverner Choir, dir. Andrew Parrott. EMI CDC 7
49555 2. 1989. Includes "Dum transisset sabbatum" (5vv),
"Loquebantur variis linguis."
Mass for Four Voices, Motets. Oxford Camerata, dir. Jeremy Summerly.
Naxos CD DDD 8.550576. 1992. Includes "O Sacrum Convivium,"
"Loquebantur variis linguis."
Spem in Alium/Lamentations. King's College Choir, Cambridge dir.
Stephen Cleobury. Argo CDD 115496. 1989.
Taverner, John. *Missa Gloria Tibi Trinitas.* The Tallis Scholars, dir. Peter
Phillips. Gimell CDGIM 004. 1984. Includes "Dum transisset
sabbatum."
Missa Mater Christi. A liturgical reconstruction. Christ Church
Cathedral Choir, Oxford dir. Stephen Darlington. Nimbus CDNI
5218. 1987. Includes Motet, "Mater Christi Sanctissima."
Tomkins, Thomas. *Cathedral Music.* Choir of St. George's Chapel,
Windsor, dir. Christopher Robinson. Hyperion CDA66345. 1989.
Includes "Above the stars my saviour dwells"; "My beloved
spake."
The Great Service. The Tallis Scholars, dir. Peter Phillips. Gimell CDGIM
024. 1991. Includes Third Service; "When David Heard";
"Almighty God, the fountain of all wisdom"; "O sing unto the Lord
a new song."
Domine, tu eruisti animam meam; "O God, the proud are risen"; "O
Sing unto the Lord a new song"; "When David heard." On *When
David Heard.*
Tye, Christopher. *Cathedral Music.* Winchester Cathedral Choir, dir.
David Hill. Hyperion AC KA66424. 1990.
Mass in Six Parts, "Euge Bone." Choir of King's College, Cambridge,
dir. Philip Ledger. EMI AC TC-ASD 4104. 1982.
Vaughan Williams, Ralph. *Five Mystical Songs.* [Texts by George
Herbert.] On *Serenade to Music,* Sixteen Soloists, Corydon Singers,
English Chamber Orchestra, dir, Matthew Best. Hyperion CD
A66420. 1990.
Vecchi, Orazio. *L'Amfiparnasso,* with *Il Convito Musicale* (1597).
Ensemble Clément Janequin, dir. Dominique Visse. Harmonia
Mundi CD 901461. 1993.
Victoria, Thomàs Luis de. *Tenebrae Responsories.* Pro Cantione Antiqua,
dir. Bruno Turner. Harmonia Mundi CD 77056–2–RG. 1990, [P]
1979.
Weelkes, Thomas. "All people clap your hands"; *Laboravi in gemitu meo;*
"Gloria in excelsis Deo"; "Hosanna to the Son of David"; "O

Jonathan, woe is me"; "O Lord, arise into thy resting place"; "O
Lord, grant the king a long life"; "When David Heard." On *When
David Heard.*

Ninth Service and Anthems. Christ Church Cathedral Choir, Oxford,
dir. Stephen Darlington. Nimbus Records CD NI 5125. 1988.
Includes "Alleluia, I heard a voice"; "Give ear, O Lord"; "Give the
King thy Judgements"; "Gloria in excelsis Deo"; "Hosanna to the
Son of David"; "O Lord, Grant the King a long life."

"The nightengale, the organ of delight." On *All at Once Well Met.*

"Thule, the period of Cosmographie." On *"Draw On Sweet Night."*

White, *Lamentations of Jeremiah.* The Clerkes of Oxenford, dir. David
Wulstan. Nonesuch LP H-71400, 1982, [P] 1977.

Wylkynson, "Salve Regina." On Eton Choirbook: *Stabat Mater.*

Bibliography

MANUSCRIPT SOURCES, BY LOCATION

[C] Cambridge, England
  [CUL] Cambridge University Library.
    Ely Cathedral MS 1, 4, 28–29.
    Ely Treasurer's Account Book, EDR 3/1/2.
  Christ's College
    Account Books, 1625–32.
  Fitzwilliam Museum
    The Fitzwilliam Virginal Book: see Fuller Maitland, J. A.
    Mu 689 (Edward Herbert's lute-book).
  King's College, Rowe Library
    Rowe 9–17, the Norwich part-books.
    Rowe 316 Elizabethan medius part-book labelled "Contratenor."
    Rowe 321 Bassus part-book, Latin and English.
  Peterhouse, Perne Library
    [P] Peterhouse "Caroline" part-books (two sets).
    Peterhouse 40, 41, 31, 32, "Henrican" part-books.
    Printed Book G.5.30, with MS music interleaved.
  St. John's College
    St. John's 180–81, c. 1630
  Trinity College, Wren Library
    R. 16. 29. George Handford, *Ayres*, 1609.
    R. 2. 58. George Loosemore, *Graces/ Of the Collects for the day made to be sung upon Feast-dayes in Trinitie Colledge hall in Cambridge by the Clerks and Choristers. Composed/ By George Loosemore Master of Choristers and Organist in the same Colledge. 1664.*
[D] Durham
  Durham cathedral part-books (c. 1620–70).
[E] Edinburgh
  [EU] Edinburgh University MS D. C. 1.69.
[L] London
  [BL] British Library
    Add. 10337.

Add. 11608. Lawes, Hilton, Ramsey, Deering, Lanier, numerous dialogues.

Add. 15117. Lute-book with a few anthems, songs for lute and solo voice, early seventeenth century.

Add. 17792–17796, early seventeenth century. Cover stamped "I. M."

Add. 29372–7, the Myriell part-books; see Myriell.

Add. 29427 (Milton, Pierson, Ravenscroft, Warde, Weelkes, Hanford, et alia).

Add. 34049, cantus only, early seventeenth century.

Add. 53723 Henry Lawes, Songs, autograph, 1634.

Egerton MS 2013.

Harley 6346. Anthems used in the King's Chapel.

Dr. Williams' Library, Gordon Square
  MS Jones B 62 (see Charles, Amy).

[LA] Los Angeles, William Andrews Clark Memorial Library
  C6967 M4, English songs, begun 1639.
  Mus. C6968 M4, *c.* 1650.

[NY] New York, New York Public Library
  Drexel 5469, *c.* 1630 ("Henry Loosemore's Organ Book").

[O] Oxford
  [B] Bodleian
    Eng. poet. d. 49.
    Mus f. 11–15, The Hammond part-books (*c.* 1630–40).
    Mus. Sch. e. 420–22, Wanley part-books.
    Rawl. Poet 23, anthems from the Chapel Royal, 1635.
    Tanner 307, press copy of Herbert's *The Temple*.
    Tenbury 34–41, *c.* 1600.
    Tenbury 791, "Batten Organ Book," *c.* 1630.
    Tenbury 1018 and 1019.
    Tenbury 1382, 1617.
  Christ Church
    MS 21.
    Music MSS 56–57 (Amner, Weelkes, Hooper, Jones, Ward, et alia).
    MSS 736–38, containing Ford's anthem from Donne's *Lamentations* and Jenkins' settings of Herbert.
    MSS 979–83, late sixteenth century.

[SM] San Marino, Huntington Library
  MS EL 6863, *Rules how to compose.*

Shrewsbury, County Record Office
  Ludlow part-books.

[Y] York
  York Minster MS M. 29 (s), 1640 (Tomkins, "Above the Stars").

REFERENCE WORKS

Abraham, Gerald, ed. *The Concise Oxford History of Music.* Oxford University Press, 1979.

Arnold, Denis, gen. ed. *The New Oxford Companion to Music.* 2 vols. Oxford University Press, 1983, repr. 1984.

Benton, Rita, ed. *Directory of Music Research Libraries II: Thirteen European Countries.* Iowa City: University of Iowa, 1970.

Davies, J. G. *A Dictionary of Liturgy and Worship.* London: SCM Press and New York: The Macmillan Company, 1972.

Herbert, A. S. *Historical Catalogue of Printed Editions of the English Bible, 1525–1961.* London: British and Foreign Bible Society and New York, American Bible Society, 1968.

Hughes, Dom Anselm. *Catalogue of the Musical Manuscripts at Peterhouse.* Cambridge: At the University Press, 1953.

Hughes-Hughes, Augustus. *Catalogue of Manuscript Music in the British Museum.* 3 vols. London: Printed by order of the Trustees, 1906–09.

Jacobs, Arthur. *The Penguin Dictionary of Music.* Fifth edition. London: Penguin Books, 1991.

Jeffrey, David Lyle, gen. ed. *A Dictionary of Biblical Tradition in English Literature.* Grand Rapids: William B. Eerdmans, 1992.

Karp, Theodore, ed. *Dictionary of Music.* Evanston: Northwestern University Press, 1973.

Livingstone, Elizabeth A., ed. *The Concise Oxford Dictionary of the Christian Church.* Oxford University Press, 1977.

The New Grove Dictionary of Music and Musicians, ed. Stanley Sadie. 20 vols. Washington, DC: Grove's Dictionaries of Music, 1980.

The New Grove High Renaissance Masters and *The New Grove Italian Baroque Masters* (Reprints from *The New Grove Dictionary,* cited by article.) New York: W. W. Norton, 1984.

The New Oxford History of Music, editorial board J. A. Westrup, Gerald Abraham, Edward J. Dent, Dom Anselm Hughes, Egon Wellesz. 10 vols. Oxford University Press, 1854–90.

The New Shorter Oxford English Dictionary, gen. ed. Lesley Brown. Oxford: Clarendon Press, 1993.

[OED] *The Oxford English Dictionary.* First edition, ed. James A. N. Murray, Henry Bradley, W. A. Cragie, and C. T. Onions. Second edition prepared by J. A. Simpson and E. S. C. Wiener, with supplement by R. W. Burchfield. Oxford: Clarendon Press, 1989.

[RISM] *Répertoire international des sources musicales.* The International Musicological Society and the International Association of Music Libraries. 12+ vols. Bärenreiter, Kassel, Basle, London, 1971–92.

[RISM, Series B] *Recueils imprimés XVIe–XVIIe siècles,* ed. François Lesure. Vol. 1: *Liste chronologique.* München-Duisburg, 1960.

Robertson, Alec, and Denis Stevens. *The Pelican History of Music,* vol. 1: *Ancient Forms to Polyphony.* Harmondsworth: Penguin Books, 1960; repr. 1978.

Squire, William Barclay. *Catalogue of Printed Music Published between 1487 and 1800 Now in the British Museum.* 2 vols. London: Printed by order of the Trustees, 1912.

Wooldridge, H. E. *The Oxford History of Music,* vol. 11: *The Polyphonic Period.* Second edition Oxford: Clarendon Press, 1932.

PRINTED PRIMARY SOURCES

Amner, John. *Sacred Hymns.* Six part-books. London, 1615.
"Thus sings the heav'nly choir" (Part 1) and "The heav'ns stood all amazed" (Part 2), ed. J. A. Pilgrim. London: Stainer and Bell, 1959.

Andrewes, Lancelot. *CXVI Sermons,* ed. William Laud and John Buckeridge. 1629.
Sermons on the Nativity. Grand Rapids: Baker Book House, 1955.

Anon. *A new and easie method to learn to sing by book.* London, 1686.

Aubrey, John. *"Brief Lives," chiefly of Contemporaries,* ed. Andrew Clark. 2 vols. Oxford: At the Clarendon Press, 1898.

Authorized or King James Version [1611] of the Holy Bible, including Old and New Testaments. Philadelphia: A. J. Homan, n.d.

Bacon, Sir Francis. *The Essayes or Counsels, Civill and Morall,* ed. with intro. and commentary by Michael Kiernan. Cambridge, MA: Harvard University Press, 1985.

Baird, Julianne C., ed. and trans. *The Art of Singing, by Johann Friedrich Agricola.* Cambridge Musical Texts and Monographs. Cambridge University Press, 1995.

Barber, Abraham. *A book of psalme tunes in four parts.* York, 1687.

Barnard, John, ed. *The First Book of Selected Church Music, consisting of Services and Anthems such as are now used in the Cathedral and Collegiate Churches of this Kingdom.* London, 1641.

Battell, Ralph. *The Lawfulness and Expediency of Church-Musick Asserted in a Sermon Preached at St. Brides-Church, Upon the 22d. of november, 1693. Being the Anniversary Meeting of Gentlemen, Lovers of Musick.* London, 1694.

Batten, Adrian. Fourth Service. In *Adrian Batten,* ed. Maurice Bevan. London: Oxford University Press, 1957.

Baxter, Richard. *A Christian Directory: or, A Summ of Practical Theologie.* London, 1673.

Boethius, Anicius Manlius Torquatus Severinus. *De institutione musica,* printed 1491–92; excerpts in Strunk, *Source Readings,* 1: 79–86.

[*BCP*] *Book of Common Prayer, 1559,* ed. John E. Booty. Washington: The Folger Shakespeare Library, 1976. [This scholarly edition does not

include the Coverdale Psalter, which is quoted from various
    editions.]
Brady, Nicholas. *Church-Musick Vindicated. A Sermon Preach'd At St. Bride's
    Church, on Monday November 22. 1697* . . . London, 1697. With
    Estwick, S[ampson]. *The Usefulness of Church-Musick.* Augustan
    Reprint Society Publication Number 49. Intro. James E. Phillips, Jr.
    Los Angeles: William A. Clark Memorial Library, University of
    California, 1955.
Brieger, Peter H., trans. *The Trinity Apocalypse: An Introduction and
    Description.* London: Eugrammia Press, 1967.
Browne, Sir Thomas. *Works,* ed. Geoffrey Keynes. 4 vols. University of
    Chicago Press, 1964.
Buckeridge, John. *A Sermon Preached before his Maiestie At Whitehall, March
    22. 1617, being Passion Sunday. Touching Prostration and Kneeling.*
    London, 1617.
Bullinger, Heinrich. *Fiftie godlie and learned sermons divided into five
    decades, conteying the chiefe and principall pointes of Christian religion*
    . . . London, 1577. Repr. *The decades of Henry Bullinger,* trans. H. I.,
    ed. Thomas Harding. 4 vols. Cambridge, at the University Press,
    1849–52. Repr. New York: Johnson Reprint Corp., 1968.
Butler, Charles. *The Principles of Musick.* London, 1636.
[*BE*] *The Byrd Edition.* Gen. ed. Philip Brett. London: Stainer and Bell,
    1963–. Vol. i: *Cantiones Sacrae: 1575,* ed. Craig Monson; vol. ii:
    Cantiones Sacrae I:1589, ed. Alan Brown; vol. iii: *Cantiones Sacrae II:
    1591,* ed. Alan Brown; vol. iv: *The Masses,* ed. Philip Brett; vol. v:
    Gradualia I: The Marian Masses, ed. Philip Brett; vol. vi:a *Gradualia,
    1605,* ed. Philip Brett; vol. viii: *Latin Motets: I,* ed. Warwick
    Edwards; vol. xa: *The English Services: I,* ed. Craig Monson; vol. xb:
    The English Services: II: The Great Service, ed. Craig Monson; vol. xi:
    The English Anthems, ed. Craig Monson; vol. xiv: *Psalmes, Songs, and
    Sonnets (1611),* ed. John Morehen; vol. xvi: *Madrigals, Songs and
    Canons,* ed. Philip Brett.
[*BF*] *The Collected Works of William Byrd,* ed. Edmund H. Fellowes.
    London: Stainer and Bell, 1937– .
Campion, Thomas. *Babylon's Streams.* 1613.
Cartwright, Thomas. *A Replye to an Answere made of M. Doctor Whitegifte,
    agaynst the Admonition to the Parliament. By T. C.* Wandsworth,
    1574.
    *Second Replie . . . agaynst Master Doctor Whitgiftes second answere touching
    the Church Discipline.* Np., 1575.
Case, John. *The Praise of Musick.* Oxford, 1586.
Castiglione, Count Baldassare. See Hoby, Sir Thomas.
[Church of England.] *A Collection of Articles, Injunctions, Canons, Orders,
    Ordinances, and Constitutions Ecclesiastical* . . . , Anthony Sparrow.
    Second edition. London, 1671.

Constitutions and Canons Ecclesiastical, 1604, intro. and notes by H. A. Wilson. Oxford: At the Clarendon Press, 1923.

Clifford, James. *The Divine Services and Anthems Usually Sung In His Majesties Chappell, and In all Cathedral and Collegiale Choires in England and Ireland.* Second edition. London, 1664.

A Collection of all the Anthems Daily us'd in Divine Service throughout the year in King's Coll. Chappel in Cambridge, 1706.

Cowley, Abraham. *The Collected Works of Abraham Cowley,* ed. Thomas O. Calhoun, Laurence Heyworth, Robert King, Allan Pritchard, Ernest W. Sullivan II. 2 vols. Vol. II includes the musical settings of *The Mistress.* Newark: University of Delaware Press; London and Toronto: Associated University Presses, 1993.

The Complete Works in Verse and Prose, ed. Alexander B. Grosart. 2 vols. New York: AMS Press, 1967.

Crashaw, Richard. *The Poems English Latin and Greek of Richard Crashaw,* ed. L. C. Martin. Oxford: At the Clarendon Press, 1957.

Croce, Giovanni. *Musica Sacra: To Sixe Voyces. Composed in the Italian tongue by Giovanni Croce. Newley Englished.* 6 part-books. London: Thomas Este, 1608 and H. L. for Mathew Lownes, 1611.

Day, John, printer. *Certaine Notes Set forthe in foure and three partes.* London, 1560 [bass part-book only].

Morning and Evening Prayer and Communion set forthe in foure partes. London, 1565.

Donne, John. *The Complete Poetry,* ed. John T. Shawcross. Garden City, NY: Doubleday, 1967.

Devotions upon Emergent Occasions. Repr. Ann Arbor: University of Michigan Press, 1959.

Letters to Severall Persons of Honour, ed. Charles E. Merrill. New York, 1910.

Paradoxes and Problems. Repr. of the 1633 edition. London, 1923.

The Sermons of John Donne, ed. George Potter and Evelyn M. Simpson. 10 vols. Berkeley: University of California Press, 1953–62.

Dowland, John. *Complete Psalms for S. A. T. B.,* ed. Diana Poulton. London: Stainer and Bell, 1973.

Dryden, John. *The Works of John Dryden,* gen. ed. H. T. Swedenberg, Jr.; vol. III, ed. Earl Miner. Berkeley: University of California Press, 1969.

[*EECM*] *Early English Church Music,* gen. ed. Frank Ll. Harrison. London: Stainer and Bell 1962– . Vol. III: *Orlando Gibbons: I,* ed. David Wulstan; vol. V: *Thomas Tomkins: Musica Deo Sacra: I,* ed. Bernard Rose; vol. VII: *Robert Ramsey: I: English Sacred Music,* ed. Edward Thompson; vol. IX: *Thomas Tomkins: Musica Deo Sacra: II,* ed. Bernard Rose; vol. XI: *Sir William Leighton: The Tears or Lamentations of a Sorrowful Soul,* ed. Cecil Hill; vol. XII: *Thomas Tallis: English Sacred Music I: Service Music,* ed. Leonard Ellingwood;

vol. XIV: *Thomas Tomkins: Musica Deo Sacra: III*, ed. Bernard Rose; vol. XX: *John Taverner: I: Six-Part Masses*, ed. Hugh Benham; vol. XXI: *Orlando Gibbons; II: Full Anthems, Hymns and Fragmentary Verse*, ed. David Wulstan (includes Wither, Hymns and Songs of the Church); vol. XXVII: *Thomas Tomkins: Musica Deo Sacra: IV*, ed. Bernard Rose; vol. XXX: *John Taverner: III: Ritual Music and Secular Songs*, ed. Hugh Benham; vol. XXXV: *John Taverner: IV: Five-part Masses*, ed. Bernard Rose; vol. XXXVII: *Thomas Tomkins: Musica Deo Sacra: V*, ed. Bernard Rose; vol. XXXVIII: *Thomas Morley: I. English Anthems; Liturgical Music*, ed. John Morehen; vol. XXXIX: *Thomas Tomkins: Musica Deo Sacra: VI*, ed. Bernard Rose. Suppl. vol. I: *The Sources of English Church Music 1549–1660*. ed. Ralph T. Daniel and Peter le Huray. 2 parts. 1972. Suppl. vol. II: *Latin Music in British Sources, c. 1485 – c. 1610*, compl. by May Hofman and John Morehen, 1987.

East, Michael. *The Fovrth Set of Bookes . . . To 4. 5. and 6. Parts. Apt for Viols and Voyces*. London, 1618.

The Third Set of Bookes. London, 1610.

[*EL*] *English Lute-Songs*, ed. Edmund H. Fellowes, rev. Thurston Dart. London: Stainer and Bell, *c.* 1959– .

[*EM*] *The English Madrigal School*, ed. Edmund H. Fellowes. London: Stainer and Bell, 1913–24; revised as *The English Madrigalists* by Thurston Dart, 1956– .

Engle, Lehman, ed. *Renaissance to Baroque*, vol. III: *English Music*. Delaware Water Gap, PA: Harold Flammer, 1940, 1967.

Este, Thomas, publisher, *The Whole Booke of Psalmes . . . composed into foure parts*. London, 1592 and 1604.

Estwick, S[ampson]. *The Usefulness of Church-Musick . . .* London, 1696. See Brady, *Church-Musick Vindicated.*

The Eton Choirbook, ed. Frank Ll. Harrison. *Musica Britannica*, vol. X (1956); XI (1958); XII (1961). London: Stainer and Bell.

Fayrfax, Robert. *Collected Works*, ed. Edwin B. Warren. 3 vols. Vol. II: *Magnificats and Motets. Corpus Mensurabilis Musica* 17. American Institute of Musicology, 1964.

Fisher, John. *Treatise concernynge the . . . Seuen penytencyall psalmes . . .* London, 1508.

Fludd, Robert. *Utriusque cosmi maioris scilicet et minoris metaphysica, physica, atque technica historia*. Engravings by Johann Theodor de Bry. 2 vols. Vol. II: *Tomus Secundus de Supernaturali, Naturali, Praeternaturali et Contranaturali Microcosmi historia in Tractatus tres distributa*. Oppenheim, 1617–19.

Fuller Maitland, J. A., and W. Barclay Squire, eds. *The Fitzwilliam Virginal Book*. With introduction, notes, and German translation by John Bernhoff. 2 vols. London and Leipzig: Breitkopf and Härtel, 1899.

Gerard, John. *The Herball or Generall Historie of Plantes*. London, 1597.

Facsimile edition, 2 vols., Amsterdam and Norwood, NJ: Walter J. Johnson, 1974.

Gesualdo, Carlo. *Responsoria et alia ad Officium Hebdomadae Sanctae spectantia*, 6vv. Gesualdo, 1611.

Gibbons, Orlando. *First Set of Madrigals and Mottets of 5 Parts: apt for Viols and Voyces*. London, 1612.

The Gostling Manuscript, compiled by John Gostling, forward by Franklin B. Zimmerman. Austin and London: University of Texas Press, 1977.

Greening, Anthony, ed. *A Sixteenth-Century Anthem Book: Twenty Anthems for Four Voices*. London: Oxford University Press, 1973, revised 1988.

Greer, David, ed. *Alfonso Ferrabosco, "Ayres," 1607*. In *English Lute Songs, 1597–1632: A Collection of Facsimile Reprints*, gen. ed. F. W. Sternfeld. Vol. V: Menston, England: The Scolar Press, 1971.

Hawes, Steven. *Pastime of Pleasure*. London, 1554.

Henry, Avril, ed. *Biblia Pauperum*. Facsimile edition with transcriptions and annotations. Ithaca: Cornell University Press, 1987.

Herbert, George. *The English Poems of George Herbert*, ed. C. A. Patrides. London: Dent, 1974.

The Latin Poems of George Herbert: A Bilingual Edition, trans. Mark McClosky and Paul R. Murphy. Athens: University of Ohio Press, 1965.

Herrick, Robert. *The Poems of Robert Herrick*, ed. L. C. Martin. London: Oxford University Press, 1965.

Heywood, James, and Thomas Wright. *Cambridge University Transactions during the Puritan Controversies of the 16th and 17th Centuries*. 2 vols. London: Henry G. Bohn, 1854.

Hoby, Sir Thomas. *The Courtyer of Count Baldessar Castilio . . . Done into Englyshe by Sir Thomas Hoby*. 1561. Repr., intro. Walter Raleigh. New York: AMS Press, 1967.

Hooker, Richard. *Of the Lawes of Ecclesiastical Polity*, ed. Georges Edelen. *The Folger Library Edition of the Works of Richard Hooker*, gen. ed. W. Speed Hill. Vols. I and II. Cambridge, MA: The Belknap Press, 1977.

Howel[l]s, James. *Dendrologia. Dodona's Grove, or the Vocall Forest. The last Edition*. London, 1649.

The Pre-eminence and Pedigree of Parlement. London, 1649. Bound with *Dendrologia*.

The Hymnal 1982, According to the use of The Episcopal Church. New York: The Church Hymnal Corporation, 1985.

James I. *The Workes of the Most High and Mighty Prince Iames*. London, 1616.

Kepler, Johannes. *Harmonice Mundi* (1619), trans. A. M. Duncan (in progress).

Lafontaine, Henry Cart de, ed. *The King's Musick: A Transcript of Records Relating to Music and Musicians (1460–1700)*. London: Novello, 1909; repr. New York, 1973.

Lake, Arthur. *Sermons with some religious and diuine meditations*. London, 1629.

Lawes, Henry and William. *Choice Psalmes put into MUSICK, For Three Voices*. London, 1648.

A Paraphrase upon the Psalms. 1638.

Le Huray, Peter, ed. *The Treasury of English Church Music, 1545–1650*. Cambridge: Cambridge University Press, 1982.

Lowe, Edward. *A Review of some Short Directions for performance of Cathedrall Service*. Second edition. Oxford, 1664.

Mace, Thomas. *Musick's Monument*. London, 1676.

Marbeck, John. *A Booke of Notes and Common Places with their expositions*. London, 1581.

Cranmer's First Litany, 1544, and Merbecke's Book of Common Prayer Noted, 1550. Facsimile with introduction by J. Eric Hunt. London: Society for Promoting Christian Knowledge, 1939.

Marenzio, Luca. *Madrigali Spirituali a cinque voci . . . libro primo*. Rome, 1584; Venice, 1588 and 1606; Antwerp, 1610.

Motecta festorum totius anni . . . liber primus. Rome, 1585; Venice, 1588.

"Occhi lucenti e belli," ed. Franklin B. Zimmerman. Hanover, New Hampshire: Dartmouth Publications, 1968.

Marsden, John H. *College Life in the Time of James the First*. c. 1851.

Marvell, Andrew. *The Complete Poems*, ed. Elizabeth Story Donno. Harmondsworth: Penguin Books, 1978.

The Poems and Letters of Andrew Marvell, ed. H. M. Margoliouth. Second edition. 2 vols. Oxford: Clarendon Press, 1952.

Mazzoni, Jacopo *On the Defense of the Comedy of Dante*, trans. Robert L. Montgomery. Tallahassee: University Presses of Florida, 1983.

Mersenne, Marin. *Traité de L'harmonie universelle*. Paris, 1627. Trans. John Bernard Egan in "A Critical Translation of the Second Book," University of Indiana dissertation, 1962.

Milton, John. *The Complete Prose Works of John Milton*, gen. ed. Don M. Wolfe. 8 vols. New Haven: Yale University Press, 1953–82.

John Milton's Complete Poetical Works Reproduced in Photographic Facsimile, ed. Harris Fletcher. 4 vols. Urbana: University of Illinois Press, 1943.

[*PL*] *Paradise Lost*, ed. Merritt Y. Hughes. New York: The Odyssey Press, 1962.

The Poems of John Milton, ed. John Cary and Alastair Fowler. Harlow: Longman, 1968.

Samson Agonistes and Shorter Poems, ed. A. E. Barker. Arlington Heights: AHM Publishing Corporation, 1950.

[*SM*] *The Student's Milton*, ed. Frank Allen Patterson. New York:
　Appleton-Century-Crofts, 1933.
[*CM*] *The Works of John Milton.* gen. ed. Frank Allen Patterson. 18
　vols. + index. New York: Columbia University Press, 1931–40.
Monteverdi, Claudio. *Madrigali Guerrieri et Amorosi . . . Libro Ottavo.*
　Venice, 1638. Vol. VIII of *Tutte le Opere,* revised version.
Opera omnia, a cura della Fondazione Claudio Monteverdi. Facsimile
　edition. Cremona: Athenaeum Cremona, 1970.
Selva Morale e Spirituale. Venice, 1640.
Tutte le Opere, ed. Gian Francesco Malipiero. 17 vols. Asolo, 1926–42.
　Revised version, Universal Edition: Vienna, 1967.
Morley, Thomas. *First Book of Ballets.* London, 1597.
A Plain and Easy Introduction to Practical Music (London, 1597), ed. R.
　Alec Harmon. New York: W. W. Norton, 1973.
[*MB*] *Musica Britannica.* London: Stainer and Bell, 1951– . Vol. V: *The
　Keyboard Music of Thomas Tomkins,* ed. Stephen D. Tuttle; vol. VIII:
　John Dunstable: Complete Works, ed. Manfred F. Bukofzer (American
　Musicological Society. Studies and Documents 2) revised by M.
　Bent and B. Trowell; vol. X: *The Eton Choirbook I,* ed. Frank Ll.
　Harrison; vol. XXIII: *Thomas Weelkes: Collected Anthems,* ed. D.
　Brown, W. Collins, and P. le Huray.
Myriell, Thomas, collector. *Tristitiae remedium. Cantiones selectissimae
　diuersorum.* From 1616. BL Add. MSS 29372–7.
North, Roger. *Roger North on Music.* London: Novello, 1959.
Palestrina, Giovanni Pierluigi da. *Le Opere Complete,* ed. Raffaele
　Casimiri. Rome: Fratelli Scalera, 1941.
Parker, Matthew, Archbishop. *The Whole Psalter translated into English
　Metre.* London: John Day, ?1567.
Pepys, Samuel. *The Diary of Samuel Pepys,* ed. Robert Latham. Berkeley,
　University of California Press, 1970– .
Petti, Anthony G., ed. *The Chester Books of Madrigals, 1. The Animal
　Kingdom.* London: Chester Music, n.d.
The Chester Books of Motets: The English School. The Second Book, for 4
　voices; *The Ninth Book,* for 5 voices; *The Sixteenth Book,* for 6 voices.
　London: Chester Music, 1977–82.
Plato. *The Dialogues of Plato,* trans. B. Jowett. 2 vols. New York: Random
　House, 1937.
The Republic of Plato, trans. Francis MacDonald Cornford. London:
　Oxford University Press, repr. 1975.
Playford, John, ed. *Cantica Sacra: contayning hymns and anthems for two
　voices to the organ, both Latine and English. 3 vols.* London, 1674.
An Introduction to the skill of musick, in two books . . . . London, 1679.
Prynne, William. *Histrio-Mastix.* London, 1633. Repr. New York:
　Garland, 1974.
*The Psalter of David, with Titles and Collects according to the matter of each
　Psalme.* London, 1655.

Ode on St. Cecilia's Day (1692), ed. Michael Tippett and Walter
Bergmann, London: Schott, *c.* 1995.
Puttenham, George. *The Arte of English Poesie.* London, 1589. Facsimile
reproduction of 1906 repr., ed. and intro. Baxter Hathaway. Kent,
OH: Kent State University Press, 1970.
Ravenscroft, Thomas. *The Whole Book of Psalmes: with the Hymnes
Evangelicall, And Songs Spirituall. Composed into 4. parts . . . with
such seuerall tunes as . . . are vsually sung in England, Scotland,
Wales, Germany, Italy, France and the Nether-lands . . . .* London,
1621, 1633.
Rimbault, E. F., ed. *The Old Cheque-book, or Book of remembrance of the
Chapel Royal from 1561–1714.* Camden Society, vol. III, 1872.
Salkeld, John. *A Treatise of Angels.* London, 1613.
Sandys, Edwin, set by Robert Tailour. *Fifti Select Psalms of David and
others, paraphrastically turned into English verse. And by Robert Tailour,
set to be sung in Five parts, as also to the Viole, and Lute or Orph-ariaon.*
London, 1615.
Sandys, George. *A Paraphrase vpon the Divine Poems.* London, 1638.
*A Paraphrase vpon the Psalmes of David. And vpon the Hymnes Dispersed
throughout the Old and New Testaments.* London, 1636.
and Henry Lawes. *A Paraphrase vpon the Psalmes of David.* London,
1638.
Shakespeare, William. *The Complete Works,* ed. G. B. Harrison. New York:
Harcourt, Brace, 1952.
Sherlock, W. *A Sermon Preach'd at St. Paul's Cathedral, November 22. 1699.
Being The Anniversary Meeting of the Lovers of Musick.* London, 1699.
Sidney, Sir Philip. *An Apology for Poetry,* ed. Forrest G. Robinson.
Indianapolis: Bobbs-Merrill, 1970. See also Anon., above.
Slatyer, William. *The Psalmes of David in 4 Languages . . . 4 Parts.* London,
1643.
Sternhold, Thomas, John Hopkins, and others. *The Whole Booke of
Psalmes. Collected into English meeter . . . conferred with the Hebrew with
apt notes to sing them with all.* London, 1640.
Stevens, Denis, ed. *The Penguin Book of English Madrigals: for Four Voices.*
Harmondsworth: Penguin, 1967, repr. 1983.
The Second Penguin Book of English Madrigals: for Five Voices.
Harmondsworth: Penguin, 1970, repr. 1977.
Strunk, Oliver, ed. *Source Readings in Music History.* Repr., 5 vols. Vol. I:
Antiquity and the Middle Ages. II: *The Renaissance.* III: *The Baroque Era.*
New York: W. W. Norton, 1965.
Tallis, Thomas, and William Byrd. *Cantiones Sacrae.* 1575. 6 part-books
in facsimile repr., dir. Leslie Hewitt. Leeds: Boethius Press, 1976.
Taverner, John. "Dum transisset sabbatum," ed. Philip Brett. Oxford
University Press, 1975.
Tomkins, Thomas. "Above the stars my saviour dwells" (secular
version), ed. John Milsom. Oxford University Press, 1990.

Traherne, Thomas. *Centuries, Poems, and Thanksgivings*, ed. H. M. Margoliouth. 2 vols. Oxford: At the Clarendon Press, 1958.

[*TCM*] *Tudor Church Music*, ed. P. C. Buck, E. H. Fellowes, A. Ramsbotham, R. R. Terry, and S. Townsend Warner. 10 vols. London and New York: Published for the Carnegie United Kingdom Trust by Oxford University Press, H. Milford, 1922–29. Vol. I: *John Taverner, Part 1*; vol. II: *William Byrd: English Church Music*: vol. III: *John Taverner, Part 2*: vol. IV: *Orlando Gibbons*; vol. V: *Robert White*; vol. VI: *Thomas Tallis* (New York: Broude Brothers); vol. VII: *William Byrd: Gradualia*; vol. VIII: *Thomas Tomkins, Part 1: Services*; vol. IX: *William Byrd: Masses, Cantiones and Motets*; vol. X: *Hugh Aston, John Marbeck, Osbert Parsley*.

Tudor Church Music: A collection of fourteen anthems and motets. London: Novello, 1969.

Vaughan, Henry. *The Complete Poems*, ed. Alan Rudrum. New Haven: Yale University Press, 1981.

Vecchi, Orazio. "Benedicite," edited for this study by Patrick O'Shea from *Sacrarum Cantionum quinque, sex, septem, & octo vocibus: liber secundus*. Venice: Angelo Gardano, 1597.

Walton, Izaak. *The Lives of John Donne, Sir Henry Wotton, Richard Hooker, George Herbert, & Robert Sanderson*, intro. George Saintsbury. London: Oxford University Press, 1927, repr. 1956.

Watson, Thomas. *The first sett, of Italian madrigalls englished, not to the sense of the originall dittie, but after the affection of the noate*. London: T. Este, 1590.

Weelkes, Thomas. "Alleluia, I heard a voice," ed. S. Townsend Warner, rev. Roger Bray. London: Oxford University Press, 1976.

"Gloria in excelsis Deo," ed. Walter S. Collins. London: Oxford University Press, 1960.

Whitgift, John. *An answere to a certen Libell intituled, An admonition to the Parliament*. London, 1572.

The Defense of the Aunswere to the Admonition, against the Replie of T. C. London, 1574.

Wienandt, Elwyn A., ed. *Opinions on Church Music: Comments and Reports from Four-and-a-Half Centuries*. Waco: Markham Press Fund of Baylor University Press, 1974.

Willett, Andrew. *Harmonie vpon the First Booke of Samvel*. London, ?1607.

Wither, George. *A Collection of Emblemes, Ancient and Moderne* (1635). Facsimilie edition, intro. Rosemary Freeman, bibliographical notes by Charles S. Hensley. Columbia, SC: University of South Carolina Press, 1975.

The Hymnes and Songs of the Church. London, 1623.

SECONDARY SOURCES

Alter, Robert. *The Art of Biblical Poetry.* New York: Basic Books, 1985.
Aplin, John. "The Origins of John Day's 'Certaine Notes.'" *Music and Letters* 62 (1981): 295–99.
"Structural Devices in English Liturgical Music, 1545–1570." University of Reading dissertation, 1977.
Bald, R. C. *John Donne: A Life.* New York: Oxford University Press, 1970.
Barker, A. E., ed. *Milton: Modern Essays in Criticism.* London: Oxford University Press, 1965.
"The Pattern of Milton's Nativity Ode." *University of Toronto Quarterly* 10 (1941): 167–81.
Basile, Mary Elizabeth. "The Music of *A Maske.*" *Milton Quarterly* 27 (1993): 86–98.
Benet, Diana Treviño. *Secretary of Praise: The Poetic Vocation of George Herbert.* Columbia: University of Missouri Press, 1984.
Benham, Hugh. *Latin Church Music in England, c. 1460–1575.* London, 1977.
Bent, Margaret. *Dunstaple.* London: Oxford University Press, 1981.
Blackwood, Easley. *The Structure of Recognizable Diatonic Tunings.* Princeton University Press, 1985.
Blessington, Francis C. "'That Undisturbed Song of Pure Concent': *Paradise Lost* and the Epic-Hymn." In Lewalski, ed., *Renaissance Genres.*
Bloch, Chana. *Spelling the Word: George Herbert and the Bible.* Berkeley: University of California Press,1985.
Brennecke, Ernest, Jr. *John Milton the Elder and his Music.* Repr. of *Columbia University Studies in Musicology* 2 (1938). New York: Octagon Books, 1973.
Brett, Philip. "Homage to Taverner in Byrd's Masses." *Early Music* 9 (1981): 169–76.
Brown, Cedric. *John Milton's Aristocratic Entertainments.* Cambridge University Press, 1985.
Budick, Sanford. *The Dividing Muse: Images of Sacred Disjunction in Milton's Poetry.* New Haven: Yale University Press, 1985.
Bukhofzer, Manfred M. *Studies in Medieval and Renaissance Music.* New York: W. W. Norton, 1950.
Byard, Margaret. "'Adventrous Song': Milton and the Music of Rome." In Di Cesare, ed., *Milton in Italy.*
Caldwell, John. *Editing Early Music.* Oxford: Clarendon Press, 1985; second edition, 1995.
Caldwell, John, Edward Olleson, and Susan Wollenberg. *The Well-Enchanting Skill: Music, Poetry, and Drama in the Culture of the Renaissance.* Oxford: Clarendon Press, 1990.
Carpenter, Nan Cooke. *Music in Medieval and Renaissance Universities.* Norman: University of Oklahoma Press,1958.

Chan, Mary. *Music in the Theatre of Ben Jonson.* Oxford University Press, 1980.

Charles, Amy M. "George Herbert: Priest, Poet, Musician." *Journal of the Viola da Gamba Society of America* 4 (1967): 27–36. Repr., Roberts, *Essential Articles*, 249–57.

A Life of George Herbert. Ithaca: Cornell University Press, 1977.

The Williams manuscript of George Herbert's poems: a facsimile reproduction. Delmar, NY: Scholars' Facsimiles & Reprints, 1977. [London: Dr. Williams' Library, Gordon Square, MS Jones B 62.]

Colie, Rosalie. *"My Ecchoing Song": Andrew Marvell's Poetry of Criticism.* Princeton University Press, 1970.

Connolly, Thomas. *Mourning into Joy: Music, Raphael, and St. Cecilia.* New Haven: Yale University Press, 1994.

Corse, Sandra. "Old Music and New in 'L'Allegro' and 'Il Penseroso.'" *Milton Quarterly* 14 (1980), 109–13.

Dart, Thurston. "Henry Loosemore's Organ Book." *Transactions of the Cambridge Bibliographical Society* 3.2 (1960): 43–51.

Davies, H. Neville. "'Laid artfully together': Stanzaic Design in Milton's 'On the Morning of Christ's Nativity.'" In Røstvig, *Fair Forms.*

Di Cesare, Mario A. "God's Silence: On Herbert's 'Deniall.'" *George Herbert Journal* 10 (1986/1987): 85–102.

Di Cesare, Mario A. ed. *Milton in Italy.* Binghamton: Medieval and Renaissance Texts and Studies, 1991.

Evans, J. Martin. "A Poem of Absences." *Milton Quarterly* 27 (1993): 31–35.

Evans, Willa. *Ben Jonson and Elizabethan Music.* Repr. New York: DaCapo Press, 1965.

Henry Lawes: Musician and Friend of Poets. London: Oxford University Press, 1941.

Fellowes, Edmund H. *The English Madrigal Composers.* London: Oxford University Press, 1948.

English Madrigal Verse, 1588–1632. Third edition, revised and enlarged. Oxford: Clarendon Press, 1967.

Fenlon, Iain, ed. *Cambridge Music Manuscripts, 900–1700.* Cambridge University Press, 1982.

Finney, Gretchen. *Musical Backgrounds for English Literature, 1580–1650.* New Brunswick, NJ: Rutgers University Press, 1962.

Fish, Stanley. "Wanting a Supplement." In *Politics, Poetics, and Hermeneutics in Milton's Prose,* ed. David Loewenstein and James Grantham Turner. Cambridge University Press, 1990.

Francis, Richard, and Peter Klein. *The Organs and Organists of Ludlow Parish Church.* Leominster: Orphans Press, 1982.

Freer, Coburn. *Music for a King: George Herbert's Style and the Metrical Psalms.* Baltimore: Johns Hopkins University Press, 1972.

Friedman, Donald M. "Marvell's Musicks." In *On the Celebrated and*

Neglected Poems of Andrew Marvell, ed. Claude J. Summers and Ted-Larry Pebworth. Columbia: University of Missouri Press, 1992.

Gottlieb, Sidney. "The Social and Political Backgrounds of George Herbert's Poetry." In *The Muses Common-Weale: Poetry and Politics in the Seventeenth Century*, ed. Claude J. Summers and Ted-Larry Pebworth. Columbia: University of Missouri Press, 1988.

Greene, Thomas. *The Descent from Heaven: A Study in Epic Continuity*. New Haven: Yale University Press, 1963.

Grossman, Marshall. *Authors to Themselves: Milton and the Revelation of History*. Cambridge University Press, 1987.

Hayes, Albert McHarg. "Counterpoint in Herbert." *Studies in Philology* 35 (1938): 43–60. Repr. in Roberts, *Essential Articles*, 283–97.

Heninger, S. K., Jr. *Touches of Sweet Harmony: Pythagorean Cosmology and Renaissance Poetics*. San Marino: The Huntington Library, 1974.

Hollander, John. *The Untuning of the Sky: Ideas of Music in English Poetry, 1500–1700*. Princeton University Press, 1961.

Hutton, James. "Some English Poems in Praise of Music." *English Miscellany* 2 (1951): 1–63.

Jacobus, Lee. "Milton Hero: The Rhetorical Gesture of Monody." In *Reconsidering the Renaissance*, ed. Mario A. Di Cesare. MRTS vol. 93. Binghamton, NY: The Center, 1992.

Jorgens, Elise Bickford. *The Well-Tun'd Word: Musical Interpretations of English Poetry, 1588–1651*. Minneapolis: University of Minnesota Press, 1982.

Kerman, Joseph. *The Elizabethan Madrigal: A Comparative Study*. New York: American Musicological Society, 1962.

"The Elizabethan Motet: A Study of Texts for Music." *Studies in the Renaissance* 9 (1962): 273 ff.

The Masses and Motets of William Byrd. London: Faber and Faber, 1981.

King's College Chapel. Norwich: Jarrold and Sons, 1989.

Klause, John. "The Two Occasions of Donne's Lamentations of Jeremy." *Modern Philology* 90 (1993): 337–59.

Knight, Frida. *Cambridge Music*. Cambridge: Oleander Press, 1980.

Labriola, Albert C., and Edward Sichi, Jr. eds. *Milton's Legacy in the Arts*. University Park: Pennsylvania State University Press, 1987.

Le Huray, Peter. *Music and the Reformation in England, 1549–1660*. Cambridge University Press, 1978.

Leonard, John. *Naming in Paradise: Milton and the Language of Adam and Eve*. Oxford: Clarendon Press, 1990.

"'Trembling ears: the Historical Moment of *Lycidas*," *Journal of Medieval and Renaissance Studies* 21 (1991): 59–81.

Lewalski, Barbara Kiefer. *"Paradise Lost" and the Rhetoric of Literary Forms*. Princeton University Press, 1985.

Protestant Poetics and the Seventeenth-Century Religious Lyric. Princeton University Press, 1979.

Lewalski, Barbara Kiefer, ed. *Renaissance Genres: Essays on Theory, History, and Interpretation.* Cambridge, MA: Harvard University Press, 1986.

Lieb, Michael. *Poetics of the Holy: A Reading of "Paradise Lost."* Chapel Hill: University of North Carolina Press, 1981.

Luckett, Richard. "The Legend of St. Cecilia in English Literature: A Study," University of Cambridge dissertation, 1972.

"St. Cecilia and Music." *Proceedings of the Royal Musical Association* 94 (1972–73): 15–30.

Lull, Janis. "George Herbert's Revisions in 'The Church' and the Carnality of 'Love' (III)," *George Herbert Journal* 9 (1985): 1–16.

McColley, Diane Kelsey. "The Copious Matter of My Song." In *Literary Milton: Text, Pretext, Context,* ed. Diana Treviño Benet and Michael Lieb. Pittsburgh: Duquesne University Press, 1994.

A Gust for Paradise: Milton's Eden and the Visual Arts. Urbana: University of Illinois Press, 1993.

"The Poem as Hierophon: Musical Configurations in George Herbert's 'The Church.'" In *A Fine Tuning,* ed. Maleski.

"'Tongues of Men and Angels': Ad Leonoram Romae Canentem." In *Urbane Milton: The Latin Poetry,* ed. James A. Freeman and Anthony Low. *Milton Studies* 19 (1984): 127–48.

McGinn, Donald Joseph. *The Admonition Controversy.* New Brunswick: Rutgers University Press, 1949.

Mackerness, E. D. *A Social History of English Music.* London: Routledge and Kegan Paul, 1964.

Maleski, Mary A., ed. *A Fine Tuning: Studies of the Religious Poetry of Herbert and Milton.* Binghamton, NY: Medieval and Renaissance Texts and Studies, 1989.

Mander, M. N. K. "Milton and the Music of the Spheres." *Milton Quarterly* 24 (1990): 63–71.

"The Music of L'Allegro and Il Penseroso." In Di Cesare, ed., *Milton in Italy.*

Marotti, Arthur F. *John Donne: Coterie Poet.* Madison: University of Wisconsin Press, 1986.

Masson, David. *The Life of John Milton: Narrated in Connexion with the Political, Ecclesiastical, and Literary History of his Time.* 7 vols. New York: Peter Smith, 1946.

Maynard, Winifred. *Elizabethan Lyric Poetry and Its Music.* Oxford: Clarendon Press, 1986.

Mellers, Wilfred. *Harmonious Meeting: A Study of the Relationships between English Music, Poetry and Theatre, c. 1600–1900.* London: Dennis Dobson, 1965.

Milsom, John. "Music." In *The Cambridge Guide to the Arts in Britain,* ed. Boris Ford, vol. III: *Renaissance and Reformation.* Cambridge University Press, 1989.

Monsom, Craig. *Voices and Viols in England, 1600–1650: The Sources and the Music*. Studies in Musicology 55. Ann Arbor: UMI Research Press, 1982.

Morehen, John. "The Sources of English Cathedral Music, *c.* 1617 – *c.*1644." University of Cambridge dissertation 6740, 1969.

Morehen, John, ed. *English Choral Practice, 1400–1650*. Cambridge Studies in Performance Practice. Cambridge University Press, 1995.

Morris, Brian. "'Not Siren-like to tempt': Donne and the Composers." In A. J. Smith, ed., *John Donne: Essays in Celebration*. London, 1972.

Moseley, C. W. R. D. *The Poetic Birth: Milton's Poems of 1645*. Brookfield: Scolar Press. 1991.

Nardo, Anna K. *Milton's Sonnets and the Ideal Community*. Lincoln: University of Nebraska Press, 1979.

Novarr, David. *The Disinterred Muse: Donne's Texts and Contexts*. Ithaca: Cornell University Press, 1980.

Ostriker, Alicia. "Song and Speech in the Metrics of George Herbert," *PMLA* 80 (1965): 62–68. Repr. in Roberts, *Essential Articles*, 298–310.

Parry, Graham. *Seventeenth-Century Poetry: The Social Context*. London: Hutchinson, 1985.

Patrides, C. A. "'Something like Prophetick strain': Apocalyptic Configurations in Milton." In *The Apocalypse in English Renaissance Thought and Literature*, ed. C. A. Patrides and Joseph Wittrich. Ithaca: Cornell University Press, 1984.

Pattison, Bruce. *Music and Poetry of the English Renaissance*. London: Methuen, 1970.

Payne, Ian. "Instrumental Music at Trinity College, Cambridge, *c.* 1594–1615: Archival and Biographical Evidence." *Music and Letters* 68 (1987):128–40.

"The Musical Establishment at Trinity College, Cambridge, 1546–1644." *Proceedings of the Cambridge Antiquarian Society* 75 (1985): 53–69.

Phillips, Peter. *English Sacred Music, 1549–1649*. Oxford: Gimell, 1991.

Poulton, Diana. *John Dowland*. Second edition. Berkeley and Los Angeles: University of California Press, 1982.

Radzinowicz, Mary Ann. *Milton's Epics and the Book of Psalms*. Princeton University Press, 1989.

Raynor, Henry. *Music in England*. London: Robert Hale, 1980.

Revard, Stella. "From the State of Innocence to the Fall of Man: The Fortunes of *Paradise Lost* as Opera and Oratorio." In Labriola and Sichi, eds., *Milton's Legacy in the Arts*.

Roberts, John R. *Essential Articles for the Study of George Herbert's Poetry*. Hamden, Connecticut: Archon Books, 1979.

Roche, Jerome. *The Madrigal*. Second edition. Oxford University Press, 1990.

Roebuck, Graham. "Donne's Visual Imagination and Compasses." *John Donne Journal* 8 (1989): 37–56.

Røstvig, Maren-Sophie. "Elaborate Song: Conceptual Structure in Milton's 'On the Morning of Christ's Nativity.'" In Røstvig, ed., *Fair Forms*.

Fair Forms: Essays in English Literature from Spenser to Jane Austen. Cambridge: D. S. Brewer, 1975.

Rudrum, Alan. *A Critical Commentary on Milton's "Comus" and Shorter Poems.* London: Macmillan, 1967.

"Henry Vaughan, the Liberation of the Creatures, and Seventeenth-Century English Calvinism," *The Seventeenth Century* 4 (1989): 33–54.

Rumrich, John P. *Matter of Glory: A New Preface to "Paradise Lost."* University of Pittsburgh Press, 1987.

Schleiner, Louise. *The Living Lyre in English Verse from Elizabeth through the Restoration.* Columbia: University of Missouri Press, 1984.

Schoenfeldt, Michael. *Prayer and Power: George Herbert and Renaissance Courtship.* University of Chicago Press, 1991.

Scholes, P. S. *The Puritans and Music.* New York: Russell and Russell, 1962.

Shapiro, Alexander H. "'Drama of an Infinitely Superior Nature': Handel's Early English Oratorios and the Religious Sublime," *Music and Letters* 74 (May, 1993): 215–45.

Shephard, John Harley. "The Changing Theological Concept of Sacrifice, and Its Implications for the Music of the English Church, c. 1500–1640." University of Cambridge dissertation 13357, 1984.

Slights, Camille Wells. *The Casuistical Tradition in Shakespeare, Donne, Herbert, and Milton.* Princeton University Press, 1981.

Stapleton, Laurence. "Milton and the New Music," in Barker, *Milton: Modern Essays*, 31–42.

Stevens, Denis. *Thomas Tomkins.* New York: St. Martin's Press, 1957.

Tudor Church Music. New York: Merlin Press, 1955.

Stevens, John. *Music and Poetry in the Early Tudor Court.* London: Methuen, 1961; repr. Cambridge University Press, 1979.

Stubbs, Charles W. *The Story of Cambridge.* London: J. M. Dent, 1905.

Sullivan, Ernest W., II. *The Influence of John Donne: His Uncollected Seventeenth-Century Printed Verse.* Columbia: University of Missouri Press, 1993.

Summers, Joseph. *George Herbert: His Religion and Art.* Cambridge, MA.: Harvard University Press, 1954.

Temperley, Nicholas. *Music of the English Parish Church.* 2 vols. Cambridge University Press, 1979.

Toft, Robert. *Tune Thy Musicke To Thy Hart: The Art of Eloquent Singing in England, 1597–1622.* University of Toronto Press, 1993.

Tomlinson, Gary. *Monteverdi and the End of the Renaissance.* Berkeley: University of California Press, 1987.

Tuve, Rosamond. *Essays by Rosamond Tuve,* ed. Thomas P. Roche. Princeton University Press, 1970.

A Reading of George Herbert. University of Chicago Press, 1952.

Waddington, Raymond. "A Musical Source for *L'Allegro?*" *Milton Quarterly* 27 (May, 1993): 72–74.

Walker, D. P. *Studies in Musical Science in the Late Renaissance.* Vol. XXXVII of *Studies of the Warburg Institute,* gen. ed. J. B. Trapp. London: The Warburg Institute/University of London, 1978.

Wayment, Hilary. *King's College Chapel Cambridge: The Great Windows: Introduction and Guide.* Cambridge: Published by the Provost and Scholars of King's College, 1982.

The Windows of King's College Chapel, Cambridge. Corpus Vitrearum Medii Aevi, Great Britain, Supplementary Volume I. London, 1972.

Werblowsky, R. J. Z. *Lucifer and Prometheus.* London: Routledge and Kegan Paul 1952.

Whiting, George Wesley. *Milton and this Pendant World.* New York: Octagon Books, 1969.

Wilcox, Helen. "'My Mournful Style': Poetry and Music in the Madrigals of John Ward." *Music and Letters* 61 (1980): 60–70.

"'The Sweet Singer of the Temple': The Musicians' Response to Herbert." *George Herbert Journal* 10 (1986/1987): 47–60.

Wilson, E. C. *Prince Henry and English Literature.* Ithaca: Cornell University Press, 1946.

Wilson, John. *Fairfax: A Life of Thomas, Lord Fairfax.* London: J. Murray, 1985.

Winn, James Anderson. *Unsuspected Eloquence: A History of the Relations between Poetry and Music.* New Haven: Yale University Press, 1981.

Woods, Susanne. *Natural Emphasis: English Versification from Chaucer to Dryden.* San Marino: Huntington Library, 1984.

Wulstan, David. *Tudor Music.* Iowa City: University of Iowa Press, 1986.

Zickler, Elaine Perez. "John Donne: The Subject of Casuistry." Bryn Mawr doctoral dissertation, 1992.

Zim, Rivkah. *English Metrical Psalms: Poetry as Praise and Prayer, 1535–1601.* Cambridge University Press, 1987.

Zimmerman, Franklin. *Henry Purcell, 1659–1695.* London: Macmillan; New York: St. Martin's Press, 1967.

Index